African American Cultural Theory and Heritage
Series Editor: William C. Banfield

George Russell

The Story of an American Composer

Duncan Heining

African American Cultural Theory and Heritage

THE SCARECROW PRESS, INC.
Lanham • Toronto • Plymouth, UK
2010

Published by Scarecrow Press, Inc.
A wholly owned subsidary of The Rowman & Littlefield Publishing Group, Inc.
4501 Forbes Boulevard, Suite 200, Lanham, Maryland 20706
http://www.scarecrowpress.com

Estover Road, Plymouth PL6 7PY, United Kingdom

British Library Cataloguing in Publication Information Available

Library of Congress Cataloging-in-Publication Data
Heining, Duncan, 1953–
  George Russell : the story of an American composer / Duncan Heining.
    p. cm. (African American cultural theory and heritage)
  Includes bibliographical references and index.
  ISBN 978-0-8108-6997-4 (hardback : alk. paper) — ISBN 978-0-8108-6998-1 (ebook)
  1. Russell, George, 1923- 2. Jazz musicians—United States—Biography. 3.
Composers—United States—Biography. I. Title.
  ML410.R96H45 2010
  781.65092—dc22
  [B]   2009025401

∞ ™ The paper used in this publication meets the minimum requirements of
American National Standard for Information Sciences—Permanence of Paper for
Printed Library Materials, ANSI/NISO Z39.48-1992.

Printed in the United States of America

To George and Alice Russell,
and to our mutual friend, musician and author Ian Carr

~

Contents

~

Preface

George Russell is a unique figure in jazz. He is a theoretician, a composer of note, a working musician, and an educator. Long before his first record, *The George Russell Smalltet—Jazz Workshop* (1956), he had begun his life's work developing the Lydian Chromatic Concept of Tonal Organization. One of a rare breed of thinker-musicians, he has had—through his ideas and music—a remarkable influence on the development of jazz after 1950. From his early composition with Dizzy Gillespie of "Cubano-Be, Cubano-Bop," through the changes wrought by modal jazz as a consequence of his ideas, to his impact on the Scandinavian and European scenes, his achievements are among the most outstanding in the music.

His life story weaves its way through contemporary jazz intersecting with the lives of many of its most colorful characters. Charlie "Bird" Parker, Dizzy Gillespie, Miles Davis, John Coltrane, Bill Evans, Gerry Mulligan, John Lewis, Gil Evans, Charlie Mingus, and Carla Bley were not just Russell's contemporaries. They were his peers, his colleagues, and his friends. He touched their lives and music and, in turn, was encouraged by them.

This is a tale of a potential realized despite obstacles of birth, discrimination, ill health, poverty, and neglect. Russell's early life and career were acted out against the dramatic landscape of America's racial divide. It is an important part of American mythology that the United States is the land of opportunity—where, if you have it in you, you can and will succeed. Seen from certain angles, Russell's life would seem to bear this out. The truth is always more complex, however.

Though his struggle has often been more concerned with developing the Lydian Concept than with seeking recognition for his music, his success has come despite the American Dream rather than because of it. An African American child born in an inner city experiences a very different world from a WASP born with a trust fund in place, let alone the scion of an oil dynasty. To quote the novelist Ross MacDonald, "In a puritanical society, the poor and fatherless, suffering the quiet punishments of despair, may feel themselves permanently and justifiably damned for crimes they can't remember having committed."[1]

From his adoption by Bessie and Joseph Russell, he was confronted by racism in his native Cincinnati and beyond. Some writers have found the whole circumstances of his birth and adoption "mysterious," and the story Russell was told about his origins has achieved an almost mythic significance in reference to his work. As will be seen, most interesting is what Russell made of his life and talents and where these came from *in fact*, rather than in fantasy.

By his twenties and despite suffering from two bouts of tuberculosis, he had established himself in New York within the core of the Jazz Bloomsbury that gathered in Gil Evans's apartment on West 55th Street. It was in the course of a now-famous conversation with Miles Davis that the idea of an overarching musical concept was born. Asked what his musical aims were, Davis replied, "Learning all the changes." Knowing Davis knew the changes already, Russell realized he meant something else. "I felt that he was looking for a new way. Maybe a way that was more of a chord scale unity that would give him time so he didn't have to play complex changes but could have a lingering melody that stretched over a good period of time."[2] And so a lifelong study began that would lead Russell to question the musical and philosophical basis of Western music and propose instead a system based on the relationships between scales and chords. The theory would lead jazz into modal playing and anticipated the jazz-rock of the sixties and seventies.

"Cubano-Be, Cubano-Bop," written in 1947 for Dizzy Gillespie and His Orchestra, fused Afro-Cuban rhythms with jazz. Generally accepted as the first avowedly modal piece in jazz, it was followed by "A Bird in Igor's Yard," written for Buddy DeFranco and His Orchestra. Considered by the record company to be far ahead of its time, the track wasn't released until 1970! Russell wrote and arranged for Earl Hines, Charlie Ventura, Artie Shaw, Claude Thornhill, and singer Lucy Reed and wrote for Teddy Charles, Hal McKusick, and Lee Konitz. But the Concept proved a demanding mistress. In fact, although he published his thesis in 1953, it wasn't until 1956 that Russell made his first record, *Jazz Workshop*, an astonishing album full of dense textures and rhythms.

Working on and refining his Lydian Concept, Russell put the principles of his theory into practice with his own music. A series of groundbreaking recordings followed that included *Jazz in the Space Age*, *New York, N.Y.*, and six albums for the Riverside label, including the brilliant *Ezz-thetics* with Eric Dolphy. By then his Lydian Concept was acknowledged for its impact on the work of such seminal figures in jazz as Miles Davis, John Coltrane, and Bill Evans. Davis had by then released *Kind of Blue* and Coltrane was forging his own take on modality. The direction Russell had initiated had become preeminent in modern jazz.

By 1965 Russell had become increasingly alienated by both the aggressively political stance of the Free Jazz movement and by America's increasing involvement in Southeast Asia. Russell accepted an invitation to work in Sweden, and his influence there proved decisive for a new generation of musicians in Scandinavia and beyond, including Jon Christensen, Palle Mikkelborg, Terje Rypdal, Arild Andersen, and a very young Jan Garbarek. He also had a child by a Swedish woman, but despite his success in northern Europe he could not settle.

In 1969 Russell took up composer Gunther Schuller's offer to teach in the Jazz Department of the New England Conservatory. Since then, he has taught some of the most able and searching musicians. Players like Don Byron, Ricky Ford, and John Medeski have studied the Concept, and others, like Randy and Michael Brecker, studied Russell's ideas through his former student and musical colleague, Dave Baker. He has worked and recorded with his Living Time Orchestra for Blue Note, Soul Note, and Label Bleu, and has toured North America, Japan, and Europe. In some ways, he is more feted abroad than at home, but any disregard Stateside has not stood in the way of both Guggenheim and MacArthur fellowships. George Russell has written both short and extended works for jazz orchestras and groups. He has written ballets and choral works and his influence continues to be felt.

This biography will explain why George Russell is perhaps less well known and less highly regarded than his achievements deserve. It will examine a career that has been sustained over seven decades without any loss of artistic integrity and without the rewards sometimes received by lesser talents. So where does he belong in the jazz firmament? This biography hopes to restore some balance and will weigh Russell's gifts and contributions to jazz. And perhaps at the end, readers will agree that George Russell has earned his place in the pantheon.

Notes

1. R. MacDonald, "Writing the Galton Case," in *On Crime Writing* (Santa Barbara, CA: Capra Press, 1973).

2. Duncan Heining, "A Meeting with a Remarkable Man," *Avant* 7 (Summer 1998).

Acknowledgments

I would like to thank all of the musicians and interviewees who gave their time and help in creating this book. I particularly wish to acknowledge Jack Reilly, Ben Schwendener, and Dwight McPheeters, whose assistance has been exceptional. Others whose advice proved particularly valuable include Stuart Nicholson and Len and Marion Holden. Finally, the greatest debt is owed to my partner, Annie, for her unstinting intellectual, emotional, and financial support. George Russell has had a number of wonderful women in his life, none more so than his wife Alice. I have been especially fortunate in having just one.

CHAPTER ONE

~

From Such Beginnings . . .

George Russell was clearly upset. We were at Stone Mill in the Berkshires, where Jimmy and Juanita Giuffre live. Juanita had been married to George back in the fifties, and I was interviewing her for the biography I was writing on him. They had remained friends, and Alice and George Russell were staying with the Giuffres that weekend. Jimmy suffers from Parkinson's disease, so I was unable to talk to him, but I was looking forward to speaking with Juanita.

As I waited for Juanita to finish attending to Jimmy, Russell started talking about something that had happened in Cincinnati, when he was a young man just starting out as a professional musician. He'd told me the story before—and that was the problem. Now he did not want it in the book. It concerned a young white bassist whom Russell and his mother had befriended and who was severely beaten one night by two white men. By their dress—dark suits, white shirts, dark ties, and fedoras—and attitude, it seemed clear who and what these men were. Russell was convinced they were police officers. Sixty years later he was expressing his fears about how white citizens and officials in Cincinnati might react if they read this accusation.

For me, the story was pivotal in Russell's life. Not only did it indicate the cost for someone such as him of growing up as an African American in a racist society, it also revealed what it meant for him as an individual, as someone who was an unusually sensitive human being. But more than that, it explained how he finally came to leave the Midwest and head for New

1

York. We talked and eventually reached what seemed a mutually acceptable compromise.

Reflecting later, I wondered what had disturbed Russell so much. I had just returned from Cincinnati bringing pictures from his life back in the Midwest. Photos from childhood taken at a school where he had been bitterly unhappy, including some of a childhood friend who had been in the same tuberculosis ward as he and who later died of the illness. A report card from a school where he had experienced discrimination and felt constantly worthless and undermined. These were all reminders of difficult times and of a place he had chosen to escape as soon as he could. It was not surprising that the issue Russell picked to express his discomfort concerned events that led to his leaving home. Maybe he was expressing the fear of being dragged back there in some way. As Alice Russell would later say when she and I talked about this, "George doesn't like to look back. He likes to go forward. He's happy to reminisce, but that's different. He just doesn't like to dwell on things that for him lie in the past."[1]

The conversation provided a salutary lesson about the process and nature of shaping a biography. It could be a flattering process but also a threatening one. It could evoke positive memories and experiences but also equally negative ones half-repressed or happily consigned to oblivion. And it raised the question: *Who owns a life?* The subject? The biographer? The fans and other readers?

The story of someone in Russell's position extends beyond him. He cannot own it, or the manner of its telling, entirely. What our lives say about us, they also say about others and their potential. They talk about forces and themes much greater than us. Those themes are universal and cannot be owned by the subject of a biography.

I understood Russell's discomfort, both in terms of an understandable fear about what might be said about him and in terms of a feeling that he had somehow lost control of his own story. Someone else was walking around in his life and in his memories. He had not lost control of the themes that dominated his life or the external forces that might have shaped it; these were never under his control. Yet it was important to be sensitive to his discomfiture, to respect his feelings, and to maintain his confidence, in both senses.

For Russell, the Lydian Chromatic Concept of Tonal Organization had to be central to the book. That, rather than half-forgotten events from his past, was ultimately what mattered. To exclude it would be like talking about Einstein without relativity or Darwin without evolution or Freud without the unconscious. And as with Freud, Darwin, and Einstein, Russell did not invent—he discovered—and like them he used his discovery to explain to us how relationships within his area of study were different from how we had understood them previously. Like them, his ideas are not without controversy and remain the subject of debate. But ideas are advanced by discussion and disagreement only as long as the dialogue remains open.

This book is therefore concerned with how ideas are developed, disseminated, challenged, and debated. It is about influence, about the way that new ways of seeing or thinking often arise in special contexts where particular personal, creative, and professional relationships are present. Russell's thinking evolved through the complex interaction of his life and personality, his relationships, his environment, and wider social, economic, and cultural forces. In his case one of those wider forces is racism, both in its systematic, political sense and at the very personal level of individual experience.

But there are also themes that emerge about what is or is not jazz and where its place lies in modern culture. There are themes about influence and the transmission of ideas, both in terms of the influences on Russell himself and in terms of his influence on others and on the development of jazz. There are points to be made about who owns jazz and whether it is now a world music or still quintessentially an American or indeed African American music. There are questions to be addressed about education and jazz, and how jazz or any creative enterprise can be taught. And perhaps most important of all, there runs through all of this the history of a truly beautiful and remarkable art and the place of George Russell in its story.

George Allen Smith came into the world at 8:00 p.m. on June 23, 1923. He was born in an apartment at Helena Flats, 1339 Lincoln Avenue in the Walnut Hills district of Cincinnati. The block housed some eleven African American families.[2] It is unclear in which precise apartment Russell was born, and there is no apparent connection between his or his birth mother's name and the names that appear on census records for the block. The doctor certifying the birth was Louis A. Cornish, MD. Russell's mother gave her name as Mary Smith and her place of birth as West Virginia. She was nineteen and single, and the birth certificate records her as "Colored." The space for the father's name is left blank.

It seems likely that "Mary Smith" was an alias given to Dr. Cornish. The doctor was either quite happy not to pursue this further or saw no reason to question her identity. Since there are no apparent connections by name to other residents at 1339 Lincoln Avenue, it seems a reasonable assumption that "Mary" was staying with friends or relatives with a different surname. Perhaps she was estranged from her own family or sent away to give birth due to her family's desire to retain an image of respectability. Speculation perhaps, but it would certainly fit the story Russell was told much later about his birth and origins.

On January 23, 1924, George was adopted by Mr. Joseph A. and Mrs. Bessie O. Russell. He had been with his adoptive parents since June 25, two days after his birth, according to the adoption petition. The mother's consent form gives her name as "Grace Smith" and the witness's name was given as "J. H. George." The adoption certificate states that "George Allen, an illegitimate male child" was, with the consent of his mother, adopted by the Russells. With this document, signed by probate judge William H. Leeds, secured in the public record, George Allen Smith became George Allen Russell. It would not be until he was in his mid-teens that Russell would learn about his origins. Even then, he would never see any reason to pursue his birth mother or birth father or seek any connection with their families.

Mrs. Bessie Russell—she always insisted on that form of address from strangers—was a nurse who worked for Dr. Eli Miller. Miller was a very well-respected physician who would later play a leading role in the Planned Parenthood movement in Cincinnati.[3] She was an active member of the African Methodist Episcopal Mount Zion Church in Walnut Hills. This was one of the most significant of the black churches in Cincinnati, and its minister, Reverend Gilbert,[4] one of its most important community leaders and spiritual figures. As a woman of some standing in her own community, and with her work for Dr. Miller, it seems likely that Mrs. Russell would have insisted that correct procedures for the adoption be followed.

Joseph and Bessie Russell wed on Christmas Day, 1916, in St. Louis, Missouri, so they had been married for six and a half years when they adopted George. They were childless, though whether this was due to an inability on their part to conceive or some other reason is unclear. How the adoption came about remains a mystery. Certainly, there is no reason to assume that Mrs. Russell attended "Mary Smith" during her pregnancy in a professional capacity. Nevertheless, the potential connections are there. The Russells might have known her or her parents as part of an extended family or as friends. They might have attended the same church. However, it seems at least possible that the connection might have come through Miller. It is a reasonable assumption that two white doctors working in the African American community would have known each other, and Miller would have known that the Russells were looking to adopt. Alternatively, Mrs. Russell might have known the nurse attending "Mary." But there are other reasons to wonder about a connection between the Russells and "Mary Smith," and also about the possible part Miller might have played in the adoption. Melbourne Terrace, where the Russells lived, was just a few blocks from Lincoln Avenue, where George was born. It also leads into Reading Road, close to Miller's practice. It is therefore possible that although Cornish attended the delivery, "Mary" might have come under Miller's care during her pregnancy. Whatever the connection might have been, this is now lost and, as noted, George never felt a need to know.

During the nineteenth century, Walnut Hills was a fairly wealthy area of the city, attracting bankers, merchants, and lawyers to its elegant streets. Cable cars arrived in the 1880s, followed by faster and more reliable electric streetcars in 1898. The increased accessibility of the area from downtown both reduced its exclusivity and brought the development of less expensive housing for middle-income families, and from the 1890s to the 1920s there was an expansion of row houses, apartment buildings, and modest single-family dwellings. While the 1930s brought a greater influx of black families into the area, some blacks had been living there since the 1860s. Up through the mid-twentieth century, black families could usually move only into neighborhoods where other black people resided. Although now quite run-down (its days of decline appear to be behind it, however), at the time of George's birth, it was a respectable neighborhood that attracted African Americans who had good jobs and who were keen to see certain standards of propriety maintained.[5]

Lieutenant Commander Dwight McPheeters, one of the Tuskegee Airmen and a childhood friend of George Russell's, recalls,

> It was an all-black neighborhood apart from a couple of grocery stores. There was one on Kerper and the lane leading to Washington Terrace and another at the end of Kerper Avenue, but those were the only white people who—not lived—but were in that neighborhood. But I'll tell you one thing: We didn't have any crime in that neighborhood. People watched out for one another. It wasn't well-to-do or upper middle class. It was a whole bunch of folks that were struggling, but at the same time they were very disciplined about their families and their neighborhood. We had a couple of good policemen who used to be around there that everybody understood and respected.[6]

William R. Davis, now retired from his post at Loyola University, Chicago, also knew George and lived in the area. "It was very close. The people at that time, everyone knew each other. We might live a block away or two blocks away, but you knew each other." Though it was not an affluent neighborhood, in Davis's words,

> The people in neighborhood, the men worked. Most of the women that were able to, if the father had a good job, could stay at home and take care of the

children. My mother was a domestic worker. I had an aunt that did live across the court from us that did never have to work because her husband had a better job, but then we had people who were just postmen, we had people who were railroad Pullman porters, and we had people who worked for the U.S. Postal Service delivering the mail. We had a few teachers and a few social workers in the neighborhood and those were the people who had had the opportunity to go to college and become teachers and social workers, etc. Most of the people there in the neighborhood were just plain ordinary working people, blue-collar more or less.[7]

Mrs. Bessie O. Russell was born in St. Louis in 1883 and, according to Russell, she was one of the first nurses of color in Cincinnati.[8] Mr. Joseph Russell was born in 1879 and was a chef on the B&O Railroad. He and Bessie were both in their forties when they adopted George. Given their age and childless status, it is a little surprising that they had not adopted a baby sooner. This might suggest that it was the opportunity to adopt George himself that presented itself to the Russells, and again that there might have been some family connection between one of the Russells and "Mary." Though he does not know why his parents were childless, Russell says that theirs was not a happy marriage. They had separate bedrooms and, in Russell's words, Joseph's "marriage to Bessie had most of the time been strained." Describing his father, Russell says, "He was an intelligent man. He had street knowledge. He didn't need any official colleges or high schools. He was a gentleman and he could talk well and [was] a good man, but they had a bad relationship. I never saw them kiss or hug or sleep together."[9]

Bessie's work for Dr. Miller also became a source of dissention in the marriage.

He still supported us—as my mother did—but at one point he asked my mother to stop working for Dr. Miller and I think that had to do with their marriage, you know. And she had to stop working for Dr. Miller. Nurse that she could be—she was probably the best nurse in Cincinnati. She knew her nursing up and down because I saw her save lives of people.[10]

It seemed that Joseph was threatened by her working for Miller rather than her working per se.

The relationship between my mother and Dr. Miller was very tight. I don't know how tight because Dr. Miller was married and he was a man of scruples and they both were. My father might have thought something was going on there because "she's not giving it to me." If there was a fight, my mother would win. She had muscles. She was a strong lady. Once there was . . . she had a gun, so he started crying and went to his room.[11]

From all his comments, it's clear that Russell loved and admired both his parents deeply. But there's also a powerful vein of sadness that runs through his account of their marriage. "He'd come in, he'd lay down the food he'd gotten, the great food he'd gotten from the train that he hadn't used, and he'd go up stairs and start playing the races. He played the races a lot."[12] And:

> I was sad that they didn't have a happy life together, that there wasn't more of a rapport between them. You kind of felt the distance between these two wonderful people. Both were wonderful. My father went to the third grade. My mother graduated, was the first black woman to graduate from Mihara University from Atlanta, Georgia, in nursing. My father used to . . . I played cards with him a lot. I loved cards. He loved cards. When he was sick I played cards with him. He'd fix me, I forget the name of the drink, but it had ginger ale and whisky and sugar. What's that called? Boilermaker or something. We'd have fun playing, but it got so that getting down the stairs must've been an ordeal and he slept upstairs. But he left me with a lot.[13]

Being a railroad man, Joseph was frequently away, though he sometimes took George on trips with him. Bessie was, however, perhaps the more constant and significant figure in his life. McPheeters remembers her fondly. "She had the sweetest disposition you ever saw and I think she spoiled George; that was my opinion. But she was a very, very nice lady. I never met his father."[14]

William R. Davis has a similar recollection. "His mother and my mother were friends. We all belonged to the same church. All I remember was that she was one of the nicest people in the block. You see, the families were very close in that neighborhood, especially those that belonged to the church."[15]

At that time the Russells were living on Kerper Avenue, and although their area of Walnut Hills was predominantly black, Russell speaks about Bessie's German origins on her mother's side. He also has early recollections of a family friend, "Aunt Nee," who had blonde hair and was married to a "black feller." These memories suggest that the racial divisions in Cincinnati were sometimes less clear-cut than might be assumed. He recalls, "Because my mother had a number of friends, people who were white people, I knew white people better than I knew colored people."[16]

Russell told Vivian Perlis in a 1993 interview for the American Music Series that as a child he would often bring "some little ragamuffin home" and Bessie would take care of him. "[M]y mother would kind of adopt him, as a friend of mine, sometimes for long times, or some kid whose home life was horrible, she'd take him in and he'd become a playmate. But not for a terribly long time, maybe for a year even, she'd do that."[17]

One of Russell's earliest memories is from when he was five. Bessie had sent him to get a haircut at the barber's across the road from Dr. Miller's surgery. "I went to the barbershop. Came out, I didn't see any cars. One car turns a corner and slams into me and ran over my face."[18] He was carried to Dr. Miller's surgery, where one patient—a Mrs. Tannenbaum, a member of the Jewish-German family who owned Cincinnati's main department store—rushed him in her car to the hospital nearby.

> It was a Jewish hospital, and in Cincinnati at that time blacks were not allowed into that hospital. She got to [the] Jewish hospital and the attendants kept saying . . . I don't know how they could tell what kind of race I was, but she must've said, "I have this little colored boy with me." They said, "Colored boy? He's not going in here." She said, "The hell he isn't." (laughs) She said, "You get the hell out of the way." She got me to the operating room and the doctor said to the assistants there, "Get your ass moving. We got to help this kid." That was beautiful. I guess they had to sew on my ear. For some years, I had the streaks where the car had run over me, the impressions it made.[19]

It was a lucky escape for Russell and he was in hospital for some weeks. He recalls being treated well by the hospital staff despite being "the first person of color to be admitted" to the hospital. "The cook made special dishes for me and they treated me royally. I hated it when they dismissed me because they'd done all they could do. My mother was visiting all the time. I had the time of my life and I almost cried the day they took me home, because they celebrated me."[20]

The accident seems to have set Russell back at school and held back his physical development. "The next impression I had was of Hoffman School, Kindergarten. I'm not sure I have this right, but I must've started Kindergarten a year later than the average person. My age thing got all messed up with the accident."[21] Dr. Robert Moore, who began research for a biography of George Russell in the eighties, spoke to a number of people in Cincinnati who had known Russell as a child.

> [W]hen he was very young the kids nicknamed him Kelly. I guess that as a result of that accident, of being hit by a car, I guess maybe naturally that he wasn't as gifted or as physically adept as some of his playmates and he'd always be the last one picked to play baseball or whatever and he was rather awkward physically. They nicknamed him Kelly because of a baseball player for the Cin-

cinnati Reds—I think his name was Red Kelly—who wasn't particularly good, who was usually cited as a problem on the team. So that name followed him, and George spoke of this in the context of his getting an interest in playing the drums. In the Boy Scout troop he was the second best drummer and he took great pride in that and that became his thing to excel in.[22]

The incident at the hospital also made Russell aware that his color set him aside from other parts of the world he lived in. "The negativity of the world begins to start with incidents like this. However, being unconscious and everything, it doesn't make a deep impression until you're able to go back on it. While it's happening you don't think anything of it."[23] He had also begun to appreciate that there were differences between life at home and life on the street.

> I did have an impression that things on the street weren't exactly like things in your house. Things on the street were disconnected from your house. It was a separate language to survive. For example, my mother, beautiful Bessie, growing up and being Dr. Miller's nurse, she used technical terms like "rectum." This is your *rectum*. This is your . . . whatever. Kids being kids, one day one guy kicked me right in the ass. I said, "You've kicked me in my rectum! *(laughs)*" All the kids around said, "What?" And they broke out laughing. That taught me. That was the beginning of something else in me I suppose. It's a different language in the street, so I began to learn street survival and street language.[24]

At Kindergarten, Russell says the first thing he did the first day was to kiss the girls—white or black. It was a mixed school, as were many of the city's schools. In racist societies, people of color need to develop special skills to negotiate the different worlds with which they must have contact. There are different codes, different ways of speaking—and Russell seems to have begun to learn this quite young.[25]

> So, the impression between home and the street was just beginning to grow. Especially when the guys did the rectum thing. That started in me a new compulsion to speak the language of the street until I could finally speak it better than they could. And still today, if I lose something I say, "Where the fuck . . . ?" The part of you that cares about protecting you, the red light goes on between the streets and your own essence. At home I felt relatively safe. In the streets, even when things got normal and everything was done, the same day I realised the differences, not to the extent that . . . well, [I suppose] it did mess with my psychology that I was different, but not as formidably as it did later on. I mean a little later on. Like, my father was from Georgia, went to the

third grade in school, but he was a third-degree Mason. He was an intelligent man, chef-cook on the railroad. I remember him meeting a cracker, a fucking policeman, who said, "Boy, what you doin' wearing that pin?" My father just said, "Oh!" Took the pin off, or else.[26]

This sense of difference, of being in an alien environment, was fostered by Russell's experiences of school. Cincinnati had begun to integrate the school system—or at least to allow schools to integrate their pupils—in the twenties. As Davis recalls, "The high schools were always integrated. You went to the high school for the district you lived in. If you went to the high school that I went to you had to take an examination at the sixth-grade level, and for Walnut Hills at the seventh-grade level. If you passed the exam and [then you could] go [on] through the twelfth grade. Walnut Hills had a reputation of being one of the better high schools in the nation. I had the opportunity to go there."[27] And yet in most other respects de facto segregation was the day-to-day order of life. Ohio had been a free state since its inception. However, it bordered on Indiana and, more importantly, Kentucky, which was a slave state and had fought on the side of the Confederacy. Describing the postbellum situation in the Midwest, C. Vann Woodward notes in *The Strange Career of Jim Crow*,

> Generally speaking, the farther west the Negro went in the free states the harsher he found the proscription and segregation. Indiana, Illinois and Oregon incorporated in their constitutions provisions restricting the admission of Negroes to their borders.[28]

As early as the 1830s, Alexis de Tocqueville was shocked by depth of racial bias he saw in the North, writing that "the prejudice of race appears to be stronger in the states that have abolished slavery than in those states where it still exists; and nowhere is it so intolerant as in those states where servitude has never been known."[29]

It's a point made eloquently by McPheeters: "Cincinnati is a bigoted town and it's barely underneath the surface at this time. These people are one step away from Dixie."[30] Davis echoes this comment.

> It has always been that way. Racism is a very strong factor in the life there, and although they have organizations that have tried and are still trying to alleviate some of the friction between the races, there is something there that I would say—having been gone for fifty years, I'm still in contact [and] I have four sisters that are there—most of the people are still alienated against one another. That may be because of the influence of southern Indiana and

Kentucky, which is immediately across the river from Cincinnati. A lot of the traffic that you get coming into Cincinnati for buying goods, trading, and entertainment comes from Kentucky and Indiana and Tennessee. Some of them come from as far away as Tennessee just to see a baseball game. We have those kind[s] of influences that are still there and it's difficult to change the mores of people who have been brought up with those kinds of differences in their minds.[31]

Russell went from the Kindergarten to Hoffman Elementary and was one of the small minority of African American students attending the school. Hoffman had been recently desegregated, and although the option of him attending a blacks-only school existed, Bessie Russell rejected this for her son. As a professional woman who seems to have had the ability to function effectively in both black and white worlds, she appears to have wanted Russell to be able to do the same. On balance, he seems to have felt that was the right choice, as he told Perlis:

I could have gone to any of the other schools. Some schools weren't desegregated. But my mother insisted that I go to Hoffman, which was an integrated school. So in a way we were—we few who went to the school, the integrated school—were much more faced with the reality of things—which is good—than the kids who didn't go to the integrated schools.[32]

At the same time, it was clearly not a happy experience and he felt constantly undermined and undervalued because of his color.

I think what finished me at Hoffman in the eighth grade, the teacher who had a book and she had different people reading it. It was a book about slavery—one of the famous books—the word "Nigger" was all through the book, and she pointed at me and asked me to read the book to the class. I read maybe five words that had "Nigger" in and slammed the book down and left the class.[33]

Such insensitivity was commonplace, and when he was fourteen, Russell was chosen for a part in the school play. It was *Gone with the Wind* and his role was that of Aunt Jemima.

Dwight could've killed me. I tried to explain to him. He said, "What the hell did you do that for? It's a disgrace." I'm smart enough to act Aunt Jemima. I'm smart enough to see the pattern. [But] I too, of course, felt belittled.[34]

McPheeters recalls the event well, though his view has softened over the years.

Yeah. I really panned him. I think maybe our friendship suffered because of that. I didn't think that George should do that. I thought that he was degrading himself and all of us by doing that, but like Hattie McDaniel in the movies, we did the same—kind of ridicule of her—but she paved the way for a lot of us to get into the movies.[35]

Russell describes another incident that took place on a field trip, which perhaps reveals the complexity of thoughts and feelings that go through a young African American's mind in a world of such divisions.

It's things like—when you're in a class with whites and you feel that they're special or something. Even incidents like the eighth-grade class, which made me thirteen or fourteen or so, going out on a nature thing and being on a mountain and this girl slipped and I happened to be there at the drop-off of the mountain and I caught her and her arms were around me. I associated that with, "Let's see how the crowd reacts?" You know? Would they appreciate what I'd just done? My teacher did, because he was Jewish, but would the others or would they want to say, "What are your arms doing around that white woman?" I was saving her life.[36]

If the divisions in Cincinnati, and Ohio as a whole, were marked, as a young boy Russell was still surprised by his first experience of traveling south with Bessie to visit Joseph's family.

The big one was when we took a train, my mother and I going south to see his family. The train was nice. The food was nice on the train. After we left Cincinnati, we went to the next town in Kentucky. Nothing happened there, but then at the next stop further south we had to go, my mother and I, both light-skinned, had to go to the back of the train, which was full of black people. Then I said, "Oh, I get it." So it grew on me, this difference, because of these incidents.[37]

He was seven at the time, and he recalls being told very clearly not to leave the family's farm under any circumstances. He was too young to understand what precisely they feared might happen to him but remembers the palpable sense of danger the warning implied. Returning to the North, or rather the Midwest, he understood for the first time the implications of segregation: "Then when I got back north and all the theaters were segregated. I understood all that then. I understood I was really different."[38]

It's hard even now to understand what this means for a young African American, growing up in a world where the routine humiliations of everyday

discrimination demean but where in some situations those same racist impulses can place physical safety in jeopardy. There's a story from their time in
high school, that both Russell and McPheeters tell, that illustrates this very
well. Russell remembers it as a Boy Scout trip to Indiana, while McPheeters
recalls that they were at a YMCA camp in the state. Though there are other
differences in their recollection, the substance of the account remains the
same. Their teacher or scout leader was an African American man named J.
Harvey Kerns. As McPheeters tells it,

> So we stopped in Liberty, Indiana, and they were having a street carnival
> there, and before we could get out of the car a state trooper came up and said
> to Mr. Kerns, "What do you boys want?" Mr Kerns said, "We want to see the
> carnival." And the state trooper said, "Well they don't allow colored people
> in this town after 6 o'clock." So, Mr Kerns said, "This is America and I'm go-
> ing to see the carnival." I was scared to death and so was everybody else. So
> was George. Everybody was scared but J. Harvey Kerns. He was like a banty
> rooster. The crowd started following us and there was this thing with this
> sledgehammer; you were supposed to hit it and ring the bell. This guy sees us
> and he blocked our way. He was the concession owner. He said, "Want to try
> this thing, boy?" So he gives the hammer to Mr. Kerns and he hit it a couple
> of times and it didn't go up. Kerns was a little guy. Then one of the people in
> the crowd walked up and says, "Hey boy, let me show you how to do it." And
> he showed him, and Mr. Kerns hit it again and rang the bell, and the conces-
> sion owner grabbed a cigar and shoved it in his mouth, and he didn't smoke.
> (laughs) Then we went to get something to eat and all you could hear was,
> "Nigger. Nigger. Nigger." I tell you, I wanted to get out of that place. I didn't
> want to hang around. And so we went into this restaurant and the waitress
> wanted to know what we wanted, and we said we'd like to have something to
> eat. So, she didn't know what to do and went over to talk to the manager, and
> the manager took us and put us at a table right by the kitchen door. Boy, they
> were washing dishes and clanging pots and pans in the kitchen, so you couldn't
> hear yourself talk or think. But they served us. And the crowd gathered out-
> side, and I said to myself, "Oh God, I don't know if we're ever going to get out
> of here alive or not." But we went out the back door, got in the car, and went
> on back to the retreat. But those were the days, and anybody who says, "Those
> were the good old days" is a damn liar.[39]

As Russell recalls, they were told to get out of town for their own safety.
"One man said, 'You better leave town.' I think it was a policeman. I think
that was the home of the KKK. So we did. We left."[40] He told musician,
broadcaster, and writer Ian Carr in 1992:

I saw them humiliate this beautiful man, who was very much a gentleman and very much a soft-spoken, very sensitive individual. You know, "Hit it, boy!" But he picked up the hammer . . . one of those things you hit, a hammer and a bell, to see if you can get the iron ball up to hit the bell. And he nearly shot that bell up through the [top] when they called him "boy." And they called him other things you know that were not very nice, you know.[41]

On the one hand, one might wonder at the risks that Mr. Kerns took with his young charges. They hardly bear thinking about. But from another perspective, he taught them a powerful and valuable lesson that is still heard in McPheeters's words: "I've been determined for practically all my adult life that any unwritten law which was made for me or mine is going to be broken. I will not accept those kinds of things."[42] In a way, it's a timeless message, one that was clearly not lost on Russell or on their mutual friend William Davis. In his work as a specialist lecturer to underprivileged, bright-but-failing young people, Davis tries to express it to his students in this way: "There is opportunity, which I always vouchsafed to the students and children there when I was working in Cincinnati, being prepared as well as anybody else is prepared regardless of your race or religion or whatever, and if the opportunity is there you can grab it."[43]

But despite the prejudice of many, there were also children and adults who felt able to cross America's Great Divide of race and color. Russell remembers a small but, for him, puzzling and even touching incident at Hoffman.

This eighth-grade student—his name was Bentley—passed a note to me, and the note was from the girl who was considered one of the smartest girls in the class—Marion Laing—and she was very beautiful, and the note said, "I've always loved you." She had given it to Bentley to give it to me. I just understood that because—I think she was German—I was on the football team.[44]

And how did the other football players react to him being black? "Oh, we didn't have any problems."[45]

Russell went from Hoffman to Withrow High, as did Dwight McPheeters. William Davis, on the other hand, went to Walnut Hills, a more prestigious establishment. McPheeters had also been intended for Walnut Hills. "I had missed going to Walnut Hills High School. They had a test for people to be eligible to go there, but I had the measles when they were giving that test. I don't know if I would have passed it or not. The Walnut Hills kids came from all over town depending on if they passed the test."[46]

For Russell, and also for McPheeters, Withrow High holds few happy memories. A homeroom photograph in the 1939 yearbook shows Russell crouching at one side, six feet from the rest of his contemporaries. It seems to echo his feelings about the experience.

> I really didn't belong to that except for the grace of one good kid. I remember him still today. His sister was the story lady on the radio. She told stories for kids. Wendell Gabrick was his name. Wendell and I were real tight because he loved cooking and I loved cooking. This all happened at Withrow. It ended up with us being the two guys in the room with the rest being thirty women, with the average ignorant shit coming from people, "Oh you sissies!" I was used to being degraded. Wendell wasn't, but he'd come home with me, by himself, and he'd go back by himself. In the black neighborhoods at the time the blacks were scared to do anything to white people. In white neighborhoods it was much more scary for black people.[47]

The stupidity of the informal but overt discrimination and segregation that operated was something that did not escape all white children. As Davis remembers: "I was in the Boy Scouts and we were doing some merit badge projects and I had three friends who were white, and we would go hide in the woods near school to do these projects and nobody knew what was happening until they were all done and the inspectors would come to check them out."[48] This contrasts markedly with Dwight McPheeters's experience of trying to attend a Scout Jamboree at the Civic Center in Cincinnati. "I heard about it and I was a Boy Scout, so I thought I'd put on my Scout uniform and go down. I went to the door and this white man said, 'What are you doing here?' I said, 'I'm a Boy Scout and I'm here for the Jamboree.' He said, 'This is for whites. Go have your own black Scout Jamboree.'"[49]

It was not that children could not be cruel or reflect the prejudices of their parents. As Russell told Carr, "They were all under the same thing too. I mean they were given roles to play in life, you know, but without realizing they're just roles."[50] But for some white children, like Wendell Gabrick, the differences just didn't accord with their own experiences of the world. And not all adults were quite so ignorant either. McPheeters recalls a teacher named Mr. Surdo, who ran the Withrow Special Chorus and Glee Club.

> Surdo was a little man who wore a toupee, but he was a tyrant and he was as fair and square and straight as an arrow. I know I was invited along with everybody in the Special Chorus to Mr. Surdo's house for a party he was having. Well, I didn't go, and I think that Leonard Williams was also invited and we didn't go. When I went back to school the following week, Mr. Surdo called me to his office and wanted to know why I didn't come to his party. I told him that I didn't think that I would be welcome. Well, he gave me what for and he told me that

his house was open to all of his students and he says, "Your color doesn't mean a thing to me. As far as I'm concerned, you're a part of the group of children that I teach and I don't teach color one way or the other. I teach music. When I have a party, I want all the students that I teach to be there."[51]

Sadly, Surdo left shortly after, and his replacement was, in McPheeters's words, "a latent bigot but it showed."[52] But both he and Russell recalled teachers and lessons that did offer some inspiration. For McPheeters it was English with Miss Atkins, and for Russell it was government. "I only cared about a course called government. I got A in that and Ds in everything else."[53] Russell also sang in the Boys' Glee Club and the school's A Cappella Choir, though in a photograph of the former his name appears as "George Russel" and he doesn't seem to have been physically present. He didn't take any other formal musical training at Withrow, and his academic record was, to say the least, undistinguished. As he says, Ds and C-minuses predominate on his report cards, though physical geography also stands out as one of his better subjects. He told Carr, "The school didn't like me and I didn't like it, you know."[54] Though the school was integrated, Russell remembers that out of several thousand pupils fewer than twenty were black. According to him, his lack of any more formal musical training, despite his involvement in the Boy Scouts drum and bugle band, was in part due to one of the teachers: "The music teacher there, Mr. Smithee, told me that I'd never be allowed in the band, you know, and that I didn't belong in music."[55]

And some white teachers made no effort to hide their racist attitudes, as Robert Moore recounts in an article for the *Trotter Institute Review*:

> Racism and racial discrimination played a most important part in Russell's life, as it did in the lives of most of his peers. Interviews conducted with some of his early associates—musical and others—revealed that racism cut quite deeply into all of their lives. Every interviewee had a collection of horror stories to tell. George recalls being pushed down the hall by the gym teacher at the Hoffman School who yelled at him, "You ain't nothing but a Nigger." He was discouraged from participating in the high school band.[56]

A sense grew in Russell that there was a gap between what he experienced and saw and felt and what he was being taught at school. Again talking with Carr in 1992, he noted, "At an early, very early age, I had a feeling that I wasn't hearing the whole story and I was hearing a colored story. *(laughs)* Colored in favor of the people who were the dominant race [who] were running the culture as they saw it. So there was already a cultural clash."[57]

Such feelings could only be reinforced in Russell by experience. "Dwight and I were in the Hoffman choir when the YMCA in Cincinnati invited the choir to come and swim except for me and Dwight. *(laughs)* Everybody in the class must've been fifty people. The Young Men's Christian Association! That woke me up to religion."[58]

If the issue about mixed-race swimming sounds laughable, then it should be noted that throughout the high schools in Cincinnati, African American students always swam last period on Fridays. The pool was then cleaned. Both McPheeters and Davis recall this vividly, nearly seventy years on. McPheeters's voice still shakes with fury as he says,

> To show you what we were up against to some extent, and this is just to some extent, they allowed the black students to swim on the last period on Friday and after they swam they would drain the pool and . . . yeah, they would drain the pool.[59]

And Davis, who was on the Walnut Hills swimming team, laughs at the absurdity:

> On occasion you find a great deal of integration—some things we did inter-racially that showed how ridiculous more or less the segregation idea was. I had a very good friend by the name of Reginald Brown. Reginald Brown and I were swimmers and track men. I played football, ran on the track team, played basketball and swam. Reggie and I were swimming in a competition with our homeroom, which was all-white. The African American students' regular swimming periods at that time were the last period on Friday. Over the weekend they cleaned the swimming pool. We used to laugh at that, and some of the white boys laughed too because we were swimming together every afternoon after school and yet we couldn't swim in class with them during the week. It was stupid, but there were grown people that controlled the thing—we didn't.[60]

Home life and community was one set of experiences growing up. School and the white world was a whole other universe of often—or even mainly—negative events. Both made you who you were in differing degrees. For some—Russell, McPheeters, and Davis—it presented a set of challenges to overcome. For others, perhaps these challenges were just too overwhelming.

Russell was sixteen when his father, Joseph, died. It was Russell himself who found him on September 12, 1939.

He was done in. I don't know if you've ever experienced negativity, serious negativity. It pulls you down, you know. So, one morning, for some reason, I got up early and I walked in his room. And he was sitting like this (*demonstrates posture: one knee raised pulled against his chest with both arms around it*) looking right in my eyes, but dead. I looked at him for a long time, you know. I said, "Mom"—they slept in different rooms—"Mom, I think that Dad is dead." He was holding his frickin' leg . . . because he was in terrible pain. He had arthritis, rheumatism, all of it together, and he wasn't hollering or crying. He didn't do that. I think that was due to his being a Mason. And my mother screamed. So that made me the man. Mom took up [child] nursing. People wanted to take a vacation, she'd take care of their children. She did that most of her life, the rest of her life.[61]

As to what Russell gained or learned from Joseph, he identifies an important kind of knowledge—"He gave me an idea of what I cannot be, and he was a real father."[62] But Joseph also loved music, and when in his teens Russell was playing drums with a neighborhood orchestra, he'd come and listen to them practice, very much the proud father. And there's something in both the quiet dignity and the caution Russell describes about Joseph that he has also perhaps developed. When a "cracker" sheriff Down South tells you to take off your Masonic Pin, it's foolhardy to argue. Dignity and self-respect, after all, lie within.

By the time of Joseph's death, things at Withrow were deteriorating. As he explained to Carr, "You know that feeling of the way the dominant class was thinking, that there was something suspect in it was born early on. . . . And it made a rebel out of me. A quiet one, but a rebel."[63] And he qualifies this very slightly, adding, "If you wanted me to act a certain way and it's life-threatening, I'll act that way, you know. If you want me to say 'Yessa boss,' I'll say 'Yessa boss'—if it's life-threatening, you know. But I'll get you somewhere up the line."[64] His rebellion at Withrow High took the form of an increasing extracurricular involvement in playing jazz and absenting himself from school, both physically and psychologically.

The music . . . I talk about that in something I'm writing about the past and how it grew. For the instant I heard jazz music, I said, "I have to have a part in that," and that was actually in high school—Withrow High School in Cincinnati. . . . I attended school but I wasn't really there with the type of material the school was talking about . . . and I, in a sense, rejected the academic knowledge and went for instinctive knowledge from the very beginning. My aim was to somehow live a spiritual life. That was a big help that saved me.[65]

His rejection of the school's white cultural values also involved a sartorial assault on the school's informal dress code. As he recalls it now, "I was rebellious to begin with and I probably set off the fashion period down there because I wore high-draped pants and shoes that were oh so mellow."[66] And as he told Carr, "I began to have troubles when the principal would call me in his office quite regularly and ask me why I was wearing those high checkered pants and purple pants with red checks in them, and why am I wearing that goatee to school?"[67]

The school's initial response was to refer him to a psychologist for the usual panoply of assessments and Rorschach tests but "psychologizing" the "problem" he presented clearly didn't work. Russell remembers, "And them sending me to a psychiatrist for a Rorschach test, which I managed to make as ugly as possible. I mean you just play that game, all of that crap."[68] Or, as he told Perlis in 1993, "[T]hey managed at school to send me for one Rorschach test too many. Even then I thought it was idiotic, and I still think they're absolutely idiotic. [Because] I would say anything weird just to shock the person administering the test."[69]

For Russell, from his early encounters of racism at Hoffman Elementary to his even more humiliating experiences at Withrow High, his sense of alienation from and antagonism toward education grew. He described it to Perlis as "a creative conflict with the establishment." Up to that point, he says, he had not really identified with any ethnic group, feeling that he had been "well-protected, insulated from all of that." Increasingly he saw himself as "antiestablishment," and his admiration for others he saw as being against the system increased, whether they were musicians, artists, or gangsters. He was determined not to fit the mold that he felt education was shaping for him.

> I knew—I knew that I felt inside a revolution; that I wanted to revolt. I felt a strong feeling of revolting. And that's really what I did. (laughs) I wanted to rebel, the result of those experiences has made me a rebel. In some way I wanted to rebel against this kind of stupid ethnocentricity, which I didn't know anything about that word at the time. I just knew the feeling of being called a "Nigger" or being the butt of stupid jokes and remarks, and the feeling that if you were white you had a natural right to a mind, and, well, most of those minds hadn't had an original thought, ever. They never had the imagination to be a rebel at all. They were cogs in the wheel.[70]

It is worth taking a moment to think in more depth about the processes Russell is describing. The social psychologists Peter Berger and Thomas Luckmann suggest that where "acutely discrepant worlds are mediated in primary socialisation, the individual is presented with a choice of profiled identities apprehended by him as genuine biographical possibilities." They continue, "[T]here may be a socially concealed asymmetry between 'public' and 'private' biography." Russell, like his peers McPheeters and Davis, seems to have developed a strong sense of himself from his life at home with Joseph and Bessie and within the rich community life of Walnut Hills. This is broadly what Berger and Luckmann mean by primary socialization. As they note, "The original reality of childhood is 'home' and all later realities are 'artificial' in comparison." Secondary socialization refers to those forces such as education that ideally build upon "successful" primary socialization and mirror it to a greater or lesser extent. What psychological impact must this have had on young black people back in the thirties (and probably still does today), where the social "knowledge" imparted by the education system devalues and denigrates the individual, in the face of the positive experiences of home and community? What Berger and Luckmann describe above as a failure of effective socialization must, in the context of Russell's experience, be an "effective" adaptation.[71]

Raising questions regarding socialization and race is by no means new. Evidence was given by a number of leading American sociologists and psychologists to the Supreme Court in 1954 on the effects of segregation in education on black children. This evidence was a key factor in the subsequent desegregation of education and training in America.[72] More recently, in the *Journal of Black Studies*, W. Oliver has discussed the issue of failures in socialization of black males and how these can be addressed through what the article describes as "Afro-Centric Socialization."[73] Adaptation and socialization in the context of inequality and racism are hugely complicated matters. In George's situation, he told me that he was brought up knowing as many white people as black, and by a mother he describes as "70 percent German." He developed a strategy for dealing with police officers who would stop him at night with the demand, "What are you, boy?" He would say, "I'm Greek-Italian," and with his "swarthy" complexion registered and computed, they would let him pass. As noted, young black males in the thirties (then as now) needed intricate negotiating skills to survive in the world. Writing about the impact of attributions upon an individual where there is a severe disjunction between how one is perceived and how one sees oneself, psychiatrist R. D. Laing notes,

> It is an achievement to realize one is not necessarily who others take one to be. Such awareness of discrepancy between self-identity, being-for-oneself, and being-for-others, is painful. There is a strong tendency to feel guilt, anxiety,

anger or doubt if self-attributions are disjunctive with attributions made about self by others, particularly when attributions are taken as injunctions.[74]

Interestingly, Berger and Luckmann also look at the additional "socialization" needed by priests, revolutionaries, and musicians (!).[75] Extending the point they are making but slightly, it is a reasonable supposition that from the age when Russell began playing professionally, the most positive and "effective" secondary socialization he experienced was through the community of musicians in which he moved. This perhaps provided a psychological, emotional, and social counter to the negative experience of mainstream education. Music made sense in a world that did not.

By the time he was fourteen, Russell was playing drums regularly in a nightclub with a pianist backing a singer, and the clothes—purple highwaisters, zoot suits, set off with a goatee and mustache—he wore for school reflecting the demimonde he inhabited. The periodic summonses to the principal's office continued, and Russell remembers that he was on the verge of expulsion. It was possibly on the last such occasion that something peculiar happened. The principal told him

> that he had gotten a call from my father asking how I was doing in school and how he hates to have to tell him that, you know, I'm on the verge of being expelled. Well, that was rather strange. That was a strange day in my life because my father had been dead a year, you know.[76]

Or, as he later recalled,

> The last dealing I had with Withrow was the president [principal] Mr. Peoples saying, "Your father called." My father probably did call, I guess he's from West Virginia, but he wasn't the father I knew. I never saw him in my life and Mr. Peoples telling me that they were letting me go from school because they didn't like the way I dressed—long drape pants. It was too "out" for them.[77]

It is unclear whether the principal's comment was simply malicious and made out of ignorance or whether Russell's biological father was actually following his progress "from afar." My suspicion is that the former was the case. Russell, however, has always believed the latter. Either way, it was this that led to his discovery that he was adopted.

Russell admits he had suspicions that Bessie and Joseph were not his birth parents. A "cousin" had let something slip when he was twelve. "Actually, my mother protected me from finding out, and we had a little suggestion when I was twelve in the Boy Scouts drum and bugle corps in Cincinnati.

That probably came from my cousin, Juanita, who was, I believe, adopted by another family, but we used to play as cousins but weren't really cousins."[78] And, "I suspected but the truth came out when . . . she said, 'I'm not your real mother.' I said, 'You are because you have been.' And she remains my mother, with no hard feelings against what I call 'the kids.'"[79]

Following the confrontation with the Withrow principal, Bessie told him the story of his origins. As he describes it, he was the "love child" of a white music professor at Oberlin College and a light-skinned African American student from a wealthy background in Kentucky. Some children might have reacted badly to such news. Bessie and Joseph had, after all, kept the truth from him for sixteen years. Some children might have felt that their biological mother—and father—had abandoned or disowned them. But any anger he felt, or feels, seems only to be directed immediately toward the school principal, but primarily to a system that would not allow his biological parents to be together. He talks of "the kids":

> That was a pretty huge shock for me because that really even before my mother said "I'm not your real mother"—although in my experience she's the only . . . she was totally a real mother—but the "kids" she was standing in for didn't have a chance because she did come from an upper-income family [who] made sure that her decisions were as close to white as could be at the time.[80]

Russell still seems genuinely touched that his biological father might have contacted his school to express an interest in his progress. "So, my father, a white music professor, had that much of an interest, but the times were really rough. The rules were absurd. (laughs)"[81] And in the dining area of his condominium in Boston, there's a photograph of a group of African American students. In the front row, a light-skinned black woman is sitting on the ground. "It's funny that picture has about three tiers to sit on and my mother was in the front row, and if I show it to people they usually pick her out pretty easily."[82] The resemblance is striking.

On the front of the photograph is written "Class 1920 B.C.I." During research for this book, two names were found on the back of the photograph—Lettie E. George (written underneath "Class Philo. . . . 1920") and Kathaleen George. The latter were only revealed when Russell's wife, Alice, removed the photograph for copying in connection with this biography. From this it proved possible to trace "BCI" and identify that it was a school for African American children in West Virginia. The 1920 U.S. Census revealed that Nannie K. (Kathleen) George was the daughter of James H. and Lettie W. George, and that Lettie E. was their niece, who lived with them in North Fork, West Virginia. J. H. George was, of course, the witness to the consent to adopt. Further research, with assistance from archivists at Oberlin College, confirmed that Nannie Kathleen George attended Oberlin in 1922–23 but left during her first year. She was a student of music. Although this does not confirm the story Bessie Russell told her son, it is certainly consistent with that account.

Ultimately, it matters little whether the story of his origins is true or not. What is significant is the way Russell has used the story. It is as if the stability and love that Bessie and Joseph gave him has been in some way projected onto "the kids." In a way, the story of his origins, far from leaving him feeling abandoned or betrayed, gave him a sense of security in a world that was becoming increasingly insecure. In a positive sense, it was as if his origins as a "love-child" of a white man and a black woman allowed him to inhabit both the white and black worlds. The lack of bitterness is quite remarkable, even in respect to the insensitive and indiscreet way in which the school principal dealt with him and which led to his discovering that he was adopted. But this is also part of a pattern in his life where he "consciously" transcends potentially negative experiences and turns them into positive and sometimes life-changing events. It's true of the childhood car accident, of the way he handled Bessie and Joseph's emotional coldness toward each other, of how he learned to manage the differences between street and home and between the white world and the black. It is evidence of an attitude to life—involving simultaneously a kind of spiritual certainty and also an intellectual and emotionally intelligent questioning—that seems to have sustained him.

Notes

1. Interview with Alice Russell, November 2004.

2. The apartments' residents listed in the Cincinnati City Directory for 1923 were Stanley Cohen, Wendell E. Mitchell, Edward Turner, Sally Dowlin, John W. Hodges, Ernest Montgomery, Clifford W. Reid, Hosie Hand, Matty Gibbs, James Jones, and G. W. Byrd.

3. Dr. Elizabeth Campbell, a pioneer in the area of sexual hygiene and birth control in Cincinnati, also had her residence on Reading Road, where Dr. Miller's office was located. See Marguerite Wykoff Zapoleon, "Cincinnati Citizens: Elizabeth Campbell (1862–1945) and M. Edith Campbell (1875–1962)," *Queen City Heritage* 43, no. 4 (Winter 1985): 4–20.

4. See Wendell P. Dabney, *Cincinnati's Colored Citizens* (Cincinnati, OH: Dabney Publishing, 1926).

5. Geoffrey J. Giglierano and Deborah A. Overmyer, with Frederic L. Propas, *The Bicentennial Guide to Greater Cincinnati: A Portrait of Two Hundred Years* (Cincinnati, OH: Cincinnati Historical Society, 1988).

6. Interview with Dwight McPheeters, June 2004.

7. Interview with William Davis, August 2004.

8. Interestingly, Dabney does not include Bessie Russell in his list of "colored" health professionals. He does, however, note Joseph Russell and his profession. See Dabney, *Cincinnati's Colored Citizens*.

9. Interview with George Russell, June 2004.

10. Ibid.

11. Ibid.

12. Ibid.

13. Ibid.

14. Interview with McPheeters.

15. Interview with W. Davis.

16. Interview with G. Russell, June 2004.

17. Vivian Perlis, interview with George Russell, American Music Series, December 8, 1993, Oral History Project of American Music, sponsored and supported by the National Endowment for the Arts Special Jazz Projects.

18. Interview with G. Russell, June 2004.

19. Ibid.

20. Ibid.

21. Ibid.

22. Interview with Robert Moore, July 2004.

23. Interview with G. Russell, June 2004.

24. Ibid.

25. G. John and D. Humphrey, *Because They're Black* (Harmondsworth, UK: Penguin, 1971).

26. Interview with G. Russell, June 2004.

27. Interview with W. Davis.

28. C. Vann Woodward, *The Strange Career of Jim Crow* (New York: Oxford University Press, 1966), p. 19.

29. Quoted in ibid., p. 20.

30. Interview with McPheeters.

31. Interview with W. Davis.

32. Perlis, interview with G. Russell.

33. Interview with G. Russell, June 2004.

34. Ibid.

35. Interview with McPheeters.

36. Interview with G. Russell, June 2004.

37. Ibid.

38. Ibid.

39. Interview with McPheeters.

40. Interview with G. Russell, June 2004.

41. Ian Carr, interview with George Russell, June 1992.

42. Interview with McPheeters.

43. Interview with W. Davis.

44. Interview with G. Russell, June 2004.

45. Ibid.

46. Interview with McPheeters.

47. Interview with G. Russell, June 2004.

48. Interview with W. Davis.

49. Interview with McPheeters.

50. Carr, interview with G. Russell, June 1992.

51. Interview with McPheeters.

52. Ibid.

53. Carr, interview with G. Russell, June 1992.

54. Ibid.

55. Ibid.

56. Robert E. Moore, "George Alan Russell: Jazz's First Theorist," *Trotter Institute Review* 2 (Summer 1988): 15–19.

57. Carr, interview with G. Russell, June 1992.

58. Interview with G. Russell, June 2004.

59. Interview with McPheeters.

60. Interview with W. Davis.

61. Interview with G. Russell, June 2004.

62. Ibid.

63. Carr, interview with G. Russell, June 1992.

64. Ibid.

65. Interview with George Russell, June 2003.

66. Ibid.

67. Carr, interview with G. Russell, June 1992.

68. Ibid.

69. Perlis, interview with G. Russell.

70. Ibid.

71. P. Berger and T. Luckmann, *The Social Construction of Reality* (Harmondsworth, UK: Penguin, 1981), particularly pp. 149–88.

72. See K. B. Clark and M. P. Clark, "Racial Identification and Preferences in Negro Children," in *Readings in Social Psychology*, edited by E. E. Maccoby, T. M. Newcomb, and E. L. Hartley (New York: Holt, Rinehart & Winston, 1958). The Supreme Court decision was *Brown v. Board of Education*.

73. W. Oliver, "Black Males and Social Problems: Prevention through Afro-Centric Socialization," *Journal of Black Studies* 20, no. 1 (1989): 1–19.

74. R. D. Laing, *Self and Others* (Harmondsworth, UK: Penguin, 1975): 152.

75. Berger and Luckmann, *The Social Construction of Reality*, 164–65.

76. Carr, interview with G. Russell, June 1992.

77. Interview with G. Russell, June 2004.

78. Interview with G. Russell, June 2003.
79. Ibid.
80. Ibid.
81. Ibid.
82. Ibid.

CHAPTER TWO

~

On Class and Culture

This world of daily humiliations that was life in the Midwest for African Americans had economic, political, social, cultural, and psychological implications. It would leave emotional scars even on those who eventually transcended its imposed limitations, but many others less talented, resilient, or resourceful would remain trapped in its grip. Most, if not all, would to some degree internalize the image of themselves that the dominant white culture imposed upon them. As George Russell puts it,

> [It] made me feel inferior and it made actually the race feel inferior because we used to berate each other. "Oh, nigger you can't do that." You know. It was stupid; we were beginning to accept the fact that we were stupid when we weren't. But I guess we grew more stupid by believing that there was no way out.[1]

Russell is describing a psychological process that functions at both individual and broader social or cultural levels. The capacity to impose such definitions on others—sometimes in the face of opposition—requires the power and authority, as well as the mechanisms, to do so. School, the education system, control of the media of mass communication and, ultimately and more directly, the offices of enforcement and repression—all these were in the hands of white people, and in particular those with wealth and political influence. But Russell's point goes a step further in its insights. The fostering among African Americans of a self-image of inferiority was then reinforced within their communities themselves. Sadly, this is a story that is all too common and is documented and examined extensively in the academic literature of sociology and psychology.[2]

Such images of African Americans held by white people—and, as Russell suggests, by black people as well—were in sharp contrast to the richness of cultural activity in the Walnut Hills area where George Russell, Dwight McPheeters, and William R. Davis lived. In his interview with Vivian Perlis, Russell looked back with some fondness to a childhood that in cultural terms was far from underprivileged. "Anyway, as much and as boring as Cincinnati could be, and I look back on it now, and as much as one would think I was born into an underprivileged situation, I was born in an overprivileged situation. I had culture booming out of every nook and cranny of that town and in my neighborhood."[3]

First of all, there were those activities centered around the church. In Russell's and Davis's case, that was the African Methodist Episcopal Mount Zion Church. As Davis remembers:

> At the time that we were in the church, George sang in the boys' choir. We had a wonderful choirmaster there who organized this boys' choir. We had forty-seven boys in that choir. At that time I was seven years old, so George was about six. We stayed in that boys' choir until our voices began to change during our mid-teenage years. At that time we were probably going to high school, so we sang in the chancel choir with the adults after that point. But George was a good singer.[4]

Mount Zion had at that time a very forward-thinking minister in Rev. Gilbert, and the church was a focus for the community in a number of ways. For one thing, it had indoor recreational facilities, as Davis recalls. "One of the things that happened at the church was that we had a full-size gymnasium in the basement. That church and one of the schools, Douglas School, were the only places you could go for indoor recreation in Walnut Hills, that particular section of the city."[5]

Sports were as—or more—important than music within the African American community in Walnut Hills. Russell had been on the football team at Hoffman, and William Davis was a football player, swimmer, and track star. And within the area, there were those whose sporting success motivated the young men in the community. Davis's vivid memory again notes:

> There were various playgrounds throughout the city. We had one young man who was the 1924 broad jump champion in the Olympics who lived right be-

hind us, and he would come down to the little playground in our neighborhood and show us things about running and jumping. He was one of some very good track people in that neighborhood. His name was DeHart Hubbard. His record stood from 1924 until Jesse Owens won the broad jump in 1936. That's how long his record for the broad jump—the long jump as they call it now—lasted. But we had people like that in the neighborhood. We had some football and baseball players who were inspirational to us as well.[6]

Russell remembers Mount Zion well, and he notes that his mother insisted that he attend services. But he was more drawn to another church, probably Pentecostal, two blocks away.

I used to sneak down there without my mother knowing. It was near a big hole, a deep hole, like a working pit. And the people lived down there; it was a pretty rough place. They used to have these Holy Roller services. It was shocking sometimes. They went into trances and things. I used to lie on my stomach and look in the windows. But the rhythm was incredible, man, and that's what influenced me.[7]

And as he told Ian Carr:

In the traditional Baptist churches, they had very good gospel music. And the sanctified music I heard because there were churches in what was called "the hollow," which was kind of a ravine that was close to our house, and down in this hollow there was a sanctified church. And there'd be storefront churches. When I did venture downtown in what they called the "Black Bottom" there would be these storefront churches and this enormous rhythmic thing would be coming out.[8]

At some point Russell's mother turned toward a more fundamental "Holy Roller" Christianity and became a follower of Bishop Mary Mack.

What I remember about Bishop was her weight—she weighed nearly four hundred pounds. She was big and fiercely black. She owned a Rolls-Royce, with accommodations in the back for a throne. She owned two mansions very close to us. She had a chauffeur. My mother and Bishop became very good friends. My mother was consulting with Bishop when she was going through troubled times. And I do remember Bishop, and I became good friends with Bishop's grandkid, his name was Sam. So, they were going to the World's Fair in 1933, and I was ten. And so, they took me along—it was a big thing for me in the Rolls-Royce with the chauffeur, Marvin.

He continues,

> In the meantime, she owned churches all over the United States—I'm not
> kidding—and in Hawaii. She was touring her churches at the same time we
> visited the World's Fair. I had to go to services with her in her own church;
> she had her own network of churches. What happened in those churches was
> that she healed people; the music was incredible. It was the music that affected
> me.[9]

Asked to describe the music by Perlis, Russell said it was "more primitive than gospel," though clearly gospel-based with "fierce rhythms," and
members of the congregation "would get the tongue and faint and have
water thrown on them."[10] Robert Moore's research confirms that the family
attended "Mount Zion African Methodist Evangelical Church," as did "a
number of Cincinnati's Black Elite." He also notes that Bessie and George
Russell also traveled and attended revival meetings with Mack, though
Moore notes that it was Mary Mack's son, rather than her grandson, whom
Russell befriended.[11] Again, the attraction for Russell lay more in the music
than in the religious experience itself. He hinted, in fact, in his interview
with Perlis that by the time he was sixteen he'd had experiences with Mack's
church that discouraged him from "becoming a devout believer as I was on
my way to being." Unfortunately, Perlis did not pursue this line of inquiry
in the interview.

And there were plenty of opportunities to hear and make music in Walnut
Hills. Dwight McPheeters and his sister both took music lessons.

> George was more interested in music. I was interested in music too. My sister
> and I were both given music lessons. I was too stubborn, stupid, or whatever to
> take it because I had an ear for music, because when I was given piano lessons
> my piano teacher would play a piece over [and] I could play it right behind
> him. But when it came to reading the notes, that was out. I didn't want to
> practice. After piano lessons I was given violin lessons and I did not practice
> and did something or other to the bow and the bow went to pieces and my
> father said, "That's the last music lesson you're gonna get out of this house."
> But I always had a good voice. I had a baritone voice and I sang in the choruses
> at Withrow High School and so did George.[12]

Russell had also had music lessons with a Professor Ryder, a very strict
teacher, when he was about seven or eight. It had not been a happy experience for the young and sensitive boy. He describes Ryder as a "knuckle-
cracker" who responded to wrong notes with a sharp crack on the back of a

child's hands with a ruler. That was pretty much it for Russell as far as any formal musical education was concerned.

But jazz was all around Cincinnati and Walnut Hills. Cincinnati was, after all, at a crossroads in the Midwest. Musicians would pass through and head on to St. Louis or Kansas City, north to Chicago, and on to New York. Or maybe west to Los Angeles and San Francisco or southeast to New Orleans. And there were the riverboats that headed up and down the Ohio en route to the Mississippi and the Missouri. Many of those passenger steamers featured bands. Bessie Russell loved music and took her son on trips on the boats, and it was on one of those trips that he first heard jazz. Years later he recollected that it was Fate Marable's band he had seen and that it was the drummer that most held his attention.[13] Many articles have noted Marable's significance in Russell's very early musical development.[14] While this makes for a charming tale, any influence was probably far less important than the cumulative effect of seeing the various riverboat orchestras. There were others Russell recalled with just as much clarity. When he spoke with Carr of these riverboat trips, it was Noble Sissle who stuck out in his memory, and it was again his drummer who made the greatest impression—and not only for his musical skills.

> Cincinnati was very music conscious, and my mother used to take me on these riverboats that used to pass. It usually'd start in New Orleans and go up the Mississippi to St. Louis, then on to the Ohio, up to Cincinnati and Cairo and then Pittsburgh, you know. Bringing culture all the way. I know I heard the Noble Sissle band because—I forgot his name—but the drummer and my cousin had an affair . . . but he was a dandy. I was impressed by all this, you know. These guys were very glamorous to me. And they dressed beautifully and they looked beautiful and they got all the women. So I thought, this [is] it—you know, this is the life for me.[15]

Russell also talked to Perlis about the impact of hearing and seeing these riverboat jazz bands. Again, it was Sissle he remembered, and the rhythm of the drums.

> **GR:** And when she took me on these boat rides, they always had a band. It was always a band that came from either St. Louis up the Ohio River to Cincinnati or they had originated in New Orleans and come up the Mississippi to St. Louis and then up the Ohio to Cincinnati and then on up to Pittsburgh. They were the boat bands. So, you know, that's a real part of Americana. They were transplanting this music wherever they went, and of course by 1923 jazz had really established itself as an art form in America, although it wasn't taken

seriously, you know. Here it was taken seriously, in Europe . . . and I was always impressed with the drummers. Drums became my first instrument . . . .
VP: Was it a lot of early Dixieland jazz and ragtime also, or . . . ?
GR: It was pretty organized big-band jazz. It really wasn't . . . the musicians were reading arrangements. So these were schooled musicians; I know one of the bands was Noble Sissle. Noble Sissle was a legend.[16]

Of at least as much importance was a man by the name of Zack Whyte. Whyte had an orchestra with the wonderful name the Chocolate Beau Brummels. William Davis recalls that Whyte was a near neighbor of the Russells.

Further down on that porch was a gentleman by the name of Zack Whyte who had his own orchestra, the Chocolate Beau Brummels. They all lived right there in close proximity, not more than twenty or thirty yards apart. Those kind[s] of things could have been an influence on him because those people were right there.[17]

Or, as Russell himself recalls, "[In] my neighborhood [was] Zack Whyte, one of the first people to have a band on a riverboat that went from Cincinnati up the Ohio to St. Louis and then down to New Orleans. It was bands like that that really began to get to me. They were really attractive and the music was attractive."[18]

The riverboat orchestras played Dixieland, as Russell remembers it.[19] Swing had not yet arrived, or at least hadn't crossed that far into the mainstream, though it had by then developed into a sophisticated big-band form of the music. Cincinnati jazz historian Bill Lawless Jones echoes this in his sleeve notes for two CDs featuring Cincinnati jazz of the modern era:

[T]he 20's saw the expansion of the normally small jazz band of 5 to 7 pieces, which played "Dixieland Style," into the big band of 10 to 12 instruments with arranged scores. Fletcher Henderson of NYC's Roseland Ballroom is generally credited with having organized the first big band. Well, perhaps Mr. Henderson was a year ahead of anyone else, or maybe he got the publicity virtue of being in America's largest city. Anyway, right here in Cincinnati in 1927, a man by the name of Zack Whyte organized a big band.[20]

One of Whyte's musicians was Melvin James "Sy" Oliver, who proved influential both as a trumpeter and as an arranger, first for Whyte and later for Jimmie Lunceford and Tommy Dorsey. So Russell's recollections to Vivian Perlis and, more recently, to me are clearly borne out by Lawless Jones. And, as the historian adds, while with Whyte, Oliver "composed such tunes as 'Stomp It Off' and 'Dream of You' and arranged traditional melodies like 'Swanee River' and 'Dear Old Southland.'"[21] Dixieland it might have been, but it was already in a process of transformation into highly sophisticated large-ensemble arrangements. Many of the musicians were readers, as James Lincoln Collier notes about Fate Marable: When Marable took the young "unschooled" Louis Armstrong into his band, it was essentially an exception in his usual hiring policy.[22] This was the kind of music that fired Russell's imagination. It was full of glamour and excitement, and it moved with the rhythms of the popular dances of the time.

It is not surprising that it was the drums Russell was attracted to, and his first opportunity to develop that interest in rhythm came through playing in the Boy Scouts marching band.

> And of course the other drummers—some of them were quite good—and they, even if they played the orthodox march music, they played it in a way that was . . . had something else in it, had this rhythm, you know. And it was this rhythm that really stuck with me. This Americanized African rhythm will always intrigue me, and that being the most obvious kind of musical impression that weighed on me heavily, I turned to playing drums and started off with just sort of youth bands.[23]

He acquired his first drum set through Dwight McPheeters, who had got them from his godparents.

> I said, "Yes, I'd like to have them." My mother was not really favorable to that. It was a set of trap drums. They weren't regular band drums. Anyhow the noise that I made around the house drove my mother up the wall and so she decided on her own, and since I was not taking any lessons regarding the drums, that she would get rid of them. So, she called Mrs. Russell—she called her "Sweets," that was her nickname—and she asked if George wanted the drums and Mrs. Russell said, "Yes," George would like to have the drums. So, she gave my mother five dollars for the drums and those were the first set of drums that George ever had. I like to think that I was responsible (laughs) for everything that followed.[24]

Davis also remembers the drum set: "I remember when she bought George that drum set and I don't remember who influenced her to buy him a drum set, maybe it was because he was in the Boy Scouts and they had a drum and bugle corps. George and my brother and others were playing these snare drums and blowing bugles for parades and things like that."[25]

One of the most important local musicians living in Walnut Hills was tenor saxist Jimmy Mundy. Mundy played with Paul Whiteman, Earl Hines, and Benny Goodman, though his greatest claim to fame was that he wrote "Travellin' Light" for Billie Holiday. He lived a couple of doors down from Russell's family, and his return from a tour was always a source of excitement in the neighborhood.

> Jimmy had written for all the bands. We were going so fast, that I forgot to mention that Jimmy was a great inspiration. I told you how he'd come home in his big car, park it out in front of his door—and these are just little houses built for . . . I forget what they call them, but they've got a name for them—but for people with just modest incomes. As soon as Mrs. Critten and his mother saw him, she'd throw a fit—"Jimmy's here." Then he'd go up and put on his bedroom shoes and his fancy nightwear and drive his car to Kerper Avenue to the main street and go to one of the bars and have a drink, and everybody would know that Jimmy's in town.[26]

It was Mundy who first suggested that Russell might pursue a career in music. "I didn't know how great Jimmy was, but Jimmy was a great, great guy, and he wanted me to go to a Battle of Music with Benny Goodman. My mother wouldn't let me go because I was sixteen years old, so I didn't hear that, but Jimmy said, 'I'll go over and talk to your mother.' He told her, 'Look George belongs in music.'"[27]

Davis also remembers Mundy very well. "But right next to George on that same row of apartments in that building, there was another family and the man in the family was the son of a lady about Mrs. Russell's age who became the arranger for Benny Goodman, and that was Jimmy Mundy, and he may have been one of the influences that inspired George to go into music."[28]

Art Tatum had a cousin with the wonderful name of Spaulding Givens (later known by his Muslim name, Nadi Qamar), who lived nearby, and Tatum would play locally when he was in town, as did Fats Waller. Once again, from William Davis's impeccable memory: "There were other entertainers that came by there in the neighborhood. We all used to go round and listen to them. Fats Waller used to come there and play at a speakeasy that was not far from there, right down the hill from where George would live."[29]

Nelson Burton, a drummer and stalwart of the Cincinnati scene, tells in his memoirs how Waller lived and worked in Cincinnati during the Great Depression.[30] As well as his own show on "The Nation's Station," Cincinnati-based Radio WLW, Waller played organ on the schmaltzy *Moon River* show. It was a performance on the latter that got Waller fired from the station. Supposed to play suitably nocturnal accompaniment for host Peter Grant's poetry recitation, an inebriated Waller swung the hell out of his

Wurlitzer. The next day after Waller had gone, the cleaners found a pile of gin bottles in the back of the instrument.

Russell's mother actually got him on a bill with Waller at the YMCA, singing "Moon Over Miami" accompanied by "some lame piano player," as he told Carr. "I must've been nine years old and I was always a very naive person, but I wasn't naive enough to know that this was a very corny thing for me to be doing, to be singing 'Moon Over Miami,' you know."[31] One writer, Francis Davis, recounts this tale with wonderful embellishment and has Fats Waller, "a friend of the family," accompanying Russell, but sadly, as so often is the case, the truth was more mundane.[32]

William Davis also talks about Peg Leg Bates, the dancer. "He wasn't a musician. He was a one-legged dancer, a one-legged tap dancer. That was his nomer because he had one peg leg and one normal. He had a cousin that lived in the neighborhood too."[33]

Traveling musicians with limited access to hotels because of formal and informal segregation would stay with black families when on tour, and Russell's family was no exception. And from time to time Russell's mother would leave him with friends who took in itinerant performers. "This brings up something that I didn't focus on, but one thing with my mother being a nurse, [she] had to board me with people, and many times they were musicians. So I was born sort of sleeping with musicians, so guys used to tell me things."[34]

But there were other influences around. Russell tells how Nadi Qamar (at the time known as Spaulding Givens) brought some records to his house one day. "It was this *Festivals of Debussy*. That may have been the first time I really heard what struck me as modern symphonic music. And I was very impressed. And I didn't let it go. I pursued it from then on, you know."[35]

William Davis supports the idea that culture and talent in the neighborhood extended beyond jazz.

> We had some very talented people. And in our church we had this Mr. N. W. Ryder who was a very, very good leader, a good composer, a good conductor, a good choirmaster. We had two violin players that played with our choir. Emile Burbanks ended up playing with the Cincinnati Symphony Orchestra. Those kind[s] of people were around us where we grew up.[36]

As well as singing in the Glee Club and choir at Withrow, Russell and Dwight McPheeters were in a semiprofessional vocal group together. "George and I sang in a quartet. The person who played for us and arranged

our music was a lady by the name of Marie Gerard. There was George Russell, Leonard Williams, George Bassard, and myself. We tried to model our
singing after the Modernaires and that group that Tommy Dorsey had, and
we sang those songs."[37]

And even then, racism intruded.

> Well Marie and a couple of people from the YMCA made arrangements for
> us to sing before a group of politicians, of Republicans in this town. They told
> Marie that we were not to sing any modern songs. We were told to sing only
> spirituals. So Marie began to give us some music and we sang spirituals, but
> we always thought that with the group that we had if we hadn't been black
> we could have been as famous as the Modernaires, because we were good. We
> were very good. We didn't have a name, but when we were called on to go to
> these places, Marie would call us and tell us that we'd got to go to this place
> or that, so we did.[38]

By his teens Russell was working regularly as a drummer and McPheeters's
mother commented often to her son about the late nights he was keeping.

> He was in his mid-teens. My mother used to say that he ought to be home in bed.
> He's out all night and he has to go to school the next day. He's going to get sick.
> He probably was on that road, but we didn't run around together. We knew each
> other. We were good friends but we seldom were in the same group because he
> was always working. George has worked in music practically all of his life.[39]

According to McPheeters, by then most of Russell's friends were in the
music business. "He was very, very loyal to the music world," he recalls, "and
everything else was secondary."[40] Russell's aptitude for music had developed
as much through his associations as by his application and practicing, but
he had reached the point where his skills had advanced sufficiently for
him to work regularly around Cincinnati. His closest associates were Teddy
Weatherford and the Gaston brothers, Harold and Roger, and according to
McPheeters, the group, though still in school, was making a regular income
from music. William Davis also remembers Roger Gaston as a track star, but
the whole Gaston family seems to have been very talented.

Photographs from the Withrow High School yearbook for 1939 reveal a
smiling, handsome young Harold Gaston. It's not hard to see character and
intelligence in that face, and a real self-assurance as well. Other pictures
show him performing in the orchestra and with the choir, and playing double
bass in the Minstrel Show band. There is, of course, no irony or sense of the
ridiculous in the yearbook reviewer's comments:

Tapping toes, smiling ponies, greasepaint, the strains of a hit tune, Smittie's grin of delight, costumes galore, the query, "Do I look alright?," idiotic end-men in their colorful array—these phrases spell Minstrel Show. To the expectant audience of amazed parents and more amazed teachers, the Minstrel means more than all these: it means an appreciation of hard work, of the numerous beautiful costumes, of the professional appearance throughout, of the fact that a high school can produce a hit to a full house for five nights. And to the Minstreleers themselves, the show symbolizes abundant fun, new friendships made, pleasant memories, and, at the end, a sigh of satisfaction.[41]

And white people dress as black people and mug a grotesque caricature for the mainly white adult audience, and black students still get to swim last period Friday afternoon, after which the pool gets cleaned. But Harold Gaston is there, as if the chance to play music is much more important in the long run and any fresh insult is just another among many. And if that were his rationale, he was probably right, because everything Russell and Davis and McPheeters remember about him suggests that Harold was a quite remarkable individual. It was he who would famously teach Russell the rudiments of music theory a few years later, when they were both in a sanatorium suffering from tuberculosis. Harold was the effective leader of the group of semiprofessional young African American musicians of which Russell was the youngest member. As Davis recalls,

> Then in the neighborhood we had a group of very talented high school young men who were musicians. They had a club called the Rhythm Club—we called the band the Rhythm Club. And they were all accomplished musicians while they were in high school. George ended up playing drums with them before he went with one of the other orchestras. They played high school dances and other kinds of events around the city of Cincinnati, but then they ended up having to get into the union. The union people didn't want them to play certain places because they were not union musicians, but they all ended up being in the union. The Rhythm Club began to break up because of the war, and I know George got that job with another band and began to travel and that.[42]

The Rhythm Club had more than its share of bright young talents, as Davis again recalls.

> We had another man there who played piano for this Rhythm Club by the name of Andrew Johnson. Andrew Johnson was the only person that Duke Ellington let rehearse his band when he came to Cincinnati. Andrew Johnson was a most talented young man but he never left the city of Cincinnati. He married and began to raise a family, and though he had opportunities to go

away, he never did. George grew up around a bunch of very talented young men. Ralph Green—did he mention Ralph Green? Ralph Green lived in the same building that I lived in. Ralph Green was a high school track star, football player, he played the trombone and the piano. He played the trombone and the piano in this Rhythm Club that they had. There was another boy by the name of Oliver McLean. Now, Oliver played with the Lionel Hampton Band when it came to Cincinnati and did not have a tenor sax player. Oliver McLean belonged to our church, and he was another musician that George grew up with. Oliver played every reed instrument you could name, including the oboe. He was an excellent musician. These guys were a little bit older than us, but we used to go and listen to them. They would let us listen to them rehearse on Tuesday afternoons. There was another young man by the name of Charles Lewis who was an excellent trumpet player, and Charles left Cincinnati to go to New York and I don't know what happened after he went to New York, but every time Louis Armstrong came to Cincinnati they had this trumpet contest and Charlie would win the trumpet, he'd win the trumpet every time. They would give a trumpet to the winner of the contest. And they were the people that George was associated with as a youngster. That's the thing that I see that contributed in helping him to want to be a good musician, because the guys that we grew up with were all good. I mean they were exceptional, very much so.[43]

By then Russell was quite confident in his abilities as a drummer and was working six nights a week backing a singer in a club. His schoolwork and attendance were, as already noted, clearly suffering, but as he put it to Vivian Perlis, "In the meantime I had felt music, especially drums, very strongly." Describing Harold Gaston as an "African" and "a star in their school orchestra, both the symphony orchestra, and any other kind of orchestra," he talked about rehearsing with the jazz band Harold had formed.

And he asked me to play drums with that orchestra. [So] I'm going to rehearsals of a, let's say, young, very excellent orchestra that impressed me very much, young orchestra, it was called the Rhythm Club, and they rehearsed in my neighborhood so I used to go and listen to their rehearsals. In the meantime, I am sneaking down to the Cotton Club at Six and Mound, and listening to the bands that come through and feeling more and more that music is what I want. The regular school was not going good. When I went to high school I was really only good in one subject. I'd learned what I'd wanted to learn from school and . . . I read in a magazine about Hemingway, and he said, "If you want to be a writer, you don't need to go to school." That impressed me very much, and the whole thing was building up to make music the number-one priority in my life, and so that's all I can say.[44]

It was just what Russell wanted to hear, and it made perfect sense to a young African American by then completely alienated by an education system that treated him as a second-class mind being prepared for a life sitting at the back of the bus. Though Hemingway's words rang true, Harold Gaston's impact on Russell's life would, in some ways, prove both more direct and lasting.

According to Nelson Burton, Gaston studied at the Cosmopolitan School of Music founded in Cincinnati by pianist Artie Matthews, composer of "Weary Blues" and other early blues and ragtime pieces. Burton notes that blacks could attend the uptown white conservatory only if they were light enough "to pass," and Matthews set up the Cosmopolitan School of Music to provide young African Americans with "an equal chance to get their formal musical training." He adds that back then, black areas of Cincinnati held a greater mix within them of people and that "teachers, tradesmen, ministers, and well-respected figures like Dr. Matthews provided role models for the children." Saxophonist and Basie Orchestra leader Frank Foster was another student who attended the school.[45] Burton's comments about Harold Gaston (or Gastonia, as he refers to him) reveals the impression the young man made on those that knew him.

> Many fine musicians, educators and choral directors came out of the Cosmopolitan School of Music, including a bass player, Harold Gastonia, who caught Duke Wellington's [sic] eye at age seventeen. Gastonia died of tuberculosis before he got the chance to join the Duke. TB was a common disease back then. Penicillin wasn't invented yet so they didn't know how to treat it other than to put patients in a sanatorium. Even though Gastonia died young, memories of his great playing still linger in my mind.[46]

Russell's recollections of Gaston also remain very vivid after so many years. "I was there when Jimmy Blanton died, Ellington's bass player, and I was playing with the band as a drummer. That band was so good, and it was conducted by a dear friend of mine, Harold Gaston."[47]

And again, a year earlier, he remembered:

> [W]hen Jimmy Blanton died at twenty-one [sic], a wonderful bass player, it was Harold Gaston that got the message from Ellington. That's how good he was. His family was, his entire family, first of all they were artistic. They had a very African kind of appearance, very tall . . . Watusi tall and dignified. Harold was like that. He's the only black guy who played . . . they had the good sense to have him play with the Cincinnati Symphony Orchestra.[48]

Burton is quite correct when he notes the direct influence that Harold Gaston had on his younger sanatorium roommate. In fact, it is a debt Russell has always acknowledged. He told Ian Carr in 1992 about the time they were hospitalized together: "And he being in the hospital too, he could pass the time teaching me the elements of music, chords and basics . . . intervals, basic techniques of writing, you know."[49]

Burton's memories of Russell are less kind. However, his comments are interesting in the distinction he makes between Gaston's influence on Russell in teaching him music and the distinct differences in the music Gaston wrote and that which Russell would later compose.

> George Russell, now a famous jazz innovator, was Gusto's roommate, and I suspect that some of the music Gastonia left in his trunk helped Russell get his foot in the door in Cincinnati. Once Russell got to New York, his music took off into a different orbit. It was, and still is, way out there, real strange and progressive, and nothing like Gusto's.[50]

Additionally, Burton's clearest recollections of Russell are not about his music at all. They refer instead to another aspect of the young man's personality and behavior.

> In those early years, I remember more about Russell's personal style and natty dressing than I do about his music, which didn't seem so outstanding. He never wore hats because he had such nice wavy hair. Everything always matched— scarves, gloves, shoes, and all. Look at him now. He's a star and people can say, "Yeah, George Russell. He came from these parts."[51]

Robert Moore tells another story that arose in an interview he did with Nadi Qamar:

> Nadi was a little older than George but they did play a few gigs in Cincinnati. There was one particular occasion George talks about when they were playing at some little club and they started without any preparation, just started playing in a generally free manner, something that was out of the ordinary and I remember Nadi telling me about that particular evening. They were playing the changes to "Rosetta" and Nadi said he did not remember too much about that night because he had come across some kind of intoxicant which led him to play things that he'd never played before.[52]

Russell said something similar to Vivian Perlis in 1993. "We played at this place in a sort of poor white neighborhood. And every night what we sort of . . . we just improvised, that's what we did. We were improvising, and we'd get into some pretty wild stuff and when we'd get too wild, fights would break out in the audience."[53]

Well, jazz has always been a pretty dangerous music.

As already noted, Qamar introduced Russell to Debussy and symphonic music, both important in his development as a composer, and Russell remained in touch with his friend. Although never one of the great names in jazz, Qamar has his own place in jazz history in several respects. Firstly, he played piano with Charles Mingus, and the bass/piano duets (as well as a few trio sides with Max Roach) they recorded are released on the Mingus Debut Records box set. Secondly, Qamar was something of a pioneer of world jazz and he developed an interest in African percussion instruments such as the kalimba or thumb piano. Saxophonist T. K. Blue, who has played with Abdullah Ibrahim and Randy Weston, speaks of encountering Nadi Qamar and Don Cherry on the New York downtown scene in the seventies and says that Qamar influenced him to take up the kalimba.[54] Though Qamar's own history in jazz falls far behind that of Russell's, his achievements do suggest that his significance within the music world Russell inhabited goes far beyond that of being simply Art Tatum's less talented cousin. Rather, he was a part of the rich cultural milieu in which Russell moved in Cincinnati.

Qamar told Ben Young of WKCR in 1998, in a tribute to Russell on his seventy-fourth birthday, about life in Cincinnati.

> We were just completely surrounded by good musicians, both black and white, even though there was . . . the color line was there in the conservatories and things but the musicians . . . . Black musicians had musicians who were capable of teaching other black musicians anything they wanted to learn. So George and myself were surrounded by very fine musicians.

He also mentions relatives and others who were "very musical in both European classical and jazz" and speaks of a community that was "well evolved into African American and European cultural influences."[55]

And there was one other musical influence that rarely gets acknowledged in the telling of this story. Given that some writers assume he was influenced in some way by a biological father and professor of music whom Russell had never known, it is ironic that the direct influence of his adopted father, Joseph, should be ignored. As Russell recalled to Carr:

> [W]hen he came home his chief love was to play the piano, you know. But he didn't have . . . he had a left hand but he didn't care what he hit in the left hand. He played stride but he didn't (*laughing*) care about what the chord was.

So he came up with some pretty incredible music, 'cause he would sing along with this very, very outgoing piano.[56]

At other times, Russell has jokingly referred to his father's playing as being "like Cecil Taylor before Cecil Taylor." The strange thing about Russell's description of Joseph's piano style is that it could almost describe the sound of his own highly rhythmic approach. It is a point that is not lost on Robert Moore.

> Did George mention that Joseph Russell liked to play the piano? He was not a trained musician. Did he tell you about his particular style of playing, which kind of reminds me of a similar story I think I heard, a similar story with Ives, with the composer Ives, whose father played in a similar fashion? Very chromatic! (laughs) The impression I got was that he played a kind of Stride. The important thing is to keep the rhythm happening. If you play things with a certain confidence, no matter what your playing skills, it's going to be valid in some way. (laughs)[57]

And did it strike him that if the "amateurish" tag was removed it could be a description of Russell's playing as well? "Exactly. Exactly. I think so."

Russell made a very similar point to Vivian Perlis.

> GR: One of his delights was to play—I'm sort of thinking of Ives in this situation, I think Ives's father played a kind of pretty, I don't like the term "dissonant," but dissonant piano that influenced Ives's harmonic sense, you know?
> VP: Yes, he even talked about "piano drums," which amused me, because I think you did that a little later on too?
> GR: Yes, my father played and sang. He might have been lucky with one or two notes of a melody. About as close as he came to the melody in accompanying himself was to, was actually his singing of the melody, because he hit very few notes in the melody in the right hand that corresponded to the song he was singing. And the left hand was totally, totally anything. Just wherever the fingers fell, playing stride piano. So he influenced . . . my sense of the seed of being progressive was planted within. He was just having a good time. He didn't know anything about harmony or melody or anything. He liked the sound of the piano and he kind of let the fingers fall wherever they happened to be.[58]

Cincinnati's race-political divisions were reflected in its music scene. The place was—like the United States itself—a mass of contradictions. Its integrated schools enforced all manner of informal segregations, and even though it had always been a "free" state, de facto and formal separation of the races operated throughout the city, including in its jazz and nightclubs. Vine Street, a long stretch that runs from east to west in the city, was the effective dividing line. In many ways it still is, though it now separates the ghetto of the Over-the-Rhine district from prosperous downtown. Back in the thirties, the East Side was set aside for white musicians belonging to Union Local 1, and club owners operated a policy of "Only Caucasians Need Apply." Inevitably, the economic implications of this segregation for black musicians were severe. As Nelson Burton points out, if you were not a big star among white audiences or working at the Cincy Cotton Club, "you'd be scuffling."[59]

But as Bill Lawless Jones points out, Cincinnati loved music and loved jazz.[60] Because of its unique geographical position, Cincinnati was at a crossroads for traveling musicians, white and black. Russell confirmed this in conversation with Perlis:

> So Cincinnati was a very critical town, maybe that's because of its German, largely Germanic influence. The sister cities where Germans settled were St. Louis and Cincinnati, possibly Minneapolis, and going on up the Mississippi. Very culturally minded towns, very strict demands on musicians of all stylistic trends. So the audiences there were really tough, so they called Cincinnati "the graveyard of bands." Many bands didn't make it, didn't pass Cincinnati. They came there, and they broke up because the audiences would let them know if they were really innovative. These people knew and demanded innovation.[61]

Lawless Jones notes the irony that "segregated" Cincinnati had an integrated Cotton Club, while "liberal" New York's more famous club of the same name did not allow black patrons and made its black artists use the servants' entrance. And it was located in Harlem![62] Cincinnati's Cotton Club always allowed black and white musicians and fans to fraternize. Musicians from touring bands would fetch up there for after-hours sessions of drinking, carousing, and music making. As Burton writes, when you got the call from the Cotton Club, you knew you'd arrived as far as Cincy was concerned. And from time to time, Russell got the call. Once again the glamorous life of the jazz musician was spread out before him, with all the current and past sounds and styles of jazz.

In his *Trotter Institute Review* article, Robert Moore wrote about the world of music that was unfolding for Russell and in particular the attractions of the Cotton Club.

> By the age of 14, Russell's interest in music, coupled with his adolescent interest in exploring the adult world, took him far beyond the boundaries

of Walnut Hills. He began making the long four mile trek down Gilbert Avenue to downtown Cincinnati and the Cotton Club. Although "Cotton Clubs" were to be found in just about every American city with a sizeable black population, Cincinnati's was known throughout the black entertainment world. Jimmy Lunceford, Cab Calloway, Earl Hines, Andy Kirk, and others of that stature appeared there. The Cotton Club became school for George as his attendance at Withrow High School dropped precipitously. Finally, at the age of 16, George dropped out of high school and began working at a downtown department store in the day and playing at night.[63]

Russell now describes the Cotton Club as "his school," and he played there as a "dep" on several occasions. In a letter to me, Russell wrote:

Situated in what was called the "Black Bottom," (deep downtown) of Cincinnati, the club was noted as the "Graveyard of Bands," due to the ever-present demands of audiences to hear something hot and new. If a band lacked something new and lacked that spark, it didn't last long with the Cinci audience. It was located on the ground floor of the Hotel Sterling. Lee Morgan, the black owner, was married to a white woman who sometimes worked at the club. It was a hang for the Cincinnati police (black and white) who managed to maintain law and order. The bands were mainly middle-sized groups that had made a name as river bands coming up from New Orleans to Kansas City, St Louis, Cincinnati and up the Ohio River to Pittsburgh; these were historically important bands such as Noble Sissle, Zack Whyte, McKinney's Cotton Pickers, Andy Kirk, the Sweethearts of Rhythm (all girl band) and the Chick Webb Band. I first played there as a sub with the Alabama State Collegians, and then was hired when other bands came through needing a drummer.[64]

By the age of sixteen, Russell had committed himself to a career in music. As Robert Moore notes, it was a hard life. His days were spent working in a department store and nights into the early hours passed playing jazz. Joseph was dead, and school was behind him. The life Russell had first observed on the riverboats was opening up before him.

Returning to the question of Russell's musical influences, with the rich musical and cultural milieu that was the community of Walnut Hills, it seems quite unnecessary to focus on the occupation of his biological father in explaining his talent.[65] One of the earliest pieces to emphasize the latter was a 1960 biographical article for Broadcast Music Inc. by Nat Hentoff,[66] and it seems certain that Russell himself is the source of the misunderstanding. Whether this was consciously or unconsciously so is unclear, but it is an error that has been repeated ever since, including in an article I wrote in 1998.[67]

The fact that Russell himself may be ultimately responsible for this erroneous assumption does not excuse a certain laziness in the lack of adequate research that has added to the confusion. Given that Russell has also spoken often of his adoption, it invites speculation that some writers have placed undue emphasis on the birth father he never knew as a primary influence on his subsequent development. Allowing that the story Russell was told—for which there is no actual evidence—is true, any influence from his biological father can only be inferred.

By contrast, evidence of significant influences from within his community is extensive. Even though identifying influence can be a tricky business, there is more than enough in Russell's story itself, and in his own insights into his life, to allow us to focus on some key individuals and factors in his development as an individual and as an artist.

Harold Gaston certainly gave George something very valuable in teaching him the rudiments of musical theory, but his contribution would seem to have been much broader than that. By all accounts he was not only very gifted, he was also dedicated and committed to his music. As an older boy, Gaston took Russell into his circle and even acted as a mentor for him. His influence was perhaps as much by example as in what he actually taught Russell, and that dedication and concentration of focus is apparent in Russell's development of the Lydian Concept and in his writing. On the other hand, and as Nelson Burton notes, there was no apparent stylistic influence that Russell derived from Gaston.

Russell has also noted the impact Nadi Qamar had upon him in introducing him to Debussy and symphonic music. In fact, Russell considered this important enough to include it in his biography for the French Record company Label Bleu, for whom he recorded two albums in the eighties and nineties.[68] Additionally, Russell played drums in a trio with Qamar, including on the night where they discovered the possibility of improvisation that did not rely in some way on chord progressions. It seems reasonable to assume again that Qamar was an important figure in Russell's intellectual and cultural development. It is also important to note the impression made by those other members of the Rhythm Club mentioned by William Davis—pianist Andrew Johnson,[69] trombonist Ralph Green, saxist Oliver McLean, and trumpeter Charles Lewis.

But there's also the broader influences of musicians within the community: people like Zack Whyte and Jimmy Mundy, who offered both positive role models, and, in Mundy's case, direct encouragement to Russell. They also promoted a sense of adult glamour. As Russell has said, they looked great, the girls loved them, and they commanded respect. Russell identified powerfully with these men, and in Burton's description of him and his attention to detail in his mode of dress, we have a graphic illustration of that process of identification: You gotta walk it like you talk it.

And there were countless other musical influences that contributed both to Russell's musical development and his choice of a career in music. What he absorbed unconsciously is hard to gauge after all these years, although he has often spoken articulately about what influenced him on a more conscious level. However, it is a reasonable assumption—given his subsequent career and approach to music—that he took then, as later, from what he heard and observed. This is more than some kind of psychological-cultural soup he imbibed. It's evident from quite early on in his career—even before he began to develop the Lydian Concept—that he had an open-minded attitude to music and culture and was quite selective in what he took from his observations. In so far as the Concept draws first and foremost from the practice of musicians, it is an empirical theory. Even though Russell's abilities to theorize and conceptualize were not at that juncture developed, it's unlikely that that ability was not present in some degree. It is a particular way of seeing the world, and, as he points out in other respects, he has always had a mind to question.

And there were the positive cultural values he encountered in Walnut Hills and the broader black community in which he lived. This was a blue-collar to lower-middle-class area, but one that also contained its share of black professional people such as teachers and social workers. It was a "respectable" neighborhood with low crime rates and a strong sense of community. Religion and Christian values were clearly important within it, as was the desire for self-improvement and, to some degree, mutual encouragement and mentorship. The behavior of 1924 Olympic broad jump champion DeHart Hubbard, who according to William Davis would come down to the little playground and show the kids "things about running and jumping," was an example of this. According to both Davis and Dwight McPheeters, there were also other track and football stars keen to share their expertise with local youth. These same impulses could be seen in the African Methodist Episcopalian Church's provision of indoor recreation facilities, in the formation and pooling of resources of the Rhythm Club, and in the altruistic acts of Harold Gaston in sharing his musical knowledge with others, including Russell. One could suggest that there is no evidence that these were typical, and yet it is these positive features of community life that Dwight McPheeters, William Davis, and George Russell recall, and which contrast with the racism experienced in most of their dealings with white society. It is perhaps to these formative influences that Russell owes much of his sense of identity as an African American.

As for the negative effects of white racism, these have been detailed in the previous chapter at length to show the obstacles placed in Russell's way by the highly stratified society into which he was born and to emphasize his achievement. But their inclusion is also intended to show Russell's own response to racism. In various ways, he made something distinctly personal from these events. Though these will be dealt with in later chapters, here it needs to be noted that they inspired in him an understandable hatred of racism and racists, not of white people or of America. Russell, like McPheeters and Davis, has been prepared to challenge and confront prejudice and discrimination but has never descended into such behavior or attitudes himself. It has given him a hatred of intolerance, authoritarianism, and totalitarianism and made him a questioner of authority. As he contrasted his reaction to his expulsion from school to that of his mother, "The getting expelled from school made my mother feel, 'Well, this child is disturbed.' . . . but I took it as a badge of honor."[70]

And what of his origins and upbringing? Russell learned quite late that Bessie and Joseph were not his biological parents. Yet far from reacting with any sense of betrayal, abandonment, or loss of identity, he transformed this experience into a positive one. He talks of "the kids" who were kept apart by society's rules and describes himself as a "love-child." He made it work for him and turned a potential negative into a powerful positive. Although he has never said this, he seems to have been able to identify with his birth father's musical ability and chosen career and with Joseph as a strong immediate father figure. His birth mother he sees as a victim forced to give up her child, not as the woman who abandoned him. He chose not to seek out his birth mother or birth father, or to trace his origins. It seems that the story he was given by Bessie sufficed, and perhaps he unconsciously, or at least without acknowledging it to himself, avoided searching out his origins to allow Bessie's version of his history to prevail.

In some ways, Russell gives the impression of a self-assured and self-confident individual. In others, he does seem to share with many other adopted children the sense of displacement, dislocation, and insecurity that the knowledge of "abandonment" can cause. He describes himself as a "loner," and his single-minded focus on the Lydian Concept and his own spiritual searching suggest a desire to make connections with something greater than himself. Yet even if this assessment is accurate, his adjustment is both remarkably successful and creative in its outcomes for him and for his music. And this is the observable pattern of Russell's life: He turns potentially negative experiences into positive ones and crises into opportunities.

Notes

1. Interview with George Russell, June 2004.

2. There's a huge body of literature within what is generally described as phenomenological or interactionist psychology and sociology that explores these same processes. See, for example, R. D. Laing, *The Divided Self* (Harmondsworth, UK: Penguin, 1971) and *Self and Others* (Harmondsworth, UK: Penguin 1975); E. Goffman, *Stigma* (Harmondsworth, UK: Penguin, 1968); and H. S. Becker, *The Outsiders Studies in Sociology of Deviance* (New York: MacMillan, 1966). There is also a body of literature in psychology that deals with the experience of concentration camp victims (Bruno Bettelheim), hostages (the term "Stockholm Syndrome" was coined by psychologist Nils Bejerot to describe the behavior of those held captive during the famous Norrmalmstorg bank robbery of August 1973; the syndrome develops out of the victims' attempts to relate to their captor or gain the kidnapper's sympathy; in this case, the victims kept on defending their captors even after their six-day physical detention was over, and they showed reticent behavior in the legal procedures that followed), and of victims of colonialism (see F. Fanon, *The Wretched of the Earth* [Harmondsworth, UK: Penguin, 1969] and *Toward the African Revolution* [Harmondsworth, UK: Penguin, 1970]) and the way in which the oppressed internalize a debased image of themselves through identification with their oppressors.

3. Vivian Perlis, interview with George Russell, American Music Series, December 8, 1993, Oral History Project of American Music, sponsored and supported by the National Endowment for the Arts Special Jazz Projects.

4. Interview with William Davis, August 2004.

5. Ibid.

6. Ibid.

7. Interview with George Russell, December 2003.

8. Ian Carr, interview with George Russell, June 1992.

9. Perlis, interview.

10. Ibid.

11. Robert E. Moore, "George Alan Russell: Jazz's First Theorist," *Trotter Institute Review* 2 (Summer 1998): 18.

12. Interview with Dwight McPheeters, June 2004.

13. Most notable here is George Russell's response to a questionnaire sent in preparation of Leonard Feather's 1960 edition of *The Encyclopaedia of Jazz*, where it notes, "First infatuated with Jazz when mother took him on River Boat Excursion featuring Fate Marble [sic] Orchestra from St. Louis. Was especially intrigued with drummer."

14. See, for example, Moore, "George Alan Russell"; Robert Palmer, "A Jazz Visionary Eyes the Evolution of Life on Earth," *New York Times*, April 28, 1985.

15. Carr, interview with G. Russell, June 1992.

16. Perlis, interview.

17. Interview with W. Davis.

18. Interview with George Russell, June 2003.

19. Interview with George Russell, June 2004. See also Nelson Burton, *My Life in Jazz* (Cincinnati: Clifton Hills Press, 2000).

20. Bill Lawless Jones, sleeve notes to *Cincinnati Jazz Collection Volume I* (1998), J Curve Records J71098. Whyte's lineup for two 1929 recording sessions was William Benton (d), Floyd Brady (tb), Herman Chittison (p), Montgomery Morrison (tba), Sy Oliver, Bubber Whyte, Henry Savage (t), Clarence Paige, Ben Ricardson, Earl Tribble (as), Al Sears (ts, bs), and Zack Whyte (bj, ldr).

21. Ibid.

22. James Lincoln Collier, *The Making of Jazz—A Comprehensive History* (Basingstoke, UK: Papermac, 1981), p. 145. See also Wikipedia entry for Marable. Fate Marable (December 2, 1890–January 16, 1947) was a jazz pianist and bandleader. Marable was born in Paducah, Kentucky, and learned piano from his mother. At the age of seventeen he began playing on the steamboats plying the Mississippi River. He soon became bandleader for boats on the Strekfus Line, which ran several paddlewheelers that held dances and excursions along the river from New Orleans, Louisiana, to Minneapolis, Minnesota. Marable appreciated the new "jazz" sound being played by the New Orleans musicians, and the bulk of his band members were recruited from that city. Members of Marable's bands were expected to be able to play a wide variety of music, from hot numbers to light classics; to play both by head and from sheet music; and above all to keep the dancers happy. Noted musicians who spent time in Marable's bands included Red Allen, Louis Armstrong, Baby Dodds, Johnny Dodds, Pops Foster, Al Morgan, and Zutty Singleton, among others. In addition to piano and bandleading, Marable played the boats' steam calliope, a contraption that could be heard for miles up and down the river and poured down so much water from condensing steam that Marable performed wearing a raincoat and hood. Marable died of pneumonia in Saint Louis, Missouri. See also A. Shipton, *A New History of Jazz* (London: Continuum, 2001), pp. 111–14; and G. Schuller, *The Swing Era* (Oxford: Oxford University Press, 1989), pp. 785–87.

23. Carr, interview with G. Russell, June 1992.

24. Interview with McPheeters.

25. Ibid.

26. Interview with G. Russell, June 2004.

27. Ibid.

28. Interview with W. Davis.

29. Ibid.

30. Burton, *My Life in Jazz*.

31. Carr, interview with G. Russell, June 1992.

32. Francis Davis, "George Russell: The Intellect of the Heart," *Jazz Times*, December 12, 1984.

33. Interview with W. Davis.

34. Interview with G. Russell, June 2004.

35. Carr, interview with G. Russell, June 1992.

36. Interview with W. Davis.

37. Interview with McPheeters.

38. Ibid.

39. Ibid.

40. Ibid.

41. Withrow High School yearbook, 1939.

42. Interview with W. Davis.

43. Ibid.

44. Perlis, interview with G. Russell.

45. Burton, My Life in Jazz, chap. 10.

46. Ibid., pp. 62–63.

47. Interview with G. Russell, June 2004.

48. Interview with G. Russell, June 2003.

49. Carr, interview with G. Russell, June 1992.

50. Burton, My Life in Jazz, p. 64.

51. Ibid.

52. Moore, "Jazz's First Theorist," p. 18.

53. Perlis, interview with G. Russell.

54. See the T. K. Blue Official Web Site, www.tkblue.com.

55. Ben Young, interview with Nadi Qamar, WKCR Radio, New York, 1998.

56. Carr, interview with G. Russell, June 1992.

57. Interview with Robert E. Moore, July 2004.

58. Perlis, interview with G. Russell.

59. Burton, My Life in Jazz, p. 64.

60. Lawless Jones, sleeve notes to Cincinnati Jazz Collection Volume I; also sleeve notes to Cincinnati Jazz Collection Volume II (1999), J Curve Records J7005.

61. Perlis, interview with G. Russell.

62. Lawless Jones, sleeve notes to Cincinnati Jazz Collection Volume I and Cincinnati Jazz Collection Volume II.

63. Moore, "Jazz's First Theorist," p. 18.

64. George Russell, letter to author, October 13, 2004. Russell's memory may be faulty regarding McKinney's Cotton Pickers. The group apparently disbanded in 1934, when George was only eleven.

65. See, for example, Max Harrison, "George Russell—Rational Anthems (Phase 1)," Wire (Spring 1983): 30–31; Robert DiNardo, "Jazz Prophet," Boston Globe Sunday Magazine, June 12, 1983; Ian Carr, program Notes for a Contemporary Music Network tour (1992); Howard Mandel, "The Mathematical Musician," Washington Post, September 27, 1987; John Fordham, "Send Off the Clones," Guardian (Manchester), March 5, 1998, and "King George's Gold Blend," Guardian (Manchester), September 1, 1989. What is interesting here is that a number of different and in the main highly talented writers either make an assumption that George knew and was brought up by his music professor father, for example, Howard Mandel and Max

Harrison, or, like John Fordham and Ian Carr, understand the nature of George's relationship with his biological father, an unspecified influence.

66. Nat Hentoff, "George Russell," *Broadcast Music Inc.* (1960).

67. Duncan Heining, "A Meeting with a Remarkable Man," *Avant* 7 (Summer 1998).

68. The Label Bleu Web site notes, "Still in Cincinnati, a pianist among his friends, Spaulding Givens (who will work with Charles Mingus and will be called later Nadi Qamar) lets him hear Debussy's records, preceding his discovery of Stravinsky." See http://www.label-bleu.com/artist.php?lng=e&artist_id=46.

69. Lawless Jones mentions Andrew Johnson in relation to the access or lack of access for black students to music colleges and the development in the black community of "professors" who taught piano or other instruments. Johnson's father was one such, as were Noah Ryder and Wendell P. Dabney. See also Burton, *My Life in Jazz*.

70. Perlis, interview with G. Russell.

CHAPTER THREE

~

Cincy Blues

How did it feel for sixteen-year-old George Russell, walking those streets free of the school he hated and now a part of the adult world in fact, if not by virtue of age of majority? We can guess it felt exhilarating, exciting, and full of possibility. Home was becoming increasingly a place to refuel and re-charge. It was not that Bessie was irrelevant. She was and is the only mother Russell knew, and he loved her. However, it would be surprising if she had much more influence over her son than most parents, then or today, have over their teenage children. She was a disciplinarian with strong moral val-ues. She was, nevertheless, by one account—that of Dwight McPheeters and his mother—somewhat indulgent of her child.[1] That is not a criticism—the balance of parenting is a fine one, not a perfect one. Did she know where George was and what he was doing, even half of the time? She would be an unusual parent if she did, and with her involvement with Bishop Mack's ministry she was not always around.

There is another issue. Entry to the world of manhood was anyway achieved at a younger age for African American males than for whites. Young George was working, which any mother would expect and hope, and was probably not that different from his peers within his race and class. He worked by day as a lift operator in a department store in Cincinnati. In fact, George, given his background, was never afraid of hard, "blue-collar" work. Later he would work whenever he needed to, but never to the point that it got in the way of his more important activities in music.

Music had been more important than anything else when he was at school. He had been a semiprofessional musician from the age of fourteen or fifteen. Now, every night he could he played the drums.

> As I said, I got kicked out of school and began doing night gigs with singers in clubs and not getting paid much money but learning all the time. Anyway, the kids, especially the black kids and to the lesser degree the whites, they wanted jazz. We had some fabulous musicians come into that town. The era . . . was amazing. I had gone to school, as you know, and out of school had to [get] a job being an elevator man in a department store in downtown Cincinnati. That was okay. So I was working nights as a drummer and days as an elevator man.[2]

It was hardly a healthy lifestyle, and Russell blames this and the experience of playing in smoky jazz clubs for his first bout of tuberculosis. "I was working nine to five at Klein's in Cincinnati, the department store. I would come home, get a little food down, and go to work in a night club four or five blocks from my house with my mother, yeah. When we were working between something like nine-thirty and two, and coming back home and then getting up too early to have a decent breakfast."[3]

It was around this time that Russell was invited to Wilberforce University, about fifty miles north of Cincinnati, to audition for the school's Collegians jazz band. According to Russell, the reason he got the call was due both to the school's need for a drummer and the positive reputation he was building in the clubs around town. Students from the college came to Cincinnati and heard him in the Cotton Club. "Students told the Collegians, 'Hey, this guy can play.' I got a letter from Wilberforce. They asked me to come up, and that's what I did."[4]

At that time, he was playing in a club over the river in Kentucky owned and run by the mob, "a Dillinger," as Russell tells it. Nelson Burton confirms that "across the river was a common expression on both sides of the Ohio but it had different meaning depending on the direction." He describes crossing the river as a "Jekyll-and-Hyde sort of thing."[5] "Mobsters knew they no longer had the law in their pockets when they crossed to Cincinnati, so their behavior was beyond reproach." However, "[b]y keeping the prostitutes and the gamblers on the other side of the river, Cincinnati had a clear conscience on the surface of being the goody-goody-two-shoes that she wasn't."[6]

Here the story becomes a little confused, due to both the distance in time and Russell's memory. Certainly, things didn't work out at Wilberforce first time. Whether Russell failed the audition, as Ernie Wilkins, a Collegian at the time, told Robert Moore,[7] or whether, as Russell remembers, he was asked to return later because the band leader was initially unhappy with his playing, is uncertain. According to Russell's recollection, "The first semester I really wasn't playing that well" and "they weren't satisfied with my playing."[8] Wilkins has suggested that part of the reason Russell failed at Wilberforce the first time stemmed from the kit Russell was using,[9] which was the one his mother had bought him as a child. This seems quite possible, as that set was subsequently lost in a fire around this period, forcing Russell and his mother to replace it. However, when school started in the fall semester of 1940, Russell was again invited to join the Collegians. He celebrated the night before his departure, playing blackjack with his older bandmates in "Dillinger's" club. He told me he believed it was his mob-connected employer who encouraged the band to let him win the money back,[10] but gave Vivian Perlis a slightly less elaborate version before talking more generally about his time at Wilberforce.

GR: So, I was again working both in the day and at night in some joint across the river from Cincinnati owned by some gangster in Newport, Kentucky. I had managed to save up a little money, I would guess, certainly, and then I took all the money—I needed some money, just a small bit to register—and I gambled that night, the night before I was going to Wilberforce and lost it all in a blackjack game (*laughing*) but with other musicians. They must have known, because they stayed on, and they sort of let me win it back. And I not only won it back, but I had money to spare. The next day I drove up to Wilberforce and registered. Wilberforce was to be my home then, really, from the time I was seventeen or eighteen, until . . . not seventeen, sixteen to about nineteen, playing in their world-class college orchestra with other musicians who would become very well known, like Ernie Wilkins. This was a band, its roster read like a Who's Who in American jazz. So that was quite an experience.
VP: Was it necessary for you to study other things in order to get through?
GR: Yes, a lot of other things. Wilberforce was kind of a prep school for upper-middle-class blacks, especially for the kids who tended to get in trouble, especially older kids. So it had a number of older, really, they were men, there, who were all taking business administration. Most of them eventually practiced it in the underworld, what they learned at Wilberforce. (*laughing*) So there was the orchestra and the bus trips, following the football team around in the fall, especially, and playing Battles of Bands after the game with the other school's orchestra. So we might drive from Zena, Ohio, down to Tuskegee, where the football players would have the Saturday playing a game with their team, [the] Tuskegee Institute, and at night there'd be a dance with two orchestras going with each other.[11]

Russell has always minimized any influence on or benefit to him from formal education; this clearly stems from his experiences at Woodrow. He has always portrayed himself as essentially an autodidact. At that time, Wilberforce, still today a private African American college, had a university and a high school. As Russell had not completed his elementary education, he attended the high school, studying the general academic curriculum. His report card made troubling reading for Bessie Russell. Out of 206 days, Russell was absent 34 and tardy 31. Apart from a couple of Bs in music, Cs predominate, and there's more than a spattering of Ds and Es! As for "effort," that was graded as "D," "below average, unsatisfactory but passing."

There is a rather poignant letter on file from Bessie to one of the teachers, Mr. B. H. Heard.

> Dear Sir,
>
> I received my son's Report Card / Geo Allan Russell/ I can't say I am any more pleased than you are with it. But there is a slight improvement from the first one and we hope he will continue to make more or better improvement than the last one. I do know he had dental trouble and I do hope he can hold up until school is over to have the rest of the work attended to. As soon as I can make it convenient I will come up and have a talk with you. I have been very sick since the Boy was home. Enclosed Mr Heard you will find two dollars, $1.65 for Physical Geography Text and Laboratory Field Manual and weekly periodical scholastic and please give him balance left which is 35c. I do thank you for your patience and interest shown him and I will continue ask please help and encourage him for my sake. I want him to finish school above all things.
>
> Respectfully Yours
> Bessie O. Russell[12]

Her wish would not be granted. The first semester, Russell continued to live in Cincinnati and commute to Wilberforce, working at the same time in a department store.[13] During the second semester, he continued to trek back to Cincinnati to gigs. He recalls that he was living on the Wilberforce campus at the time and working at Wright-Patterson Air Base to earn money.[14] How he actually found time to do any studying at all during his eighteen months at the college is in itself remarkable. It was obvious that his only real interest was playing in the Collegians and in the clubs of Cincinnati.

How much Russell actually gained from his studies at Wilberforce is a matter of conjecture. Interestingly, Dr. Anna M. Terry was his teacher of music at the school, and she would later serve on the Board of Trustees of the New England Conservatory, where Russell taught from 1969 until 2004.

When Ian Carr asked Russell about Terry, an educator of some standing, Russell minimized what he learned at school, instead referring to his later period in hospital due to TB with Harold Gaston. "She [Terry] helped me out in talking to me but I still didn't learn music formally from her. I learned music formally in a hospital."[15]

While Russell's account may be accurate, it is likely that by the time he came to learn "the rudiments of arranging," as he has put it, from Harold Gaston in the tuberculosis sanatorium, he had sufficient knowledge and understanding to take advantage of what Gaston had to teach. Also, there are those Bs and Cs in music at Wilberforce, suggesting that he learned a little more at Wilberforce than he has since allowed.

I am not alone in this assumption. Robert E. Moore interviewed Terry for his *Trotter Institute Review* article on Russell, though he refers to her as "Anna." He wrote, "It was at Wilberforce that he received his first formal instruction in music frm Professor Anna Terry, mentor to a long list of distinguished African-Americans. About Russell, Professor Terry related: 'When he came to me he didn't know a thing . . . what a staff was. I had to teach him all of the fundamentals."[16]

Two photographs of the Collegians in the 1942 and 1943 college yearbooks show Russell dressed in bolero-jacketed uniform, white shirt, and straight dark tie behind a kit with "Wilberforce Collegians" written on the bass drum. Oliver McLean, the Collegians' alto player, was highly regarded in Cincinnati and the Midwest. However, aside from McLean, Russell and tenorist/arranger Ernie Wilkins were the only members of the band to make careers of note in jazz.

Having worked on his drumming between his first and second invitations to Wilberforce, it was playing with the Collegians that Russell really enjoyed about his time at the college. "In the meantime, I had—in that six months—I had really learned how to play drums. So when they got me back it was wonderful. You know, we had just a great time."[17]

Recalling the band's roll call of past stars—inaccurately, as it happens, including Fletcher Henderson and Coleman Hawkins[18]—Russell notes that all the black universities of the period had "incredibly exciting jazz orchestras."

And one of our most enjoyable tasks was to follow the football team around in the fall, they going on their bus and we going on ours to these various universities. And on Saturday the football team would play the football team and then at night there'd be this battle of the bands between . . . with the Wilberforce Collegians and, let's say, the Alabama State Collegians, with Lucky Thompson and . . . oh, Willy . . . you know, Willy Cook.[19]

At that point, for Russell, playing jazz mattered more than anything, even more than clothes, cars, or girls, or any of the things that drive an eighteen-year-old young man. Although "handsome" George Russell, as he is dubbed in one of the yearbook photos, clearly already had an eye for the women who were attracted to jazzmen and their lives.

On December 8, 1941, following the Japanese attack on Pearl Harbor, the United States declared war on Japan. As Russell recalls, "It was around '41 that I was called up for the draft. In that . . . at the draft you know, the World War II thing, I volunteered for the Marines 'cause they told me I'd be playing in the Marine Band. Hardy har, har, har, you know."[20]

Russell wanted to fight and was swept up in the patriotic fervor that followed Pearl Harbor, though with hindsight he wonders if he would have been up to demands of the Corps.

> I wanted to [fight] . . . not knowing all of the things I would have had to go through if I'd made it, because in those days the Marine Corps demands were rough, very rough. I was with a friend, a pianist, and we were in a room of three thousand people, naked men, who had taken these examinations, and then I heard my name called. But before that we had told a Marine colonel that we wanted to join and he was delighted and he showed us the way to where they examined me. They took my friend but they told me I had tuberculosis; saved my life in a lot of ways.[21]

As he told Carr, "But they spared me a few, a few of their most interesting parties—Iwo Jima, Guadalcanal."[22]

Russell remembers meeting his pianist friend Bobby, who was drafted, in Chicago a few years later. "He was a piano player but couldn't play piano when he got back. Just had this look on his face. If you saw it you would never forget it. That was a knockout blow for me to see him in that state. Didn't speak. Just the way he looked."[23]

Russell was admitted to the Branch Hospital in Cincinnati. He describes it as a "good hospital, wonderful hospital," where he had a private room with a veranda; it was nevertheless a segregated facility. One of the other patients was Harold Gaston, Russell's school friend and colleague in the Rhythm Club. In a broadcast for WGBH Radio in Boston, Russell summarized his six months in the hospital.

> I went into the hospital and one of the patients was Harold Gaston. We used to pass the time with him coming in and teaching me music, the rudiments of music. Harold and I were part of a group that began to protest the segregated poli-

cies in the hospital lunchroom. The chief doctor said, "I think you are both well enough to be dismissed." I was glad to hear it, even though it was a big lie.[24]

That is the expurgated version. The real story tells something about the racial fault lines in American society. There are always those who, whatever their reasons, will explore the margins of social divisions and will sometimes cross the line far beyond what is considered acceptable. Prescribed six months of bed rest, Russell's experience was surely not what his doctor had in mind.

> Each patient had their own room with a beautiful view, but whites on one floor, blacks on another. There had to be some nurses that liked that, and one of them—the head nurse—used to come in the room and look at me and not ask me what's wrong but just look at me for a long time. Finally, a nurse came in who was from Kentucky and she did it all. I sucked her breast.[25]

And: "The nurses had infiltrated to the patients . . . and this is a segregated facility . . . and the guys, the black guys used to get visits at night from some of the nurses, and I managed to do that just in time before the hospital clamping down on any kind of integration."[26]

In some ways, what is most amazing is less the fact that white nurses were having sex with black patients but that they were doing so with patients who had tuberculosis!

> At the same time, this woman from Kentucky, she was a nurse and she took a liking to me . . . she was white . . . as did a number of nurses there who made boyfriends of the patients. And the head nurse walks in in the middle of the night and catches me at it.[27]

Gaston and Russell passed the time—when not engaged in other such therapeutic and recreational activities—with Gaston teaching Russell musical theory and arranging. "And he being in the hospital too, he could pass the time teaching me the elements of music. And from him I learned the elements of music—chords and basics, intervals, basic techniques of writing, you know."[28]

The senior nurse who caught Russell *in flagrante delicto* had not kept matters to herself. With Gaston and Russell trying to desegregate the hospital in other ways, it was more than the hospital administration could bear. "We were being rebels and trying to integrate the food facility there at the hospital. They would have none of that. But Gaston was a rebel, got kicked out of the hospital. The hospital changed president [director] and the new president came from Mississippi and that was it. He released us."[29]

Neither he nor Gaston was cured of the disease, and it is with a bitter tone in his voice that Russell recalls that this amounted to a death sentence for his friend. Although Russell recognizes that his lifestyle may have contributed to his contracting tuberculosis, the disease was rife across America, in particular in poorer areas where people lived in close proximity.[30]

Gaston and his entire family died of the disease. In Gaston's case, it seems that he had received a call to replace the great Jimmy Blanton in Duke Ellington's orchestra shortly before his final illness. Both Russell and Burton have referred to this, though Russell has elsewhere mentioned Lionel Hampton as the bandleader calling on Gaston's services.[31] It is one of those cases of "what might have been" had that doctor from Mississippi followed his oath rather than his prejudices. Given that Russell played with Gaston and no doubt visited his home, it is possible that this is where he caught tuberculosis, though that too is conjecture. Like many such diseases, tuberculosis is no respecter of class, race, gender, or religion.

Russell's two stints in the hospital for tuberculosis figure significantly in interviews he has given over the years. There is no doubt that they were genuinely life-threatening and life-changing events. In one interview, he actually noted that when talking about his periods in hospital, "I'm just mentioning a few of the things that shaped my life."[32] It was during his second bout of tuberculosis that Russell first elaborated his Lydian Concept. But it is perhaps worth considering for a moment Russell's experiences in relation to the way he and others have told his story. Such considerations may say something about the rather formalized and archetypal form in which such stories are told in our culture.

For example, the Jungian writer Joseph Campbell has described in detail common themes from myths and biography that recur in the telling of the lives of exceptional individuals, as if there is an unspoken and unconscious format to which such stories must conform. According to Campbell, symbolic rites of passage, chance encounters, perilous journeys, isolation and misunderstanding, difficult trials, secret helpers, atonement with the father—all of these often feature in "hero" biographies. Through these "transformative" events, the "hero" emerges a changed person, "possessing the power to bestow great benefits upon his fellow man."[33] Virgin or mysterious birth origins also feature. It is not about questioning "the frequent kernel of biographical truth," to use Frank J. Sulloway's phrase about another "hero," Sigmund Freud.[34] It is how this is understood and the context that is constructed for it that requires thought. Overreliance on such archetypical forms may cause the biographer to miss important issues and fresh insights.

Here, it suffices to note again Russell's origins. In his program for the BBC on Russell, Ian Carr begins as follows:

> [George Russell is] one of the most mysterious and unorthodox figures in jazz. His ideas have been hugely influential, yet he has been for the most part a shadowy presence on the sidelines. It may be that his *covert genius has its roots in the secrecy surrounding his birth* in Cincinnati in 1923. (my italics)[35]

Though the story he was told does bear scrutiny and certainly seems to contain more than a "kernel of biological truth," inquiries into his background proved comparatively easy. It is a not uncommon American story of its time—an attractive, talented, and respectable young woman of color is seduced by—here we assume—an older, white authority figure.[36] Their association, given the social and political culture of the time, was taboo. Russell's origins are not shrouded in mystery. However, the truth does fit the hero myth of a kind of virgin birth, for, to all intents and purposes, his biological father is the shadowy, (holy) ghostlike figure here.

Russell's bouts of tuberculosis are his perilous journeys. His experiences at Withrow High, in racially divided Cincinnati, and in its jazz clubs are his rites of passage. But, as we shall see, even more pertinent is the inward journey Russell took in the hospital when he "discovered" the Lydian Concept. It is that voyage of (self-)discovery that also predominates within the hero myth. It will later be seen that other aspects of Russell's story fit the "hero myth." However, Russell's life is, in reality, fascinating enough and his achievements significant enough that neither requires or benefits from such a telling. It is more useful to try to understand both within a more objective contextual account. We will return to these questions later.

It is obvious from his account that for Russell, still in his teens, the experience of being in the hospital—of having sex with nursing staff, of challenging the system, and of learning the "rudiments of music"—was both exhilarating and liberating. It was, in all senses, a "rite of passage." Tuberculosis saved him from fighting, and, even as it threatened his life, it possibly saved him. The regret at having to leave is obvious in his comment: "The hospital became like a school to me and it was a hard thing to be fired from a hospital and being a patient who was actually not cured."[37] At the same time, there is an understandable anger in his voice as he notes that this was, for Gaston, a death sentence. As he also told Vivian Perlis, "Harold was actually on his way. When I came back three months after that he was dead. And all of this was really completely needless, it was murder, actually, 'cause the doctor knew he wasn't gonna live. . . . So, I'm getting more and more radicalized."[38]

From the hospital, Russell returned to work and to the jazz clubs of Cincinnati and Kentucky. In the hospital, he had written his first composition, "New World," and he sold it to A. B. Townsend and his orchestra. Around this time, Nadi Qamar, who had been living in Los Angeles, returned to Cincinnati. Some fifty-plus years later, Qamar recalls playing with "one of his [Russell's] small bands on Central Avenue in Downtown Cincinnati Ohio." In an interview with Ben Young for WKCR, Qamar's recollections were still quite clear: "We didn't really play anything together until I went to the West Coast. I was out there for a while and met Charles Mingus, and when I came back to visit my mother in Ohio, we got together and started doing some things around Cincinnati, Ohio—not too many."[39]

What surprises most of all is what he appears to be saying about Russell's music back in Cincinnati.

> When I saw him again, he was, to me, . . . he was totally into himself. He wasn't playing drums with other people's music, he was playing with his own quintet or writing, when I saw him again, but he was very open too. You could bring in arrangements and the band would try 'em out. You know, like that he was really into himself, what he wanted to do, and what he wanted to write. To me, he remained that way all through the years.[40]

In the interview, Qamar's account wanders between midforties Cincinnati and meeting Russell again in New York in the early sixties with his new sextet. However, Young presses the issue, and it certainly seems that Qamar is referring to playing with Russell in their hometown.

As noted in chapter 2, Robert Moore also interviewed Qamar, and he confirms that Qamar played with Russell. Qamar continues in his interview with Young to suggest that Russell's music, even then, involved "very complex rhythms and scales and harmonic clusters."

Russell also told Carr about the period after his hospitalizaton:

> **GR:** And [I] concentrated on writing when I came out of the hospital because then I had found something that I knew I could do well, you know.
> **IC:** What? Arranging?
> **GR:** Arranging, composing . . .
> **IC:** How long did it take you to realize that you could do them well? I mean . . .

GR: Well, right away, because when I wrote my first arrangement, I wrote it in the hospital with no piano and the person who got the arrangement he bought it, you know. So that . . . that was always a sign that you were doing something right, if they paid you, you know.[41]

By this point, Russell had clearly advanced considerably as a musician and as a composer/arranger. Russell has been at some pains to stress that he knew very little prior to Harold Gaston's tuition in the sanatorium. He has stressed that he learned little about music at Wilberforce and has generally downplayed the early pre-Concept period in his work. Qamar's comments are crucial because they suggest a more consistent and coherent history of Russell's musical development than he has himself offered. To accept Russell's version at face value, with less than six months tuition from his friend, he wrote and sold his first composition to a leading regional orchestra. It also ignores his school reports from Wilberforce. If one believes Russell's version, it almost begins to echo the kind of transformation stories about other major black musicians, including Robert Johnson and Charlie Parker, who went from novices to masters, also within similar time frames.[42] What is more, barely five years later Russell composed the remarkably advanced "Cubano-Be, Cubano-Bop" for Dizzy Gillespie and two years later the even more startling "A Bird in Igor's Yard" for Buddy DeFranco. Qamar's account would fill the gap and suggest a musical intelligence that was already advancing and building rapidly on his experiences with both Gaston and Professor Terry at Wilberforce.

As we have seen, Russell's formal education left him little reason to view such learning positively, and Papa Hemingway's injunction had already struck a chord in him. He admired Gaston, and his sense of loss at the pointless and neglectful way the young man came to die is palpable even now. Unconsciously, Russell preserves Gaston's achievements within the context of his own story. There is perhaps also, in line with Campbell's thesis, an unconscious tendency to fall into preexisting frameworks in the way we tell our stories. But more than that, we weigh and place value on aspects of our memory according to a range of criteria that are subjective as well as objective in nature.

By this point, around 1943, Russell had begun to outgrow Cincinnati. His first break came through bandleader and saxophonist Benny Carter, as he told Ian Carr: "It was a time when drummers were scarce, and Benny Carter came through and he had heard about my drumming. He hired me."[43]

Trombonist J. J. Johnson was Russell's roommate, and they quickly became friends. Russell tells of one occasion when he and Johnson missed the whole first set of a gig. They had been smoking marijuana and were completely stoned. One of the band had needed to deputize for Russell, and Carter, by all accounts a tolerant man, was understandably unhappy.[44]

After three weeks out on the road, the band played Cincinnati, and Russell saw his friend Harold Gaston. "Harold was elated because Ellington had sent him a wire saying that he wanted him to join the orchestra, you know. But he didn't look well and he sensed that he wasn't able to accept this. And maybe two months after that he died, you know."[45]

The tour took in New York and Russell heard for the first time the new jazz that Bird, Dizzy, and others were making in the clubs of Manhattan, and as a drummer, he was particularly struck by the playing of Max Roach. "There was a new music developing on 52nd Street and it was bebop. I went down to the street and heard this really fantastic music. And the drummer was Max Roach. I'm looking at Max, and he just moved his wrist and got all this energy and I had to really swing to get all that, to really fire up a big band, a professional big band."[46]

Of his own playing at the time, Russell recalled for WGBH Boston, "I could play time really beautifully but I wasn't a show drummer. I couldn't throw the sticks. I wasn't a great solo drummer. There was this exciting music on 52nd Street, and I remember going down to hear Dizzy and Bird and Max and I heard Max play and I said, 'There's a drummer. There's really a drummer.'"[47]

While Russell enjoyed the experience of playing gigs like the Apollo Theater in Harlem, he noted to Vivian Perlis that he felt, for the first time, "a disenchantment with drums."

Benny Carter had a similar experience on that tour.

During that tour in Boston, Benny called me in and said, "I hate to tell you this, but I found a drummer." (laughs) I was shocked in a way and relieved in a way. I was tired of carrying those drums around. I said, "Who's the drummer?" He said, "Max Roach." (laughs) So that was just about the beginning of my writing career.[48]

And:

Benny called me into the room at the Apollo Theater in Harlem, where we were, and he said, "George, I have to give you two weeks' notice. (laughs) I've a new drummer coming in." He'd been to 52nd Street, heard Max play, and knew that he had to have that drummer—and I agreed with him! (laughs) Once I heard Max I realized I'd never be anywhere near as good a drummer as him.[49]

Asked about Benny Carter, he says, "I didn't really know Benny. We weren't chummy. He wanted a job done. He wanted it done well, and with me he wanted it done well enough to get by. And I did that. I filled that spot for the time he needed me and I agreed with him with the two weeks' notice."[50]

The band played the Howard Theatre in Washington, and two weeks later Roach took over the drum chair. Russell did the only thing he could: headed for home. "So I played with the band for two weeks more. I got out as fast as I could and took the train back home and began to do what I should be doing, which was write. I started writing, then, maybe the first day I got back home."[51]

And to Perlis:

> So after the two weeks at the Howard, I left and went back to Cincinnati and dove headfirst into writing music, and actually writing for the Benny Carter Orchestra, the piece was called "New World." I didn't know when or where I'd see him. And then I also started playing with a band around. First this "New World" piece, I tried it out with the band at the Cotton Club and it sounded great. So I said, "I'll put a big band arrangement on this for Benny Carter."[52]

This again seems to confirm Nadi Qamar's memories of Russell and the music he was making when he again caught up with him in Cincinnati.

It is clear that Russell was already aware of the new music coming out of New York, and he had certainly heard "'Round Midnight" on the radio. He had told Ian Carr that it was this song that had made him want to head for the Big Apple. "That struck me as incredibly . . . as an incredibly profound new piece of music or new music, you know."[53]

One incident in particular seems to encapsulate his latter-day experiences in his hometown and crystallized in him the desire to leave for good.

> Spaulding and I and a bass player got a job downtown in a nightclub and something had happened to our regular bass player, and a fellow named Fitz was passing through town, totally white and a good bass player and this was novel. . . . My mother practically adopted him. . . . He had been stranded in Cincinnati. He stayed with us and played with us at night. Anyway, we had this trio at a club downtown, essentially white clientele, and one night this guy comes down and sits in with us and he said he noticed two rather big men in the back of the club, white men. He wondered why they were watching him. This is all because he was living with us. One night after we had packed up, Fitz was taken out by these two guys that were Cincinnati police detectives, and about four in the morning there was a knock on the door . . . about four

or five . . . a kind of weak knock on the door, and there before you stood the most bloody, beaten person. He said, "They threatened to throw me in the river." He said, "They kept asking me . . ."—they asked him either whether he was black or white. He said, "I'm white." I don't know why, but there seemed at the time to be a kind of relief period when the Cincinnati police probably were . . . had a limit to what they would go to, but these guys passed the limit. My mother, being a nurse, she . . . he had to be cleaned up, and there was no way we could . . . what we did is the very next day we went back to the club and played and these guys walked in. And none of us . . . we all gave 'em dirty looks. I tried to get other people interested in dealing with this.[54]

Russell and Nadi Qamar, the trio's pianist, apparently tried to raise this issue within the community and in wider Cincinnati, but without success. It was this incident, combined with what he saw as the indifference of local politicians to it, that encouraged Russell to leave Cincinnati once and for all. It was 1944, and although the Big Apple seemed to be the main draw, Russell headed to Chicago rather than to New York.

As he told Vivian Perlis about this "ghastly story": "Incidents happened, not really worth discussing, made me realize I had to get out of Cincinnati. The hatred there was just unbelievable."[55]

Again speaking with Perlis, Russell describes the bitter irony: "This was the same irony I ran into the first day of school, and I said, 'Somehow there is a way out of this.' So I picked up a few weeks later and went to Chicago, where I ran into the Benny Carter band, at the downtown theater, and I had my 'New World' arrangement, and they played it, and they loved it, and they bought it."[56]

Speaking to me in 2003, Russell remembered, "Cincinnati got to be unlivable, so I went to Chicago and started out playing with a band in Chicago—the Paradise Ballroom Band—and that held me over. That was maybe three or four months later that Benny came through Chicago, where I was living at the time. I told him I had worked on a piece for the band. He took the band down in the basement of the theater and said, 'George has a piece. Let's hear it.' It was called 'New World.' He bought it. He loved the piece. He didn't give me a lot of money, but I was off to writing."[57]

It was the same tune he had already sold to A. B. Townsend. According to Russell, "New World" in this incarnation "was rather impressionistic, beautiful chords and put together in a nice way. Benny liked it and gave me $25.00 for it! I was living with a girl in Chicago, and that helped enormously."[58]

As Russell told Ian Carr, "I kept rearranging the same composition, you know, until it got better and better. (laughing) And I also kept selling it to a lot of different bands, over and over again." Carr asked him if that was legal, to which Russell replied, chortling to himself, "Well, I made it legal. It was legal for me, you know. I sold that to a lot of bands—Cab Calloway, Earl Hines. That was my bread and butter for a couple of years."[59]

Perhaps fortunately for Russell, none of the four or more bands (Dizzy Gillespie was another customer) to whom he sold the piece recorded it. Had they done so, not only would his subterfuge have been exposed, but a valuable source of income would have been lost!

> I sold that piece many times. That piece kept me alive when I went back to New York. Because we didn't have any money. Three of us lived in a hotel room in Harlem on 125th Street and Lennox Avenue. We had gotten out of Chicago and were living in New York, but it got more and more difficult because we were barely surviving. But we made it in our own way.[60]

In 1944 and still in Chicago, Russell got work writing for Earl Hines.

> They had opened up a new club at the big hotel there on 63rd Street in what was then the black community of Chicago, right in the center. They were presented by the Panther Room of the Hotel Shermann in downtown Chicago, which was at the time mostly a white audience, and they had a show. It was opening night and it [the club and the scene in Chicago] was mostly run by gangsters and they [Hines and his manager] asked me to write music for the show. I took from here to there. I stayed up four nights—took from this thing and that thing, a little Debussy, a little Ravel—and wrote the show music. The point was, I was really tired. I didn't go to bed for four nights—but I wasn't the only one who was tired, because when the band started playing the music it sounded absolutely ridiculous, just terrible. For one hour, with the gangsters looking on. It was one day before the club opened, but they were looking a little angry, I should say. One good thinking person in the band said, "What key is this in?" Well, the copyist had put the wrong key signature. I was really worried, because those guys were for real. We played the music and it was beautiful enough to get a very good review in a Chicago newspaper. I think it was the *Tribune*.[61]

To Carr in 1992, Russell recalled that the "lavish nightclub" was the El Grotto in the Hotel Persian, and it was an uptown take on the downtown, white Panther Room. He described the initial rehearsal as being like "a combination of Webern, Ran Blake and Charles Ives" and says that it was the longest hour of his life as the gangster owners looked on. The copyist had transposed the music correctly but had failed to put the transposed key signatures on the sheets.[62]

The point about Debussy and Ravel is important. Speaking to Carr, Russell is quite specific about the influence and refers to the *Nocturnes* (1897–99), an orchestral piece in three sections, which Russell names correctly as "Nuages," "Fetes," and "Sirenes." This was just two years or so after his discharge from the hospital. This was clearly quite sophisticated music, and either Russell's progress from learning "the rudiments of music" with Harold Gaston in the sanatorium was beyond remarkable—or he was not quite the neophyte he describes. Whatever the case, he was clearly by this point drawing on an unusual range of sources and upon music to which Nadi Qamar had introduced him prior to his teens.

It is worth taking a moment to consider what Russell might have heard in this suite that he could use as a jazz composer. While Billy Strayhorn brought Ravel to his own compositions and to the attention of Duke Ellington, generally in jazz criticism the influence of such European composers is contained in the epithet "musical impressionism." In fact, there is much more in that term that needs to be unpacked for it to make real sense. Debussy's concern was to convey ordinary, everyday emotions—the feeling one might get watching clouds, for example ("Nuages")—primarily using the tone colors and harmonies of an orchestra or a single instrument. That brings us to the possibility of using a jazz orchestra and its range of colors in a similar way. But more than that, such conceptions can be translated into chords and scales. The second section of Nocturnes draws on Gamelan and uses a pentatonic scale in its simple tune. That section is also rather static in the way the orchestra is used, with only flute and harp suggesting movement. Finally, Debussy uses various orchestral techniques that certainly Russell—but also Strayhorn and Ellington and Gil Evans—would utilize. He divides the strings, just as Russell in later years would divide his jazz orchestra. Key centers are implied rather than fixed in Debussy's music, and he tends to use brass muted to create softer textures. Again, there is a parallel in Russell's, Ellington's, and particularly Evans's work. But perhaps most significant in Russell's case is Debussy's extensive use of percussion, almost to the point, in "Fetes," of suggesting a sense of swing, but more generally as a means of providing additional color. Understood this way, the idea that European art music does not have anything to contribute to jazz is utter nonsense.[63]

As Russell explained to Carr, "And that was it, you know. Then I had my ticket, you know." For many musicians of his generation, New York was the big pull, and, like them, Russell was willing to accept any amount of hardship to try and make it in what had become the home of the new jazz era.

> Then after hanging around Chicago for a year, and I had heard a little bebop when I was in New York with Benny, but I had two young friends, Little Diz and Little Bird—Robert Gay and Henry Pryor—and they played Bird and

Monk until I really heard it. And especially Monk I heard. Then I said, "It's time to move on to New York." So, we had fifteen dollars between us and we all jumped on a bus for New York.[64]

Notes

1. Interview with Dwight McPheeters, June 2004.
2. Interview with George Russell, June 2003.
3. Ibid.
4. Ibid.
5. Nelson Burton, *My Life in Jazz* (Cincinnati, OH: Clifton Hills Press, 2000), p. 33.
6. Ibid.
7. Interview with Robert Moore, July 2004.
8. Interview with G. Russell, June 2003.
9. Interview with Moore.
10. Interview with G. Russell, June 2003.
11. Vivian Perlis, interview with George Russell, American Music Series, December 8, 1993, Oral History Project of American Music, sponsored and supported by the National Endowment for the Arts Special Jazz Projects.
12. Letter from Bessie O. Russell to Mr. B. H. Heard, March 3, 1941.
13. Ian Carr, interview with George Russell, June 1992; also interview with G. Russell, June 2003.
14. Interview with G. Russell, June 2003.
15. Carr, interview with G. Russell, June 1992.
16. Robert E. Moore, "George Alan Russell: Jazz's First Theorist," *Trotter Institute Review* 2 (Summer 1988): 18.
17. Carr, interview with G. Russell, June 1992.
18. Ibid. Horace, Fletcher's brother, formed the Collegians, and Benny Carter was also in the orchestra at that time as Russell rightly notes. Fletcher, however, attended Clark University and then took his masters at Columbia in chemistry. However, he found his job prospects in chemistry to be very restricted due to his race and turned to music for a living. (See Frank Driggs, liner notes in *The Fletcher Henderson Story*, Columbia CL419.) Coleman Hawkins attended Washburn College. See J. Chilton, *Song of the Hawk* (London: Quartet, 1990).
19. Carr, interview with G. Russell, June 1992.
20. Ibid.
21. Interview with George Russell, June 2004.
22. Carr, interview with G. Russell, June 1992.
23. Interview with George Russell, October 2003.
24. *George Russell—A Jazz Portrait*, WGBH Radio, Boston.
25. Interview with G. Russell, June 2004.
26. Ibid.

27. Ibid.

28. Carr, interview with G. Russell, June 1992.

29. Interview with G. Russell, June 2004.

30. Burton, *My Life in Jazz*, p. 62. Although Burton is wrong regarding when penicillin was discovered, which was in 1928, the drug was not synthesized effectively until the late thirties or available in injectable form until 1941. (See R. Bud, *Penicillin—Triumph and Tragedy* [Oxford: Oxford University Press, 2007].)

31. Interview with G. Russell, June 2003.

32. Interview with G. Russell, June 2004.

33. Joseph Campbell, *The Hero with a Thousand Faces* (London: Fontana, 1993); Frank J. Sulloway, *Freud, Biologist of the Mind* (London: Fontana, 1980), p. 447.

34. Sulloway, *Freud*, p. 446.

35. Ian Carr, *George Russell—The Invisible Guru*, BBC Radio 3 broadcast, July–August 1994.

36. Burton, *My Life in Jazz*, p. 25. Intriguingly, Burton also discovered in his teens, after his father's death, that his biological father was a white doctor named S. P. Nelson. Just as Russell was told that his mother gave him her surname as his first name as a connection to her, Nelson Burton was given his biological father's surname in similar fashion.

37. Interview with G. Russell, June 2003.

38. Perlis, interview with G. Russell.

39. Ben Young, interview with Nadi Qamar, WKCR Radio, New York, 1998. See also Dom Cerulli, "George Russell," *Down Beat*, May 29, 1958. Discussing his second hospitalization, Russell states, "I had experimented scantily with polytonality before but on the piano in the library of the hospital, I really began an intensive research into tonality." This suggests a greater degree of continuity in Russell's musical development than the composer has sometimes acknowledged and provides some confirmation of Qamar's recollections.

40. Young, interview with Qamar.

41. Carr, interview with G. Russell, June 1992.

42. See G. Marcus, *Mystery Train* (London: Omnibus, 1977); P. Guralnik, *Searching for Robert Johnson* (London: Pimlico, 1998); and R. Russell, *Bird Lives* (Aylesbury, UK: Quartet, 1988).

43. Carr, interview with G. Russell, June 1992; interview with Moore.

44. Russell told this story over dinner in a club in Boston in October 2003 in my presence.

45. Carr, interview with G. Russell, June 1992.

46. Perlis, interview with G. Russell.

47. *George Russell—A Jazz Portrait*.

48. Ibid.

49. Interview with G. Russell, October 2003. Interestingly, J. J. Johnson described Russell as "a fine big-band drummer, with excellent time and imagination." See Burt Korall, "Who Is George Russell?" *Down Beat*, February 16, 1961.

50. Interview with G. Russell, October 2003.

51. Ibid.

52. Perlis, interview with G. Russell.

53. Carr, interview with G. Russell, June 1992.

54. Interview with G. Russell, June 2003.

55. Perlis, interview with G. Russell.

56. Ibid.

57. Interview with G. Russell, October 2003.

58. Perlis, interview with G. Russell.

59. Carr, interview with G. Russell, June 1992.

60. Interview with G. Russell, October 2003.

61. Ibid.

62. Carr, interview with G. Russell, June 1992.

63. See, for example, D. J. Grout and C. V. Palisca, A History of Western Music (New York: Norton, 1996), pp. 681–82; also K. Anderson, sleeve notes for Debussy—Prélude à l'après-midi d'un faune, Nocturnes, La Mer (1990), Naxos CD 8.550262.

64. Carr, interview with G. Russell, June 1992.

CHAPTER FOUR

~

New York, N.Y.

It was May 1945, the war was still on, bebop was at its height in New York, and George Russell and his two friends Little Bird and Little Diz had just arrived in the city. With fifteen dollars in their collective pocket, they faced a simple choice. Two of them could get a room, but the third was out on the streets. So they moved into the Hotel Barada, right behind the Apollo at 125th Street and 7th Avenue, and Russell would sneak in after dark to share the room. After a week the money had run down to five dollars and, to make it last, they moved into a cheaper room at the Braddock Hotel, on 134th Street, one without windows. It was high summer, which in New York is about as humid and sticky as it gets in the Northern Hemisphere, and Russell decided he would be more comfortable sleeping in nearby Gracie Park.[1]

It all sounds quite jolly, one of those experiences that was hell at the time but looking back was character forming. The trio ate at a local Catholic Mission for fifty cents, but even that got too expensive. "In the days I would go to one of Mrs. Kramer['s]. . . . There was a woman who owned several hotels in New York and she featured the big bands you know. She had nice washrooms. I'd go there to wash up."[2] And,

> Mrs. Kramer was a lady who owned some big hotels in town, and what she must have thought of people like me, down-and-outers, who would use those lovely lush bathrooms. So you could stay clean, scrape a little here and there, and eat at the automat. About the third night, I began to realize that I wasn't up for this kind of adventure for too long.[3]

Back in Ohio, it must have been late 1942 or more likely 1943, Russell had gone to Dayton to see the Duke Ellington Band. Several of the musicians could not find a hotel, due to "color bar" problems, and so Russell invited Ray Nance, Betty Roche, Al Hibbler, and Skippy Williams to stay at his home with the redoubtable and always welcoming Bessie. "And Skippy said, 'If you're ever down and out in New York, give me a call.' That's what I did. He said, 'George, I remember you, come on over.' I stayed with him, and took my arrangement of 'New World' over to Dizzy. He said, 'I'm glad to get this because I'm starting a big band now, I'll try this.' They tried it and Dizzy gave me like $25 or $30. I sold this arrangement to just about everybody!"[4]

In fact, Russell has telescoped events slightly here. By other accounts he has given, to Ian Carr and to me, for example, he had by that point met up with Max Roach. The drummer seems to have adopted Russell as a protégé and introduced him to Bird, Diz, and everyone on "the Street." As he once said, "When I was in New York with Skippy, I don't know what got into Max, because he didn't have to do it but he introduced me to everybody as an arranger."[5] It was Roach's introduction and the credibility that went with the title that provided Russell with the opportunity to sell Gillespie "New World," and, as Russell remembers, "it was kind of my passport into the group of musicians that were doing this fantastic . . . that were part of this incredible revolution."[6]

What is striking about Russell's account, and that of others such as Gil Evans and Gerry Mulligan, is the openness of that group.[7] Bebop was a virtuoso music, rhythmically and harmonically adventurous and often played at breakneck tempos that discouraged all but the most confident and able. Yet, despite the cool, the hip vernacular, the drugs, the clothes, and the attitude—all meant to exclude the straight world—genuine talent, black or white, was welcomed. As Russell notes, "The one entrée to the group was talent. So people who later on were talented were welcomed."[8] And musicians shared their ideas and knowledge, which was great for someone like the twenty-two-year-old midwesterner, as Russell told Carr: "It didn't last, but it was the prevailing feeling at the time, a feeling of great openness, you know."[9]

Much of that spirit Russell attributes to Charlie Parker. "I don't know what the cause of that was particularly, but, one thing, it was like Charlie Parker was the center of that. And I think it was his spirit, and generous spirit, that encouraged very much this community feeling around what was happening mainly because of him."[10]

The money from selling "New World" was enough to get Russell his own room. "With the money, I moved to my own place on 48th near 6th Avenue, just one room. There's all these guys working the Street, nobody had thought to rent a room or anything. I had Bird in my room, well, a lot of other people too. The landlady was going crazy. She said, 'I don't like all of those strange people coming in here.' I said, 'They're just like me.' *(laughs)* I think she didn't know I was black or something."[11]

Although he had only been "on the Street" a few months, Russell had by now met Miles Davis as well, and by his account had been invited to join Charlie Parker's quintet on drums. That room on 48th was used by just about everyone playing the clubs around 52nd Street. Charlie Parker would come by between sets to cook up and shoot heroin.

> Bird used to ask me, "George, do you want some of this [smack]?" I said, "Bird, I don't think I can take it." He said, "Okay." I knew that people like Fats Navarro—talented people—losing a hundred pounds in weight and just getting eaten up from the inside with these drugs, and Bird himself. Dizzy stayed pretty free of that, though. I just knew that I didn't have the stamina to take that. Something wanted more of me than to just come have a nice time, an interesting time for half a life, and die.[12]

Russell did, however, drink quite heavily during the forties and fifties. He was never an alcoholic, but attitudes toward alcohol were somewhat different back then. According to Russell's wife, Alice, he told her that he would open a fifth of scotch in the morning and drink his way through it during the day. In the evening, he would go to a club and drink some more. He also smoked a pipe despite having had tuberculosis. Again, the association between tobacco and health problems was less well known then. And Russell also enjoyed smoking pot. Dwight McPheeters remembers a car ride up to Harlem with Russell and some other guys.

> I remember when I was going to photo school in New York, George asked me if I wanted to go up Minton's Playhouse and so I said, "Yes." So I jumped in this car with George and about three or four other guys and it was really cold and they had all the windows shut. Even with all these guys in the car and the car would heat up with all these bodies in it, but they wanted the windows shut. The reason why they wanted the windows shut was because they didn't want the smell of pot to get out onto the street. George asked me, "You coppin'?" I said, "Uh-uh!" I got a big headache out of it, that's all, so I never got into pot. I smoked a lot of cigarettes in my life, but I tried smoking pot once but it did nothing for me.[13]

Russell seems to have hit it off particularly well with Davis, although the trumpeter was three years his junior and, though still a student at Juilliard, was playing in Charlie Parker's quintet at night. "Miles and I hit it off really good. He'd invite me to get a one-room apartment, in the West Nineties or something, and we'd sit down and play chords. He liked my harmonic sense and I loved his harmonic sense and we tried to see what kind of chords we'd come up [with]."[14] It was in the course of one visit to Davis's apartment and one such conversation that Russell discovered his course in life. Russell has told this story many times over the years. It has become one of those little legends or myths, true though it may be, that life and jazz thrive upon, almost acquiring a Zenlike truth, a story that encapsulates something universal.[15]

> We were having a session, you know, where musicians trade off ideas. He'd play a chord, "How do you like that?" "I like that." I played some chords and he, I think he liked my harmonic sense, and, of course, he was extraordinary, you know. But I said, "What's your aim musically, what do you really wanna do?" And he said, "I wanna learn all the changes."[16]

Knowing that Davis was already a highly gifted melodic improviser whose grasp of the changes was second to none, Russell was presented with a paradox. "I think everybody then who knew about Miles knew he knew how to play the changes. So it occurred to me to look for a new way to relate to chords."[17]

For some reason Russell was unable to keep the apartment on 48th, probably because he could not make the rent. So he moved in with a couple of other musicians who had a place over on the West Side of Manhattan, around the Seventies. "We lived on Cream of Wheat every morning. We lived on Riverside Drive in a huge apartment, but we didn't have any money. I remember laying out in the sun one day on Riverside Drive and this big [gurgling] in my chest started."[18]

Russell had already been to the doctor with a nagging cough that had been diagnosed as a "bad cold." It was, however, his uncured tuberculosis flaring up, and that gurgling sensation was "a hemorrhage coming on."[19] By now it was late summer of 1945. In just a few months, Russell had established himself within that group of musicians who were shaping the new jazz, but now he was really in a bad way. He was admitted to St. Joseph's Hospital in the Bronx, and that was to be his home for the next fifteen months. This time there was no private room, and this time the nurses—mainly elderly nuns—reserved their hands for more strictly medical procedures. With fifteen chronically and critically ill men on the ward, Russell would turn over in his corner bed, face the wall, and go deep inside his own thoughts. And that puzzle that Davis had set for him kept coming back to him.

I went to the hospital at 143rd and Brook Avenue, St. Joseph's, and it was a very dreary Catholic hospital. At the first opportunity I got a chance—it was a room with fifteen patients—I got a chance to get a bed in a corner where I had no one next to me, at least on one side, and made a little cozy pad for myself, and then focused on what Miles had said—he'd wanted to learn all the changes. So I had a lot of time in bed to think about it. In the meantime, they are coming and visiting me, Dizzy, Miles, Max, which was nice, and J. J. I reasoned that if there just could be a scale that sounded, projected the sound of a chord. and not in the way the major scale projects the sound of a C-major chord. The scale of an almost harmonic unity. This idea just stayed with me, it wouldn't go away, that there was a scale that was closer to the sound of the chord than any other scale.[20]

The first six months involved complete bed rest, but, as Russell told Ian Carr,

Traditional music [theory] gave us the key signature and from this arbitrary key signature it builds chords up from the tonic. I had a feeling that there must be another way to approach playing chordally, that's all. And the first impression I got was that for every chord there had to be a scale that sounded a unity with that chord and that, more so than any other scale, it projected the sound of that chord.[21]

After those six months, Russell was able to get up, and at first he used the piano in the solarium to test his ideas. Unfortunately for the other patients who had nowhere else to go, those experiments involved fairly interminable explorations of the C-major chord, the C-major scale, and the latter with a raised fourth. After a couple of days of this, the patients revolted and started hurling the remains of the lunchtime meal and their loved ones' gifts of grapes and other fruit in Russell's direction. Fortunately, one of the sisters of mercy came to his—or rather, his fellow patients'—aid and moved him into the library, where he could experiment to his heart's desire.

In repeatedly playing these scales, it was as if Russell was engaged in a scientific experiment, weighing notes against each other, examining sounds and tones in the most minute detail and testing their correspondence to each other. As he told Carr,

And I finally decided that the major scale just doesn't cut it. It doesn't make it, you know. It doesn't sound a unity with its major chord. And then I began to look for reasons why it didn't. And then I found it wasn't a ladder of fifths. It wasn't a ladder of perfect fifths like the Lydian on the tonic, because the Lydian did sound a unity. But the major scale always sounded this effortful feeling of striving for the tonic, striving to become a unity.[22]

Russell then related this to himself and his own sense of the world. "And that had something to do with, in a way, this feeling that had always bothered me about life, you know, is that I was having to adopt a way of being and a way of thinking that was put on me by the church, by education, you know, that didn't conform to my essence."[23] Obviously, we all reinterpret and rearticulate our experiences in the light of a changing understanding. As Russell acknowledges, "I didn't make any philosophical associations with it early on, but I was very curious that the Lydian Scale was a ladder of fifths and the major scale wasn't."[24] It is a human quality that "knowledge," in particular those things we discover for ourselves, seems to resonate continually and acquire new and deeper meanings for us over time through the process of reflection.

Apart from the diversion of occasional visits from Miles, Dizzy, Max, and J. J. Johnson, Russell had little to do but continue his experiments with chords and scales. The only satisfactory way of describing Russell's breakthrough discovery is to allow him to tell it in his owns words, as he explained to Vivian Perlis.

Finally, I realized that because of the first four tones of the C-major scale, the C major-scale could in no way be in unity with that C-major chord because of the Do, Re, Mi, and Fa, Fa itself was a Do. That doesn't sound Do, a "C" Do, that sounds the Fa Do. But what led me to play the G-major scale was that the second tetra chord of C-major scale is G-A-B-C, and that *does* sound C. The following tetra chord in G is D-E-F#-G, and that at least resolves to a tone that is in the C-major chord. So it led me to say, "Well, let's try the G-major scale." As I said, I began to accept the G-major scale as actually sounding closer to the tonality of a C-major chord than the C-major scale. The problem, thinking practically, how can I tell musicians if you see a C-major chord, play a G-major scale? So then I began to understand that the first mode of the G-major scale, the Ionian, playing that with the chord presented this problem of having musicians playing a G-major scale. Then the Dorian, the same problem, kind of. Then the Phrygian, finally the Lydian—C-D-E-F#-G-A-B. I said, "I don't care what anybody says; this isn't just the Lydian mode of the G-major scale, this is the C-Lydian scale, the closest scale to the C-major chord."[25]

Aside from Russell's explanation of the Concept, he makes two additional sidepoints. The first focuses on his understanding that the Concept challenged traditional thinking; it was, if not new knowledge, knowledge that had been lost. The second point indicates his reluctance to tell the world of his discovery. In this context, he doubted, understandably, that a black man would be taken seriously in presenting such a challenge to Western musical theory and the institutions upon which it is based. Without questioning either the issues for a black man in a racist society in facing such a challenge, the reader may be interested to note that Joseph Campbell in his examination of the "hero myth" refers to this process at some length and calls it "Refusal of the Call."[26]

In *The Black Composer Speaks*, Russell was asked what features of his music are uniquely "black." He replied these were the substitution of F# for F-natural and the conviction that the Lydian scale is a "much more scientifically profound scale upon which to base a world of music." In relation to a question about the role of the black artist, he responded that it was to "show a new path to human evolution based upon his ancient high African Heritage."[27] Russell had always been aware that what he was exploring was a different set of musical traditions that drew on folk music from around the world as opposed to the formalized musical structures of Western music. The point he is making above refers to his understanding of humanity's roots and origins in Africa, a point he would later make in interview with Ben Young of WKCR and even more eloquently in his work *The African Game*. What Russell is saying here is that African Americans brought with them a different set of musical ideas based on a different tradition, and through jazz and blues gave those to America and the world. He is not making a political statement in any simplistic sense, but is instead commenting on what he sees as the scientific basis of music and of his theories and their basis in the natural world and the very origins of our species.

The scientific foundations of Russell's ideas are open to question. However, the approach he describes below and elsewhere—of reading, studying, and experimenting musically, of observing and reflecting—is a scientific one. In terms of scientific research, this process would be described as inductive, that is, observation leading to theorization, rather than deductive, which involves reasoning from a priori assumptions.[28]

So I began reading a little bit—books—and I found that the interval of the fifth in the overtone series is the first biased interval. Strike the fundamental, the next overtone is the fundamental an octave above and the third partial is an interval of a fifth and the tonic of an interval of a fifth, if anyone, no one in the world would agree that it wasn't the lower note. If you build a ladder of continual fifths you don't get C-G-D-A-E-B-F, you get C-G-D-A-E-B-F#. You get the Pythagorean, the start of the Pythagorean twelve-tone ladder of fifths. So that was the day when I said, "A ladder of fifths confirms the Lydian scale as the scale of unity for that tonic chord."

The rest of the time in the hospital was spent examining the modes of the Lydian scale and finding out what I call were their principal chords, what were the most highly evolved harmonic chords that they produced within the context of the Lydian scale and so the D7 chord—D-F#-A-C-E-G-B is the highest evolved principal chord, so in my thinking the seven chord is not the dominant five, it's the two chord of the Lydian scale. Each mode produces its own principal scale. Beside the Lydian, there is the "Lydian augmented" that gives us all of the augmented chords, C-D-E-F#-G#-A-B, which gave the scale its name. Then the "Lydian diminished" C-D-E♭-F#-G-A-B which furnishes the diminished chords with the Lydian itself producing major on I, seventh on II, minor on VI, and that scale being a complete unity with those chords.[29]

Grand theories—that is, theories that make claims for comprehensiveness within a whole area, such as Marx in economics or Freud in psychology—invite criticism. We will see later that Russell and his ideas have their critics. However, it suffices to note here that Russell was hearing something different in music, as well as hearing music differently. This led him to question the relationship, as traditionally understood, between chords and scales, between scales and their tonic, between different scales and how a musician or composer might move between these different scales in ways that challenged accepted notions of the antagonistic relationship between tonality and atonality.

As an aside, one of the other patients on the ward Russell befriended was Eddie Roane, the trumpeter who had played with Louis Jordan. Roane died of tuberculosis in Russell's arms. Russell was truly fortunate to survive. In fact, at one point, Russell recalls that a priest came to give him the last rites; he shouted at him that he was an atheist and told him to get lost.[30]

We have already noted Campbell's identification of the "Refusal of the Call" as an element within the hero myth. Here it may be added that other aspects he refers to are near-death experiences, the inward journey, and seeking of knowledge.[31] Once again, this does not make Russell's account inaccurate or mythical in itself. It may, however, mean that the construction or form of the tale has certain mythologized features to it. A more prosaic telling is actually no less remarkable. Had Russell not survived, we would simply not have the Lydian Concept, jazz would have missed out on his contribution to its development, music like *All About Rosie* and *The African Game* would have been denied to us, and this book would not be written! Circumstances were such that Russell did survive, and his achievements speak both of his efforts, then and later, and of our good fortune.

Russell came out of hospital around Christmas 1946 and went to stay with Max Roach and his family. Keeping track of Russell's living arrangements from the late forties into the early fifties is a demanding activity in itself. However, for much of the next period he lived variously with Roach and, at one point, with Roach's mother. Living conditions were quite squalid, according to Russell, but he is still grateful for Roach's support and generosity. He was in all respects treated as a member of the family.

> Well, when I got out of the hospital, Max invited me to stay in Brooklyn with him, and I stayed at his house on Monroe Street for about nine months. And it was back there, when you got out of hospital, there was a program in place run by the New York Welfare Department where you got subsidized and they even sent you to school or something. It's through that program that I started to study with Stefan Wolpe in New York. But they took care of the . . . you know, paying Mrs. Roach for my lodging and food. And so when I hear people put down the welfare system, you know, I think that's ridiculous, because I know I'm a product of that.[32]

Stefan Wolpe was a German socialist composer who had worked with Hans Eisler in the workers' music movement and who fled his homeland in 1933 to escape Nazi persecution both as a socialist and a Jew. Having studied with Webern in Vienna, he went first to Palestine and then, in 1938, to New York. As a teacher, friend, or colleague, Wolpe was a huge influence on the whole postwar generation of American composers, including Elliott Carter, John Cage (who was president of the Stefan Wolpe Society at one point), Morton Feldman, and Milton Babitt. Saxophonist John Carisi, arranger Eddie Sauter, clarinettist Tony Scott, and Elmer Bernstein also studied with him. What Russell drew from him was both the older man's life experience and his knowledge of contemporary music theory.

> He knew I was a kid who didn't know much about anything and didn't know a lot about life. My interest was in talking to him chiefly about life, but I wanted to know his principal concepts of music. The two things that impressed me, that caused me to think in a new way, were his theory of the rate of chromatic circulation as a means of destroying any tonical integrity and the principle of the thirdless sound.[33]

In fact, Russell is quite specific in identifying the *Jazz Workshop* album, "Lydian M-1," and *All About Rosie* as examples of compositions that used Wolpe's ideas and influence. Along with a host of other composers and musicians, Russell provided his comments for a centennial memorial publication for Wolpe. Even allowing for the fact that such remarks are invariably fulsome in their praise of the dear departed, Russell's final words are quite touching and seem to reflect very genuinely what the young man found in Wolpe at a more personal level.

Wolpe's overall effect on me was immensely positive. I felt a living, breathing force in this man that was extremely life-positive. You couldn't be around him without that force entering you. To that extent Wolpe and the two principles that stuck with me and his forceful being are part of *me* now, and they always have been, and always will be. He's alive in those of us that he touched.[34]

Despite being introduced by Roach to his peers as "an arranger," his only contribution to the city's music had been the piece he had written back in Cincinnati in the hospital and had sold at least four or five times already. It was certainly too early for his Lydian Concept to have achieved anything other than "work in progress" status. A pattern had already emerged where Russell would compose only when he had someone or something to write for. Otherwise his work would, from this point on, focus on the Concept. Now out of the hospital, Russell was about to produce something that would cement his reputation even outside the bebop inner circle.

Dizzy approached me one day and he said that he was getting very interested in Afro-Cuban drumming and music, and there was this wonderful drummer in town, Chano Pozo, and he had a theme and maybe it would be possible for me to put a suite around it, you know, encompass it in a suite. And it was a beautiful theme. So it didn't take long for me to get the idea of what to do with it, and the whole introduction then was modal.[35]

The use of modes had been around in jazz and in other musical forms for ages. However, what Russell did with "Cubano-Be, Cubano-Bop" was to use modes consciously, and through this and his subsequent work, both as a theorist and as a composer, he made the jazz community aware of modes and their potential in jazz. Also, as he himself put it, "It was the first application of modality using the Concept. The 'Cubano-Be, Cubano-Bop' thing sort of got the reputation rolling."[36]

Premiered at Carnegie Hall at a concert promoted by British-born critic Leonard Feather on September 29, 1947, Russell conducted Dizzy Gillespie's Big Band in front of a sellout crowd. Charlie Parker played with Gillespie in a quintet at the same gig but sat in the audience for Russell, Gillespie, and Pozo's number, and also for John Lewis's "Toccata for Trumpet." Ella Fitzgerald also sang with Gillespie and, as *Down Beat*'s headline put it, "Despite Bad Acoustics, Gillespie Concert Offers Some Excellent Music." Critic Michael Levin saw "Cubano-Be, Cubano-Bop" as a definite "stand-out," writing, "The crowd unquestionably liked the 'Cubano-Bop' number with its added bongo and congo [*sic*] drum soloists the best, illustrating a point the Beat has often made that there is much jazz can pick up on from the South American and Afro-Cuban rhythm styles."[37]

After Carnegie Hall, the band took the show up to Boston's Symphony Hall, and Russell traveled with the band. He recalls that Chano Pozo was sitting at the back and began this African chanting. "I said, 'Dizzy, you know, you should open the whole middle section up, bring Chano out front, let him do this.' We built a whole thing out of it, you know."[38]

The African American contingent in the audience, however, was embarrassed by this. Looking back on the incident, Russell identifies this as a consequence of the way black people were taught to be ashamed of their culture, and later, in his conversation with Ian Carr, he related this directly to a process of ethnocentricity that is "literally messing up the planet": "The black people in the audience were very noticeable because they started to laugh when Chano came out on stage in his native costume. It's like Louis [Armstrong] when they sent him to Africa, you know. Louis said, 'Damn, these people really do climb trees like monkeys.' (laughing)"[39]

Whilst it is hard to know how far Russell and Gillespie articulated to themselves at the time their purpose in including this section in the performance, it does seem that their intention was to celebrate Africanness and the origins of jazz. In a way, and several decades before Afrocentrism emerged as an important element in American education, it was clearly an attempt to say to an audience: This is something special and something of which we should be proud. It was an early attempt to take a stereotype and transform it by framing it in a positive rather than a negative context. In that sense, it links with Russell's disagreement with his friend Dwight over his playing Aunt Jemima in their school play *Gone with the Wind*.

Whatever the audience's reaction, "Cubano-Be, Cubano-Bop" was Russell's first significant contribution to jazz composition, and it remains a marvelous piece and was, as Gillespie noted, a wonderful collaborative effort. "That was a collaboration. That was a collaboration of all three. I think that was the most successful collaboration I've ever seen with three people. I can see what I wrote. I can see what George wrote and I can see the contribution of Chano Pozo and then George Russell came back and spread out what I had written and what Chano had done."[40] The fact that these three potentially disparate elements hang together so well is a tribute to Russell, as Gillespie appears to acknowledge in that last sentence.

Recorded in the studio on December 22, 1947, it remains a highly symphonic work, with "harshly incantatory ensemble passages," "its juxtaposition of very different textures and types of motion," and the "disconcertedly independent of convention" ways it used the "jazz orchestra's resources," as

Max Harrison has noted. He adds, "It is consistent but accords with laws then unfamiliar."[41] Ingrid Monson's detailed analysis of the piece in the *International Dictionary of Black Composers* is also well worth reading by students of music. Her final paragraph, however, suffices for our purposes:

> Fifty years after its first performance, 'Cubano-Be, Cubano-Bop' remains a model of innovative writing for Big Band. Its collaborative genesis, a synthesis of Afro-Cuban rhythms and Bebop and its imaginative use of modes 12 years before the emergence of the term "modal jazz," collectively explain why George Russell must be included in the first rank of composers writing for jazz orchestra.[42]

Anyone doubting the significant advance represented by this piece should hear it followed by Gillespie and Pozo's "Manteca," written around that time and in a similar vein. However well this stands on its own, compared to "Cubano-Be, Cubano-Bop" it sounds frankly ordinary.[43]

Notes

1. Vivian Perlis, interview with George Russell, American Music Series, December 8, 1993, Oral History Project of American Music, sponsored and supported by the National Endowment for the Arts Special Jazz Projects.

2. Ian Carr, interview with George Russell, June 1992.

3. Perlis, interview with G. Russell.

4. Ibid.

5. Carr, interview with G. Russell, June 1992.

6. Ibid.

7. Stephanie Stein Crease, *Gil Evans—Out of the Cool* (Chicago: A Cappella, 2002). See also M. Harrison, "Gerry Mulligan," in *These Jazzmen of Our Time*, ed. R. Horrocks (London: Jazz Book Club, 1959).

8. Interview with George Russell, October 2003.

9. Carr, interview with G. Russell, June 1992.

10. Ibid.

11. George Russell—A *Jazz Portrait*, WGBH Radio, Boston.

12. Interview with George Russell, June 2003.

13. Interview with Dwight McPheeters, June 2004.

14. Perlis, interview with G. Russell.

15. J. Campbell, *The Hero with a Thousand Faces* (London: Fontana, 1993).

16. Ian Carr, interview with George Russell for BBC Radio 3 broadcast The Trailblazer—George Russell, July 1994.

17. George Russell—A *Jazz Portrait*.

18. Perlis, interview with G. Russell.

19. George Russell—A *Jazz Portrait*.
20. Perlis, interview with G. Russell.
21. Carr, interview with G. Russell, June 1992.
22. Ibid.
23. Ibid.
24. Ibid.
25. Perlis, interview with G. Russell.
26. Campbell, *The Hero with a Thousand Faces*, pp. 59–68.
27. D. Baker, L. B. Baker, and H. Hudson, *The Black Composer Speaks* (Metuchen, NJ: Scarecrow Press, 1978), pp. 277–89.
28. Popper, *The Logic of Scientific Discovery* (New York: BasicBooks, 1959).
29. Perlis, interview with G. Russell.
30. Carr, interview with G. Russell, June 1992.
31. Campbell, *The Hero with a Thousand Faces*.
32. Carr, interview with G. Russell, June 1992.
33. Perlis, interview with G. Russell.
34. A. Clarkson, ed. *On the Music of Stefan Wolpe* (New York: Pendragon, 2003).
35. Carr, interview with G. Russell, June 1992. NB. Pozo's real name was Luciano Gonzales.
36. George Russell—A *Jazz Portrait*.
37. Michael Levin, "Despite Bad Acoustics, Gillespie Concert Offers Some Excellent Music," *Chicago Tribune*, October 22, 1947. Russell also arranged 'Relaxin' at Camarillo' for Gillespie's band for the concert. Part of the concert, including both 'Cubano-Be, Cubano-Bop' and 'Relaxin' at Camarillo', as well as five numbers performed by Gillespie with Charlie Parker, have been issued by Blue Note as Diz N' Bird at Carnegie Hall (724385706127).
38. Carr, interview with G. Russell, June 1992.
39. Ibid.
40. Dizzy Gillespie, quoted in *The Invisible Guru*, BBC Radio 3, July 1994.
41. Max Harrison, "George Russell—Rational Anthems," *Wire* (Spring 1983): 30.
42. Ingrid Monson, "George Russell," in *International Dictionary of Black Composers*, ed. S. A. Floyd Jr. (Chicago: Fitzroy Dearborn, 1999).
43. Dizzy Gillespie, *Dizziest*, Bluebird Records 5785–1-RB (Double LP).

CHAPTER FIVE

~

A Bird in Igor's Yard

Despite the critical acclaim received by "Cubano-Be, Cubano-Bop," George Russell received only a fairly small payment from Dizzy Gillespie. Additionally, he was hardly picking up much extra work as a result of the success of the piece. Asked by Ian Carr whether Russell did other arrangements for Gillespie's band, Juanita Giuffre, Russell's first wife, noted, "He didn't. He didn't work that steadily. He wrote 'Cubano-Be, Cubano-Bop' for him and I think Dizzy gave him a very nominal amount of money for it. It was a big success."[1]

It was certainly a hand-to-mouth existence, and Russell did what he had done back in Cincinnati. He took occasional jobs in stores or in catering, but whereas in Ohio there was regular work playing drums to supplement his earnings and relieve the drudgery, several patterns began to emerge that would mark Russell's responses for the next ten years—and, in fact, for the rest of his life. The first of these was that his pursuit of the Lydian Concept would become his overriding concern and his life's work. Second, Russell was never afraid of work—Joe and Bessie had instilled that virtue in him—and would take menial jobs when necessary to survive, albeit only as long as absolutely essential to pay the bills. Third, he would compose only when he had something or someone to write for. Russell has never been one of those composers who appears driven to write music; it would always take second place to the Concept. Despite his pride in works like *The African Game* and *All About Rosie*, the sense one gets from talking with him is that these are incidental to the main feature: the Lydian Concept. Of course, he welcomed the income from composing for others and from making records. From time to time, in the fifties and sixties, a record date could mean enough money to live on for up to six months or even a year. It also provided an opportunity to test out his ideas. Speaking about his contract with Riverside Records in the early sixties, Russell told Ben Young of WKCR,

> I was thirty-five years old before I could say I was earning money from music. That all started with the RCA Victor album, and things were touch and go in-between. So the offer from Riverside meant a few months of being able to pay the bills and also a chance to create. Well, the offer from Riverside stretched out not only into one album but into two or three or four albums and that was good for a couple of years of security and at the same time being able to test, because I always was working at the Concept, and being able to test the new ideas coming from the Concept in music, check them out and I would never let anything go without being satisfied with it aesthetically.[2]

This modus operandi has continued, albeit with a full-time teaching post and occasional grant now replacing income from recording, up to the present. But as Russell also explained to Young, the Concept has a life of its own almost separate from the music-making process.

> Well, for me the Lydian Chromatic Concept was an obligation that I took on and I took it on . . . rather than just use it as an instrument for me becoming a composer ten years ahead of his time or something and being able to afford all the pleasurable creamy and delightful things that money can buy. I didn't choose that way at all because I knew I had something to offer and, as I said, I debated about whether I should really part with it. The thing that convinced me is that it does deal with gravity and it deals with gravity behaving and controlling music and therefore you can't keep gravity a secret without really going against nature. So I'm obligated and have been obligated to take time away from the music to work on the Concept. I'm always working on the Concept. Like this time, for example, the book has to be finished now, so I don't want or need any commissions. They do interfere. I don't have time for that. The book is very important to get out there. So we're working very hard on that. And all through my musical life, and the Concept was the beginning of it in 1945—the Lydian Concept—I've dropped composing from time to time to devote to that. But then with having worked on it and having worked it up to another level, I use that level to then compose from it, and if I have to drop it for a while, I'll do it and work it up to another level.[3]

Or on a more prosaic level, as Russell told Carr, "When I was with Max, his mother told him, 'Max, this boy never sleeps, you know. He's always working on the theory.'"[4]

"Cubano-Be, Cubano-Bop" may not have transformed Russell's finances. However, if nothing else, it had done two things—it had put Russell's name out there and it had begun to open doors for the young man. One door it opened fairly quickly was that of a basement apartment under the St. Regis Hotel on 55th Street, or, as Russell described it to Carr, "Gil Evans's Church of the Aesthetic." This was the late forties, and having led jazz into the postwar era with bebop, the musicians centerd around Evans were looking to see how much further they could push the boundaries.

It is worth stressing that the success of "Cubano-Be, Cubano-Bop," however advanced the composition, had to have a context in which it could be appreciated. This required an articulate and progressive audience of musicians, critics, and the public. This had been prepared not only by bebop but by the open-mindedness of the previous generation of musicians, both black and white. It is far too simplistic to suggest that jazz prior to bebop was somehow conservative and mainstream. One only has to think of Duke Ellington and Billy Strayhorn, of Russell's erstwhile employers Benny Carter and Earl Hines, of Fletcher Henderson, or of white bandleaders like Claude Thornhill, Benny Goodman, Artie Shaw, and the much maligned Stan Kenton. These musicians were quite familiar with modern composers such as Copland, Stravinsky, Milhaud, and Ravel, many of whom were themselves influenced by jazz. And Russell was, as noted, one of a number of jazz musicians who chose to study with Wolpe.[5]

The "Bebop Divide," as poet and critic Phillip Larkin called it, or the "Bebop Revolution," to use a more common epithet, is better understood as a coalescence of ideas and currents that had arisen within a particular social, cultural, and economic context. Periods of social change raise expectations within oppressed groups and within artistic communities. New ideas, philosophies, and practices begin to find a ready audience. The war years and those that immediately preceded them saw America come out of its economic slump as the economy geared itself for war. There were jobs for white women and African American and Hispanic men and women in industries that were previously closed to them. There was an eager anticipation that America and the world would be a different place—more prosperous and perhaps more equal.

At the same time, the war years had also seen a different set of behaviors emerge within the African American and Latino communities. Groups of black and pachuco youths, who identified strongly with jazz as dance music, marked themselves as outsiders through the clothes that they chose to wear, primarily the zoot suit. There were, of course, "zoot suit riots" in Los Angeles and other centers along the West Coast, involving black and Mexican youths and the predominantly white U.S. servicemen stationed along the coast. These riots spread to other urban centers, including Detroit, Pittsburgh, and New York. Stuart Cosgrove in his article "The Zoot-Suit and Style Warfare" suggests that one consequence of the recruitment of men into the armed forces and women into the defense industries was a reduction of the extent of parental supervision of black and Mexican youth. At one point, Cosgrove notes there were as many as 15 million civilians engaged directly in "war work" and 12 million military personnel "on the move" in the United States.[6] By any standards this is a major social upheaval for any society, and its consequences were both negative in heightening racial divisions and positive in terms of their longer-term consequences in creating the potential for social change and greater equality.

It must be stressed that zoot suit–clad youth were not the vanguard or even in the vanguard of racial politics. It was more that their dress, musical tastes, and lifestyle represented a "refusal," to use this term in its sociological sense, of the dominant white attitudes and culture. There does seem also to be a relationship between the zoot suit youth and the emergence of the "hip" or "hep" and of a body of signifiers of that cultural attitude. These included a love of jazz, use of drugs, an enjoyment of clothes/style beyond function, freer attitudes toward sex and sexuality, interest in literature and art and in particular poetry, and in some cases an enthusiasm for radical political ideas. The forties also saw groups of white and black youths, some middle class but others from impoverished backgrounds, begin to cross racial and social divisions in search of "kicks" and excitement. The media would dub them the "Beat Generation."

While bebop did break with past jazz in significant respects, it is better to see it as the outcome of a series of merging aesthetic, social, and economic currents rather than a "revolution" or a "divide." And the musicians who gathered around Gil Evans were a highly literate and articulate bunch. As Russell noted to Young,

> [T]he company I was keeping at that time . . . was Gil Evans's 55th Street conclave with John Lewis, Johnny Carisi, Miles, and Gerry Mulligan and myself being sort of the . . . forming the particular spearhead of that group and, of course, Gil Evans being the patron saint of that way. We used to listen to all kinds of music in that little one-room apartment and, as the title insinuates, I think one of our favorite pieces was *Sacré du Printemps*, and I was particularly amazed at that piece and still am, and at the same time Bird being in the same company because Bird used to frequent that 55th Street one-room apartment of Gil's under the St. Regis Hotel in the basement with a cat named Becky.

Charlie Parker was often there. I think we all were influenced not only by that but we listened to Schoenberg and *Pierrot Lunaire* and we went up to Juilliard as a group to hear a rehearsal for Hindemith concert and then we'd go to the concert and watch Hindemith conduct it.[7]

But it was also a self-critical and challenging environment:

[A]nd I was always attracted to people who came along and were and are some of this music's greatest innovators, and I learned from them and I had this intensity to experiment. I was in the right circle to do that. Mulligan did it in his way. Miles did it in his way and John [Lewis], of course, with the Modern Jazz Quartet, but it helped being in that environment. And something always saw to it that I was in an environment that goaded me into not being satisfied with the latest work but to take it further and not to experiment on the audience but to only release that that I had in essence thought was my very best at that time.[8]

As for Evans himself, Russell describes him in the following terms: "He was the father, the patron. He was the head, the body, the heart and the spirit of those times. The wise man." And the "wise man" held open house day and night.

It was a big room in the basement and with practically every musician in New York coming in at any time after the gig at maybe 4 o'clock in the morning and it would still be available and we'd talk with Gil and that was the place where the "Cool" was born. Mulligan and I, many times, we worked all night on pieces. Gil was, as I said, he was the caretaker there to see that some beautiful music was made. He wouldn't let go and we would march up to Juilliard if a classical composer like Hindemith was going to give a concert . . . . He did a piece called *History of the Soldier* there. We attended the rehearsals a couple of days before that. We could sit in on the rehearsals at Juilliard. I watched Hindemith's assistant put the piece together. If it was Stravinsky, we'd be there. We played it down in the basement. We played all kinds of music.[9]

Maybe it is just the benefit of hindsight, but Russell says he did feel that history was being made down in that basement.

Well, I personally thought I was part of that history. I was accepted, certainly, but that idea was a living fact. Yeah, there was no way it could be otherwise. The music had to go somewhere, and it came out of that basement. He had Miles Davis, Gerry Mulligan, John Carisi, John Lewis, the Modern Jazz Quartet there every night practically. So there was something came out of that. Plus

Gil himself and his band and his writing. Music was the thing that we did and every aspect of life was devoted to music. I think we thought of ourselves as a kind of club, and they were good days.[10]

It was an elite circle, but not elitist. Anyone with talent was welcome, but Russell was still scuffling a living and despite the success of "Cubano-Be, Cubano-Bop"—no commissions rolled in as a result. Nor did he seem to be keen to sell himself. As he told Carr, "Well, I was really practicing that legendary art that I think many artists are forced to get acquainted with, and that is living off the graces of a nice lady, you know." Russell told Carr that he lived with a woman and her husband on Park Avenue, and when Carr described her as his "patron," Russell concurred.[11] However, in a more recent interview, he explained the situation in more detail: "I did live with . . . there was this woman who took a liking to me. She lived on Park Avenue, Anita Kushner. She was very much involved in the arts. She had a husband and they were very nice people. When I came into the picture I lived with them."

Asked if this were *une menage a trois*, Russell replied,

It sounds like that and it was like that. *(laughs)* I don't want to say anything damaging about her. She was wonderful woman. She took a liking to me and she wanted me there. Her husband went along with it. That lasted maybe a year. She had a good piano and I wrote "A Bird in Igor's Yard," it's one of the things I wrote on her piano for Buddy DeFranco.[12]

When that came to an end, Russell moved in with the lyricist Jack Segal, writer of the popular songs "Scarlet Ribbons" and "When Sunny Gets Blue." Their apartment also became a hangout for the members of Evans's circle as well as other artists like Harry Belafonte and Tony Bennett. Segal was interested in the ideas of psychologist Wilhelm Reich and actually had an "orgone box" in his living room, according to Russell.[13]

What might have proved a big break came for Russell in April 1949. In fact, in comparison with the absence of paying work over the previous two years, Russell actually sold two compositions and one arrangement between April 1949 and January 1950. The first of these was "A Bird in Igor's Yard." Buddy DeFranco had just formed his own big band. DeFranco was more than just a fine clarinet player. An established player with the big bands of Tommy Dorsey, Gene Krupa, and Boyd Raeburn, he was equally at home with the new sounds of bebop and played with Miles Davis, Lee Konitz, Bud Powell, Max Roach, and J. J. Johnson. He also had a vision for his new band that encompassed both the new music and the "progressive" sounds of Stan Kenton. "A Bird in Igor's Yard" should have fit perfectly into that vision.

Featuring a band that included Konitz, Al Cohn, Serge Chaloff, and Oscar Pettiford, it did not, however, prove quite the heaven-made match anticipated. There were four tracks recorded for Capitol, Stan Kenton's label, at that session, including Russell's. The others, arranged by Gerry Valentine and Manny Albam, included "The Boy Next Door" and "This Time the Dream's on Me." Neither of these is that remarkable, though they are perhaps less upbeat than much of the more popular big-band material of the forties. "A Bird in Igor's Yard" stands out both in terms of the complexity of its arrangement and the unusual sonorities it pioneered. Russell's attempt to make Stravinsky dance with Bird would receive a better and more convincing reading seven years later on his own *Jazz Workshop* date. That said, the DeFranco performance is a fascinating slice of modernism, and it's hardly surprising that it remained in Capitol's vaults for twenty more years.

The myth has grown up that the piece was so far advanced and ahead of its time that Capitol refused to release it. Reality may be more complex. First, Capitol had little apparent difficulty with some of Kenton's "progressive" jazz at that time. So it seems unlikely that the label would have rejected the performance on those grounds alone. Second, none of the pieces recorded at that date were actually released until much later, and one could hardly claim that these were in any sense that "advanced." Third, the recording itself is not that well balanced, and the opening ensembles sound rather frayed. Finally, DeFranco seems to have been rather unhappy with the result and his own playing. As he told *Down Beat* in 1951, "That was one attempt at pioneering I never should have made."[14]

An acetate of the piece was obtained by the DJ Symphony Sid and broadcast regularly on his show. This no doubt helped to fuel the myth surrounding "A Bird in Igor's Yard." What does matter about "A Bird in Igor's Yard" is what it says about Russell's ambition, even this early in his career. He was drawing on composers like Stravinsky, Debussy, Schoenberg, and Ravel quite consciously and was deliberately bringing their ideas and harmonic language into jazz and into contact with improvisation. In doing so, he emphasized the written elements of jazz in creating a symphonic sound for the jazz orchestra, just as he would later stress the chamber elements of the small jazz group. This was years before John Lewis and Gunther Schuller coined the term "Third Stream." Russell might not have been alone in wishing to expand the scope of jazz in this respect. Gil Evans had already taken such steps with Claude Thornhill, Ellington and Strayhorn had stretched the vocabulary of jazz, and Kenton had pressed its case for a place in the concert hall as well as the dance hall. And classical composers like Gershwin, Copland, and Stravinsky had taken bold steps toward jazz. Nevertheless, a case can be made that "A Bird in Igor's Yard" is perhaps the most "advanced" and coherent such statement up to that point. What is more, its statement of intent is unequivocal and explicit.

Another Russell piece, "Similau," was recorded by Artie Shaw during that period, and he also did an arrangement of "Caravan" for Charlie Ventura. Both were big-band recordings. Shaw's band of 1949 (the recording was actually made early in 1950) was known as his Bebop Band and included players like Zoot Sims, Al Cohn, and guitarist Jimmy Raney, just as earlier Shaw bands had contained the talents of Barney Kessel, Georgie Auld, and pianist Dodo Marmarosa. Two points should be made here. First, like fellow clarinetist DeFranco, Shaw was an adventurous and forward-thinking musician who reacted positively to bebop. Second, his attempts to meet the challenge of the new music were met by commercial failure. That emphasizes a further point that what happens in New York or out on the West Coast does not necessarily catch on with Middle America.

When Russell was interviewed by Ben Young for WKCR, he recalled that the Charlie Ventura performance of "Caravan," like that of "A Bird in Igor's Yard," was held back by the record company. He also spoke of an arrangement he had done around 1948 for Ella Fitzgerald of "How High the Moon."

> Charlie Ventura asked me to arrange "Caravan," just as Ella Fitzgerald asked me to arrange "How High the Moon." She came out with that record about 1948, actually, and they both suffered the same fate because Ella ended up in the Decca studios; I had overwritten, overextended myself, and had written some things for her to sing. She just took the first chorus of it and Ray Brown quickly came up with some kind of ending, not my ending, but the chorus, I mean, the first chorus of it is my arrangement. So she was very, very annoyed at me in the studio, you know, but later on, about five or six months later I bumped into her on the street—she and Ray. She said, "I want to take you to dinner." The record sold something like 10 million copies with a fragment of my arrangement. So the same thing with Charlie Ventura, turned out to be . . . they weren't angry because they knew it was the best I could do and it was a good, exciting arrangement, but it wasn't . . . the company decided it wasn't commercial enough. That happened with "A Bird in Igor's Yard," so "Caravan" was released twenty, thirty years after it was written.[15]

"Similau" is qualitatively different from the other fifteen or so sides Shaw recorded with this band around 1949. The listener need only contrast it with

John Bartee's "Afro-Cubano," clearly a tip of the cap to "Cubano-Be, Cubano-Bop," or bop pianist/composer Tadd Dameron's "So Easy." While these tunes are delightful examples of big-band playing, with Shaw frighteningly good on his instrument, they are of their time and genre. "Similau" seems to have more in common with Stravinsky or Schoenberg than with any writer for big band. It has a truly filmic quality with discordant brass and its dark and somber mood. If that were how it sounds now to us, how at odds would it have sounded to the listening public brought up on Miller and Dorsey?[16]

Russell's recollections are that he approached Shaw with the piece he had written.

> At the time I was just very relieved that he was such a gentleman, you know, such a nice guy. I can't say I was close with Artie, but afterward, when he had recorded "Similau," I would see him in different places, once on a horse in upstate New York. He said, "Hello." I didn't recognize him but I finally saw the smile and that was Artie. People question me about it but I really didn't know the chap.[17]

Asked if he liked what Ventura had done with his arrangement of "Caravan," Russell replied, "I liked everything that I gave to people. I liked it. Especially the things I gave to people at that level." In terms of payment, as he acknowledges, "I can't say I made money. After a piece was gone, I can't say I kept up with it. I'm not a business man, so I can't follow up these things and see if I'm getting cheated or not."[18]

This has also marked the pattern of Russell's career, at least until the seventies when his third wife, Alice, began to take care of business. Not only does he rarely compose without a commission or recording date, he has shown a lack of concern for material gain or pursuit of fame. His work on the Concept and its expression in his music from time to time has been enough, it seems.

Jazz was now beginning to move on from its bebop phase in new directions that should have suited Russell's talents. Miles Davis had met Gil Evans toward the end of 1947 when Evans had asked the trumpeter's permission to orchestrate Davis's "Donna Lee" for the Claude Thornhill Band. Already impressed with Evans's ideas and chafing at the simple arrangements that bop relied upon—in contrast with the demanding soloing required—Davis began pushing Evans and his circle to put their ideas to test. Hiring halls and calling up the musicians, Davis proved the catalyst and driving force that would lead to the famous *Birth of the Cool* sessions. The rehearsals continued through 1948, leading to live performances at the Royal Roost in September. The personnel changed according to availability, but Davis, altoist Lee Konitz, Gerry Mulligan, Max Roach, John Lewis, and Gil Evans were fairly constant. The lineup drew heavily from the Thornhill band. Mulligan, Lewis, Evans, and saxophonist John Carisi wrote and arranged the material.

According to Robert Moore, bassist Red Mitchell told him that Mulligan said Russell had provided a couple of tunes, but that these had not been used as they were considered "too difficult."[19] Though not perhaps part of that circle, Mitchell played with Mulligan a few years later. Russell himself has no recollection of this. Gunther Schuller, who played French horn on one of the sessions, believes this may have been the case, as his son George comments,

> Gunther does have a vague memory of George having written something for the Birth of the Cool band but he's not sure if that was something written specifically for one of the three sessions or if it was a chart that was rehearsed prior to those sessions. Gunther was in the last session. Gunther also said that perhaps whatever George wrote for the band might have resulted in a later composition like "Lydian M1" or one of those pieces he wrote for the small group RCA recordings.[20]

Certainly Pete Welding's original liner notes mention Russell as part of the pool working on the material, and Gerry Mulligan's memories from 1971 note Russell as one of the regulars at Gil's: "George Russell, our resident innovator. (Wrote a couple of fine, interesting charts for Claude Thornhill's band that I suppose there's no trace of now.)"[21]

It is easy to overestimate the immediate impact of these sessions. It was not a regular working band and, apart from a couple of 78s issued from the sessions, it was not until 1954 that eight tracks were released on a 10-inch LP and another three years before all twelve made it on to an album. They were, however, influential within the jazz community—in New York at least—and in terms of the expansion of the possibilities of jazz. Perhaps they also began to open up an audience for what, unsatisfactorily, became known as "Cool Jazz." Konitz was already working with blind Italian American pianist Lennie Tristano and a group of like-minded musicians such as guitarist Billy Bauer, bassist Peter Ind, and tenor player Warne Marsh. In the early fifties Lewis would form the Modern Jazz Quartet and Gerry Mulligan would debut his pianoless quartet with trumpeter Chet Baker. All of these would also help to create a small audience for Russell when he finally recorded in his own right in the mid-fifties.

However, it seems fair to say that—at that time, at least—neither the record companies nor the buying public seemed ready for such experimentation. French horn player and composer Gunther Schuller met the young composer during this period. Their meeting would prove important for Russell's future in several respects over the years.

> I met George Russell about three weeks after I'd met John Lewis, which was 1948. We went to George's apartment and as I entered the place I was hearing Alexander Scriabin's *Prometheus* on the record turntable. Well, I was bowled over because jazz musicians didn't listen generally to Scriabin's *Prometheus* or any . . . some people listened to classical music but it was still a rarity in those days. So, I realized almost immediately that George was obviously a broad-gauged composer, musician, and thinker. Anyway we got on wonderfully and then he told me already at that time he was embarking on this attempt to create a theoretical concept for jazz, which as we all know he has spent the rest of his life on and is about to embark on another edition.[22]

Around that same period, Russell had met Juanita Odjenar, a beautiful young woman of Irish, Mulatto, Cherokee, and Filipino extraction. She was about nineteen and had met Dizzy Gillespie at a gig. He had phoned her and visited her at her parents' home. Reluctantly her parents and grandmother, protective of their only child, agreed that she could go with Dizzy to meet his arranger in Jamaica, Long Island. That was John Lewis. They took the cab that Gillespie had left outside, its meter running while Dizzy played the family piano and chatted.

> So we went out and John was not at home, and Dizzy walked in and yelled for John and we heard a voice in the bathroom. "I'm here, but it's not John." And I had to go to the bathroom so badly at the time, that Dizzy said, "You go on in." There sat George in the tub with depilatory on his face because he was so delicate with shaving burns. He didn't like that and had something wrapped around his head. Well, all of a sudden I didn't have to go to the bathroom. I just bounced back I was so shocked. He said, "Hello, how are you?" That's how I met George Russell, under those circumstances.[23]

It was a couple of years later before Russell introduced himself properly. They began dating and Juanita became pregnant. Juanita explains, "Then, in 1950, we got married. It was like one of those funny little marriages that took place because I was pregnant. So it was something my family didn't know. They weren't particularly happy about this musician who walks in to my grandmother and says, 'Do you have a flair for drama? We're getting married.' My grandmother said, 'You have a flair for what? How much money do you have? My granddaughter's been well taken care of.' She brought him to tears."[24]

Despite their concerns, her parents gave their permission and Russell married for the first time. Juanita was working for an insurance company but also
studying art part-time. From the outset, Juanita took on the role of provider.
As Russell told Ian Carr, "In the early part of that marriage we had this deal
that I should work on the music."[25] Partly to prove to herself—but mainly
to her parents—that "money wasn't that important" and that love conquers
all, Juanita did so gladly. She also had a sense that George had an important
contribution to make to music and the world.

> Even as a young person, I knew that there was something important he had to
> do and say, and so that became *our* goal. It wasn't just his goal; it was *our* goal
> at that point to see this thing to fruition, whatever it was. We didn't know
> if it would be just composing; the Concept was always there in some form or
> another. In a sketchy sense it was always there. I knew without even under-
> standing what it was that there was something very deep he was reaching for,
> and I felt as though this is a goal that should be accomplished.[26]

It was, however, a situation Russell found conflicting. His upbringing
with Joseph and Bessie had taught him different standards. He told Carr that
he felt after a time that he should work as well. He also acknowledged his
frustration at the lack of progress of his career in music. "I was twenty-three
when I conducted Dizzy in Carnegie Hall, you know. So, I had to contend
with this feeling. . . . I felt I'd reached a certain plateau."[27]

Life was certainly a struggle for Russell and his young wife. They were
living in a one-room apartment in the Beechwood Hotel down on 23rd St
between Lexington and 3rd Avenue. They shared bathroom and kitchen
facilities with the other residents. All human life was there, as Juanita remembers:

> There were all kinds of people at this hotel, starting with hookers who were
> really pretty decent women. There was a sailor who would always come home
> to this place. You would have to put your food and lock it up in this commu-
> nity refrigerator. The stove that everybody used had cockroaches jumping out
> of it. But I'd never ever lived like that before. It was like an adventure for me.
> Even though I was embarrassed about it, this was a learning experience I never
> would have gotten any other way about people. There was one guy, a doctor,
> and he was working for the Mafia and he would disappear. We would hear him
> walking down the hall at night. He would disappear and it turned out that
> when he was studying, he was on internship and wasn't ready to practice yet,
> he'd operated on his wife, some emergency thing he just had to take care of
> himself, and she died and he lost his license. He ended up with the Mafia going

out digging out bullets or whatever you do for the Mafia. We had a stripper there that was quite fond of George.[28]

Juanita had a miscarriage not long after the marriage and also developed lupus, which damaged her kidneys. As a result, she has never been able to have children. With hindsight, Juanita realizes how problematic it would have been had she carried the baby to full-term and beyond.

> And not only that, George didn't want children at that time. Later it was differ-ent. But then he really didn't want children and luckily for the children neither of us felt that we were capable of handling it. Were we going to take a child into the Beechwood Hotel, and who knows—there are just some people that are just not meant to be parents, and if they admit it at the beginning that's all well and good. I think it's that much better for the children that might have been in that kind of relationship. I've seen relationships where that would happen, where the woman would kind of force the man or the man will force it if they want children very badly. In this case, nobody was terribly anticipating that it would be a good idea. Because you'd have the extra trauma of trying to make a living in music, which is already bad enough. It's as big enough a child as it is. Then to bring a child into that kind of uncertainty is kind of crazy.[29]

According to Russell, initially they lived "in an apartment that was by the river, a very nice apartment." They could not make the rent one time and did a moonlight flit. "The rent was a little high, so . . . we had to move one night. We just had to get out. We were down to the last penny and we ended up in the Hotel Beechwood, which was another trip because that was one step away from the Bowery, but we made it nice."[30]

Russell recalls that one day, Juanita ran down a hill near their apartment and the next day started hemorrhaging and then lost the baby. As he put it, "She had enough babies to watch over, you know. *(laughing)*"[31]

Russell's contact with Lee Konitz through the *Birth of the Cool* sessions did, however, yield a further commission. In early 1951 Konitz was recording a ses-sion with a group that contained fellow Tristano alumni Sal Mosca on piano, Arnold Fishkin on bass, and Billy Bauer. Max Roach was on drums and the trumpeter was Miles Davis. Konitz notes that the word "commission" suggests a degree of formality greater than was really the case. As he put it, "Somehow he knew that I was doing this date and he made them available and I was very pleased to try to play them. George had written at least two tunes that were very challenging to play. Miles wasn't on top form at that time but I was very grateful that he was willing to be a sideman with me. George's pieces were very original and very interesting to play and very difficult."[32]

The two pieces were "Odjenar," named after Juanita's maiden name, and "Ezz-Thetic." It was the latter that really stood out for Konitz.

> Yeah, "Ezz-Thetic" after a boxer named Ezzard Charles and it was based pretty much on the standard "Love for Sale," and it was a very difficult line at that fast tempo and I think Miles had borrowed a trumpet for the date and he was really kind of on his toes trying to get all the notes. So I was concerned with getting my notes right and I was praying that he got his right and it came out pretty good, I think, but those were some interesting times and George certainly contributed to that.[33]

In fact, difficult though "Ezz-Thetic" might have been, it was "Odjenar" that was unusual as a jazz recording for the time. It is a strange, ominous piece beginning with unaccompanied alto and trumpet that moves, some might say uneasily, between classical and jazz styles. Davis's playing here has always disappointed Russell, as it was the only time the trumpeter actually played one of Russell's compositions. He was, however, badly strung out on heroin at the time and actually tried to leave the session. Juanita, who was present, made him stay. Russell recalls, "As he was going out the door she ran over and grabbed him by the back of the neck, the collar and drug him back in. And she said, 'You're staying here until you finish this and I'm going to see to it.' He wasn't in much of a condition to do battle. (laughing)"[34]

Davis cannot even manage the tricky melody line on "Ezz-Thetic," playing only a counter line. Konitz, however, is quite astonishing both in the speed and fluidity of his performance and in the way he builds his solo. Of the rest of the sextet, Roach swings and drives the music on and Billy Bauer and Sal Mosca are in fine form. It is just a shame that Davis needed to score more than he wanted to play. It is also sad that Charlie Parker, who played "Ezz-thetic" at gigs, did not record the piece. There is apparently a score for strings in existence, which may have been intended for the *Bird with Strings* album but that obviously came to nothing.[35]

After six years in New York, Russell had had four compositions and one arrangement recorded, plus another half if we include Fitzgerald's recording of "How High the Moon." "New World" had not made it into the studio and "A Bird in Igor's Yard" lay in Capitol's vaults. Though he was still working on the Concept, money was tight and Russell realized he had to find some work, preferably work that would not interfere too much with his musical research. Macy's, the department store, provided the answer. "Because Juanita was pulling in all the money and, you know, I couldn't get away with saying, 'Well, let's have a deal and, when I make it, then you can lay back and relax.' It really isn't that way, anyway. So I did take the job at Macy's."[36]

Working in the wallpaper department was undemanding but Russell was less happy when he was switched to men's toiletries. However, it was then that he realized that nobody knew or cared that much where he was. It also meant that he could avoid the embarrassment of seeing people he knew from the business, like the time he had to serve his friend MJQ bassist Percy Heath.

"So I'd walk in. I'd get there on time in the morning. Punch the clock and go home and work on the Concept all day, you know. That seemed fair. Then, I'd walk in about five minutes of nine at night."[37] One day, Juanita came home from work unexpectedly. "He swore I was from Macy's until he saw my smiling face and such fear as you've never seen before! *(laughs)* He would do little odd jobs here and there just to keep us paying this small rent at this hotel."[38]

Other jobs included working as both a counterman and a cook in various diners around the five boroughs. In his scrapbooks, there is a note from those times with details of his work schedule. Interestingly, it is scribbled on a copy of the review of the Gillespie Carnegie Hall concert, acting as both a message about the ironies of life and a reminder not to forget where he came from.

Russell published the first edition of *The Lydian Chromatic Concept of Tonal Organization* privately in 1953. It was a photocopied affair bound in a ring binder. As Russell told Ben Young, it was not a best seller. In fact, it did not even get into double figures. Quite how Russell's ideas spread through the jazz community is therefore in part a matter of speculation. A comment Russell made to Young suggests both a gradual filtering process initially and one that perhaps led to some misunderstanding of his intentions.

> When I completed the Concept in the first edition in 1953, what it had to say became available by osmosis practically. "Oh, George uses modes. He doesn't use chords." Okay, that's a mistake because I always use chords, but chords are modes. Chords come from modes, which wasn't really perceived at that time. So this idea is released in the jazz community, and not only in the jazz community but in modern music. It was released that you've got to take modes seriously because, if you have a scale, you have modes, because modes are simply the scale begun and ended in its natural order in any one of the scale tones.[39]

He continued, "So, that information got disseminated in 1953 and then I came out with the 1959 publication, and by that time I had a conversation with Miles about it before he did 'Milestones.'"[40]

These comments suggest that Russell is quite unclear about how his ideas spread, and also how effectively. He did have a few students in that period, but this fact does not account for their spread either. Nor were his compositions well known enough to put his ideas over to a wider audience. His comments in a WGBH radio broadcast on the subject attempt an explanation, but seem inadequate.

> In 1953 I published the Lydian Concept. I think I sold one book. Not everybody had $120. Somehow the knowledge itself was spread by word of mouth—you know, "Hey, man have you heard of that book? That George is into something else." That's how it spread and became what Archie Shepp called "The Bible of the Avant Garde." The writing was simply an expression of the Concept and if I couldn't integrate the writing and the Concept I would work and work and work until I could, because that's what made the Concept grow.[41]

"Word of mouth" as a description of the dissemination of Russell's ideas actually becomes more accurate and convincing if one bears in mind the context. Four points need to be noted here. First, there was a hunger for new ideas. Earlier discussion of "Gil Evans's Church of the Aesthetic," of which Russell was a part, has demonstrated this. What is more, there was widespread interest in how jazz was going to develop among musicians and critics. This is evident from even a cursory read of *Down Beat* circa 1949–1953. Second, the jazz community—at least as far as the number of musicians—was actually quite small. Most of the players knew each other and connected via gigs, clubs, and hangout joints. Third, Russell's connection with and important role within that grouping of the most forward-thinking musicians in New York provided a mechanism for his ideas to spread, even if only truncated form. Finally, Russell's ideas, at least to his more perceptive peers, drew on the practice of jazz musicians. It is a point John Lewis made to Ian Carr in 1992 when asked whether he considered the Lydian Concept to be a significant breakthrough: "It was, but not for me and not for the same generation that he and I both belonged to, because the things he was using were the way we both played and thought. This was really for the next generation of people."[42]

John Benson Brooks amplifies this point in a *Jazz Review* article on Russell's Lydian Concept.

> The boppers of the 'forties inherited the jazz scale—natural major with traditional options on the flat 3rd, flat 7th and flat 9th (or flat 2nd) and put the blue note, freedom squawk, or fly in the ointment (a feature absolutely essential to jazz's life) on the so-called flatted fifth, of F# in the scale of C. Notice

that the last two options in the history of the scale are enharmonically tonic and fifth of the F# scale.

Inevitably this soon had everybody playing around with polytonality and if you were blowing in a C gravity while the bass was in F# then, crazy. And why worry, since the circle of perfect fifths was an equilibrium with a magic gravity that would carry you through?

Benson Brooks then refers briefly to the contribution of Schillinger, continuing,

Tunes which had chord circles with several tonic stations (like "How High . . . ," "All the Things . . ." etc.) were the thing and everybody was trying to work out a chromatic mobility (12 tonics) that would make melodic sense.

It is to George Russell's everlasting credit that he did it.[43]

Russell has never hidden his debt to the musicians he observed. This is clear from his analysis of the different melodic approaches of Coleman Hawkins, Lester Young, John Coltrane, and Ornette Coleman in chapter IV of *The Lydian Chromatic Concept of Tonal Organization* and his examinations of solos by Miles Davis ("Four"), Eric Dolphy ("245"), and John Coltrane ("Giant Steps") in chapter V.[44] Although I will later question some of Russell's scientific claims for his ideas, I would suggest that what we are seeing in his practice is actually the "scientific method" of observation leading to hypothesis to testing and further theoretical refinement.[45]

Given the closeness of the group—Evans, Mulligan, Miles, Carisi, Lewis, Schuller, et al.—this seems a fair assessment. That said, it must be remembered that Russell first published the Lydian Concept six years after "Cubano-Be, Cubano-Bop," and it would be another five years before Miles recorded the classic "Milestones." It may well be that it was Russell's own recordings in the fifties and his writing for others that did more to disseminate the use of modes, if not his deeper theoretical concerns, than the book itself. Certainly, it was hardly a rapid process.

It was another three years before Russell got what turned out to be his most significant break so far. Vibraphonist Teddy Charles was recording an album for Ahmet Ertegun for Atlantic Records and had commissioned a number of writers to provide material. Gil Evans arranged "You Got to My Head," saxophonist Jimmy Giuffre provided "The Quiet Time," and Russell contributed "Lydian M-1." Featuring a ten-piece band with four saxes, trumpet, and a five-piece rhythm section, the album was in the modernist vein of the times. Highly arranged, well prepared, and beautifully played, its seven tracks sound much of a piece and bear comparison with the MJQ, *Birth of the Cool*, and the music Mulligan and Chet Baker were making. Unsurprisingly, the pieces commissioned from Evans, Giuffre, and Russell are the meat of the record, and "Lydian M-1" revealed how far Russell's writing had progressed, albeit in the absence of any real recorded or performance outlet. As Teddy Charles recalls, "I felt his 'Cubano-Be, Cubano-Bop' for Dizzy was a breakthrough to new music and a new harmonic, tonal, and rhythmical territory. Again, "Lydian M-1" was extraordinarily challenging. His personality was very different from our contemporaries."[46]

"Lydian M-1" was also one of the only Russell recordings that underwent major editing, as Russell told Ben Young. It seems the band struggled with the music, and the engineer, Tom Dowd apparently, then battled to achieve a satisfactory cut.

> GR: "Lydian M-1," which was the piece that enabled me to . . . sort of put me on the map in terms of getting record dates, either to compose music for other people or featuring my own group, that piece "Lydian M-1" had . . . now I forget the engineer, but he worked for Atlantic and he's very famous, Tom. . .
> BY: Tom Dowd?
> GR: Tom Dowd, his hair turned grey practically overnight because there were fifty-six splices on the piece, lasting just six minutes long. *(laughs)*
> BY: Were there problems putting it together? Were the musicians goofing up the solos?
> GR: Yeah, to have it turn out right, it took that and he was completely immersed in tape. He had tape attached to his belt, around his neck. Sometimes he looked like Tarzan.
> BY: Were you directing the edit?
> GR: Well, I was with him and wouldn't let him get away with anything in terms of shortcuts. Actually, it worked out. It doesn't really sound that way, but Tom really sweated that.[47]

Time magazine liked Charles's album, noting, "Vibraphonist Charles, not content with rhythmic exploration, exploits harmonic possibilities developed by Duke Ellington, uses dissonance to create color and mood rather than sheer shock. The album ranges from familiar ('Nature Boy') to far-out ('Lydian M-1')."[48] Teo Macero, later Miles Davis's producer, commented in *Metronome*, "'Lydian M-1' was by George Russell. This is my first association with his work. I felt that the composition did not come up to the level of [Gigi] Gryce or Charles' compositions but that it was well-worth hearing. He has potential as a composer but needs more of a 'classical' approach in developing his musical ideas."[49]

"Lydian M-1" was heard by a young alto player called Hal McKusick. Apart from his involvement with Russell, McKusick has been largely overlooked as a musician, but he made some fine records in his own name, with a sound somewhere between Paul Desmond and Lee Konitz. McKusick was doing a date for RCA Victor and had a budget that allowed him to recruit a number of writers for the project. The altoist had been working with a quartet of Barry Galbraith on guitar, Milt Hinton on bass, and Osie Johnson on drums. Apparently, he had met Russell in the street and asked him to write something for his group. Eight months later, Russell rang him and told him the piece, "Lydian Lullaby," was ready.

McKusick knew Gil Evans from their time with the Thornhill band and Evans gave him "Blues for Pablo," later made famous by Davis, and "Jambangle." For the rest, the record carried a couple of Giuffre tunes, and others by Johnny Mandel and Al Cohn, and featured a quartet on some tracks and an octet on the remainder. The octet, incidentally, included Jimmy Raney on guitar and Sol Schlinger on baritone, both of whom had been on the Teddy Charles album. *Hal McKusick - Jazz Workshop* is a remarkable record. It is imaginative and forward looking, and is as concerned with the role of composition in jazz as it is with improvisation.

Russell contributed three tunes, "Lydian Lullaby," played by the quartet; "Miss Clara," performed by the octet; and "The Day John Brown Was Hanged" with the quartet and Russell himself on drums. (He also contributed tambourine on Evans's "Blues for Pablo"). On "Lydian Lullaby" the interplay between McKusick and Galbraith is marvelous, but the tune then shifts abruptly into a second, slower, bluesy movement and from there into a swinging third section before returning to its opening theme. Its suite-like quality, with Russell using the quartet much as a classical composer might, creates a sense of thematic development. It's a quality that Stephanie Stein Crease has described as Russell's "advanced structural sensibility."[50] That same sensibility is even more evident on "The Day John Brown Was Hanged," as Russell later noted: "That was the period when I wrote short pieces. Each one's a little vignette. I like to think of it as a play that says something, that has different moods and different doors and different atmospheres, you know. From then on it was set."[51]

Each of its three movements has its own subtitle. The first—"The Day John Brown Was Hanged"—features Galbraith playing the melody of the "Battle Hymn of the Republic" while McKusick wails a mournful spiritual in the distance, contrasting the formal, stately expression of loss with perhaps the more immediate grief felt by those left unfree. The second section—"Some

Did a Dance"—is unironic with its gaily dancing alto over a swaying rhythm accompaniment. The third section—"Some Wailed the Blues"—builds to a mournful blues before the piece returns to a partial restatement of the opening theme.

This composition is Russell's second great contribution—after "Cubano-Be, Cubano-Bop"—to jazz and to American music generally. Two things stand out instantly. First, Russell has deliberately created a programmatic piece of music. Though others had done so before in jazz—notably Ellington, on compositions such as "Harlem Airshaft" as well as larger-scale works like *Black, Brown and Beige*—Russell's piece reveals an elaborate set of intentions. It is a highly political work, though not in any simplistic, "agitprop" sense. It is a quintessentially American work using American forms and subject matter, and derived from an American sensibility. It acknowledges division, past and current, on racial matters, in particular in its second section. It notes the ambivalence in which Brown as a historical figure is held, despite his partial appropriation by the political establishment. Russell is perhaps suggesting that so radical a figure cannot be contained within the status quo implied by the "Battle Hymn." Its sophistication lies in the fact that Russell does not state his own position but implies those held by others—slaves and emancipated Negroes, southerners, Republicans and the northeastern liberal political elite. He asks instead that listeners consider their own position in relation to those implied above. In these respects "The Day John Brown Was Hanged" goes far beyond anything before and much since in jazz. The second point that stands out is that Russell is again utilizing complex materials from jazz and classical music and bringing these together in a conscious and coherent fusion. However, here he is not writing for big band but for small jazz ensemble.[52]

"Miss Clara" sits uneasily in this company. It is, in comparison, a trifle—almost a throwaway. Described in the original sleeve notes as the kind of intentional "satire, in jazz terms, that might be associated with Fred Allen or Bob and Ray,"[53] it plays with styles. There is a little bit of Dixie interaction between the horns, a touch of blues; it sounds like an "out-of-towner's" expectation of his first night in a big-city jazz club. Like many musical jokes, it is a case of "you had to be there, I guess!"

"Miss Clara" was recorded in April 1956, four weeks after "Lullaby" and "John Brown." By that time, fate had intervened in the lives of Russell and his young wife, in the avuncular form of Jack Lewis, RCA's head of jazz, as Russell told Ian Carr:

> And Jack was doing the Hal McKusick date and he liked what I was doing, you know. So one day we invited him to lunch in our one-room suite at the

Beechwood. He took one look around. He said, "Oh man!" He said, "You know, you can't live like this." He said, "I'll get you your own record date and you can charge what you want to." So he did, you know. And that . . . that was the RCA *Jazz Workshop* record, which came out of this Hal McKusick date, you know. And with the Workshop album we were able to move out of that place and move over to Bank Street.[54]

Down Beat even carried a short news item in its March 21, 1956, issue noting that Russell was working for RCA Victor on his own album and on McKusick's, although it mentions Kenny Dorham as the trumpeter they would use rather than Art Farmer, who actually played the dates. The short item also notes that McKusick's record would include "a six-minute suite by Russell titled 'John Brown'" and refers to Russell's inactivity on the scene since 1951 and the Konitz-Davis session, which had just been reissued as a 12-inch Prestige LP, *Conception*.[55]

Russell also arranged a set of standards for the Hal McKusick Quartette—McKusick, Galbraith, Hinton, Johnson—a remarkable and innovative pianoless group. Recorded at the Brooklyn Academy of Music in November 1956, *Jazz at the Academy* was released on Coral and featured a stunning "Over the Rainbow" as a showcase for Hinton as well as beautiful versions of "These Foolish Things" and "Out of this World."

As Leonard Feather wrote at the time,

> That jazz and the academy are not incompatible, that their fusion does not have to produce a hybrid or reduce the authenticity of the resultant performance, can clearly be discerned in the present efforts of the Hal McKusick Quartette. They are the work of a skilled and well-trained leader, a compatible group of sideman, and a composer-arranger noted for his originality and resourcefulness.[56]

Russell had arrived, and two other records helped heighten his profile during this period. They were both albums by women singers. The first, *Moody Marilyn Moore*, was by Marilyn Moore, then Al Cohn's wife, and was released on the Bethlehem label. It got a five-star review in *Down Beat*[57] and from Feather, who mentions George Russell and Jack Segal's "Born to Blow the Blues" as a "little-known and valuable" choice of material. That same tune was also featured on *This Is Lucy Reed*, on Fantasy, along with other arrangements by Russell and Gil Evans. Evans played piano and Russell played drums on some tracks.

The Lucy Reed record was made partly in New York and partly in Chicago. It is a beautiful after-hours album. However, in comparison with

Evans's and Russell's efforts, the tracks recorded in Chicago and arranged by Jack English and pianist Eddie Higgins are ordinary girl singer fare. Evans's take on Cole Porter's "Love for Sale" is a delight, as is "No Moon At All," with its Thornhill-like easygoing swing. Of Russell's three tracks, "Born to Blow the Blues" is hard to take for its embarrassing lyric by Jack Segal. That said, the tune and arrangement, with some fabulous trumpet from Art Farmer and excellent guitar accompaniment from Barry Galbraith, are fine. Sol Schlinger, who played on the Teddy Charles session, was on baritone sax and bass clarinet and Romeo Penque played flute and English horn, while Milt Hinton was on bass and Don Abney on piano. Russell's arrangement of "This Is New," from Kurt Weill and Ira Gershwin, is a rich confection indeed, and, like Evans, he succeeds in creating a really full orchestral sound from so small an ensemble. However, the standout track is "In the Wee Small Hours of the Morning."

Given the defining quality of the Sinatra-Riddle version of two years earlier, it might almost seem an affront to attempt it. But Russell and Reed transform it into a subtle, quiet, yet filmic little piece. Taken even slower than Sinatra's version, Russell locates Reed's voice in the center of the ensemble, which he uses sparingly. Those points when some instruments drop out—for example, where just Galbraith, Hinton, and Russell are heard behind the voice—are spine-tingling. Such moments heighten the drama when the whole group is heard, and Galbraith is quite astonishing. Russell has described him as his "orchestra." This performance explains why.

Asked around this time by a *Village Voice* journalist what the difference between arranging and composing was, Russell replied, "It's around 95 cents. Union scale is $4.60 per four-bar page for composition and $3.65 for arrangement."[58]

Russell was being only partly facetious. Talking to Ian Carr, Russell said, "I never would get a lot of work but I'd always get enough work to pay the bills." Noting the records he would go on to make for Milt Gabler at Decca, Russell referred back to his connection with Hal McKusick. "McKusick again would get a couple of albums. And he did get a couple and but this time for Decca. So, I wrote some things for him—like 'Stratusphunk' came out of one of his Decca Recordings. That was in '58. I did a whole Brooklyn Academy record for him. And that was living money."[59] Maybe Russell had been slow to make an impact on the jazz scene. He and Juanita had struggled—but now, with the help of Milt Gabler, his fortunes were about to take a turn for the better, and his critical and artistic standing would at last begin to reflect the expectations his friends had for him.

Notes

1. Ian Carr, interview with Juanita Giuffre for BBC Radio 3 Broadcast George Russell—The Invisible Guru, July 1994.

2. Ben Young, broadcast devoted to George Russell in celebration of his seventy-fourth birthday, WKCR Radio, New York, June 23, 1997.

3. Ibid.

4. Ian Carr, interview with George Russell, June 1992.

5. See A. Clarkson, ed., *On the Music of Stefan Wolpe* (New York: Pendragon, 2003).

6. Stuart Cosgrove, "The Zoot-Suit and Style Warfare," *History Workshop Journal* 18 (Autumn 1984): 77–91.

7. Young, broadcast devoted to George Russell.

8. Ibid.

9. Interview with George Russell, April 2003.

10. Ibid.

11. Carr, interview with G. Russell, June 1992.

12. Interview with George Russell, June 2004

13. Carr, interview with G. Russell, June 1992.

14. Leonard Feather, "Dance Biz Needs Younger Leaders: DeFranco," *Down Beat*, March 9, 1951.

15. Young, broadcast devoted to George Russell.

16. See Mike Baillie's sleeve notes in *The Artistry of Artie Shaw*, Fresh Sound FSR-CD397.

17. Interview with George Russell, October 2003.

18. Ibid.

19. Interview with Robert Moore, July 2004.

20. E-mail interview with George Schuller, May 2006.

21. See sleeve notes to *Miles Davis—The Complete Birth of the Cool*, Capitol 724349455023. NB. One of these would seem to be the ubiquitous "New World."

22. Interview with Gunther Schuller, October 2003.

23. Interview with Juanita Giuffre, June 2004.

24. Ibid.

25. Carr, interview with G. Russell, June 1992.

26. Interview with Giuffre.

27. Carr, interview with G. Russell, June 1992.

28. Interview with Giuffre.

29. Ibid.

30. Interview with G. Russell, October 2003.

31. Ibid.

32. Interview with Lee Konitz, April 2004.

33. Ibid. As a side note, Lee Konitz took part in a *Down Beat* "Blindfold Test" in 1957 and one track he reviewed was Russell's "Ye Hypocrite, Ye Beelzebub" from Russell's *Jazz Workshop* LP. "I like the written part of this very much. Sounds like something George Russell might have done." That said, Konitz was less impressed with the players and gave it three and a half stars out of a possible five. Lee Konitz, "Blind Date," *Down Beat*, July 11, 1958.

34. Conversation with George Russell, October 2006.

35. See Dom Cerulli, "George Russell," *Down Beat*, May 29, 1958, p. 16.

36. Carr, interview with G. Russell, June 1992.

37. Ibid.

38. Carr, interview with Giuffre, July 1994.

39. Young, broadcast devoted to George Russell.

40. Ibid.

41. Ibid.

42. Ian Carr, interview with John Lewis, The quote is taken from Carr's notebooks.

43. John Benson Brooks, "George Russell," *Jazz Review*, February 1960, p. 38.

44. George Russell, *Lydian Chromatic Concept of Tonal Organization* (Brookline, MA: Concept, 2001).

45. See K. Popper, *The Logic of Scientific Discovery* (New York: BasicBooks, 1959).

46. Interview with Teddy Charles, October 2007.

47. Young, broadcast devoted to George Russell.

48. Review of Teddy Charles Tentet, *Same* (Atlantic 1229), *Time*, May 21, 1956.

49. Teo Macero, Review of Teddy Charles Tentet, *Same* (Atlantic 1229), *Metronome*, June 1956. Ironically, Macero was given the same track to review in *Down Beat*'s "Blindfold Test," March 6, 1957. He notes that Russell is "a very talented composer" but that here, "[h]e didn't do anything with what he had. It was all at the same level, I think."

50. Stephanie Stein Crease, quoted by A. Kramer, sleeve notes to *George Russell—The Complete Bluebird Recordings*, Lonehill LHJ10177.

51. Young, broadcast devoted to George Russell.

52. See Max Harrison, "George Russell—Rational Anthems (Phase 1, 2, 3)," *Wire* (Spring/Summer/Autumn 1983): 31.

53. John S. Wilson, sleeve notes to *Hal McKusick—Jazz Workshop*, RCA Victor LPM1366.

54. Carr, interview with G. Russell, June 1992.

55. "Russell Writing for Victor Jazz," *Down Beat*, March 21, 1956.

56. Quoted in sleeve notes to *Hal McKusick Quartet—The Complete Barry Galbraith, Milt Hinton and Osie Johnson Recordings*, Lonehill LHJ10176. *High Fidelity* magazine was less impressed: "Jazz at the Academy is in the rather monotonous vein

that McKusick had escaped from in the RCA Victor (Jazz Workshop) disc." No date but probably early 1957.

57. Leonard Feather, Review of Moody Marilyn Moore, Bethlehem LP BCP-73, *Down Beat*, March 6, 1957.

58. Bob Reisner, "Jazz Composition," *Village Voice*, July 10, 1957.

59. Carr, interview with G. Russell, June 1992.

CHAPTER SIX

~

Ballad of Hix Blewitt

The Russells' new address on Bank Street lay in Greenwich Village, which was still hip at that time but far from chichi. It was still a real step up from the Beechwood. Jack Lewis acted as quickly as he had promised, and Russell was in the studio recording the first of three sessions that would lead to his first album before Hal McKusick's record was actually finished. McKusick played alto and flute, Barry Galbraith guitar, Milt Hinton bass, and Joe Harris drums. To these four were added trumpeter Art Farmer and pianist Bill Evans. Evans would prove to be one of two musicians, significant in themselves in jazz history, whose names would be forever associated with Russell. The other is Jan Garbarek, the Norwegian saxophonist.

Russell had met Evans through Lucy Reed, a singer he had known in Chicago and perhaps had a relationship with. Reed was working in New York with Evans as her accompanist, at that time a role low on the food chain for a jazz musician. As Juanita Giuffre explains,

> Oh, Bill was a dear friend. He really was. He was a sweetheart and he looked like [a] minister's son. When we first met him, we went out on a ferry ride with a girl who had very much a big crush on George, but she brought Bill Evans anyway, and we went out on this ferry thing around New York City and Billy's standing there by the rail looking very studious and anything but a jazz musician, and this girl was saying, "He plays very well and he's quite a nice piano player"—because he at that time was accompanying her, which to us was just like accompanying—we didn't think much of it.[1]

Russell's own recollection of the experience continues:

> A singer who lived in Chicago knew me—a very sweet singer—and she brought Bill up to the 24th Street hang where Juanita and I first lived with the one room. There wasn't anything to do on Sunday in New York, it was summertime and New York is like a desert. So she introduced me to her friend, and he seemed very detached like a businessman, like he belonged to a bank, worked in a bank. He didn't seem to be very joyful. So I said in desperation, "Let's take the Staten Island Ferry," which we did, came back, and Lucy said, "This man's a piano player. Ask him to play." That's one thing we had in the place—a piano. "Yeah, why don't we ask him to play. Why not, you know?" Expecting to hear a bank teller doodle on the piano. *(whistles)* It was one of those times when you feel like you're being blown up in witnessing a very special kind of adventure, as he played piano like nobody I ever heard. I didn't expect that outta him. All that self-reserve thing, you could see in his music there was much more to him. He and I became very good friends. I got him onto Victor. I wouldn't have anybody else. I knew who I wanted to play piano on the Victor album.[2]

Evans could evoke that kind of shock and awe despite his quiet and unassuming appearance, and could do so without resorting to grandstanding or pyrotechnics. Pianist Jack Reilly, who later studied with both Russell and Lennie Tristano, first met Evans in the early fifties.

> I was at the Navy School of Music in Washington, D.C. I heard this piano playing coming from this room and I said, "What is that?" This guy said, "It's Bill." Shearing, Teddy Wilson, Bud Powell—everything but with a notch above, and a synthesis already in his playing of all three. I said, "Oh my god!" Such fluency. I got to play with him. Then, of course, I got all his recordings; I got all the ones with George especially.[3]

On March 31 the sextet went into the studio and recorded four sides—"Ye Hypocrite Ye Beelzebub," "Jack's Blues," "Livingstone I Presume," and "Ezz-Thetic." Four days later Russell was back in the studio with Hal McKusick and the octet to record "Miss Clara." "Ezz-Thetic" had been composed five years earlier, but it is unclear whether the other three pieces were already written or whether Russell finished these between Lewis's offer of a contract and the date itself. The latter seems the more likely of the two. There was then a gap of seven months before the second session took place in October, and the final four tunes were finished just before Christmas 1956.

During these gaps in recording, the musicians rehearsed every Sunday at Milt Hinton's place, as Russell recalls:

It was wonderful because we did something that a lot of groups didn't do—we practiced, because Milt Hinton opened the door to his house in Jamaica Plain. I had done all the writing of the music, twelve songs, and Milt insisted we come out every Sunday and rehearse. So we were a well-rehearsed band, thanks to Milt, when we walked in that studio. Art Farmer, Bill Evans, you know, Milt Hinton, Barry Galbraith, especially Barry. Things were gradually working, I can't see why, for me. They gradually put me on the scene. We must have done something right.[4]

Milt Hinton offers a slightly different take on events. Describing the stressful nature and pace of studio work in his autobiography, he talks of the way he and his friends would relieve the stress with weekend jam sessions. "There really wasn't much of a chance to play jazz during the week and none of us were willing to give up sessions for a steady job in a club. So getting together and letting loose was a great way to unwind." As Hinton notes, it also allowed players to keep up with their peers and before long his house on Ruscoe Street became a "regular weekend hang-out." He continues, "After a while, some of us even put thirty-five dollars apiece in a kitty so we could pay a couple of composers and arrangers we knew to write for us. We contacted people like Manny Albam, George Russell and Gil Evans and they were overjoyed."[5]

Either way, this meant that when Russell's group got into the studio they knew the material inside out. Art Farmer told Ian Carr that it was the intricacy of Russell's tunes that demanded this regime:

It took us about a year to make that album on RCA Victor. We would rehearse every Sunday if everybody was available, and then we would take the music home and study it. It was hard, and by the time we felt we were ready—or he felt we were ready—we would go in the studio and do two or three or four numbers, because they were short numbers and so we could get around twelve tunes or something like that [on an album]. It wasn't easy. I think he was writing more intricate then because whatever the structure of the song was, well, that was what you really had to improvise on. It wasn't like writing one piece and then opening the thing up to improvise. If he had a 6/4 bar in the melody then you had to deal with that when you improvised. He had these chords. Sometimes he didn't know what to call them himself. I remember one time he had the guitarist, Barry Galbraith, he said, "Barry, what would you call this chord?" He played a chord on the piano. Playing the guitar, Barry's very used to leaving out notes. So he said, "I would call this such-and-such a chord with the fifth taken out" or something.[6]

But, as Farmer also told Carr, rehearsing to this extent meant the musicians were able to contribute more in their playing and enhance and even extend the compositions.

I remember, though, that some of the things on George's record when I was playing, when I was playing solo, I had worked with the music so closely that some of the things that sounded like they were part of the piece were actually my solo. We really did take some time on that, but ironically, no matter how much time you spent on it, when you got in the studio that's where you really learned it. (laughs) If you were thinking you were just going to go out there and coast, well, it wasn't like that at all. Anyway, it turned out very good and I was very proud to be a part of it.[7]

The album remains one of the most important in jazz, and though its ideas took time to percolate through the jazz world, it heralded the extensive use of modes in jazz not only as a compositional tool but primarily as a means of opening up improvisation. It is one of the records that many musicians instantly refer to when Russell is mentioned. In the nineties, when pianist/composer Ran Blake got a petition together to request that RCA reissue the album, he had no problem getting signatures from hundreds of the major figures in the music. The album set new standards for small group playing and writing. Each of its twelve tracks is a mini-drama, complete unto itself, and the listener is instantly drawn into a world of evocative filmic images of jazz clubs, city life, and constant movement.

"Ezz-Thetic" receives a remarkably assured reading, with a sparkling solo from Evans and some sharp playing from the rest of the band, while "Livingstone I Presume" is a witty and playful picture complete with jungle sounds. However, it is with "Concerto for Billy the Kid" that the album really takes off. Paul Motian replaced Joe Harris on drums for this session. He remembers it now only vaguely, but recalls that it was not the average jazz record session that he was used to.

It was very different from what I expected or what I had experienced up to that time. It seemed like it was really different. It was kind of a small group of seven or eight musicians, something unusual for me. I don't really know about that, but I did my best and it sounds pretty good now. Bill Evans sounds incredible on that. Milt Hinton was the bass player, I recall.[8]

On "Concerto," Motian's opening cymbal ride creates an immediate sense of urgent expectation. Russell holds the listener using a rapidly repeating phrase before first Evans, then the rest of the group play with the theme, extending it or doubling its complex line. Then Evans takes his solo. Split into two sections by a brief horn chorus, it swings, it races, it twists and turns and takes the tape. It is Evans's first great solo in recorded jazz and one of the album's high points. The second take of this number from the session lacks the energy of the chosen take, but there are people who think that Evans's second solo is even better than the first, with its well-chosen quote from Thelonious Monk's "Well You Needn't."

"Round Johnny Rondo" has a fuguelike quality and uses quite dissonant counterpoint between the horns to create a sense of movement and tension. "Witch Hunt" is a helter-skelter pursuit that returns at the end to its starting point. Whether Russell was making a political point, given the tenor of the times, with its title is unclear. However, it is the four pieces from the final session in December that seem in some ways the most ambitious. On that occasion, Osie Johnson on drums and Teddy Kotick on bass replaced Motian and Hinton.

"Ballad of Hix Blewitt" requires some explanation, because Russell has always published his music under the name of Russ-Hix. The composer's own notes refer to the "memory of a friend with a legendary quality." Russell goes on to describe a man who combined "the West, the Blues and good Dixie humor in his character." According to Russell's third wife, Alice, he knew Hix Blewitt from his and Juanita's time at the Beechwood Hotel.

> Hix was a Texan. He played clarinet with [I believe] the Bob Crosby Orchestra. Hix left the Orchestra because he left his dentures in a hotel room in Chicago, and couldn't afford to replace them. In New York, he found a gig transcribing tunes for a wealthy man who thought himself a songwriter. Although he couldn't read music, he would sing the melody and lyrics and Hix would write it all down. He was a dedicated alcoholic who was fond of saying "Hix Blewitt, and no one heard it."[9]

The composition is a beautifully elegiac piece that sets McKusick's lovely flute playing against a soft, delicate guitar and piano accompaniment before the rest of the group comes in. It plays around with the overall tonality and seems to move between keys, its classical, pastoral feel recalling something of Copland and Ives. The ballad indicates Russell's capacity for empathy with people often from very different worlds and experiences than his own, and how their histories feed into his own vision and art.

"Knights of the Steamtable" doffs its hat respectfully to Russell's former colleagues in the catering industry and to his friend Gerry Mulligan, who had written a tune called "Knights of the Turntable," dedicated to New York's jazz DJs. It is marked by the way it uses polytonality as Farmer's trumpet solo improvises in A-minor against the overall key of the piece in B-flat minor. "Sad Sergeant" draws on an old spiritual but adds a martial feel to what is essentially a blues number. Like several of the compositions on the album, it has an episodic quality, with Russell creating a series of short, dynamic movements within the short space of the tune. The most surprising piece on the record, however, is "Fellow Delegates." Featuring Russell's only recorded percussion solo, its middle section comprises a part-improvised duet with Johnson using chromatically tuned drums (Boo-Bams) made by "David Wheat's Musical Engineering Associates of Sausalito, California." When the rest of the group return to play the polytonal theme, the sense is less of jazz rather than something much more akin to the advanced contemporary composition being created in Europe and America by the disciples of Schoenberg. Although it is imbued as well with the spirit of Africa, in its use of tuned percussion, there is also something that echoes the maverick hobo composer Harry Partch. It remains one of the most unusual pieces Russell has written and recorded.

Jazz Workshop was the only album Russell made for RCA. According to him, Jack Lewis was not popular among the suits at the company and the knives were out for him. The group featured on the record was, with the exception of a TV broadcast for NBC (*The Subject Is Jazz*, broadcast on June 28, 1958), a studio band and never did any gigs. In fact, it was not till the sixties that Russell had a regular working band. Still, as a "nonperformer" and with no real wish to be in the spotlight, why would he have wanted to form his own ensemble?

Both the McKusick and Russell records were released in 1957. *Down Beat* gave McKusick five stars and Nat Hentoff commented, "I was most moved by Russell, Evans and Giuffre, particularly by Russell's extraordinarily evocative, functionally dramatic 'John Brown', the longest work in the set." The *Washington Post* also singled out the same track as the "most ambitious and successful" track in its review, on an album where "improvisation is subordinated to very well-written compositions, which are far superior to the usual jazz originals." Fred Sherman in the *Miami Herald* called "John Brown" "superlative" and C. H. Garrigues in the *San Francisco Examiner* described it as "as bitter and as topical a piece as Ellington ever wrote."[10]

Don L. McIver in the *Fort Lauderdale Sunday News* provided one dissenting voice.

> Then comes George Russell with "The Day John Brown Was Hanged", "Miss Clara" and "Lydian Lullaby." Russell's billed as a "formulator of a new set of tonal principles based on the Lydian mode" whatever that means. The result leaves the reviewer cold. If anyone had bothered to check, Russell's "new" principles can be found in the arranging system formulated by Schillinger in the early part of the century and used extensively by every modern-day com-

poser from Hindemith through Bernstein and by such jazz luminaries as Eddie Sauter and Bill Finegan.[11]

We can be certain that Russell had never intended to cause such offense! There is inevitably overlap between Russell's ideas and those of Schillinger, given the common territory they were exploring. Both were interested in the scientific and mathematical underpinnings of music, and in Schillinger's case, he proposed that certain patterns were common to music and the very structure of the human nervous system. This suggestion is examined in much greater detail in chapter 11. Neither system is prescriptive, and both lay claim to universality. It is also worth noting that McIver is wrong about when and where Schillinger's method was developed and who it influenced. Among his pupils were many from jazz, including Benny Goodman and Tommy Dorsey, and from classical music such as George Gershwin. However, Sauter and Finnegan were not, it seems, among them. Hindemith derived his own set of principles and ideas quite separately. For a time Schillinger's biggest source of influence came through Lawrence Berk, who went on to found the Berklee School of Music, where Schillinger's system was taught up to the 1960s. However, perhaps the simplest way of defining the differences between Russell and Schillinger is to note that Russell developed his ideas from studying the overtone series and the application in music of the relationship between chords and scales. Schillinger's intention was much more pedagogical in its focus and concerned with developing the range of resources available to the composer through an understanding of the relationship between mathematics and music. The other point of significant difference is in terms of compositional outcome. Russell has proved himself a composer of note and distinction, while Schillinger's own works are largely dismissed.

Metronome expressed perhaps the majority opinion and did so articulately.

> Most impressive of the writing is that of George Russell and Gil Evans. Russell, especially on "Lydian Lullaby," "John Brown" and "Miss Clara" seems to have that unique ability to portray the varieties of feeling in a given situation. It's much like turning a stone about in the sun and noticing the multiple variations of design and reflection that come to the eye.[12]

The *Village Voice* carried a short interview by Bob Reisner with Russell in its July 10, 1957, issue, in which Russell says, "The jazz composer is no different from the classical composer except that he uses the rhythmic and tonal language of jazz. He also leaves little gaps for improvisation. The best jazz composition, in fact, does not sound written but improvised." Russell was reiterating the point made in the intelligent, if grandiloquent, sleeve notes he wrote for his own *Jazz Workshop* release, from which both Nat Hentoff in the *Saturday Review* and the uncredited writer in *Jazz Today* quoted extensively in their reviews of the record. However, the point Russell makes in those notes is a useful one—the jazz composer draws on the jazz tradition of improvisation and holds this in focus not just in presenting material for the soloist to improvise but by utilizing the vitality and practice of "its strongest improvisers" and by conveying that improvisatory, dynamic spirit within the written material. There were also further interview pieces in the *Cincinnati Post*, *Jazz Today*, and the magazine of Russell's union, the *RWDSU Record*.[13]

However, in those same notes, and in discussion of his achievements by critics, Russell may have inadvertently set up a further obstacle to the reception of his music. Polly Cochran's heartfelt piece in the *Indianapolis Star* reflects a certain sense of alienation. While she clearly appreciated Russell's music, she commented, "There is much to enjoy and admire about this LP." However, she also noted, "But one look at the complicated liner notes and comes the feeling that your pleasure and/or disappointments are those of a retarded mind. You're not hip." This is no Philistine or Luddite talking. Rather, Cochran presents the dilemma facing the "ordinary fan," that modern jazz had advanced to a point where it was impossible to understand or appreciate without a degree in music and unless one was one of the chosen of an esoteric minority. She continued, "Still, these are growing pains jazz must suffer. And composers such as Russell help to nurture that growth."[14]

Others were less equivocal, however, about Russell's *Jazz Workshop*. C. H. Garrigues, again in the *San Francisco Examiner*, spoke of Russell taking jazz "out of the realm of casual improvisation and into that of serious composition." Noting Russell's intentions as expressed in his notes, *Hi-Fi Low-Down* commented, "We feel that Russell has accomplished this purpose to an amazing degree." In *Down Beat*, Leonard Feather was even more enthusiastic. Awarding the LP five stars, he noted that Russell had succeeded in extending the harmonic possibilities of jazz without resorting to atonality or the "Schoenberg mathematics of the juggled twelve-tone row." In this regard, Feather commented, "Russell has succeeded in lifting his album to a unique status and stature."[15]

Such comments were echoed in *Cash Box*, which called it a "[f]ascinating, expertly performed jazz platter," while *Billboard* commented on Russell's ability to close the gap between written and improvised jazz and called him "[o]ne of the more original composing minds in contemporary music." Memphis's *Commercial Appeal*—and what an ironic title that is in this context—on the other hand, did not like the album, calling it "dull and un-swinging."[16]

Perhaps Russell would have been better served if his supporters in the media had emphasized the sense of swing and enthusiasm that pervades these performances. They could have noted how the material creates startling and exciting opportunities for improvisation. They could have pointed out how Russell draws on the blues, spirituals, and jazz to reaffirm jazz as a music as much indebted to folk music as it is to European classical forms. They might also have stressed the drama, good humor, and wit that these twelve tunes convey. In fairness, Hentoff, Feather, and others did mention these things, and more than in passing. But somehow it got lost in the desire to grasp a music that challenged as much as it confirmed, to have a jazz that was Art with a capital A.

One of the most touching items in George Russell's personal scrapbook is a letter from Ernest Green, a sixteen-year-old African American student at Central High School in Little Rock, Arkansas. For a short time in 1957, the world watched as nine black children were determined to exercise their right to attend the school of their choice, despite the threats and jeers of white supremacists and the opposition of the state governor, Orville Faubus. So extreme and awful were the TV and newspaper reports that President Dwight D. Eisenhower called out the troops to ensure the children were safely escorted into the school building. As the veteran (white) radical commentator I. F. Stone wrote at the time, perhaps just a little presumptuously but with understandable rage and passion,

> When a station wagon guarded by army jeeps took little Negro children to and from school instead of leaving them to run the gauntlet of hate alone, the Negro felt that for the first time in American history he was being treated like a first-class citizen, that for a wonderful moment he was no longer on the outside, wistfully looking in.[17]

Ernest was the oldest and "leader" of the nine, and a newspaper clipping in Russell's files describes him as a jazz fan. Russell responded to this by sending him a copy of the *Jazz Workshop* album. Ernest's reply reads, "When I received your album I was so thrilled I hardly knew what to do." Later, he says, "I really dig your writings and the titles are the absolute *end*." Given Russell's own experiences as an adolescent at school in Cincinnati, the reader may justifiably surmise that no review ever meant as much to the composer.[18]

The reviews of *Jazz Workshop* provide a sense of jazz at a turning point, moving away from its place as a picaresque folk-based music to something more rarefied, intellectual, and serious—a music more at home in the concert hall than in the club or speakeasy. In reality, the folksy, exotic image of jazz was always an ideological and social construction that denied it status and sophistication. Jazz was bound to develop and with the (chronically slow, perhaps) breaking down of racial barriers would come a broader intellectual and social acceptance of African Americans and their cultural contributions. Sadly, admission to the Academy always comes at a price. Jazz could never be innocent again—if ever it was.

In its April 4, 1957, issue, *Down Beat* carried a short news item, "Six Works of Jazz Commissioned by Brandeis University." Brandeis was the first academic institution to commission a series of "jazz and jazz-influenced compositions." Each composer was paid $350, and three classical composers—Gunther Schuller, Milton Babbitt, and Harold Shapero—were asked to compose classical pieces making reference to jazz, while three writers from jazz were to compose pieces for jazz orchestra. The three jazz musicians, chosen by Schuller and critic Nat Hentoff, were Jimmy Giuffre, Charles Mingus, and George Russell. The concert was scheduled for June as part of the Brandeis Creative Artists Festival.[19]

Schuller apparently coined the term "Third Stream" to describe music coming either from the jazz or the classical genre that drew heavily on both traditions at a symposium following the concert. In 1955 he and John Lewis had formed the Modern Jazz Society to promote "difficult" music that was rarely heard properly rehearsed and performed in concert venues, and this subsequently became the Jazz and Classical Music Society. That same year, a concert was given by the society at New York's Town Hall featuring music from Lewis, Jimmy Giuffre, and J. J. Johnson. A second concert was planned for 1956 to feature a piece by Schuller, *Symphony for Brass and Percussion*. However, this would have clashed with another performance of the work in New York and plans were shelved. That concert finally went ahead at Brandeis in Waltham, Massachusetts, on June 6, 1957.

Of the jazz works, all three seem to have been well received. Writing in *Down Beat*, Reverend Norman O'Connor, chaplain at Boston University and a great friend to many in the jazz world, was generous in his comments about the three jazz compositions but critical of Babbitt and Shapero's efforts—"All Set" and "On Green Mountain," respectively—and diplomatic about Schuller's "Transformation." His verdict was that Russell's *All About Rosie* "was the most successful of the material by jazz personalities" and described it as "quite taut and with strong rhythmic tension." He added, "For the jazz listener, the entire program lacked the fire and excitement of good jazz. Strangely, these most valuable characteristics of jazz were the most neglected in the concert."[20] Richard Katz, writing in *Jazz Today*, was hesitant when considering whether jazz could achieve equal status with classical music in the near future, at least in America. However, he was full of enthusiasm for all of the music, except Babbitt's twelve-tone "All Set," calling it a "brainwasher." He described *All About Rosie* as "a stunning work" that "really caught fire and was extremely well-received." With Giuffre's "Suspensions," Katz noted "the charm of the deceptively simple folk-blues tinged melodies" and in Mingus's "Revelations" he drew attention to its "almost Wagnerian, brooding-like intensity." But of most importance about his comments was Katz's sense that it was an "event of far-reaching significance." If he were to have added that it would have consequences that its progenitors had not intended, he would have been seriously prescient.[21]

Among the band members were the now usual suspects Hal McKusick, Bill Evans, Art Farmer, Barry Galbraith, and Teddy Charles. Schuller conducted the orchestra, except on "All About Rosie," which Russell conducted himself. At the concert and on the recording that followed, Milt Hinton and Osie Johnson played in the ensemble, while Miles Davis had featured on John Lewis's "Three Little Feelings." Two records were later released on Columbia. *Music for Brass* included J. J. Johnson's "Poem for Brass," "Three Little Feelings," and Guiffre's "Pharaoh," as well as Schuller's "Symphony for Brass and Percussion." *Modern Jazz Concert* featured all of the pieces from Brandeis.[22]

If Katz's comments were full of foresight, Nat Hentoff's article in *Down Beat*, "Jazz's Third Stream," had the benefit of hindsight. Expressing his own initial reservations about the potential for a "durable" new music of this kind, Hentoff allows that some composers—he cites John Lewis, Schuller, Russell, and Mingus—have the potential to develop such ideas without disservice to either jazz or classical music. Discussing the Brandeis disc, it is Russell's "All About Rosie" that Hentoff singles out for praise. He calls it "brilliant" and says that it convinced him "more than any modern jazz extended form piece I had heard until then" that "a fairly long composed Jazz work could actually enhance and intensify the improvised solos within it, as in the case of Bill Evans' startling explosion in 'Rosie'" Ralph J. Gleason was similarly enthusiastic in a piece for the *San Francisco Chronicle*, though he singled out Mingus's *Revelations* for the highest praise. Again, one gets the sense from Gleason's article that the mold had been broken.[23]

Lewis and Schuller had formed the Jazz and Classical Music Society with the aim of enhancing the status of jazz as a composed music and promoting its credibility as an art form. The aim was laudable, but as Katz noted in his piece, things might have been changing but jazz was far from equal in terms of financial support, academic respectability or access to rehearsal, recording, and performance opportunities. The real significance of Brandeis and Lewis and Schuller's valiant efforts lay not just in what it would lead to but in the way it predicted the dilemma that would face jazz for the next fifty years and beyond: Is it an art music for the concert stage, one that can be taught academically alongside classical music—or is it a popular form allied to show business that is at its most potent through its connection with a pop vernacular culture and best confined to and learned on the club stage?

Of course, it is quite arbitrary to say that it cannot be both. The classical repertoire is performed in small venues, churches, and village halls by jobbing musicians and amateurs, as well as by the virtuoso professionals of the major orchestras in the grand cathedrals of culture like Carnegie Hall and the Royal Opera House. It begs question, as well: How much of that repertoire has been rendered trite by overperformance and unambitious programming? The classical audience can often be remarkably unadventurous in its tastes. Yet its support by governments, record companies, and paying public continues despite this. The difference between this reality and the world of jazz, where its major writer-composer-performers form one progressive strand, while another relies largely on retreading the past of bebop, swing and trad, is perhaps more imagined than real. In a sense, those local and small venue gigs, like their classical counterparts, keep the language alive, while the grander works extend and revitalize it. The difference, perhaps, lies in the scale and variety of the classical repertoire and in the respect in which it is held by the cultural establishment.

While some European countries have permanent big bands, often attached to radio stations, performing works by established jazz composers and newly commissioned works, the same is not true of the United States, Britain, and many other developed countries. It may be that this is the way forward for jazz and a way of realizing Schuller and Lewis's dream that would allow for regular performance of important jazz compositions and new works that would serve an existing audience, while developing a new one. Certainly, the fossilization of a jazz tradition that presents jazz as a museum exhibit and allows only those new works that fall within a canonical style will never advance its cause.

The other by-product of Brandeis would be the jazz education movement, and again Gunther Schuller and John Lewis would be prime movers in that cause. Lawrence Berk, a dance band composer and arranger, had already established the Berklee School of Music in 1945. Berk had studied with Joseph Schillinger and was one of only twelve pupils, often referred to as "the twelve disciples," authorized by Schillinger to teach his system. Called originally Schillinger House—"Boston's Progressive School of Music"—the school offered a four-year diploma course based on Schillinger's principles with a curriculum "designed for a broad range of interests": "From the writer of popular songs to the symphonist, from the arranger of tunes for dance bands to the orchestrator of television and moving picture scores, from the composer of radio jingles to the creator of tone poems."[24] As the prospectus makes clear, Berk intended his school to be broad-based and within the mainstream of popular music rather than concerned with jazz. That said, Berklee has become associated with the music of jazz and, fairly or not, with a particular style of jazz education.

In 1957 an important year in jazz continued with the first of four annual summer schools—the Lenox School of Jazz. Lewis and Schuller wanted to provide the opportunity for students to study jazz and be taught by some of the leading names active on the scene. It was in every sense a continuation of their goal to raise the profile and stature of jazz. Jazz was being put forward as a music of the concert hall, one to be taught in the conservatory, and their aim was quite different from that of Lawrence Berk.

According to researcher Michael Fitzgerald,

The School was an outgrowth of a lecture series that had been in existence in Lenox since 1950. These roundtables were started by Dr. Marshall Stearns, a professor of English at Hunter College. Stearns, who later was the founder of the Institute of Jazz Studies, now housed at Rutgers University, brought the greatest minds in music together to discuss jazz in all of its many aspects and intricacies. Their goal was to show that "Jazz is a significant contribution to American culture."[25]

As Gunther Schuller explains, "No one was teaching jazz, and though that didn't prevent the great ones from being great—they learned self-taught— but the time came when John [Lewis] thought we should have a real kind of academy where themes about jazz are taught to talented young people."[26]

In its March 6, 1957, issue, *Down Beat* printed a news item, "Jazz School's First Session at Lenox," promising a three-week jazz summer school in the Berkshire Mountains taught and staffed by "top-ranking" musicians. Planned guest lectures included Duke Ellington, George Russell, Gunther Schuller, African American author Langston Hughes, and promoter/impresario Norman Granz.[27]

Though not announced at the time, faculty members that first year included Dizzy Gillespie, guitarist Jim Hall, Jimmy Giuffre, Max Roach, John Lewis (who was executive director), Connie Kay, Percy Heath, and Milt Jackson. The school was aided by the provision of funds and premises on the estate of patrons of the arts Stephanie and Phillip Barber. Now an executive housing estate and luxury hotel, Wheatleigh Hall and its surroundings provided an astonishingly lovely setting for the school over the next four years.

During that time 122 students passed through the school, including several later figures of significance in jazz education such as Jamey Aebersold, Dave Baker, and Larry Ridley; producer Arif Mardin; journalist Don Heckman; and musicians Ran Blake, Mike Gibbs, Attila Zoller, Ian Underwood (later of the Mothers of Invention), Don Ellis, Steve Kuhn, Bob Dorough, Steve Marcus, Gary McFarland, and J. R. Monterose.

Gunther Schuller was invited by Lewis to assist in developing the course.

> John and I were very close and I had all kinds of connections that he didn't have in the managerial world and the classical world in general. So he invited me to kind of co-organize the thing with him, which we did. But it turns out that the idea was too far ahead of its time and it only lasted three years, mainly because financially it could not be supported enough. The Barbers gave a lot of their own personal wealth, not that they were all that wealthy, and income, but they finally had to give it up. But while it lasted it was about thirty, forty years ahead of its time.[28]

Russell did not teach the first year as a faculty member but gave a lecture titled "Techniques in Jazz Composition." An article in *Down Beat* in October 1957 reported that he would be on the faculty the following year. Clearly his profile in the jazz world had risen to the point where this was considered significant in itself. According to Schuller, he and Lewis had always intended to involve Russell.

> So John and I both immediately had the idea when the Lennox School of Jazz came around that—my god, here's a man who's a wonderful musician, composer, pianist, and he's a theoretician of jazz. We've never had anything like that. So it was a unique opportunity to bring that kind of thinking and that kind of a concept that we've had for hundreds of years in the field of classical music and to bring that to the school. I represented, along with Martin Williams, the teaching of the history of jazz. George was in charge of teaching his Lydian Concept to the young students and creating a theoretical consciousness, and the others were the instrumental teachers.[29]

Russell taught composition from 1958 to 1960, and the school, though planned to continue in 1961, was canceled that year due to lack of finances. It did, however, establish a model that has fostered and informed jazz summer schools, not least those run by Jamey Aebersold's organization, and permanent college jazz courses ever since.

Perhaps the most famous Lenox incident occurred in 1959, when Ornette Coleman and members of his group attended the school—officially, at least—as students. As Schuller puts it now, "The great thing was to have Ornette Coleman, who was already a fully developed genius on the frontier of jazz, and he was a student there—technically speaking."[30]

According to legend, John Lewis, already a fan of Coleman, wanted to introduce him to a wider and discerning public. Even now, Coleman is unclear as to what the whole deal was. "I didn't know it was a school. I guess maybe it was. I thought it was a retreat. I didn't really have an idea what it was." And as he notes, "I really didn't have any idea what I was doing there. But I thought it was something to do with me having to meet more musicians because I had just gotten to New York."[31]

It seemed to him at the time that "I guess what they were trying to do was analyze the quality of improvised music, [whether it] was eventually going to open up or to reveal what could be done with a different way of writing music. It was very enjoyable to be there. There wasn't a lot of things you could discover because I was already playing the way I was playing before I got there." Coleman liked the atmosphere, however, which he described as "very democratic."[32]

Hearing Coleman play for the first time that summer at Lenox is one of Russell's strongest memories of the school.

> I had heard that there was a madman coming to the school who was sensational. Jimmy Giuffre and I were sitting on a Sunday afternoon, sitting in that wonderful garden on the grass, and we suddenly heard coming from the music bar this music. He looked at me. I looked at Jim. We'd never heard music like that. It was Ornette. We'd all been expecting to hear him because John Lewis discovered him. Giuffre and I looked at each other and said, "Whoa! That's something."[33]

Russell also remembers that Coleman put him on the spot in one class with a question he asked. "I had heard about the kind of vacuous questions this fellow from the coast used to ask. So Ornette got up and begins talking. He said, 'What is the tonic?' *(laughing)* I said, 'What?' He said, 'What is the tonic?'" To make matters worse, friends and musicians like Lewis, Connie Kay, and Percy Heath were in the room. "I'm with all these guys. I don't know how I got out of that. I don't think I did. I didn't get out of it. I just felt like closing up the book and going off, you know."[34]

Hearing Coleman was important to Russell for another reason as well.

> I thought I had things pretty categorized until one very quiet, very beautiful Sunday afternoon, I hear this wild music coming out of the Music Inn up there

and it's Ornette's music. It was the first time I really heard it. Then, I realized I didn't quite have all the categories. I'd left one category out. And largely through him I incorporated that. I called it Supra-Vertical Tonal Gravity—all and everything. So it was exchange on that level where you suddenly were blown into a new dimension.[35]

Composer and trombonist Mike Gibbs had arrived in Boston from Rhodesia in 1959 to study at Berklee and enrolled at the Lenox School in 1960. He recalls both what he learned from attending Russell's classes and how this contrasted with the musical education that he was receiving at Berklee. For Gibbs, already developing as a composer, the Lydian Concept seemed more concerned with improvisation than composition. However, as Russell discussed his approach to scales with the class, an important insight struck Gibbs.

He had about seven scales all with the name Lydian in there. They all started from the Lydian scale, but the last scale was chromatic, with all the twelve notes. He even called that the Lydian Chromatic Scale, something like that, and it just suddenly hit me. Throughout my life I've always maintained that all the notes are available in a tonal situation. It doesn't have to be atonal. I just liked that as a concept and I came away from George's classes with that. It was how I was understanding what he was doing and then I decided to devise my own way to do it. In a way what I do is to devise my own way for each piece that I write. It's not really a method. It's just a concept but all the notes are available because we were learning at Berklee that you can't use this note in this tonal situation. You mustn't have a Flat 9 here. All these "must-nots." I kind of rebelled against that and was always looking for a way to do that. Then George comes up with this scale with all the notes in it and you could use all the notes in a harmonic situation. I'm really simplifying what he's saying but this was very thrilling for me. I was in awe of him because he was a name even then.[36]

Attending Lenox in 1959 were two young musicians from Indiana—trombonist Dave Baker and trumpeter Al Kiger. Gunther Schuller had met them while playing with the Metropolitan Opera in Indianapolis and had written an article he called "The Indiana Renaissance" about Baker and a then-unknown guitarist named Wes Montgomery. The next year Schuller ensured that Baker and Kiger were offered scholarships to Lenox. Both were students at Indiana University at the time and played together in Baker's group. Baker and Kiger got on well with Russell and he befriended the two musicians and kept in touch after the summer school ended, as Baker explains: "And when I got [to] the School of Jazz, of course, I was in George's theory class—I mean, his Lydian Concept class. We got to be friends at that time, even though I was hard-headed and always arguing with him about something or another."[37]

Russell went out to Indiana and began working with these very green musicians. His intention was quite clear—they were to provide the nucleus of the group he now planned to form. From Baker's group, he took Kiger, Baker, and an exceptional tenor player called Dave Young, and from Baker's big band, he took drummer Joe Hunt. Perhaps prompted by the success of Coleman's unveiling at the school in 1959, the intention was that they would play at Lenox in 1960. All four were given scholarships by John Lewis. Dave Baker remembers that Russell did much more than simply hire the four musicians.

> We were all at the School of Jazz. So when he decided to form his sextet, he came out to Indianapolis and took the group that I had been leading and then began teaching us how to play, how to make music, and he wrote arrangements and things and really just mentored us for the next . . . I don't know . . . for a month or so, before we then became the George Russell Sextet.[38]

Meanwhile, Russell's career was not standing still, as Dom Cerulli's article in *Down Beat* in May 1958 made clear. This was one of the first pieces, if not the first, to cover Russell's history and his Lydian Concept in detail. Russell also tried his hand as a critic and wrote several album reviews for the *Jazz Review*.[39] As well as working those summers at Lenox between 1958 and 1960, Russell recorded two albums for Decca under the auspices of Milt Gabler. These were *New York, N.Y.* and *Jazz in the Space Age*. Both presented remarkable opportunities for Russell. Both were to be Big Band albums using some of New York's finest musicians. *New York, N.Y.* was a tone poem and tribute to the city and to its place in jazz. As Russell recalled later,

> In 1934, my sixth grade teacher gave the class an assignment to write an essay on our favorite subject; it could be a fantasy or real life, whatever we chose. I selected New York because of its glamour and sophistication, and for what resonated in me, at that time and at eleven years of age, a tolerance for things new. I wouldn't have been able to articulate my feelings about New York then, but it was the Apple's life-positive energy which impressed me, and, eventually, magnetized me to it. The essay earned me an A+ (one of the few in my academic life).[40]

These two records were huge canvases involving extended compositional ideas and structures. As he explained to writer Burt Korall in an interview for the original liner notes for *New York, N.Y.*,

> My Lydian Concept has changed my whole mode of life. It took years, but I now feel that I function logically. At least, I'm organized and ready. I realize that music, like life, must have an inner logic. George Endrey, a scientist friend

of mine, taught me how mathematics relates to life and music. Without him, I would never have understood logic for what it is.[41]

The reference to George Endrey is important. It was Endrey who wrote the "Historical Perspective" section of the Concept, which appeared in the first and second editions of the work.[42] Russell also acknowledged a debt to "the Gil Evans composer enclave of 1949–50," Gil, John Lewis, John Carisi, and Gerry Mulligan—and to classical composers Alban Berg, Bela Bartok, Igor Stravinsky, and Stefan Wolpe. These composers, he noted, "helped shape my thinking," and, admitting that his output between 1947 and "Cubano Be, Cubano Bop" and the completion of the Lydian Concept was slim, he told Korall, "I felt I had to finish my thesis before I could say what I wanted to."[43]

On *New York, N.Y.* Russell used three standards—Rodgers and Hart's "Manhattan" and Vernon Duke's lovely "Autumn in New York" in a medley with Lane and Freed's "How About You"—alongside a number of original tunes. However, even the three standards become extended and transformed in the composer's hands. As for the band, for all three sessions between September 1958 and March 1959, it was made up of some of New York's finest—Max Roach on drums; Doc Severinsen and Ernie Royal on trumpets; John Coltrane, Phil Woods, and Benny Golson on saxes; and Bob Brookmeyer on valve trombone, alongside Bill Evans, Art Farmer, Barry Galbraith, Hal McKusick, and Milt Hinton from the *Jazz Workshop* dates.

Even more significant—and controversial—was Russell's decision to use a poem specially composed by singer Jon Hendricks to frame each of the tunes. Hendricks recalls Russell approaching him in the Turf Bar, which was part of the Brill Building and a gathering point for songwriters, both aspiring and already successful. Though unfamiliar with Russell's music, the singer was immediately taken with Russell's manners and respectful attitude, unusual in his experience among jazz musicians working New York. Russell was quite clear regarding what he wanted for the album, and Hendricks was hooked when he heard who was to be on the record.

> To get to the point, he asked me, "I hear you write lyrics?" I said, "Yes, I do." He said, "Do you also write poetry?" I said, "Well, lyrics are poetry. So, yes, I do write poetry." He said, "Because I'm working on a project called *New York, N.Y.* and I've assembled a dream band." None of them were that famous but everybody in the jazz world knew them. They were famous in the jazz world. And when he named me the band, I said, "Whoa! What would you want me to do on something with those guys?" He said, "The album is going to be called *New York, N.Y.* So I want a poem running through it that tells verbally about New York, that complements the music. Could you do that?" I said, "Sure."[44]

Hendricks attended the sessions but cut his contribution later.

> When George got through with the album he made me a tape of the entire
> album and he told me he wanted an intro for each segment. So that's where I
> got the feel of the album from, because Max breaks it up with brushes. *(imitates
> sound of Roach drumming)* I just put words to that. "Think you can lick it, get
> to the wicket, buy you a ticket"—boom! I kept repeating that from time to
> time, and that gave me the theme for it. Then for each segment I conformed
> to the musical flow. If it was slow and languid I wrote a slow and languid lyric
> about the East Side. I called it—"The East Side, the beauty and the beast side."
> *(laughs)* It was one of the finest things I've ever written and it was all inspired
> by the music and the musicians.[45]

Apparently, Milt Gabler tried to censor Hendricks's line about the
NYPD—"New York's finest/The finest money can buy"—but that and his
comment on the city's "cabaret card restriction" were allowed to stand. Russell himself felt the remarks to be entirely justified, and, as Hendricks says,
"Besides, when you make people laugh you can say things you couldn't if you
were serious."[46]

Not everyone appreciated Hendricks's words. Writing in the *Jazz Review*,
Max Harrison—British critic and Russell advocate from early on—described
the spoken commentary as "superfluous and, with repeated hearing, annoying," and found the album as a whole disappointing—"Only [Russell's own]
Big City Blues is really worthy of him, and it would be unfortunate if people
heard this record and thought it represented the best of his powers."[47] By
contrast, *Cash Box* chose *New York, N.Y.* as one of its "Jazz Picks of the
Week" and called Hendricks's narration "the hippest" and the album "one
of the most explosive jazz sets in a long while." While the *New Yorker*, using words like "pretentious" and phrases such as "precooked, frozen jazz,"
agreed with Harrison's verdict, *Down Beat* awarded the record five stars, and
a French committee presided over by Jean Cocteau gave it the prestigious
Oscar du Disque de Jazz.[48]

In *Down Beat*, reviewing it as a Jon Hendricks/George Russell disc, critic
Ralph Gleason called it "the most important album Decca has made in a
decade." "The music," Gleason noted, "is excellent, a triumph of indigenous
feeling and a concept that is bold, intuitive and soft with love all at once."
He continued, "This is music for a real life, contemporary musical cultural
expression," and, noting that music without narration and vice versa would
make the record "incomplete," he spent the rest of the review extolling
Hendricks's virtues.[49]

Decca ran an excellent and upbeat advertising campaign in the trades.

George Russell's *New York, N.Y.* is today and a little of tomorrow, drawn with rare craftsmanship and originality. It is a showcase for such major jazz soloists as Art Farmer, Bob Brookmeyer, John Coltrane, Bill Evans, Benny Golson and Max Roach; the probing wit and intelligence of Jon Hendricks; and a large star-filled jazz orchestra. This album will not soon be forgotten.[50]

In reality, *New York, N.Y.* is one of the most accessible of Russell's records and perhaps also one of his most atypical. In one sense, it is more famous for an incident that occurred during the September date than for the music itself.

That session only produced one piece—Rodgers and Hart's "Manhattan"—and was interrupted by John Coltrane. When the band reached the place for Trane's solo, he floundered and called for a break, taking his part over to a corner of the studio, studying it intently. The rest of the band, several of them with gigs or other dates to go on to, and the producer became angry, and accusations began to fly around the room that the tenor player could not read the chord changes.

Russell has written about the episode in his book[51] and in the sleeve notes for the CD reissue of *New York, N.Y.* However, in an interview for this book, he gave a concise but elaborated account of the event.

It was in that period Coltrane was melodicizing each chord to the nth degree. I had a beautiful song, "Manhattan." I had already worked with the chords in a way that I thought Coltrane had enough to work on, but he probably wanted to take every opportunity to bring the chord of the moment out. His brain was tied to the chord of the moment and it was a little too much because when he was in the studio he hadn't seen the music. So he goes over into a corner [and] probably cost a couple of thousand dollars in New York musicians' time. Bob Brookmeyer said, "I heard about him, but this guy doesn't even know his chords." That wasn't the case; he wanted to know how to . . . he wanted to apply his way of projecting that chord. That involved a lot of notes. That took time.[52]

Brookmeyer acknowledges that he was angry at the time.

Coltrane was there because we had to wait about half an hour while he learned the chords to "Manhattan." *(laughs)* Well, George and I were standing in the corner and he'd written some altered chords for "Manhattan." And John wanted to know really how the chords worked. He didn't want to just play on the top and get by. So he and Bill were over on the stage playing and playing and George and I were going, "Oh, man! That's been about a half an hour already." So, Coltrane was right. He wasn't being practical but he was being musical.[53]

It is worth thinking for a moment about Russell's influence on Coltrane, Miles Davis, and others who spearheaded the modal period of modern jazz. We might, of course, infer this from comments by the musicians themselves. However, generally jazz musicians do not think in those terms, certainly not those of the generation of Davis, Coltrane, and Russell. As the composer has noted, everyone learned from everyone else. In such a milieu, it is hard to trace an exact lineage between an idea and its subsequent appearance in other places, often transformed by other inputs. What is clear is that Russell was a significant figure in this world, one noted for his new and interesting ideas. Conversations and discussions obviously did take place. What is more important is the timing of various events. "Cubano Be, Cubano Bop" came out in 1947, and other recordings, such as Lee Konitz's version of "Ezz-Thetic," followed. And even though unreleased, Buddy DeFranco's take on "A Bird in Igor's Yard" was played regularly on Symphony Sid's show. *Jazz Workshop*, Russell's own album of modal kazz, and the music he wrote and arranged for Hal McKusick was also out there by 1957. "Milestones" was recorded in April 1958, the sessions for *Kind of Blue* began in March 1959, and Coltrane began recording his *Giant Steps* album in April 1959. In jazz as in life, timing is everything.

One more thing might be added with regard to Russell's "influence" on Coltrane. In an article for the French *Jazz* magazine, Benoit Quersin asked Coltrane how he liked Russell's music. Coltrane's reply is instructive.

> He has some good music. He has what is the type of music that seems to be coming to the fore nowadays. I've heard a few records of his, one that Eric Dolphy was on, that I heard, that I—several things on there I like very well. And he [Russell] understands quite a few of the problems that musicians are running across today and he's probably going to do a great deal to contribute to solving of such things.[54]

Coltrane's familiarity with Russell's ideas is also illustrated in Lewis Porter's article "The Atlantic Years." Referring to an article written by Coltrane in 1958—"Coltrane on Coltrane"—Porter notes the saxophonist's comments on Davis's new modal approach. The sentence he draws attention to reads: "He used tunes with free-flowing lines and chordal direction. This approach allowed the soloist the choice of playing chordally (vertically) or melodically (horizontally)." Porter's point is that Coltrane is using terminology taken from Russell's manner of describing this distinction. He adds, "(The words in parentheses reflect Coltrane's having been exposed to the music and terminology of jazz composer George Russell)."[55]

In terms of Miles Davis himself, three authorities cite Russell's influence on the trumpeter during this period. Ian Carr notes that the composer and Davis had "spent some time together, and Russell's great theoretical (and profoundly) practical work *The Lydian Chromatic Concept of Tonal Organization* had, among other things, examined the scales appropriate to certain chords. The translation of chords into scales paved the way for this later modal thinking."[56] Ashley Kahn quotes Davis discussing scalar approaches in an important 1958 *Jazz Review* article by Nat Hentoff. Of particular relevance here is: "And look at George Russell. His writing is mostly scales. After all, you can feel the changes."[57] Finally, Eric Nisenson, discussing the track "Milestones" in his biography of the trumpeter *Round about Midnight—A Portrait of Miles Davis*, writes, "The simple melody was an experiment inspired by an evening Miles had spent with the jazz composer and arranger George Russell, who at the time was working on his theoretical 'Lydian Concept of Tonal Organization.'" He adds, "Miles was fascinated by Russell's approach. Here was a means of breaking free from tonal clichés—while maintaining some amount of restraint."[58]

There is always a slight problem with proof via reference to "higher" authority. However, it is fair to note that Russell's impact on Davis is broadly accepted, and once again the issue of timing, and in particular the timing of Russell's own recordings and compositions, is perhaps the key factor here.

New York, N.Y. is certainly less striking and challenging than *Jazz Workshop*. The introduction to "Manhattan-Rico," which features drummer Don Lamond, Al Epstein on bongos, and Russell on chromatic drums, even echoes the mightier "Fellow Delegates" from *Jazz Workshop*. Max Harrison is right to assert that Russell does less than he might have done with the three standards. With the exception of "Big City Blues," there is little sense that Russell is pushing himself. Significantly, it seems that "Dimensions," from the far more radical *Jazz in the Space Age*, was written at or around the same time that Russell was working on *New York, N.Y.* On balance, it is a good but not great album. The playing from all involved is fine, and although the tenorist was apparently unhappy with his contribution, both Coltrane and Bill Evans provide some remarkable solos. Another plus focuses on the use of Jon Hendricks's narration. Here Russell is in advance of later developments in black music, such as rap and hip-hop.

New York, N.Y. is a good place for a newcomer to Russell to begin. *Jazz in the Space Age* is, however, something else again—perhaps the first genuinely "modern" big band album. To use the language of the advert for *New York, N.Y.*, it is a little of today and a whole lot of tomorrow.

Unusually for the time, in jazz at least, Russell produced music that featured two pianos as its main soloists. Russell notes that Milt Gabler initiated the recording—as he had *New York, N.Y.*—and the idea was to do something that anticipated the new decade. "Milt was behind that too. I think that followed *New York, N.Y.* It was reaching for the space age."[59]

If *New York, N.Y.* gives up its gifts too easily, *Jazz in the Space Age* requires and rewards repeated listening. Much has been made of Russell's use of two pianists—Bill Evans and Paul Bley—with their contrasting approaches, on four of the six tracks. Both play with a combination of courage and confidence, as Russell leads them into what is for both, though for different reasons, unfamiliar territory. Bley had been developing his own approach over the years that allowed him considerable freedom rhythmically, melodically, and harmonically, so the panchromatic and rhythmic elements of Russell's music were, in principle, comparatively straightforward. The writing, however, with its long and complex passages that were through-composed, drew the young Canadian into less familiar areas of form and structure. In Evans's case, Russell was again pushing him in the direction of abstraction and free playing that was outside his favored mode of operation. Needless to say, Evans had little or no problem in meeting Russell's demands.

Of at least as much significance in the longer term—for Russell's music and for jazz in general—were the ideas and devices the composer was deploying, which would be developed and extended in his later work. First, one can hear that this is definitely the same man who wrote "Cubano Be, Cubano Bop," "*All About Rosie*," "Similau," "Livingstone I Presume," and "The Day John Brown Was Hanged." Second, with repeated listening, one realizes that the writing has also reached a whole new level. The quality of the through-composed sections is *sans pareil* in jazz, but they retain all the spontaneity and intensity of improvisation. The use of solo voices is highly selective, with Dave Young on tenor getting much of the remaining space after Evans and Bley. Both the use of through-composition and the selective deployment of soloists would continue to be strong features in Russell's works such as *Othello Ballet*, *The African Game*, and *Living Time*. Finally, and perhaps most significant of all, *Jazz in the Space Age* sounds "modern" in the fullest sense. It belongs in a whole new universe or category. It does not sound like Duke Ellington or Fletcher Henderson or Claude Thornhill or even Gil Evans. It is jazz that is orchestral in the fullest sense of the term, with its resources organized less like a symphony orchestra and more like a large chamber ensemble. It is here, perhaps, that the influence of Stefan Wolpe is at its strongest.

Six tracks make up the suite. Three are titled "Chromatic Universe"—parts 1, 2, 3. These are separated by three other pieces—"Dimensions," "The Lydiot," and "Waltz from Outer Space"—this being at Russell's request, as he felt it would provide for greater variety.[60] In practice, each piece glides into the next, creating a long suite of performances. The contrasting ideas of Evans and Bley are used to powerful effect, and these then contrast magnificently with the wide harmonic and rhythmic variations of the orchestra—less a symphony perhaps and more a double concerto.

The title certainly raised eyebrows in some quarters. Nat Hentoff in *Jazz Today* put it down to "someone in the advertising department."[61] Drummer Joe Hunt, interviewed in 2004, still felt that titles like this might have put some musicians and fans off.

I mean, *The Stratus Seekers* and this idea of . . . back then, it was like even before they'd gone to the moon, you know, and this idea of space-age jazz—*Jazz in the Space Age*. I think those kind[s] of titles and things put some people off because, on the one hand, it meant that we were stretching the limits and going to the edge and pushing ourselves as musicians, but I think for the average listener it sort of put them off. Even some other musicians didn't like us because of this "space music" they'd call it, and it kind of had a bad reputation among some of the musicians. Some of the really good beboppers, they didn't like George and they still don't like Ornette or George. I mean these are like really great players too, who—I won't name names—but some of them are my colleagues and people I've played gigs with. You mention Ornette Coleman and they'll put him down. Of course, I think Ornette's a genius. So what can you do, but I also admire these guys, but they were very opinionated and I think the "space" thing, that title was detrimental in hindsight maybe. It was pretty catchy at the time, I guess. It probably got some of the curiosity seekers into the club to hear "space jazz" to see what it was like. *(laughs)*[62]

However, Hentoff was impressed, as ever, with Russell's music. "In contrast to the arranging clichés of nearly all contemporary jazz big band writing (Duke Ellington excepted), Russell's scores are considerably more variegated and surprising. Moreover, he continually pushes his soloists into stretching their imagination beyond the familiar signposts of much jazz improvisation."[63]

Russell recalls that he was quite clear about his goals with *Jazz in the Space Age*, and they were quite different from those for *New York, N.Y.* "I wanted to do a new thing, something that would make one think of the approaching era and how things might feel in that particular space-time condition and give a hint of where the music was going."[64] And to Burt Korall, Russell noted,

Jazz is changing; the 60's could well be a crucial decade. One thing is certain. A variety of sounds and rhythms, many of which are alien to what audiences are used to, will find their way into jazz. Unaccountably, things we hear around us every day, very human things, have either disappeared or been left out of jazz as we know it. Progress is inevitable. Today's musical palette is just not adequate. ALL feelings relative to life and beauty cannot be validly expressed with techniques now in vogue. What is more, Jazz is an evolving art; it is not meant to be restricted. The very nature of the music and its history indicate this.[65]

This was a statement of both principle and intent. More than any of his previous works to date, *Jazz in the Space Age* exemplifies the application of his Lydian theory in practice. It is also a prophetic statement in its anticipation of immediate and future opposition to new developments in jazz. Russell's position has always remained unaltered in this regard: He has consistently opposed any attempts to confine the music or turn it into a standardized repertoire or museum piece.

It is interesting to reprogram the tracks and play "Chromatic Universe"— parts 1–3 as one continuous suite. In fact, the rest of the orchestra enters only briefly on two occasions in part 2. For the rest, only Evans, Bley, bassist Milt Hinton, and drummer Don Lamond are heard. On part 1, Evans and Bley improvise freely around and against the tonality and 5/2 rhythm provided by the bass and drums. Part 2 opens with a free improvisation from the two pianists, with the remaining two and a half minutes being entirely scored. Part 3 is all freely improvised against a pattern and rhythm similar to that on part 1.

Interviewed by Burt Korall for the sleeve notes at the time, Russell described part 2 as "probably my most ambitious piece of music yet." His comments on part 1, which would also apply to part 3, are particularly illuminating in terms of his ideas and approach.

Bill and Paul were free to come close to the tonality—sum total of the bass notes—relate to the 5/2 gravitational pull or not. Tonality and rhythmically out in space, they were not victim to the tyranny of the chord or a particular meter. In essence, this is musical relativism. Everything can be right. The idea takes over. They worked in the realm of ideas, projecting one upon the other. This is panchromatic improvisation.[66]

Russell appears to be taking the notion of gravity in music as a scientific fact and not just as a metaphor. This point will be explored in detail later. With regard to his comments on "musical relativism," his concern is not with the imposition of a rigid system but rather with how the musician or musicians relate to the music they are playing. This notion underpins Russell's

Lydian Concept, and indeed it is in the actual practice of musicians in relating to chords, scales, melodies, harmonies, rhythms, and so on that the Concept has its origins.

Russell remembers an initial problem with Paul Bley's playing of part 2. "I was mad at Paul because he hadn't studied it. I'd written out a whole huge part of that piece for the two pianos to play, the two pianos [part], he hadn't studied it at all. I was really mad. I said, 'Go home and don't come back until you . . .'"[67]

Unsurprisingly, Bley's recollection is different.

> When George invited me to do the date he said, "I've got a lot of music. I want you to take the music home, learn it and come back in thirty days and play it for me. If you make one mistake you don't get the gig." There were pages and pages and pages of orchestral music. Not solo parts, these were extra things. Also, some of the duets that Bill and I were to play were all written out. So, like a monk I went into a room and I said to Carla, "Just put a tray under my door for the next thirty days. That's it. No phone calls, I don't want to see you, I don't expect anything." That was it. I *became* that written music *because* I wanted that date. You couldn't have made me make a mistake if you had sat on my lap or smacked me in the head. So, I went to George's house and I played the damn thing perfectly. He said, "You've got the date."[68]

According to Bley, he was not fazed by the prospect of playing with Evans, despite the pianist's reputation and involvement with Davis and Russell. After all, Bley had played with Ornette Coleman and was himself familiar with modal approaches to jazz. What bothered him was how to relate to his opposite number. Should he meet him halfway, adapt himself to Evans's style? "He was a sweet guy and a good friend. I said, 'Fuck him! Everybody loves him; he already owns 99.9% of the music piano business. I'm going to throw the kitchen sink at him from the get go."[69]

> So, I threw the kitchen sink at him and then I thought I heard what was an echo in the room because the same mode, feeling comes back at me in his phrase. I thought, "Well, it must be a lucky phrase on his part. This next one he definitely won't get. . . ." He was so "on it," he played my stuff better than I played my stuff and I got mad. It's one thing to have someone play as well as you but he played my stuff better than me! Well, George was ecstatic after the first take with the rhythm section. He said, "No-one has ever played my music like this before!"[70]

Bley and Evans also perform on "The Lydiot," this time with a full bigband arrangement, from the session recorded in May 1960. Here Russell uses the orchestra almost as a Greek chorus, warning and commenting on the solo action from Evans and Bley, who swap choruses throughout the first five minutes. Two contrasting trombone solos follow from Frank Rehak and then Dave Baker, with Baker's J. J. Johnson–influenced double-tonguing trumping Rehak's more conventional approach. Al Kiger follows with a fast series of trumpet choruses before Dave Young on tenor enters. Within a few notes, the listener realizes that he is hearing something special. There is something of Coltrane in there, what one critic called Coltrane's "sheets of sound," but any such influences are highly personalized in the maturity of Young's delivery, timing, and warm sound. Again, the piece reiterates many of the musical ideas used in "Chromatic Universe."

"Dimensions" and "Waltz from Outer Space" were recorded on August 1, 1960, without Bley and with Bob Brookmeyer on trombone and Hal McKusick on alto added to the ensemble, along with a few other changes, most notably Charlie Persip, one of the drummers from the New York, N.Y. album dates. In some ways, these two pieces are the meat and drink of Jazz in the Space Age: Beautifully crafted arrangements, complex but accessible, and the solos emerge naturally out of the ensembles with Young, Kiger, and Baker complementing Evans's wonderful playing. In fact, Evans brings to Jazz in the Space Age some of his best and most adventurous performances. But despite the availability of seasoned musicians like Rehak, Brookmeyer, McKusick, and Ernie Royal, Russell gives second billing—after Evans—to the trio from Indiana. For these young men, it was their first real experience in a recording studio, and they play with all the technique of the veteran and the fire and enthusiasm of the understudy seizing their moment. Dave Young is particularly astonishing.

Asked in an interview if he found the music difficult, Young replied, "Well, I guess for an accomplished musician it wouldn't be, but for me it was. (laughing) It was a good experience. I was around twenty-three and there I was with all these experienced New York session guys. There I was, I couldn't run and I couldn't hide, but I had to go on and face it. It was awe inspiring—all those musicians and how sharp they were."[71]

As to Bill Evans's view of the experience, the pianist was interviewed by Dan Morgenstern a few years later and talked about how different this was from his usual approach.

The only way I can work is to have some kind of restraint involved—the challenge of a certain craft or form—and then find the freedom in that. . . . I have allowed myself the other kind of freedom occasionally. Paul Bley and I did a two-piano improvisation on a George Russell record that was completely unpremeditated. It was fun to do but there was no direction involved. To do something that hadn't been rehearsed successfully, just like that, almost shows the lack of challenge involved in that type of freedom.[72]

Keith Shadwick, from whose biography of Evans this quote is taken, comments that Evans was being slightly disingenuous, noting that Russell was engaged in "a controlled experiment, not a formless, open-ended free-for-all." Shadwick's point is well made and distinguishes Russell's approach from others in the jazz avant garde. For Russell, free improvisation or freedom in music is a means to express a musical idea, not an end in itself, just as atonality has a musical function but can become wearisome if that is all that a composer has to offer.[73]

Jazz in the Space Age was the last recording Evans made with Russell until 1972, when Evans invited Russell to write and arrange a big-band album for him and his new label, Columbia.[74] Evans is forever associated with Miles Davis because of his contribution to *Kind of Blue*. Yet even here Russell had played a part, suggesting to Davis that he offer Evans a job.

I was with Miles and he said, "George. you know of a piano player?" He was at the height . . . one of his heights . . . he said, "Red [Garland] and the junkies in the band are fucking up." I said, "Yeah, I know a piano player who could really take the place of anybody." He said, "Is he white?" I said, "Yeah, he's white but he can play, you know. He wears glasses." He said, "He wears glasses? I know that muthafucker!" (*laughing*) So he says, "Bring him over to Brooklyn. We're playing a club." He told me the name of the club and I told Bill, and Bill, Barry Galbraith and I, in a little German car—a VW Beetle—we take off for Brooklyn. Big town, confusing town driving, but we did get to the nightclub and the band was Coltrane, Miles, Philly Joe Jones, Paul Chambers—all heavy on junk. In fact, that was what was worrying Miles was what irritated him. And during the intermission or something he asked Red to get up and let Bill play and that was it. Miles said, "You're going to Philadelphia with us on Saturday." That was it. It happened that way and I read books on that and they didn't get it right at all. Books that deal with history and what's happening. That's the way that Miles and Bill struck it up.[75]

Evans's period with Miles was quite short but it added the final luster upon his developing reputation and made him one of jazz's more bankable stars. In reality, throughout the fifties Evans's career was assisted by Russell's use of the young man on a number of records and performances. He played Russell's compositions and arrangements with Lucy Reed, Hal McKusick, and Helen Merrill, as well as playing on *Jazz Workshop, All About Rosie, New*

York, N.Y., and *Jazz in the Space Age*. Yet Evans never studied with Russell. Nor did he ever read *The Lydian Chromatic Concept of Tonal Organization*. However, Evans was an extraordinarily open-minded musician familiar with many styles of jazz piano and with classical music. He was already engaged in his own harmonic explorations by the time he met Russell.

Jack Reilly's comments are particularly perceptive with regard to the nature of the creative partnership between Russell and Evans: "I think Bill was so knowledgeable, and he had worked out his own horizontal approach and he came from the history of jazz piano music, that he fitted George's music like a glove and elevated it to a higher level, I think, and made it something very special."[76]

There was certainly a meeting of minds between Russell and Evans, and they kept in touch over the years, with Evans often sending postcards to Russell signed "Liberace." Evans probably did more than any other musician in the period, after Davis and Coltrane, in bringing Russell's ideas to a wider public. But this was not as a proselytizer on Russell's behalf but by virtue of his interpretation of Russell's work on those fifties recordings and by his essential role in the *Kind of Blue* sextet. Had it not been for the latter, Evans probably would not have been saxophonist Oliver Nelson's piano choice for another highly influential modal jazz album, *Blues and the Abstract Truth*.[77]

One further—and valuable—comment on Russell's relationship with and influence on Evans is found in Shadwick's biography of the pianist. Referring to Evans's arrangement of Richard Carpenter's "Walkin'" for Tony Scott's *The Complete Tony Scott*, Shadwick notes,

> In conception and method, Evans' work on "Walkin'" is strongly reminiscent of George Russell's thematic dissections and linear writing. Initially stressing the blues element of the melody's intervals, he quickly begins weaving counterpoint lines between band sections and intensifying the mood of the music by modulations and such typically Russell methods as contrary movement and imitation, even as accompaniment to the brief solos. A busy three minutes of music![78]

As Reilly again comments, "Just hearing the music, I think they all fed each other. It was a wonderful creative period of discovering things. They just wanted to contribute to each other."[79]

Metronome gave *Jazz in the Space Age* a rating of 10 and described it as "[f]ar-out funkiness that is a must for lovers of music." The reviewer focused on the music's internal coherence and cohesion, noting, "In this album, George Russell has presented an integrated product of genius" and calling

Russell "a modern jazz giant." *Down Beat* gave it four and a half stars, feeling that the record showed Russell's potential but that the composer had yet to come "to full bloom." The article, which also reviewed *George Russell Sextet at the Five Spot*, is extremely perceptive in its examination of Russell's skills and working methods. First, it notes Russell's analytical approach, his "thinking" about the music he is making, and the creation of a form that retains its links with the past but to which the composer has added new levels of rhythmic complexity, chromaticism, and unusual choices of notes and intervals. Second, and more important for the listener, is Russell's capacity to create "a musical atmosphere so pervading that most of the players he selects—and on these records he selects carefully and wisely—subordinate their own musical personalities to his." It is ironic to note here that Russell has throughout his career sought out musicians with their own distinctive sound, and yet the comment remains valid. Their sound becomes enveloped within Russell's musical world to the extent that their sound is given new depth and meaning in his sonic universe.[80]

In the October 26, 1961, issue of *Down Beat*, pianist-conductor André Previn was the magazine's guest for its "Blindfold Test," and one of the pieces he reviewed was "Waltz from Outer Space."

> Is that George Russell? I have heard better things by him but over-all he is by far the most interesting of all the guys attempting this kind of writing. I found this fascinating. It's controlled and organized and it really has something new to say within the realm of jazz. I have never studied that modal conception of his . . . that again is a label I don't think it needs. Contrary to the others you have played, here you don't have to have anything explained or pointed out. This is an attractive piece, very well played and orchestrated. I have never had the pleasure of meeting George Russell but I admire him greatly. Five stars.[81]

Perhaps the crucial promise *Jazz in the Space Age* foretold was that in Russell's hands, jazz was being reforged and, perhaps for the first time, pace Ellington, was becoming a music with a wholly new place within it for the composer-arranger. It also secured, for better or ill, Russell's position as figure of the emerging avant garde.

Whether other choices could have led to Russell's crossing over into broader areas of popular taste seems highly unlikely. Given the filmic quality of Russell's writing, one possibility might have been that of composition for film and TV. In interview with Ben Young, Russell remarked upon an offer from Milt Gabler to help him get into film and TV work. It was certainly something Russell fantasized about. He told Young how he had hoped one day to get a call from Cecil B. DeMille and how he had learned that director Robert Wise had used his piece 'Jack's Blues' to explain to composer Johnny Mandel what he was looking for from the soundtrack to the film *I Want To Live!* by way of mood. However, when the chance came to consider working "on the lot," Russell turned it down.

> I had an opportunity to deal with it because when Milt Gabler had hired me to do the *New York, N.Y.* album and he liked it, after it was finished he said, "George you know I can get you a job on the lot if you want but you gotta do all kinds of music." I said, "Thanks, Milt. I don't think it's for me." So I could have done it and probably wanted to be asked at least once to do it. Fortunately, I didn't become a career Hollywood person. It wouldn't have lasted.[82]

Notes

1. Interview with Juanita Giuffre, June 2004.
2. Interview with George Russell, October 2003.
3. Interview with Jack Reilly, October 2003.
4. Interview with G. Russell, October 2003.
5. See M. Hinton and D. Berger, *Bass Line: The Stories and Photographs of Milt Hinton* (Philadelphia: Temple University Press, 1988).
6. Ian Carr, interview with Art Farmer for BBC Radio 3 Broadcast *George Russell—The Invisible Guru*, July 1994.
7. Ibid.
8. Interview with Paul Motian, June 2006.
9. E-mail to the author from Alice Russell, July 2005.
10. Nat Hentoff, Review of *The RCA Jazz Workshop—Hal McKusick* (RCA 1366), *Down Beat*, May 16, 1957; Paul Sampson, Review of *The RCA Jazz Workshop—Hal McKusick*, *Washington Post*, May 5, 1957; Fred Sherman, "McKusick Album Is Best Thing to Come out of Jazz Workshop," *Miami Herald*, June 23, 1957; C. H. Garrigues, Reviews of *The RCA Jazz Workshop—George Russell and His Smalltet* (RCA LPM1372) and *The RCA Jazz Workshop—Hal McKusick* (RCA LPM 1366), *San Francisco Examiner*, August 25, 1957.
11. Don L. McIver, "Hal McKusick's Performance Is Good, But—," *Fort Lauderdale Sunday News*, April 28, 1957. See also "Chords and Discords," *Down Beat*, June 26, 1958. A letter from one Larry Townsend took both the magazine and Russell to task for claims made on behalf of the Lydian Chromatic Concept. Its author questions its originality and in particular refers readers to the work of Joseph Schillinger. Russell replied in the same issue in typically feisty form without really stating the differences between his approach and Schillinger's.
12. Review of *The RCA Jazz Workshop—Hall McKusick*. *Metronome*, June 1957.

13. Bob Reisner, "Jazz Composition," *Village Voice*, July 10, 1957; Nat Hentoff, "The Jazz Mainstream," *Saturday Review*, June 29, 1957; Review of *The RCA Jazz Workshop—George Russell and His Smalltet* (RCA Victor LPM1372), *Jazz Today*, September 1957. See also "1199er Wins Acclaim as Jazz Composer," *RWDSU Record*, September 15, 1957; "Drummer to Composer," *Cincinnati Post*, July 13, 1957; "Adventuring with George Russell," *Jazz Today*, June 1957. The *RWDSU* article features a marvelous photo of Russell handing over a copy of *Jazz Workshop* to 1199 president Leon J. Davis. Russell never forgot who he was or where he came from. Davis was an important labor leader on the East Coast who built the organization into a progressive force in city and American politics.

14. Polly Cochran, "Workshop Creates Learned Jazz," *Indianapolis Star*, May 5, 1957.

15. Garrigues, Reviews; Feather, Review of *The RCA Jazz Workshop—George Russell and His Smalltet* (RCA Victor LPM1372), *Down Beat*, August 17, 1957.

16. Review of *The RCA Jazz Workshop—George Russell and His Smalltet* (RCA Victor LPM1372), *Cash Box*, June 15, 1957; *Billboard*, May 17, 1957; Review of *The RCA Jazz Workshop—George Russell and His Smalltet* (RCA Victor LPM1372), *Hi-Fi Low-Down*, October 1957; *Memphis Commercial Appeal*, July 21, 1957.

17. I. F. Stone, Oct 7th 1957. "The United States as Three Nations, Not One," in *The Best of I.F. Stone's Weekly*, ed. N. Middleton (Harmondsworth, UK: Penguin, 1973), p. 106. Not for nothing did Charles Mingus write and record his The Original Faubus Fables around that time. See Charles Mingus Presents Charles Mingus Candid 9005.

18. Ernest Green went on to obtain a master's degree and eventually to become an assistant secretary of labor in the Clinton administration. He became embroiled in the so-called Chinagate investigation and pleaded guilty to a matter of income tax evasion. See entry "Ernest Green" in Wikipedia.org, http://en.wikipedia.org/wiki/Ernest_Green.

19. "Six Works of Jazz Commissioned by Brandeis University," *Down Beat*, April 4, 1957.

20. Norman J. O'Conner, "Jazz at Brandeis—Some New Areas Are Opened for Jazz by the Work of a Noted Institute of Culture and Learning," *Down Beat*, July 25, 1957, p. 18.

21. Richard Katz, "Music Festival at Brandeis University," *Jazz Today*, August 1957.

22. *Music For Brass* Columbia CL941; *Modern Jazz Concert* Columbia WL127. Reissued in 1996 as single CD with All Set and On Green Mountain omitted as The Birth Of The Third Stream, Columbia 485103 2.

23. Nat Hentoff, "Jazz's Third Stream," *Down Beat*, May 29,1958; Ralph J. Gleason, "An Album That Couldn't Have Been Made at All Ten Years Ago," *San Francisco Chronicle*, July 13, 1958.

24. 1946 brochure Ed Hazell, *Berklee: The First Fifty Years* (Boston: Berklee Press, 1995). p.22

25. M. Fitzgerald, "The Lenox School of Jazz," JazzDiscography.com, November 1, 1993, www.jazzdiscography.com/Lenox/lenhome.htm. Quote in quotes from R. A. Niccoli, "Stearns Conducts Jazz Panel Series," *Down Beat*, September 7,1951, p. 18.

26. Interview with Gunther Schuller.

27. "Jazz School's First Session at Lenox," *Down Beat*, March 6, 1957. See also "The School of Jazz," *Down Beat*, October 3, 1957.

28. Interview with Gunther Schuller.

29. Ibid.

30. Ibid.

31. Interview with Ornette Coleman, July 2005.

32. Ibid.

33. Interview with G. Russell, October 2003.

34. Ben Young, broadcast devoted to George Russell in celebration of his seventy-fourth birthday, WKCR Radio, New York, June 23, 1997.

35. Ibid.

36. Interview with Mike Gibbs, June 2005.

37. Interview with Dave Baker, April 2004.

38. Ibid.

39. Dom Cerulli, "George Russell," *Down Beat*, May 29, 1958. For Russell's reviews, see the *Jazz Review*, November 1958, for the Jimmy Giuffre 3's Travelin' Light (Russell liked it); and the *Jazz Review*, June 1959, for Johnny Mandel's I Want To Live soundtrack for the film of the same name and Henry Mancini's Music from Peter Gunn. While he enthused about the Mandel score, Russell savaged the Mancini record. Russell's writing style is heavy and ponderous, yet he does bring in elements of social criticism into the review of Mandel in commenting on the subject matter of the film, i.e., capital punishment.

40. Notes to New York, N.Y. CD reissue Impulse IMP 12782.

41. Ibid.

42. George Russell, *The Lydian Chromatic Concept of Tonal Organization* (New York: Concept, 1959). As Russell explained to J. "Hepcat" O'Brien in *Panache* magazine 18, no. 5, Issue 5—"George was on the scene in the early days. I probably met him at Gil's. We were all fascinated with George and his venturesome mind; he had inner knowledge which drew people to him. I believe he emigrated from Hungary. He was the one who first got us up to Juilliard. George was into the Schillinger System of music. The great gift he imparted to me was to respect an alternative way of thinking about things, in going for the 'outer view.'"

43. Notes to *New York, N.Y.*

44. Interview with Jon Hendricks, April 2006.

45. Ibid.

46. Ibid.

47. Max Harrison, Reviews of *The RCA Jazz Workshop—George Russell and His Smalltet* (RCA LPM1372) and *George Russell—New York, N.Y.* (Decca DL9216), Jazz Review, November 1960, p. 30.

48. *Cash Box* (no date available); *Down Beat*, September 3, 1959; *New Yorker*, Autumn 1959 (no other information). Russell's Oscar was awarded on January 15, 1962.

49. *Down Beat*, September 3, 1959.

50. See *Down Beat*, August 20, 1959.

51. George Russell, *Lydian Chromatic Concept of Tonal Organization* (Brookline, MA: Concept, 2001), pp. 177–78.

52. Interview with G. Russell, October 2003.

53. Interview with Bob Brookmeyer, October 2003.

54. Benoit Quersin, "La Passe Dangereuse," in *John Coltrane Companion*, ed. C. Woideck (New York: Shirmer, 1998).

55. Lewis Porter, "The Atlantic Years" in *John Coltrane Companion*, ed. C. Woideck (New York: Shirmer, 1998).

56. Ian Carr, *Miles Davis—The Definitive Biography* (Hammersmith, UK: HarperCollins, 1999).

57. Ashley Kahn, *A Kind of Blue* (London: Granta, 2000).

58. Eric Nisenson, *Round about Midnight—A Portrait of Miles Davis* (New York: Da Capo, 1996).

59. Interview with G. Russell, October 2003.

60. Stan Britt, notes for Affinity reissue of *Jazz in the Space Age* (1986), AFF152; Burt Korall, original sleeve notes to *Jazz in the Space Age*, Decca DL-9219.

61. Hentoff, "Jazz's Third Stream," p. 10.

62. Interview with Joe Hunt, June 2004.

63. Hentoff, "Jazz's Third Stream," p. 10.

64. Interview with G. Russell, October 2003.

65. Korall, sleeve notes to *Jazz in the Space Age*.

66. Ibid.

67. Interview with G. Russell, October 2003.

68. N. Meehan, *Time Will Tell—Conversations with Paul Bley* (Berkeley, CA: Berkeley Hills Books, 2003), p. 63. Paul Bley repeated this story in an interview with the author for *Jazzwise* magazine on June 14, 2007.

69. Ibid, p. 64.

70. Ibid.

71. Interview with Dave Young, January 2007.

72. Dan Morgenstern, "The Art of Playing," *Down Beat*, October 22, 1964. Quoted in Keith Shadwick, *Bill Evans: Everything Happens to Me—A Musical Biography* (San Francisco: Backbeat, 2002), p. 84.

73. Shadwick, *Everything Happens to Me*.

74. There are rumors that Evans and Russell took part in a project, perhaps with Gunther Schuller as well, for Riverside featuring arrangements of jazz standards. According to Steve Swallow's recollections, other members of the George Russell sextet were involved, as well as pianist Jaki Byard. Gunther Schuller remembers something

of this ilk, but nothing was ever released and the current owners of the Riverside catalog can find no trace of any tapes that might be from the session.

75. Interview with G. Russell, October 2003. See also Hentoff, Nat, "An Afternoon with Miles Davis," *Jazz Review*, December 1958.

76. Interview with Reilly, October 2003. It is sometimes pointed out that Evans had recorded a modal piece, "Aeolian Drinking Song," with clarinetist Tony Scott prior to his work with Russell. In fact, he had already played on sessions with Hal McKusick performing Russell's compositions and with Russell himself by the time this was recorded. Tony Scott, *The Touch of Tony Scott*, RCA Victor LPM1353.

77. Oliver Nelson, *Blues and the Abstract Truth*.

78. Shadwick, *Everything Happens to Me*, p. 57.

79. Interview with Reilly, October 2003.

80. *Metronome*, 1961 (no other information available); Dom DeMichael, "Spotlight Review of Jazz in the Space Age (Decca9219) and George Russell Sextet at the Five Spot (Decca9220)," *Down Beat*, June 8, 1961.

81. "The Blindfold Test—André Previn," *Down Beat*, October 26, 1961.

82. Young, broadcast devoted to George Russell.

CHAPTER SEVEN

∽

You Are My Sunshine

George Russell could look back on the fifties with some satisfaction. He had completed his *Lydian Chromatic Concept of Tonal Organization* in 1953, and it had been reissued in amended form in 1959. Its publication was greeted by the *Jazz Review* in February 1960 with a full-page dissertation on the Lydian Concept by Russell's friend, composer John Benson Brooks.[1] In practice the 1959 issue was really the first commercially available edition. Russell's original Roneo copy had barely sold at all, but this was a fine-looking ring-bound manual complete with exercises for the student to explore.

No mainstream publisher had been interested in putting out the book, and Russell did not have the resources to issue it himself. However, around this time, guitarist Bucky Wheat joined the Kingston Trio and, like many of the younger musicians on the East Coast folk scene, his musical interests extended to blues and jazz. Wheat had met Russell and had heard about his Lydian Concept, and, knowing what Russell was looking for, a backer showed some of the material to Dave Guard, founder of the trio.

> Somehow through a friend I had met one of the people who was a part of the very successful folk band—it was the folk band of the day. Dave Guard was the guy that put the band together. He saw the book and he freaked out. Bucky [Wheat] had shown him—not the full copy because it wasn't quite finished. . . . So Bucky showed it to David from the Kingston Trio. He fell in love with the Concept. One day he came over with a check for $5,000.[2]

Tom Guard, David's son and also a successful guitarist, recalls how his father enthused over Russell's ideas.

149

I always thought that the book was a new thing in 1959 since Dad gave it the financial assistance. But, like most good things that are ahead of their time, I guess it needed a push. Dave "Buck" Wheat was a godsend for the Kingston Trio. His playing and knowledge really kept my father's composing and arranging at its best. It only figures that the Lydian Concept would be shared with Dad. Neither my mother or I really know the details of when or how Russell received the $5,000, but in my mind it wasn't just a contribution. Dad bought a good number of the books from George, knowing it was a truly good investment. Our family toted around a hundred or so copies of the book.[3]

In fact, Dave drew heavily on Russell's ideas in developing his own *Color Guitar* manual for teaching guitar students. "A lot came from the latter, which was about 90 percent influenced by the Lydian Concept." Tom also acknowledges Russell's influence on his father's writing and playing. "After studying with George, all of Dad's writing involved a whole lot of chords that only jazz guys care to learn. So there is no denying it. All those wheels were turning in his head and giving his songs a lot of verve. I look at later arrangements of his Kingston Trio songs and the moving lines are just incredible."[4]

But Dave Guard did more than adapt Russell's ideas; he even included in his book a complex diagram designed around the guitar fret board that paralleled the slide rule of scales Russell included in the 1959 edition of the book. Furthermore, in his approach he changed the standard tuning of the instrument so that the intervals were all in perfect fourths. As guitar players will know, in standard tuning the interval between the third and second strings is a major third. According to Tom Guard,

This allowed the student to move a chord or scale template across the field of notes and examine how various notes change within chords/scales. It also made it easy to learn the chord inversions. If the board were designed in standard tuning with the inconsistency, the movable template would not have functioned. *Color Guitar* was more basic than the Lydian Concept but I can guarantee the similarities I mentioned advanced my understanding of musical theory in a big way.[5]

Given Dave's place on the folk scene at that time and his later role as a guitar teacher, there is an argument to be made that Russell's ideas about modes as a way of relating chords and scales entered the arena of folk music as well as jazz. This may seem quite a leap to some readers, and yet ideas often cross disciplines in the sciences, social sciences, and philosophy without it being easy to trace their trajectory. New ideas spread through the arts in a similar way. Dave Guard provides an example of Russell's direct influence, and through him a source of influence on other musicians outside jazz. And many on the folk scene were interested in jazz. In his autobiography Bob Dylan refers to listening to and enjoying Russell's music, and players like Dave Van Ronk were well versed in jazz, ragtime, and blues. Modal ideas also entered the British folk music scene in the early sixties, in particular through the music of Davy Graham, who in turn influenced guitarists like Bert Jansch, John Renbourn, Paul Simon, and Roy Harper.[6]

It is also worth remembering that rock music in America saw a different process of development from that in Britain. In Britain it started with aspiring musicians who listened to R&B and rock and roll, and with players already associated with traditional and modern jazz, not least through the localized phenomenon of skiffle. In America it was heavily influenced by the famous "British Invasion" of groups such as the Beatles and the Rolling Stones but found favor in particular with musicians involved in folk music. The Grateful Dead, Jefferson Airplane, and the Byrds are excellent examples of this. It is no accident that American rock music often had a distinctively folk-modal flavor to it that was enhanced but not initiated by the increasing interest in Indian and Eastern music of the late sixties. It is perhaps not too great a leap to suggest that Russell's ideas might have had some influence, indirectly, at least.

In early 1960 Russell was able to take out a few advertisements in the trade papers:

Now available as a correspondence Course

GEORGE RUSSELL'S
LYDIAN CHROMATIC
CONCEPT FOR JAZZ
IMPROVISATION

"The first important theoretical innovation to come from jazz."—John Lewis, musical director of the Modern Jazz Quartet.

"Important for every serious jazz musician."—Art Farmer.
Taught at the School of Jazz, Lenox, Mass.

For information write to:

Concept Publishing Company
121 Bank Street, N.Y. 14, N.Y

At the beginning of the fifties, Russell had felt that his career had plateaued with the Carnegie Hall performance of "Cubano-Be, Cubano-Bop." However, by the end of the decade he had become an important figure in jazz. There was also a lot of goodwill toward him from musicians and others involved in the music. It was, after all, quite a small, even insular world, which might have extended up and down the East Coast, while the West Coast had its own scene and the hinterland remained largely unexplored and uncolonized by the new music.

At the same time, there was a lot of interaction across the arts in general in and around New York. Any individual with any pretensions to being remotely hip or cultured would be expected to know about jazz, literature, theatre, and art. And indeed, jazz musicians mixed with their peers in other fields. George and Juanita's apartment at 121 Bank Street saw its share of parties, as Bob Brookmeyer recalls.

> Socially we spent a great deal of time together. We had parties back and forth. One of the jobs at parties was trying to get Bill Evans out of a corner. He would seek the first available corner and stay there for the party. We would attend each other's concerts—be together a lot. I don't recall us talking a great deal about music because people in those days didn't talk a great deal about music, not in my group anyway. [But] Gil Evans was there, and John Benson Brooks. It was for those days one of the "in" parties. We had a group of very happy people who enjoyed each other a lot. They were, in my memory, very mellow occasions.[7]

Juanita also remembers the time with a lot of fondness.

> Oh god yes. We gave a couple. We didn't have a lot because he was really busy and I was working, and money was not all that, you know, but we did have parties. One of them was with Manny Albam and Barry Galbraith and I think Ray Nance was there, and Gerry Mulligan, Gil Evans and his wife were there. I mean, just stardom without our thinking about it as stardom. Cecil Taylor was at one of the parties, and so was . . . who was the author? Robert Graves was there and he followed me around all night long trying to figure out what nationality I was. Everywhere! He kept naming names and I kept saying, "No." Finally, he said, "Well, it's gotta be" and he looked at me and said, "I know what it is—Canton-Greek." (laughs) They used to be crazy parties, a lot of fun. I was trying to think who else used to be at those parties—Bobby Brookmeyer, Jim Hall, all those people we hung out with.[8]

At the same time, all was not well within Russell's marriage. Probably because of everything he had experienced in his childhood, youth, and young adulthood, Russell could seem distant and emotionally reserved. Although Juanita clearly understood why he was like that, it sometimes left her feeling, as she puts it, "I needed more."

She acknowledges that Russell could be hard to get close to "sometimes, but at other times he was extremely open and vulnerable. Let's put it this way. The preoccupation with music theory and the music business and what he had to accomplish kind of was a dominating factor."

She even tolerated his indiscretions, as she explains: "It's not something that you say, 'Well, I'm going to go out and I'm gonna . . . .' Although there may have been instances when he might have been a little indiscreet, George. I mean to him it was just nothing. *(laughs)* So I had no problems with pursuing my own happiness."[9]

The event that led to the marriage breakup was that Juanita met saxophonist Jimmy Giuffre. Their paths first crossed at the sessions for *New York, N.Y.*, which Giuffre attended, but it was at the Lenox School of Jazz that their relationship blossomed. While he was angry and felt hurt at the time, Russell remained good friends with Juanita and Jimmy. "Yeah, that puts a new light on it because I can see back where it happened. It came out of the School of Jazz and she and Jimmy Giuffre got along real well, and it really was not a disaster kind of thing. And as I say, we're very close today, closer to people than back then."[10]

For her part, Juanita found in Giuffre someone she could more easily relate to and feel closer to. "When I finally met someone, you know, the two of us were really mutual, because it's hard to read George sometimes in terms of his feelings of affection. Even though he might show them here and there, he just has a certain reserved quality in that regard. Nothing bad about it. It's just what the person is." She adds, "I think there was more anger than sadness about it on his part."[11]

The only really awkward moment either George or Juanita can recall occurred when Russell appeared at the Five Spot opposite Giuffre's group. As Russell told Ian Carr, "He and Juanita were then going together, you know. That was . . . *(pause)* . . . a little sparky there, you know? *(laughing)*"[12]

Russell's decision to form a working group came at the turn of the decade. He had shown no real interest up to that point in playing live or leading a band and by his account, his reasons for doing so were largely pragmatic. As he put it, it was simply "[t]o stay alive and play music. But my main interest was in writing music, not playing it."[13]

Exactly how the idea originated is unclear. In fact, it is not a question Burt Korall found necessary to ask in a February 1961 piece for *Down Beat*. The sense that the article does convey is that it was time, as its closing quote from Gil Evans makes clear:

> George is finally out there, playing fine piano, writing for immediate situations, living in music every day. Now he can relax a bit more and make contact and more important be as diversified as he wants. Recognition . . . it has to happen for him and probably will before you know it. I don't see anything but better and better things for him. He's on the threshold.[14]

Russell has attributed the original suggestion that he form his own group to Riverside Records boss Orrin Keepnews, but has on other occasions said that it was he who approached Keepnews with the idea for a record with the musicians he had played with at Lenox.

> They were all very, very talented. It was Orrin Keepnews that suggested that I make a . . . that I should record. I think Orrin came to the School of Jazz as many people did. They came up just for the day. It was a very relaxed environment. A nightclub on campus, wonderful food, beautiful weather in that open natural environment, it was conducive to people fraternizing and socializing and having a good time. So out of that came a contract with Riverside. I never played piano in my life. So the first time I played piano was on the first date. I never really played piano.[15]

However, in an interview with Ben Young, Russell said,

> When I convinced Orrin Keepnews to record *Stratusphunk*, the first album with my personal group, I hadn't played piano before. But I did play the Concept. I played the Concept, I didn't play piano. So when you're hearing me accompany Eric Dolphy, that's the first time I ever played piano on a record at all. I never had really focused on playing piano, I just played it enough to put a composition together.[16]

Russell's recollections are out of sync; Dolphy plays on *Ezz-Thetics* from 1961, not on *Stratusphunk*. However, the actual recording sequence is quite confusing. The first album Russell made with his own sextet and with him on piano is *George Russell Sextet at the Five Spot*, which was recorded on September 20, 1960, for Decca. Orrin Keepnews then produced *Stratusphunk* for Riverside on October 18, just four weeks later. To add to the confusion, *George Russell Sextet in Kansas City*, Russell's fourth and final album for Decca, was cut on February 21, 1961, followed by *Ezz-Thetics* for Riverside on May 8, 1961. This was obviously a very concentrated period of activity for the sextet since its formation in the summer of 1960. The two final albums for Riverside—*The Stratus Seekers* and *The Outer View*—were both recorded in 1962.

Neither the *Five Spot* nor *Kansas City* dates were live; both were New York studio recordings. The reason for their titles seems to be an attempt on Decca's part to capitalize on the group's live performances at the Five Spot and in Kansas City. In terms of live work, the group debuted at the Museum of Modern Art on July 28, 1960,[17] prior to the first of two three-week engagements at the Five Spot, which came either side of the band's residency at Lenox as "group-in-residence." This was followed not long after by two weeks of dates in Kansas City. A brief residency at Birdland aside, that was pretty much it in terms of gigs for the sextet for the next twelve months. Drummer Joe Hunt remembers,

> Our work sort of trickled down. In the beginning, we had this wonderful job at the Five Spot. I guess all in all we must've played there about six weeks. We had a very good run. Toward the end—they changed bands anyway there, and toward the end, I think the business was falling off a little, and from then on we really didn't have much work in New York. We had a gig at Birdland, I think maybe that same year or maybe 1961. I remember we played at Birdland for a week. They didn't like us at Birdland. We even got some boos there.[18]

When the band first played the Five Spot, prior to their residency at Lenox, Ted Snyder was on bass, but after Lenox, Chuck Israels had joined the group. According to Hunt, Snyder had come with them from Indiana and "wasn't real crazy about being in New York," and Hunt had met Israels at Lenox. They had become friends and enjoyed playing together, which made Israels the obvious choice to replace the homesick Snyder.[19]

The Five Spot was quite a legendary New York club that had opened in the late fifties in a bar close to the Bowery. Tenorist Dave Young describes the venue: "The physical experience of it was like a local tavern, but it wasn't at all rowdy. People came in there to hear some music."[20] In fact, being close to the Village, it attracted a crowd drawn from the Apple's intelligentsia—musicians with a night off or coming down after their own gigs, artists like Willem DeKooning and Larry Rivers, journalists, and writers. Joe Hunt was amazed and horrified to see Max Roach, Ornette Coleman, Horace Silver, and Roy Haynes in the audience for opening night.

> Oh, it scared me man! *(laughs)* I was scared but we had to play. The other guys were . . . we were intimidated on the one hand but we realized we had rehearsed well and so we had to give it our best shot, so we did and we were

well received. The people liked us, you know. Ornette had already broken in the free music there.[21]

According to Hunt, the first time they played opposite Jimmy Giuffre. Money for the gig was not great, but, as he adds, it was just enough to live on.

Well, we played opposite Jimmy Giuffre's trio the first time. He had a really good trio with Jim Hall, Buell Neidlinger, and Billy Osborne a really good drummer. Most of the clubs in New York at that time had two bands. This might be interesting for you. I recollect that we made $89 a week. That was New York scale for a week's work, six nights a week. That comes down to less than $15 a night! In 1960 that would be pretty decent. You added it up and you could eat and live.[22]

Dave Young remembers Coltrane turning up one night.

On the first one that's when I met Trane. He came in with Eric Dolphy, who I had met at Slide Hampton's house. We had stayed at Slide's house the first few days there; in fact, it was when we were getting ready to do the *Jazz in the Space Age* album. Eric Dolphy brought John in. It was a very pleasant experience—he was so down-to-earth. I had admired him for a long time.[23]

George Hoefer in *Down Beat* was impressed by the group's performances of Russell's complex arrangements, noting that "[t]he playing of the Russell sextet narrows the gap between free-blowing jazz and written chamber jazz." Hoefer closed with the comment, "I believe that the Russell sextet will be a source of enjoyment and satisfaction for some time to come."[24] And *Playboy* told its readers, "We caught the nifty new George Russell Sextet at the Five Spot in New York and dug the meaty, modern jazz that came tumbling out." The unnamed writer was hugely impressed by the young band, concluding,

In all, it's a serious set of jazzmen capable of essaying fresh material like Russell's "Stratusphunk" and Baker's "Stone Nuts" and "Kentucky Oysters" with stunning style and excitement and also able to turn a jazz standard like "Woody 'n' You" inside out and back again with such dazzle and verve that even the Five Spot's waiters had to shake their heads to regain focus. Go listen.[25]

According to Kirk Silsbee's notes for the *Five Spot* CD reissue, Miles Davis, Charlie Mingus, and J. J. Johnson were also in the audience. As Chuck Israels, the group's bassist, told Silsbee, it was not unusual to see people from the other arts turn out for these gigs. "People were paying a lot of attention to us but remember, jazz at this time was connected to intelligent society, just as the work of writers and painters was. This was perfectly normal."[26]

George Russell Sextet at the Five Spot and *George Russell Sextet in Kansas City* provide a real sense of what the group sounded like live, though the rawness of the band from a tape made at their Lenox appearance suggests a looser and wilder ensemble sound. Both albums benefited from the fact that the band had played the material live for extended periods prior to recording. These are really dynamic, highly charged sets that on first hearing impress with their virtuoso playing and powerful, driving swing. They bear comparison with Art Blakey's band of the time and even with Miles Davis's group.

Another thing that strikes the listener is the quality of the sound production, even on the original vinyl—*Kansas City* has yet to be released on CD. It is bright, clear, and immediate. It is only on repeated plays that one becomes aware that the writing is of a different order from much of the jazz of the period, and indeed since.

Even Davis's "Sippin' at the Bells" from the *Five Spot* disc opens with an extended scored section where the horns play variations on the theme in unison, not unlike the way the frontline might have been used in early jazz. It closes in similar fashion, but also uses a favored Russell technique of having the soloist play out of tempo and then playing briefly a capella before the next section or solo. Russell's own piano solo—his first on record—is highly chromatic and polyrhythmic, with the closest comparison being Thelonious Monk. But it is the originals rather than the "standards"—the record also includes Trane's "Moment's Notice"—that stand out. Carla Bley's evocative "Dance Class" utilizes radical shifts in tempo, stop-start passages, and polytonality, in particular from the piano, where Russell's accompaniment is unusually free harmonically. Bley's "Beast Blues" is slightly more conventional, with a lovely opening where the horns play against each other. Yet it is also quite an unsettling blues with a slightly eerie atmosphere, again because of the unusual harmonies that are used. Russell's own "Swingdom Come" stretches the use of polytonality even further and its rhythmic shifts are rapid; both these aspects give the piece a radical, free-sounding quality not that different from early Ornette Coleman and Cecil Taylor. In fact, Russell's piano, though not as virtuosic as Taylor's, has similar chromatic and multirhythmic characteristics. The playing from the frontline is astonishing, and there is no doubt that this is an uncompromisingly professional unit. As bassist Chuck Israels told Kirk Silsbee, "It was swinging music. We were all going for that."[27] And as Dave Young explains, "I felt if I could just keep up with Al and Dave, everything would sound alright. It wasn't easy, especially playing lines in different keys at the same time."[28]

If one listens now, this music does not sound so "far out," and one wonders for a moment what all the fuss was about. But one needs to play these records alongside Coleman's *Tomorrow Is the Question* and Taylor's *Looking Ahead!* They do not sound that radical anymore precisely because the way we hear jazz has adjusted—because of these albums and what followed. In 1960 we were still five years away from the "New Thing at Newport" and the likes of Archie Shepp and Marion Brown. Coltrane had only just released *Giant Steps*, and the far more radical *Ascension* was not recorded until April 1965. Russell's sextet albums for Decca and Riverside were certainly pushing jazz into whole new areas of exploration.

It is a great shame that *Kansas City* is currently unavailable, because it complements its "live" partner well and, along with *Ezz-Thetics* and parts of *Stratusphunk* and *The Outer View*, reveals how dynamic Russell's music was during this period. These records are also classic examples of small-group playing and demonstrate how composition and improvisation can be allied without detriment to either spontaneity or art. According to Leonard Feather's sleeve notes, *Kansas City* featured "compositions that the sextet was asked to play in the course of a two-week engagement at a club called The Blue Room in Kansas City."[29] By this point trumpeter Don Ellis had replaced Al Kiger. According to Joe Hunt, "Kiger didn't like New York much either. These guys were all from Indiana and they weren't city people."[30] Kiger missed home, so he left. Fine player though Kiger was, Ellis had added a new dimension to the group's sound.

There is a wit and confidence to his playing on Dave Baker's "Lunacy" and a lightness to his solo on Clifford Brown's "Sandu," an unusual choice for this group, that Kiger might have struggled with. That said, Kiger is arguably a more interesting player in the context of Russell's group and certainly has a greater sense of Russell's aims than Ellis. Russell contributed only one tune to this record, "Theme." Described by Feather as "every man for himself in F minor,"[31] it is about the closest Russell has ever written to a straight-ahead jazz theme—hence the title, no doubt. Even then, the contrapuntal effects he obtains from the horns are quite typical of his style. Davis's "Tune Up" is given a fluid and breakneck reading, while Baker's "War Gewesen" demonstrates a point that Russell has always been quick to emphasize. The function of the Lydian Concept is to open up the individual's creativity, not to produce Lydian clones or soundalikes. Baker's piece is a tricky, slippery, and episodic blues that moves through changes in time, yet has almost a burlesque quality to it.[32]

Young again makes one wish he had recorded more. Though he does sound like Coltrane, every time he solos it is with authority and elegance. What is more, the sense is that he is on the way to achieving a sound both personal and distinct. It is, however, Carla Bley's "Rhymes" that stands out on the album. It is certainly the most "modern"-sounding tune on *Kansas City*. Modal in form and in its solos, it would not have been out of place on Davis's *Kind of Blue*, and compositionally it is more interesting than several of the tunes Davis used. "Rhymes" is marvelously atmospheric and quite lovely.

As to how the band was received in Kansas City, Russell is quoted by Feather: "The musicians in K.C. really come out to dig you," noting that Eddie "Cleanhead" Vinson, among others, turned up several times.[33] Joe Hunt also remembers the Kansas City gigs as a highlight from his time with the group. "The only place they really liked us after the Five Spot was out in Kansas City. We played at a black club in the black part of town and these people were used to hearing Kansas City Blues, right? That was a real perk for us the Kansas City gig. It was really a good gig."[34]

Dave Young's memory of the experience is different, however. "They weren't ready for our kind of music. The crowds were very slim, especially after the first night. *(laughing)*"[35] The clarity of Hunt's recollection of this and of other events perhaps gives his account the edge. Yet it is worth noting that the music this group was making was at odds with the prevailing style of the day. As Hunt had noted, the group were booed at their week's engagement at Birdland.

Musicians from the Midwest must have dreamed of playing a gig like Birdland, and one can imagine what it felt like to see that dream realized—but instead of applause to be met with catcalls. Not everyone who saw the band at the club hated it. One fan who enjoyed it was Ran Blake, the brilliant pianist-composer. Blake is one of those people who, when he likes something, he really likes it: "I went every night to Birdland. He had a one-week gig. My fifth night, he said, 'Is that you again?' You could get right up front at the old Birdland, and I tried to get as close to his piano as possible. It would have been around '61 or '62, when the first Riverside came out."[36]

Blake's enthusiasm aside, it was not a triumphal homecoming for Russell to the club where he used to hear Bird and Diz in the forties and fifties. As to why the band was met with such a response, Hunt's comment is both succinct and pertinent: "I think it was mostly the sound of the Lydian harmony. It was a pretty free band. It was new. It was different."[37]

By that time, with obvious exceptions (such as Ornette Coleman, Charlie Mingus, Cecil Taylor, Miles Davis, and Dave Brubeck, for example), hard bop was the dominant style of jazz. Even though these six albums share some elements stylistically with the music of other small groups of the period—records like *Five Spot* push and swing just as hard as albums by Horace Silver, the Adderleys, and Blakey—they are quite different in feel and approach. Kenny Mathieson in *Cookin'—Hard Bop and Soul Jazz 1954–65* rightly excludes the Russell sextet from his survey.[38] There are reasons why jazz fans are many times more likely to hear at their local jazz club a band delivering their version of Nat Adderley's "Work Song," Horace Silver's "Song for My Father," or Benny Golson's "Blues March." Of Russell's tunes, only "Blues in Orbit," "Stratusphunk," and "Ezz-Thetic" have achieved anything like standard status. The first two probably owe their relative popularity to the Gil Evans's versions rather than Russell's own, and "Ezz-Thetic" is best known due to the Lee Konitz–Miles Davis recording.

As for the reason the recordings for Decca and Riverside overlapped, Russell can no longer recall why this was. He got the opportunity to record and was paid for it, and that kept him going. He had no agent at the time, and as long as he could survive and work on the Concept, that was all he asked. The answer, if there were one, is probably about cost, timing, and opportunity. Even then there were limitations. Asked by Ben Young if he considered at the time working with a larger group, Russell replied,

> It wouldn't have been practical. I had to go to a sextet because largely the budget of the record company couldn't tolerate anything bigger. Of course, on the road it's absolutely important—a sextet is a luxury. I wasn't a strong instrumentalist in being like a superstar pianist or something. I was a background player. I did that well and I think I was hired by the record companies because of my . . . I think Orrin liked my compositions. Sort of rare.[39]

On one level, this was quite a satisfying period for Russell. He made a series of six records in a very short space of time, keeping a sextet of musicians fairly intact through that period. He taught privately and generally kept body and soul together. Live work was infrequent, however, and Russell clearly felt he was not getting his due acknowledgment. His frustration surfaced occasionally in various ways and eventually resulted in his leaving the United States for Scandinavia for five years in the mid- to late sixties.

In a sense, the records the sextet (and, on *Stratus Seekers*, septet) made are quite artificially separated by their recording dates and releases. When one considers that Russell's first album, *Jazz Workshop*, came from three sessions over a twelve-month period, in less than two years between 1960 and 1962, Russell put out six albums of new material. There is also a pattern to these six records that makes their separate consideration quite arbitrary. They were, as Russell notes, made both as a way to earn a living and keep a group together but also as experiments within the Lydian Concept. Russell needed a laboratory for that purpose and the sextet was it. In addition, Russell was very open to contributions from within the group and outside to the band's book of tunes. Composer Carla Bley contributed five pieces overall, while Dave Baker wrote six and Al Kiger one ("Kige's Tune" from *The Stratus Seekers*). Baker particularly valued the opportunity to hone his compositional skills.

> Everybody didn't take the time to write, but he encouraged us to write because he had Carla Bley writing, and David Lahm, who was a student of his at the time, too. It was a wonderful experience for me as a neophyte, somebody who's not really tasted much in the way of success as such, because I had been here in Indiana and it was very thrilling when George encouraged me to write, and on about all the albums I did with George I wrote at least one piece. It was so gracious to choose a piece to record of mine and not only could we record it but we had a chance to really internalize it because we were playing the things on the job. So by the time we record[ed] it, it was a piece which we were familiar with, it was a piece which we also felt comfortable playing, and that makes a world of difference.[40]

As for Carla Bley, she had come out to New York with her husband, Paul Bley, and had been struggling to gain any recognition as a composer in her own right. Though Carla had recorded some of her tunes, with no other validation or support she was about to give up her hopes of making it in the male-dominated music business, as she told Ian Carr.

> So I was going to a psychiatrist at that time, and the psychiatrist said to me, among other horrible things like maybe I should try shock treatment, that I should give up trying to be a composer. Because that was obviously the silliest thing he had ever heard, that somebody like me would be a composer. He said, "Is there anything else you can do?" So I said, "Well, I can sew a little bit." He said, "Well, get a job sewing." So I went home and looked in the paper for jobs as a seamstress and I applied for three of them, and while I waited to hear back I happened to take a piece of music to George Russell and he looked at it and he said, "This is fantastic. I want to record it." So he saved my life. At that moment, I was about to become a seamstress. I actually went to one of the designers and sat in his office watching that scene and wondering how I could be a part of it, but thinking I should learn to be a part of it and give up music, since the psychiatrist had told me to, but George at that moment interfered and said, "I'll record that piece." I think it was called "Bent Eagle." And so I didn't take the job as a seamstress and my whole life changed.[41]

In an interview for this book, Bley recalled,

> I knew that George had this theory about the Lydian Scale, so I made sure
> to put a sharp 11th in all the pieces. Like a tip of the hat, you know. So I
> went over to his house and I brought the tunes with me and I showed them
> to him, and he liked them and he recorded a couple of them. Oh, "Dance
> Class"—that's the piece I wrote after I met George, and that was the one with
> the sharp 11th. Because I think that "Bent Eagle" was written a long time be-
> fore that, and so was "Zig-Zag." "Dance Class" was written for George's band.
> I think I liked that one more. I didn't think "Zig-Zag" was a very good piece; I
> didn't know why he liked it. I don't even know why he recorded any of them.
> He had plenty of good music of his own. I've no idea why he recorded me and
> Dave Lahm. I mean, he was much better than us.[42]

It has been said that Carla Bley was a student of Russell's. For example,
Leonard Feather describes her in that way in his sleeve notes to the *Kan-
sas City* record, for which she composed the lovely, moody, slow-moving
"Rhymes."[43] However, she is adamant that she never studied with him.

> **DH:** Did you study with George Russell?
> **CB:** No. What does study mean? You mean like take lessons?
> **DH:** Yes.
> **CB:** No.
> **DH:** So nothing formal like that?
> **CB:** No. I never paid him any money, that's for sure.[44]

Later in the same interview, she explains that she did transcriptions for Russell. "Yes, and that could be called study because I had a good ear, so I was
able to just listen to the records and make lead sheets, you know, write out
what people were playing. That was fascinating, and I caught mistakes that
he made and everything."[45]

One number in which she found an error between the recorded version
and the sheet music was "Ezz-Thetic." Her answer goes on to clarify the nature of her relationship with Russell, which at most might be described very
loosely as that of mentor. Bley, like Russell, is *sui generis*.

> Maybe it was the old lead sheet that had the mistake, I don't know. . . . But
> also then he wrote some new pieces and I would be the copyist—this went on
> for a couple of years, and I went over to his house quite a bit. He lived near
> me on Bank Street. I would go over to his house, and I think once he did
> loan me the big book about the thing. I think he did loan it to me once and
> I leafed through it but I couldn't understand it because I was absolutely an

unschooled musician, so I really didn't understand modes or chord changes or anything.[46]

The tunes on these small-group albums made between 1960 and 1962 are highly personal. They are episodic, with unusual time signatures and changes of tempo. Soloists often play against the rhythm section rather than along with it. Key centers shift, and the music is pantonal and panrhythmic. Often the arrangements present a little drama and will contain a variety of moods. They are complete compositions with structured introductions, a middle section that is distinct from the beginning, though it follows logically from it, and a final section that is both a development and an extension of the composition. Effectively, they are performances in three or four definite and identifiable movements. This is true for Russell tunes like "Swingdom Come" and the sextet's cover of Coltrane's "Moment's Notice," both from the *Five Spot* record. In fact, if one considers Monk's "'Round Midnight" from *Ezz-Thetics* and "You Are My Sunshine" from *The Outer View*, Russell's ability to deconstruct and transform other writers' compositions is uncanny.

Stratusphunk is an album that has grown in stature over the years. There are times, however, when it does sound rather forced. The impression is that Russell was trying to show that advanced compositional techniques could combine with the hard blowing of bebop, as if Mingus or Monk had led the Jazz Messengers rather than Art Blakey. Russell's "New Donna," based on the Charlie Parker number, from this perspective seems ill at ease with herself, and the composer's "Things New" is similarly betwixt and between. The title track and Carla Bley's precocious "Bent Eagle" meet Russell's objectives more successfully, and David Lahm's "Lambskins" actually seems to push the soloists—Ellis in particular—in more interesting directions than several of the leader's compositions. The same can also be said of Dave Baker's gospel-influenced "Kentucky Oysters," which has a freshness that would have suited Cannonball Adderley's groups of the time, with Dave Young again shining on tenor.

Such reservations were shared by John S. Wilson, writing in *Down Beat* on March 3, 1961, who gave the record three and a half stars and concluded: "In view of the imagination that has gone into some of the writing (Carla Bley's 'Bent Eagle,' for instance), it is disappointing to find so much of this record devoted to essentially the same old thing that already has contributed many aimless LP's to the library of jazz records."[47]

Wilson's comments may be a bit strong—the record is certainly better than that—but it is possible to share his frustration that here, Russell was not fully utilizing his talents.

Russell has always been quite disparaging about his piano playing. Indeed, it is hard to assess Russell's qualities as a pianist, because he has played piano only in the context of his own group. As he told Ben Young, "What I did was, I played the Concept. So the Concept pulled me through that and being a drummer I could very . . . my talent was accompanying a soloist. It turned out to be my meager pianistic talent being able to accompany them and challenge them with unique environments."[48]

Referring to the Monk tune that had brought him to New York, he says, "I think that the first piece I played because I learned the chords was "Round Midnight' with the sextet. I told Monk, I said, 'I think I've messed up one of your tunes.' He said, 'Oh, you wouldn't mess it up.' I'm not a piano player. I mean I can do something on it, but I'm not a pianist."[49]

However, Russell does bring to his accompaniments and solos both a percussive, hard-driving quality and a wildness that suits his music and creates its own sense of excitement. Joe Hunt certainly enjoyed this aspect of his involvement in the sextet.

> One thing I can say too is that as a drummer that George is lots of fun to play with. He's a drummer, right? He's a great feel when he plays the piano. It's just really fun for a drummer to work with him. He's just got a great rhythmic feel. It was fun for me just to play with him as the piano player. That was good. He didn't have piano technique at all in the usual sense, but his phrasing and his feel was tremendous, kind of like Horace Silver in a way. It was like playing with another drummer. That was really fun. I just loved playing with him.[50]

And Ran Blake lists Russell as one of his favorite pianists, as he explains in his rather unusual, elliptical syntax: "I think that he would be the first to say that he doesn't pretend to have a pianistic sound à la Monk, and I know there are all those speed freaks, but Tatum doesn't speak to me. It's Thelonious that does. And I remember in the sixties feeling that George was, with Ray Charles or Mary Lou when she would do blues, maybe George is . . . I find his piano playing very rich and wonderful."[51]

Chuck Israels, his comments to Kirk Silsbee notwithstanding, seems to have been less than enamored with Russell's music:

> I was not interested in what seemed to me to be self-conscious and perhaps pretentious efforts at sounding avant garde. I know that I have participated in and been identified with a few things that are thought to represent this kind of musical point of view; George's band, an Eric Dolphy recording, and a Coltrane recording (with Cecil Taylor—that was originally issued as Cecil's date),

but they were all simply work opportunities, and I would have made other choices, given the chance.[52]

With the opportunity to join Bill Evans Trio, Israels left the sextet and was replaced by Steve Swallow, who made his recording debut on *Ezz-Thetics*.

> I was working in a coffee shop on Bleecker Street in Greenwich Village with Don Ellis and Paul Bley, and one Sunday Don Ellis said to me, "George Russell is looking for a bass player. You should call him up." That was something I had never done. I'd never solicited a gig and was very nervous and awkward about making the call, but I wanted to play George's music. So I did. I called him up fully expecting him to flunk me off. But he didn't, he paused after I'd done a little overture speech and said, "Yeah, okay. Come on by. Bring your bass." So I did, I went to his apartment on Bank Street. And we played through several of his tunes and then he said, "Fine. You're hired," which I thought was just remarkable and I was thrilled.[53]

According to Swallow, the group rehearsed in Russell's one-room apartment, and he recalls meeting Ornette Coleman there for the first time. "I remember also one day going there to get some music from George to study and he and Ornette were just sitting around talking and I joined them for a couple of hours, and that was one of the most memorable hangs I can recall. I was in awe of both of them and thrilled to be sitting with them."[54]

Ezz-Thetics introduced two new players—Swallow and Eric Dolphy on alto and bass clarinet in place of Dave Young. *Ezz-Thetics* is without doubt the best of the sextet records and one that should be in any fan's collection. This was Dolphy's only session with Russell and followed not long after the altoist had recorded *Blues and the Abstract Truth* with Oliver Nelson. Given that album's status as one of the finest examples of modal jazz, it is worth noting that Nelson's group also included Bill Evans on piano and George Barrow, who had played on Teddy Charles's recording of "Lydian M-1," on baritone.

Swallow remembers how supportive Dolphy was of the other musicians at the *Ezz-Thetics* session.

> Eric was extremely gracious and assumed a kind of leadership role on that date, a kind of secondary to George leadership role. . . . I remember Eric kind of going around from one to the other of us during the making of the date and calming us down or eliciting energy from us, as was needed. He was extremely gracious and helpful. That's my primary memory of that date, was just the remarkable social skills that Eric had, and I think they were a great factor in the success of that album, which I think is a very, very good album.[55]

And, as Swallow told Ian Carr, "George tended to be quite nervous in performing and recording situations as well. So Eric was the cool head in the studio, and he was tremendously gracious and graceful that day."[56]

Ezz-Thetics is an excellent example of how new ideas meet with tradition to produce an effective synthesis. Russell, as with other pioneers such as Ornette Coleman and John Coltrane, never eschewed the jazz tradition. Rather, his pride in the origins of his music encouraged him to foster its development. Russell seems to have had a clear understanding that jazz is a syncretic musical form. His own theoretical ideas took in not only jazz but, according to Russell at least, the whole history of equal temperament in music. In developing and expanding the range of jazz, any source was both valid and viable.

Interviewed in 1959 by Burt Korall[57] for a collection of essays and articles published as *The Jazz Word*, Russell immediately identifies the key question for jazz as the relationship between the composer and the improviser. Here, Russell is actually framing the issue in a new way, locating it in the dynamic human context of writer versus performer as opposed to the abstracted process of composition versus improvisation. He defines jazz history to date in terms of a shifting equilibrium from a position of reciprocity between writer and soloist pre-bebop to a point where the soloist (post-Bird) became the dominant figure in moving the music forward. In this later period, Russell argues, the level of compositional sophistication and technique had fallen behind the standard of improvisation.

Russell makes a further distinction between the composer who provides a framework for the improviser to say what he wishes to say and the composer who forces the improviser to say what the composer wants him to say. Russell does not give an example of the former, probably because these would include the majority of jazz composers. He does, however, cite Thelonious Monk, Benny Golson, and Gerry Mulligan as examples of the latter. For Russell, the improviser deals with melody, and the reason why jazz composers have not influenced the improviser is simple: "There have been hardly any writers with enough melodic equipment to be able to take hold of the improviser and have the improviser investigate the writer for what he is doing; so that the improviser can emerge with that new thing that the writer has." To many readers, Russell's citation of Monk in this context will be easily understood.

In the interview, Russell predicts a turning away from atonality toward what he calls "pantonality," noting jazz's roots in folk, scalar forms. Pantonality is a highly chromatic musical notion, but one that does not negate the notion of key centers or scales. It is essential that jazz retain its intuitive, improvised feel even where the music is through-composed, if jazz is to pre-serve its "intuitive, earthy dignity." He also suggests that complexity in jazz will increase rhythmically with composition "which utilizes many different meters . . . all kinds of rhythmic feelings, with music weaving a pattern over this fabric of various meters."[58] Russell is describing his own contribution and influence on jazz very precisely and presciently here. However, it is in the previous paragraph that he articulates most clearly the role of composer in jazz and her relationship with her colleagues in classical music.

> As for jazz and classical music coming together, it depends on how you define classical. If you define it as meaning music which is art, music that is intellectually developed; music that is treated intellectually and thematically—then I'd say that jazz will become a classical music and that there will be writers who will write in the jazz idiom, using all the dowry that jazz has to bring to this new music. And there will also be writers who will not use the jazz idiom. But the musics will certainly be equal. Equally good or equally bad . . . that depends on the composers.[59]

Of all the sextet recordings from the early sixties, *Ezz-Thetics* best illustrates Russell's intentions. While Russell has always maintained that each record demonstrated the best that he could achieve at a given point with available resources, he could also be quite dismissive of these albums.

> **GR:** I'm not crazy about those records at all.
> **DH:** Why is that?
> **GR:** It doesn't reflect anything profound to me. *Stratusphunk* I like.[60]

In the same interview he was also quite ambivalent about the tune "Ezz-Thetic."

> It's an old-time goody for me. It was good for the time but it wasn't ahead of them. But there's a delicate interval between what is good in different periods. If I make a record and then listen to it and it says, but you can do better, you could do more, you could explore more . . . and furthermore a lot of pieces like "Ezz-Thetic," as really most jazz is, it's lifting music from Broadway, Broadway redone.[61]

Again, Russell stresses that the groups and big bands he has led are his laboratory for testing his theories. The product is always secondary to the Lydian Chromatic Concept. Learn from it and move on. That said, he has every reason to see *Ezz-Thetics* as a tribute to both theory and practice. There are few albums to match it—from the period or since—for its bravura playing, for the complex but fluid arrangements and compositions, or for the way its authentic jazz feel is expressed within a new and fresh context.

"Ezz-Thetic" opens the record played at an incredible lick and ends with a delightful series of trade-offs between the horns. Miles Davis's "Nardis" is transformed from a nice ballad with a Middle Eastern flavor into an event rooted in the blues, and Monk's "'Round Midnight" becomes a piece of high drama full of an almost Shakespearean tension with an exceptional bass clarinet solo from Dolphy. In between, "The Lydiot" from *Jazz in the Space Age* is given a spare, loose reading for small group, while David Baker's "Honesty" is full of wit and great good humor and sounds as if the whole band were having a ball. "Honesty" also echoes the earlier point about Russell's roots in the jazz tradition with Ellis's New Orleans–inspired trumpet and Baker's use of the plunger mute. A similar point can be made about Russell's "Thoughts," which is perhaps the most typical piece on the album. It is episodic, with changes of tempo and solos played against the prevailing rhythm. Yet it also stresses Russell's idea that the composer can and should not only frame the soloist's melodic lines but shape their direction. But if there is one track here that ensures the record's status as a classic, it is "'Round Midnight." Russell was overwhelmed when he first heard Monk's tune, and he creates in this setting the most perfect tribute. It is art by any standard, from its surreal, ghostly beginning to Dolphy's beautiful opening statement of the theme and then his lyrical solo set simply by Russell and punctuated by occasional and sometimes bizarre choruses from the other horns. Even Russell's unfussy piano accompaniment is perfect.

Russell maintains that although Dolphy did not study the Concept with him in any formal sense, they discussed it together, and Dolphy took a copy of the book to read. By this account, Dolphy was very enthusiastic about what it had to offer and even wrote to Russell while the altoist was on tour in Europe to that effect.[62] Dolphy holds a rather unusual position vis-à-vis "The New Thing"—he is often seen as a part of the avant garde without actually having that much in common with it stylistically. In a sense, it seems entirely likely that he would take to the Concept because of the way it discusses and views tonality; it suggests that the combining of old and new is possible and desirable and that it is possible to be "modern" without embracing atonality.

Despite the status *Ezz-Thetics* now enjoys, it was not that well received at the time. Don Heckman, who had been a student at Lenox, wrote in *Metronome*, "This version of the group (with Ellis, Dolphy and Swallow replacing Al Kiger, Dave Young and Chuck Israels) is the best so far but, with the exception of Russell's new composition 'Thoughts,' they are better than the material they have to work with."[63]

Frank Kofsky gave the album three and a half stars in *Down Beat*, and, locating Russell firmly in the radical camp of "The New Wave," albeit as "more of a reformer than a revolutionary," he proceeds to damn the whole enterprise for its lack of any new "intellectual and/or emotional sensation their predecessors could not have done." As performers, only Russell and Ellis are singled out for any degree of praise. Though the "Record Notes" column in the *Reporter* was more enthusiastic, this was scant enthusiasm for Russell's project.[64] With little to show in the way of gigs, the Russell group became a rehearsal ensemble, coming together when they had a performance or a record date. As Swallow explains,

> At the point I joined it, the band ceased working weeklong engagements, ceased touring for more than two or three gigs at a shot. We were really kind of reduced to the isolated sort of prestige gig. Like, I remember playing in the courtyard at the Museum of Modern Art and, you know, an art center in Long Island, that kind of stuff. But it was essentially a band that just rehearsed a lot and made a recording and nobody seemed to mind rehearsing without pay for long hours.[65]

There had been a whole series of personnel changes in 1961. It is not clear why Russell dropped Dave Young. Young himself puts it down to the composer's desire to try out another tenor player, Paul Plummer. Though Dolphy had done *Ezz-Thetics*, this was just a one-off, and this group never played live. Judging by his comments to WKCR's Ben Young, Russell viewed the group as being a fluid entity in terms of its personnel.

> It was a recording band mostly. We worked two or three times and I know that a couple of times I used John Gilmore from Sun Ra's group, who I respected a lot, a very nice man and very talented. So I'd meet these different players—like, I'd use Dolphy on that famous "'Round Midnight" recording he did with us—and I'd meet these different players and that kind of interaction was wonderful.[66]

Other changes were dictated by circumstance. Drummer Joe Hunt got his callup in 1962 and was replaced by Pete La Roca. Paul Plummer came in for Dave Young, but then he too joined the army. Don Ellis left to do his own thing, and, along with Steve Swallow, proved the most successful of this generation of Russell alumni in recording terms. Ellis made a number of small-group albums and then returned to his native Los Angeles, where he established a hugely successful big band. Ellis, who had an interest in Eastern music, specialized in compositions with unusual time signatures and used electronics to powerful effect. Anyone interested should hear his astonishing *Electric Bath* and *Live at Monterey* records. How much he picked up from Russell is impossible to say—perhaps only a sense of what was really possible within the form. However, it is fair to say that his first groundbreaking music was made with the composer.

Ellis was obviously an ambitious and self-assured young musician, and Russell heard something vital in his playing even back then.

> He always seemed a little cocky to me. I hired Don because I wanted to . . . after I heard Ornette, I wanted guys that played differently. The guys that were available wouldn't have been into that kind of thing because they weren't following Don Cherry. Don and Ornette were just something else. So the nearest to me who was an adventurous trumpet player at the time was Don Ellis.[67]

Asked about Ellis, Steve Swallow laughs at the recollection: "Well, he was a bit of a martinet, but that being said, he was a fiercely dedicated and directed and disciplined young man. What I found instructive and inspiring about him was his extraordinary self-discipline and at an extremely early age."[68]

According to Swallow, while he and other young musicians saw practice as being about all-night sessions rehearsing or being on the bandstand, "Don would do that but also get up four hours later and practice for three or four hours. I was kind of remiss in the practicing area."[69]

Dave Baker remembers Ellis as being "a little egocentric at times," but adds a number of very pertinent points.

> Wonderful player. He had original ideas and was a good playing mate because he worked hard to learn the music and understand the music, even though he was already experimenting with his adventures in time and moving that way. I think the thing that attracted him to George, and I found attractive about him, he had a good historical sense of where he came from. You know, he knew the music and playing of Rex Stewart and Bubba Miley and, of course, of all of his contemporaries, so that when he formed his own big band, he drew on a vast storehouse of historical knowledge.[70]

After Ellis, the great Thad Jones—one of the three Jones brothers, along with drummer Elvin and pianist Hank—joined the group. Both John Gilmore and Joe Farrell filled the tenor spot, and Garnett Brown and Brian Trentham took over from Dave Baker on trombone at various points. Baker's story is a sad one but also an inspiring and transcendent one. Badly injured in a car accident in the fifties, Baker had had to endure reconstructive surgery on his jaw. As he puts it, "1962 was when my physical apparatus broke down from an accident I'd had ten years before. I spent, like, in and out of the hospital for eighteen months while I had all kinds of therapy and tried different ways to try to solve the problem."[71]

He was already experiencing problems when the group recorded *Ezz-Thetics* but managed to keep going and played on *The Stratus Seekers*. Though he did get some respite in the early seventies and was briefly able to play trombone again,[72] his career as a horn player was effectively over from 1962. Baker began teaching, and musicians of the caliber of Michael and Randy Brecker and Freddie Hubbard passed through his studio. Back in Indiana, he taught at Indiana University and became head of the Jazz Department, where he adopted *The Lydian Chromatic Concept of Tonal Organization* as a core text and became one of the most important educators in jazz in North America. He also continued composing and playing, now on cello. Baker was and is a remarkable musician and individual.

Nineteen sixty-one had proved quite a good year, in terms of publicity at least. Gerry Mulligan had recorded *All About Rosie* with his Concert Band in a beautiful new arrangement by Russell, noting in Dom Cerulli's sleeve notes, "The way George wrote it for us, Rosie's grown up!"[73] There had also been a number of articles on him, and he had been given his own "Blindfold Test" in *Down Beat*—he praised Duke Ellington's "Dance of the Floeadores" and J. J. Johnson's piece from the Brandeis disc but was critical of Shorty Rogers, Quincy Jones, and Stan Kenton, while being tactful about a Gunther Schuller composition performed by the MJQ. In November Russell took part in a *Down Beat* round robin panel that also included Bob Brookmeyer, Don Ellis, and Hall Overton. Its tone seems rather pompous now, and in content it seems worthy without really have much to say. Russell's participation did, however, speak loudly about his standing in jazz, on the East Coast at least.

Perhaps best of all that year was his placing in the *Down Beat* Critics Poll. He came top in the "New Stars" arranger/composer section, and his sextet came second in the "New Stars" combo section, behind Coltrane.[74] In general, Russell has fared quite well in *Down Beat* polls and reviews and articles in that magazine, and others, such as *Jazz Today*, have been fair and broadly favorable. The failure of publicity to translate itself into regular and consistent gigs has, however, been a constant feature in his Stateside career.

It was in this period that the wonderful and sadly underrecorded singer Sheila Jordan came into Russell's life. "I met George at the Page 3, this club that I sang at. That was down in Greenwich Village, and he came down because a student of his was playing on Monday nights. Monday nights was session night at the Page 3."[75]

The student was Jack Reilly. Reilly had told Russell about Jordan, and Russell stayed to listen for the whole evening.

> It was quite "out" and so George came, and then he came up to me afterwards and he introduced himself and he said, "Where do you come from to sing like that?" He said he was really moved by what I was singing. So I told him. So we became friends. And I, of course, was legally married to Duke Jordan at the time. So George paid for my divorce in Mexico. At that time you couldn't get divorced in New York City unless you could prove adultery, which I could very easily have done. *(laughing)* I didn't want to. I just didn't want to go through all that. George paid for my divorce. I went to Mexico—I guess New Mexico—and got a divorce and came back. I had a wedding dress and everything made. Were going to get married, but it never worked out.[76]

As Jordan puts it, "in the long run we were better friends than lovers," but for a time they were very close, and their one performance together on record, "You Are My Sunshine," has its own place in jazz history.

Russell wanted to see where Jordan came from, so they drove up to Pennsylvania to meet her family. The main industry in the area had always been coal mining, but now the mines were beginning to close and many of the miners were out of work. With Jordan's grandmother in tow, they went to a local social club, where the singer was pressed into performing Jimmy Davis's quintessentially American song. At first Russell accompanied Jordan, but her grandmother soon pushed him out of the way because he was not "playing it right." Jordan says that afterward he joked with her, saying, "Your grandmother sounds like Thelonious Monk."[77]

About a month later, Russell called her and showed his arrangement of "Sunshine," telling her he wanted her to sing it on his next album.

> Then we went into the studio and that's how "Sunshine" was born. But it was a dedication to the coal miners of Pennsylvania. He wanted to call it "A Drinking Song," because we were drinking and we knew the miners all drank because that was their form of recreation, and they were all out of work. It was a really sad kind of . . . in the introduction you hear that, you know. But it was like a little documentary for the coal miners and, unfortunately, we couldn't call it "A Drinking Song." They wouldn't let us change it.[78]

Jordan explains what she meant in calling the song a "documentary":

> George wanted to see the mines, even though they were closed up. He saw the towns, the poverty. He saw the whole thing where I grew up, and he associated all that with the coal mines and the miners going down into the mines. You

know, I had told him about the explosions, the mine explosions where miners were trapped in the mines and never got out and wrote their wills in coal dust on the walls. It was terrible. So he knew all that, and George was very much into people and how they lived, and that all came out in his music. That's why his music is so great. That's why I always thought of it as a documentary, a musical documentary on the coal miners. Because you can hear it, you know. You can just hear it.[79]

Recorded on *The Outer View*, the last album Russell made in the States until 1972, this performance is still astonishing in its power. It is another example of Russell's ability to transform a tune into something infinitely more dramatic and special. But it would be something far less singular were it not for Jordan's vocal, as Steve Swallow recalls.

Sheila has an extraordinary ability to move me when she sings. The take of "You Are My Sunshine"—and I can only recall one or two takes of that—was a devastating emotional moment for me. At the end of the take I was shattered, and, as I say, this is something that Sheila has always been able to do to me.[80]

If "Sunshine" is the standout track on *Outer View*, there are also strong versions of Carla Bley's "Zig-Zag" and Bird's "Au Privave." The title track has really strong piano from Russell, and the frontline of Ellis, Paul Plummer, and Garnett Brown blend particularly well. Russell's trademark stop-start and out-of-time passages and use of different key centrrs mask just how far the piece is centerd in the blues. However, after "Sunshine," it is "D.C. Divertimento" that most impresses. In this piece—commissioned for the First International Jazz Festival in Washington, D.C., in the summer of 1963, promoted by President John F. Kennedy's Music Committee—Russell pulls out all the stops. Stravinsky is again a reference point, but "Divertimento" is definitely jazz. The complex arrangement never gets in the way of the drama Russell seeks to create, and his band push and challenge each other to splendid effect. It is one of Russell's finest works, and it is surprising that its potential has not been grasped by an imaginative modern choreographer. It cries out for dancers.

The Outer View received fine reviews just about everywhere. *Billboard*, *Cash Box*, and *Music Vendor* all liked it, though *Jazz Review* for once was not convinced. Nat Hentoff in *Hi-Fi/Stereo Review* singled out "Sunshine" for particular praise and noted Russell's continued growth as a composer. *Down Beat* called it "essential listening" and awarded it five stars, but Russell must have found *Time* magazine's applause especially encouraging.[81] The album's release also coincided with the latest *Down Beat* poll, which saw Russell's sextet in strong second place in the "Talent Deserving of Wider Recognition" category and saw him third, equal with Thelonious Monk, in the arranger/composer section, behind Gil Evans and Duke Ellington.[82]

Jordan's vocal performance is one of the most striking and spectacular in jazz. She also sang it with the sextet at the Philharmonic Hall, Lincoln Center for the Performing Arts, on August 22, 1963, when the group played opposite Jimmy Giuffre's trio. The group at the time was Paul Plummer on tenor, Thad Jones on trumpet, Garnett Brown on trombone, Russell on piano, Steve Swallow on bass, and Pete La Roca on drums. Swallow also played the second set with Giuffre and Paul Bley. But the song's most famous performance was at Newport the following summer.

It was an incredibly windy, wet day, and the group's sheet music kept blowing off the stand. The rain was at its heaviest when Jordan came on stage. "I started to sing it and it was raining. I think the music started blowing around too, and of course we got the music back, but it started to rain. Oh, it was Max Roach and Abbey Lincoln. Max said, 'Who did your lighting and your sound?' Because we started out and it was raining and when we finished the sun came out. Isn't that amazing?"

With a mixture of whimsical humor and romantic fantasy, Jordan continues: "All those dead miners that had been trapped in the mines. They wanted us to know they were all right."

In fact, a bootleg recording surfaced recently that includes, alongside the original Russell sextet's 1960 performance at Lenox, four numbers from the Newport gig, including "You Are My Sunshine." The sleeve notes credit Don Ellis as the trumpeter, when in fact it would have been Thad Jones, and Dave Baker as the trombonist, when it was probably Garnett Brown. The tenor player was John Gilmore with Russell on piano, Swallow on bass, and Pete La Roca on drums. The sound quality is not good but the band sounds a lot further out than the studio recordings might suggest.

Though Russell "left her standing at the church door," as he puts it, for the daughter of his friend, composer John Benson Brooks, there were no hard feelings, and it was his intervention that kick-started her career.

> But in the meantime he did a lot for me. He was the reason I ever recorded. So it was way beyond "so, like, you jilted me" or whatever. I never felt that way about George because he was so good to me. As I said, we just weren't compatible. It would've been a disaster if we ever married, but in the meantime I got a divorce from Duke Jordan, and he had also made a demo of me. He loved the way I sang and he made a demo of me, paid for a demo and took it around to all the record

companies. He took it to Mercury—and Quincy Jones was the A&R man at the time—and he took it to Blue Note, and Blue Note bought it up right away. Then Quincy sent a letter over. He was interested to record me.[83]

That demo, which apparently featured Kenny Burrell on guitar, opened the door and led to *Portrait of Sheila.* Jordan was the first singer to record for Blue Note and for a long time was one of only two singers on the label (the other was Dodo Greene). With the great Barry Galbraith on guitar, Steve Swallow, and Denzil Best on drums, it was almost a family affair. It remains a definitive example of the singer's art.

But Russell's involvement went beyond that of midwife, as Swallow explains.

Alfred Lion brought Denzil Best into it. That was Alfred's choice. But Barry and me were chosen by George, and I remember too that the chord charts that we were playing were in George's hand. I know damn well he was responsible for the harmonization for at least most of those tunes, and he was there at the rehearsals. I don't recall that he was there at the actual recording. I have a feeling he wouldn't have been because there would have been conflict between him and Alfred, who ran a kind of tight recording ship, and Rudy Van Gelder as well, for that matter. They looked most unkindly on any visitors during their recording sessions, and I think that in particular they would have found George meddlesome, but he was guiding the harmonic content of that recording beyond a doubt, and I think that he must have had a hand in choosing the repertoire too, just because he and Sheila were together and talking about all these things a lot.[84]

Their romantic attachment may have been a factor behind Russell's motivation. However, as Jordan points out, such behavior was unusual in the jazz world but not untypical of Russell.

So the thing with George was that he really went to bat for me. I think he's known for doing that. I think he did that with Bill Evans too. He did that with a lot of young musicians, but for a musician still to go to bat for you, that was really special. I don't know if I would have ever recorded if I hadn't met George and if he hadn't paid the money—he paid for this tape—and God, I was pleased that I knew somebody that closely that was such a genius, because he writes unbelievable stuff. We always remained friends even though the romantic thing didn't work out. I got a free divorce. I have a wedding dress that I've never used and I have some beautiful memories.[85]

Writer Francis Davis tells a lovely and instructive story about Russell. The writer D. Antoinette Hardy was speaking at a colloquium on jazz at Temple

University in Philadelphia in 1984. Russell was due to deliver a lecture on the Lydian Concept at the conference and was sitting in the audience during a panel discussion on women in jazz. Handy spoke about a dictionary of black women instrumentalists that she was compiling, and when the discussion was opened to the floor Russell suggested that she had missed two very important women. Handy asked who these were, and Russell mentioned Billie Holiday. Handy pointed out that the dictionary referred to instrumentalists and Russell mumbled that Holiday had influenced more musicians than any of the artists Handy had spoken about.

Handy then asked who the other woman was that she had not included.

"Sheila Jordan," Russell replied—to embarrassed laughter from the audience, because, as Handy quickly pointed out, "Sheila Jordan is white."

Russell, who is black but has often been mistaken for white (including by Wilfrid Mellers in *Music in a New Found Land* and, I would conjecture, by many in the audience that day), grinned devilishly and paused before delivering the punch line: "Well, that depends on how you define it, doesn't it?"[86]

Notes

1. John Benson Brooks, "George Russell," *Jazz Review*, February 1960, p. 38. Though Brooks was rather underrecorded, among his albums are *Alabama Concerto* and *Folk Jazz USA*, Lonehill JazzLHJ10275. Both come recommended. Brooks also wrote the lovely "Where Flamingos Fly," which Gil Evans recorded—*Gil Evans, Out of the Cool* HMV CLP1456 and *Where Flamingos Fly*, A&M 390831-2.

2. Interview with George Russell, June 2004.

3. Interview with Tom Guard, May 2005.

4. Ibid.

5. Ibid.

6. Bob Dylan, *Chronicles, Volume One* (London: Simon & Schuster, 2004), pp. 94 and 74. See also C. Harper, *Dazzling Stranger: Bert Jansch and the British Folk and Blues Revival* (London: Bloomsbury, 2001).

7. Interview with Bob Brookmeyer, October 2003.

8. Interview with Juanita Giuffre, June 2004.

9. Ibid.

10. Interview with George Russell, October 2003.

11. Interview with Giuffre.

12. Ian Carr, interview with George Russell, June 1992.

13. Interview with Russell October 2003

14. Korall, B, "Who Is George Russell?" *Down Beat*, February 16, 1961.

15. Conversation between George Russell and the author, June 2004.

16. Ben Young, broadcast devoted to George Russell in celebration of his seventy-fourth birthday, WKCR Radio, New York, June 23, 1997.

17. Reviewing the gig for the *New Yorker*, Whitney Balliett was not impressed by Russell's orchestrations, which he contrasted negatively with those of Gil Evans: "[U]nlike those of Gil Evans, which are done in subtle oils, they appear to be fashioned out of strands of colorless lucent plastic." He was, however, impressed with the group, in particular Al Kiger, and described the performance as "a full-bodied blowing session." Review of George Russell Sexted, Jazz in the Garden, MoMA, New York, "Musical Events—Jazz Concerts," *New Yorker*, July 1960.

18. Interview with Joe Hunt, June 2004.

19. A press release from Mildred Fields regarding the Five Spot dates gives different personnel. According to this, Larry Ridley was on bass and Paul Partridge was on drums. This may have been for the opening couple of nights only. None of the other participants recalls these changes.

20. Interview with Dave Young, January 2007.

21. Interview with Hunt.

22. Ibid.

23. Interview with Young.

24. George Hoefer, "Caught in the Act (Review of *George Russell Sextet at the Five Spot*)," *Down Beat*, September 15, 1960.

25. *Playboy* (no date available but likely September 1960).

26. Kirk Silsbee, sleeve notes to reissue of *George Russell Sextet at the Five Spot* (2000), Verve 088112287–2.

27. Ibid.

28. Interview with Young.

29. Leonard Feather, sleeve notes to *George Russell Sextet Live in Kansas City*, Decca DL 4183

30. Interview with Hunt.

31. Feather, sleeve notes to *George Russell Sextet Live in Kansas City*.

32. Russell would return to the piece in the eighties on his second album for Blue Note, *So What*.

33. Feather, sleeve notes to *George Russell Sextet Live in Kansas City*.

34. Interview with Hunt.

35. Interview with Young.

36. Interview with Ran Blake, October 2003.

37. Interview with Hunt.

38. K. Mathieson, *Cookin'—Hard Bop and Soul Jazz 1954–65* (Edinburgh: Canongate, 2002).

39. Young, broadcast devoted to George Russell.

40. Interview with Dave Baker, April 2004.

41. Ian Carr, interview with Carla Bley for BBC Radio 3 broadcast *George Russell—The Invisible Guru*, July 1994.

42. Feather, sleeve notes to *George Russell Sextet Live in Kansas City*. This error is repeated by Chris Albertson in his sleeve notes to *Stratusphunk* Riverside RLP 9341.

43. Ibid.

44. Interview with Carla Bley, February 2004.

45. Interview with C. Bley.

46. Ibid.

47. John S. Wilson, Review of *George Russell Sextet—Stratusphunk* (Riverside RLP-341), *Down Beat*, March 2, 1961.

48. Young, broadcast devoted to George Russell.

49. Ibid.

50. Interview with G. Russell, October 2003.

51. Interview with Hunt.

52. Interview with Blake.

53. E-mail interview with Chuck Israels, August 2004.

54. Interview with Steve Swallow, February 2004.

55. Ibid.

56. Ian Carr, interview with Steve Swallow for BBC Radio 3 broadcast *George Russell—The Invisible Guru*, July 1994.

57. Burt Korall, "Where Do We Go from Here?" in *The Jazz Word*, edited by D. Cerulli, B. Korall, and M. Nasatir (New York: Ballantine, 1960). See also Korrall, "Who Is George Russell?"

58. Korall, "Where Do We Go from Here?" p. 188.

59. Ibid.

60. Ibid.

61. Interview with G. Russell, October 2003.

62. Ibid.

63. Don Heckman, "Review in Depth—George Russell," *Metronome*, November 1961.

64. Frank Kofsky, Review of *Ezz-thetics* (Riverside 375), *Down Beat*, November 9, 1961; *Review of George Russell Sextet—Ezzthetics* (Riverside 375), "Record Notes," *Reporter*, September 28, 1961.

65. Interview with Swallow. Such as the Jazz in the Garden concert at the Museum of Modern Art on August 23, 1962.

66. Young, broadcast devoted to George Russell.

67. Interview with G. Russell, October 2003.

68. Interview with Swallow.

69. Ibid.

70. Interview with Baker.

71. Ibid.

72. Baker played on *Living Time*, the album Russell made with Bill Evans in 1972.

73. Gerry Mulligan and the Concert Band, *A Concert in Jazz*, Verve V/V6–8415.

74. See "Blindfold Test," *Down Beat*, January 5, 1961; "Afterhours—A Jazz Discussion with Clark Terry, Don Ellis, Bob Brookmeyer, George Russell," *Down Beat*, November 9, 1961; "9th Jazz International Critics Poll," *Down Beat*, August 3, 1961.

75. Interview with Sheila Jordan, May 2004.

76. Ibid.

77. Ibid.

78. Ibid.

79. Ibid.

80. Interview with Swallow.

81. Reviews taken from Russell's private collection and papers. No dates for *Billboard*, *Cash Box*, or *Music Vendor*. Nat Hentoff, "Way Out Front with George Russell," *Hi Fi/Stereo Review*, October 1963; Review of *George Russell Sextet—The Outer View* (RLP440), *Time*, May 22, 1964; Review of *The Outer View* (Riverside 440), *Down Beat*, July 18, 1963.

82. "Critics Poll Results," *Down Beat*, July 18, 1963.

83. Interview with Jordan. See also D. DeMichael, "Newport Report," *Down Beat*, August 13, 1964.

84. Interview with Swallow.

85. Interview with Jordan.

86. Francis Davis, *Jazz and Its Discontents* (Cambridge, MA: Da Capo, 2004), p. 82.

Nannie Kathaleen George—Class of 1920. George Russell's mother is fourth from the left sitting in the front row.

George Russell—Withrow High Class of 1939 home room picture. Russell is squatting in the left-hand corner.

The Wilberforce Collegians

BUD JENKINS

Often termed "America's Greatest College Orchestra," the Wilberforce Collegians have this year enjoyed one of the most successful years since their organization. This orchestra is unique in the fact that all of its members are majoring in the School of Music. This year the Collegians have travelled extensively throughout the Southern states and have earned an enviable reputation for their inimitable renditions.

At present the orchestra is smaller than usual, but in spite of its size it still possesses some of the best musicians in the country. Feature men for the orchestra are: Ernest Wilkins on tenor, Oliver McLean on alto, Jesse Hart and Clifford King on trumpet. The rhythm section is composed of George Russell on drums, Joseph McRae on bass, and John Cotter on piano. James Wilkins plays a fine trombone, Hibonza Gray and Louis Transue compose the rest of the sax section. Flozell Fleming ably handles the vocals.

The orchestra is managed and directed by Bud Jenkins, who also plays trumpet. He is looking forward to a very promising season next year.

The Wilberforce Collegians, 1942, with the "handsome" George Russell on the drums.

George Russell in Scandinavia, 1967. Photographed by Tom Hoeg.

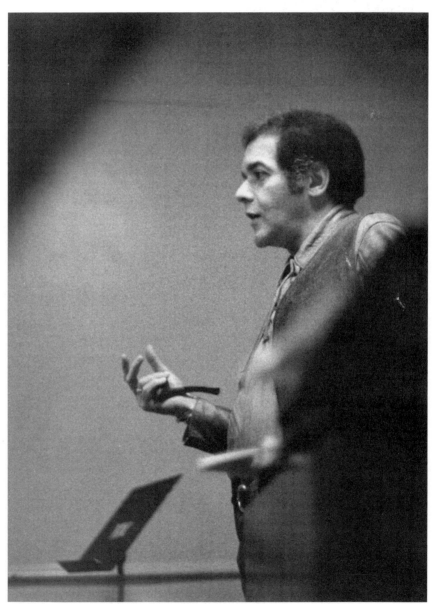

George Russell at New England Conservatory, mid-1970s.

George and Alice Russell outside the Village Vanguard with Russell's son, Jock, and club founder Max Gordon, 1978. Photographed by Ray Ross.

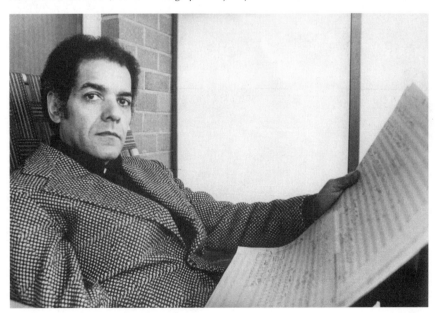

George Russell with manuscript of African Game, *1984. Photographed by Maje Waldo.*

The NEC Jazz Big Band, conducted by George Russell, premiering Russell's Timeline *(March 4, 1992). Photographed by Jeff Thiebauth.*

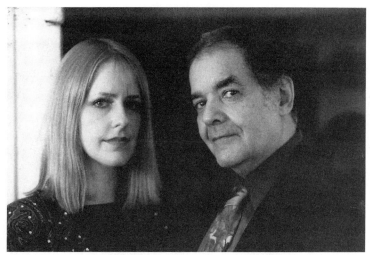

Alice and George Russell in Belgium, 1989.

George at his home in Boston with various album covers, 2003. Photographed by Hiro Honshuku.

George Russell and the Living Time Orchestra, 2008.

CHAPTER EIGHT

~

Listen to the Silence

George Russell's profile in the jazz and other press continued to be quite strong. The French *Jazz* magazine interviewed him at length for its February 1963 issue in a piece entitled, "Le Philosophe de Greenwich Village." It treats Russell as the elder statesman of the jazz avant garde, asking his opinions of Ornette Coleman, John Coltrane, and Cecil Taylor. In respect of the latter, Russell acknowledges a lack of personal enthusiasm.[1] That Russell was now seen as a figure of some significance is confirmed by invitations to take part in panel discussions for both *Playboy* and *Down Beat* in February and June of the following year. Intriguingly, given *Playboy*'s other function, its panel seems the more interesting and challenging, perhaps because of the caliber of its participants, which included Charlie Mingus and Dave Brubeck, among others.[2] However, by 1964 Russell had become increasingly frustrated at the lack of work and recording opportunities for his group. In July a duodenal ulcer had perforated, and this had been followed by a bout of pneumonia. In October *Down Beat* ran a news item, "George Russell Sends Call for Blood Donors," about his illness, noting that as a result, Russell had needed to cancel his first European tour.[3] To add a touch of irony, this ran alongside a story titled, "Dick Gregory Possible Lead in Parker Movie." In fact, the magazine was a little late in its call for blood donations to assist the composer's recovery and had underestimated Russell's recuperative powers and determination. By the time the item appeared, Russell was partway through the tour. It had, however, been touch and go as to whether he would make the trip, as Garnett Brown, the sextet's trombonist, remembers.

Before that European trip with George Wein, George had had an operation, a surgical procedure. We were rehearsing and he was recuperating. We had a point where he felt that he might not be able to make it, and he was really doubting if he was going to make the tour. We were all sad about that, because how could we do it without him? He felt that Hank Jones could do it and he always brought up Hank's name, saying, "If I can't make it, Hank'll do it." But in the end he ended up able to make it and he got stronger as the time went on because we were over there for months.[4]

Packed with stars, often in unusual and quite artificial combinations, George Wein's annual Newport Festival All-Stars trips were the ultimate jazz package tour and one of the hottest tickets in Europe. Given his health, Russell was unable to undertake the work of putting a group together, and Juanita and Jimmy Giuffre came to his aid. While most of the players had already played with him, Steve Swallow could not make the tour. At the suggestion of the Giuffres, Russell auditioned a young bassist from the West Coast named Barre Phillips, who had recently arrived in New York. This was quite a leap in Phillips's career.

For me it was quite a rush. There I am, a young free jazzer and improviser play-ing contemporary music, and then to be hired by a band like that with people like Thad Jones in it was very exciting for me. It was my first trip to Europe. So the whole trip was exciting to be with the big boys and play at the big halls.[5]

The rest of the band comprised Joe Farrell on tenor, Thad Jones on trum-pet, Garnett Brown on trombone, Russell on piano, and Albert "Tootie" Heath on drums. As Phillips remembers, all the bands on the tour played at the Berlin Festival and then toured Europe together and separately.

Miles's quintet was on that tour. I remember hanging out with them. I re-member there was an organ trio—I think it was Richard "Groove" Holmes. The plane coming over there were forty-four jazz musicians on this plane, the same plane, and all played at the Berlin Festival. Everybody played and then everybody had their tour. Some bigger than others.[6]

On several dates, the "avant garde" George Russell Sextet was on a bill with the Chicago All-Stars—Ruby Braff, Pee Wee Russell, and Bud Freeman—and the Uptown All-Stars—Coleman "Bean" Hawkins, Harry "Sweets" Edison, and Jo Jones. Of course, the musicians got on just fine. In fact, Phillips found himself depping for Ellington alumnus Jimmy Woode at some concerts due to the bassist's unexplained absences. A friendship with Bean and Sweets was cemented on a long train journey from southern France to Brussels with large quantities of the cognac Hawkins always carried with him to "cut my cold." When the musicians arrived at the venue that evening, the promoter presented a local bass player who had been hired as a stand-in. Hawkins was having none of it. He told the promoter, "No! I want Bass to do it." The tenorist had taken to calling Barre by the name of his instrument. "Bass" pointed out diplomatically that he had not brought his instrument to the hall, as he was not playing that night. At that point, Hawkins turned to the Belgian stand-in and said, "Lend Bass your bass, man." The Belgian, with typical Old World good manners, obliged.[7]

Joe Boyd, one of the tour managers employed by George Wein, recalls that he had been very impressed with Russell's sextet, and with Thad Jones in particular. He adds that "Russell's band were the surprise stars of the tour."[8] The billing was, however, not a match made in heaven, in one certain and important respect. Some nights it attracted audiences that were split between fans of the mainstream and the modern. The former were sadly not impressed by Russell's take on jazz and frequently showed their displeasure. One of the concerts in Paris, at the Salle Pleyal on October 1, 1964, was recorded for radio broadcast and came out both on a bootleg recording on an Italian label and more recently on the Spanish imprint Gambit Records. The latter includes four tracks from Bremen on the same tour and is the more intelligent purchase. Though "You Are My Sunshine" and "D.C. Divertimento" are repeated, the Bremen date adds Miles Davis's "Sippin' at Bells" and "'Round Midnight." In addition, it contains reasonable sleeve notes and the sound quality is improved.[9] Both performances suggest that live, the band sounded much further "out" than was the case on record. Everyone plays with real fire and aggression, and Russell's ability to lead and direct from the piano is really clear in this setting. While in Bremen the audience are enthusiastic and demand an encore, in Paris half the audience was cheering, but the other half sound as if they wanted blood.

With booing greeting the ending of "The Outer View," Russell walked to the microphone and said, "The next composition some of you may like even less." Then he laughed and added, "It's called 'Volupte.'" For Garnett Brown, it was the high point of his time with Russell.

So what happened was we played a couple of concerts in Paris in a big hall, I can't remember what it was, but I just remember it being large and wondering how comfortable it was going to be on the stage, as far as hearing was concerned. That wasn't really a problem, but what happened was that after we had played one or two numbers, Miles was off in the wings watching. When we finished this first tune, the people started booing George, our group. They sat there for a minute then all of a sudden the other half of the audience

started applauding. So you had this interaction of boos and applauding going on simultaneously at a raucous level. Now, George was still recovering
from the surgery he'd had in New York, so we were all wondering how that
was playing on him. George got up walked to the front of the stage took a
very determined stance, wide-legged and with his fists clenched and on his
hips. He just stood there staring at the audience—I think he was soaking it
in, loving what was going on. We never really discussed that, but that to me
was one of the more interesting, unpredictable, but rewarding things that
happened with George.[10]

It was also quite a shock for the young Barre Phillips.

In Paris it was the strongest, because they actually threw things at us. They
threw mostly pennies, which were not going to hurt you because they were
almost like cardboard. It was some very light kind of metal, some kind of pot
metal. I never got hit. Nothing fell down a saxophone bell or anything like
that. And it was incredible because people started to hoot and holler, "No!
No! No!" Then the people who were for it were saying, "Shut up! Shut up!
Shut up!" At one moment, it was just a huge roar that we were playing to. At
least that was the impression I had. It was the first time I had played on a stage
where people were shouting, "No!" (laughs) "Get off! Get off!"[11]

One of Russell's favorite anecdotes concerns the premiere of Stravinsky's
Rite of Spring on May 29, 1913, at the Théatre des Champs-Elysées in Paris,
where the performance was met with catcalls and fights broke out between
rival factions in the audience. Given his sense of the dramatic, it seems a
reasonable assumption that this story was not far from his thoughts that night
at La Salle Pleyal.[12]

The group went on to Sweden, where they were offered a residency at a
Stockholm club, as Phillips recalls.

There was two weeks of touring and then there was two weeks at the Golden
Circle in Stockholm. We had played at Stockholm at a festival and the club
said, "Can you guys stay?" So everybody checked with home and everybody
could do it. So everyone stayed for an additional two weeks and played at the
Golden Circle and went home from there.[13]

Everyone except Russell himself, that is. Russell's frustration with the lack
of work for his group had bubbled to the surface before in an interview for
the *Louisville Times* in Kentucky in April 1960. "'You can't play jazz in New
York,' says brilliant composer-arranger George Russell. 'There is no opportu-

nity to play jazz other than in the studio and I think that is really forcing the music out into the other communities of the country.'"[14]

Talking with Ian Carr, Russell recalled how rarely the group had worked live but that he had made ends meet through the opportunities to record in the studio. It seems that Russell's decision to stay in Scandinavia was essentially made on the spur of the moment.

> Well, I know that we wound up that European tour with the Newport All-Stars in Stockholm and I decided to stay there and I was offered a two-week engagement at the Golden Circle. And I took it and stayed. You know, and it was the right move because I began to work again to get . . . you know, the work just happened, working with Swedish Radio, the Danish Radio Jazz Orchestra.[15]

The reception his music had received there was obviously a factor. The caliber of the Scandinavian musicians he had heard was extremely high, and he was accorded the same respect African American musicians like Louis Armstrong, Miles Davis, Dexter Gordon, Kenny Clarke, and others had found in Europe. Speaking to Carr, Russell's friend and sometime lover Marit Jerstad contrasted what he was feeling about America with his reception in Scandinavia.

> There, you know, it was everybody should be black Negro. You had to be black, and he was very white. He had tried to become white in a way. It was very difficult, you know. Imagine. He was so light he didn't really look Negro at all. He looked like a Jew or mid-European. That alienated him from the milieu in America, which was, naturally, wanted to be fighting and very militant. Then he had no space there, because he was a theoretician and you shouldn't be that, being a jazz musician. He had written a book. That was very suspect. Coming here he was given space. He was given room for everything. Especially in Norway; in Sweden it was with jazz on the radio, here it was the new music milieu and new music composers.[16]

Speaking with Vivian Perlis, Russell acknowledged that the political situation in America in the mid-sixties was a factor in his decision to leave America.

> **GR:** Yeah, I think that had something to do with it. Things began to get rather mean, I thought, and forces were coming into the music that were nonmusical forces and musicians, and especially those who had lent themselves to various causes. I found it an ugly scene that didn't have much to do, really, with aesthetics. The art being . . . the anger being used as a kind of justification, maybe the justified anger. Anyway, anger being used as the justification for

art, actually. But for an art that—what can I say—an art that was being . . . anger was being used as a commodity, as a commodity that one could believe was justified, but at the same time behind that was a drive to power. Do you understand what I'm saying?

VP: Yes, power in the wrong sense . . .

GR: It was basically, the anger was being used by people to ride on, to get into positions of power, and not as a justifiable anger out of injustice, and wanting to see justice done. Bring about a certain shift in power.

VP: Was there more appreciation for jazz in general, more respect and more opportunity for you in Europe during that time, more understanding of what you were . . .

GR: Oh yes. Enormously much more.[17]

Russell saw much of the so-called avant garde jazz as sloppy and lazy and lacking in the values and virtues he looked for in music. He was also concerned about what he saw as the aggressive and confrontational stance taken by some African American musicians toward their white counterparts and to the jazz scene. After all, Russell counted many of those musicians as personal friends. Further, he was horrified by what he considered to be the infiltration of jazz by communist elements in America and outside. This may sound extreme or even paranoid, but he outlined his reasons for this view in an interview for *Avant* magazine in 1998.

When I left, it was a different kind of conservatism because it was people who might have been very Avant Garde but who insisted that their way was the way music was going and I never saw it that way. I always saw even the most radical serialist or so-called free players as playing in a zone—identifying a zone of music but it was merely a zone. I didn't want my music to be simply Serial or the New Thing. I wanted it to have many different colours. So, when that became politicised I left America.

Asked what he meant by the latter statement, Russell replied:

Well, actually at the time, Communism was coming in and beginning to try to exert control over the far out people and it did to a certain extent. I mean in terms of world youth conferences, that they had in Finland or wherever, and certain musicians would be there and I began to feel really oppressed by that. (*Wry smile*)[18]

On a return to New York in May 1965 on business, Russell was interviewed by *Down Beat*. He talked about teaching his Lydian Concept to a group of Swedish musicians and of forming a sextet with Swedes Bertil Lövgren on trumpet, Eje Thelin on trombone, and Bernt Rosengren on tenor, along with Polish bassist Roman Dylag and Tootie Heath on drums. The group had played in Copenhagen, Brussels, and Zurich and was due to play the Norwegian Molde Festival that summer, and also in Baden-Baden in Germany. He also talked about a possible State Department/Swedish government–sponsored tour behind the Iron Curtain.

However, it was his other comments that provoked controversy. Noting the interest in Europe for new developments in jazz, he distinguished work that he saw as being of merit from what he saw as fraudulent. "'There's a lot of nonsense involved,' he explained. 'In some ways, the avant-garde is the last refuge of the untalented.'"

The article continues, with Russell leading with his chin:

> Many of the new players, Russell said, have "an overevaluated sense of their ability to become instant composers. Composing is different from playing and always will be. The composer must take time to plan, to build structures and forms that will sustain interest. Much of what I hear is boring; there is a sameness to it all."

Furthermore, the New Thing indicated that the composer was needed more than ever: "The era of the idiocy of endless improvising is coming to an end: we need greater control in the hands of people who have an understanding of improvisation and its importance."[19]

Such comments in mid-sixties America would not go unanswered. It was Archie Shepp, a fine musician and at other times an articulate polemicist, who went into print to respond to Russell's castigation of the New Thing. In "An Artist Speaks Bluntly," which appeared in *Down Beat*'s December 16, 1965, issue, Shepp leaves no target unbloodied or unscarred. It is actually a striking "period piece" that draws Cuba, South Africa, Vietnam, racism in America, and ghetto riots, along with white critics and George Russell, into its invective. Russell is singled out in the second paragraph, not least because critic Leonard Feather had used Russell's "last refuge of the untalented" tag approvingly in a festival review: "I address myself to George Russell, a man whose work I have always respected and admired, who in an inopportune moment with an ill-chosen phrase threw himself into the enemy camp."

Russell had, in Shepp's eyes, given succor to the enemy—white America, who has murdered "Bird, Billie, Ernie, Sonny" out of "a systematic and unloving disregard." In the only direct reference to the music, Shepp stated:

> Some of you are becoming a little frightened that we—niggers—ain't keepin' this thing simple enough. "The sound of surprise"? Man, you don't want no surprises from me.
> How do I know that?

Give me leave to state this unequivocal fact: Jazz is the product of the whites—the ofays—too often my enemy. It is the progeny of the blacks—my kinsmen. By this I mean: you own the music, and we make it. By definition, then, you own the people who make the music. You own us in whole chunks of flesh. When you dig deep inside our already disemboweled [*sic*] corpses and come up with a solitary diamond—because you don't want to flood the market—how different are you from the DeBeers of South Africa or the profligates who fleeced the Gold Coast. All right, there are niggers with a million dollars but ain't no nigger got a *billion* dollars.[20]

At this point, it might have been better to leave well enough alone. Russell, however, wrote a long open letter to *Down Beat*—"Popular Delusions and the Madness of Crowds." Russell appeared hurt and frustrated at the way his comments were received, comments he stated were certainly not directed at all musicians who were or saw themselves as part of the jazz avant garde. Unfortunately, he accused the author of the original piece, Dan Morgenstern, of orchestrating his remarks into "a cantata of conservatism." Morgenstern and *Down Beat* obviously disputed the accusation, replying at some length to the charge. Whatever the truth—and one suspects it lies somewhere other than in the perceptions and misperceptions of the participants—it is a shame that a more intelligent debate could not have resulted from Russell's original remarks. Perhaps that has to be the preserve of hindsight, such were the inflamed passions of those times. If ever there were a time to talk about the relationship between art and politics, it surely was then. It was just so hard to be heard above the clamor.[21]

However, Russell did make a number of points very articulately in the interview and in his open letter, which set out his views on music and on politics. It is clear that Russell had no desire to locate himself either with the reactionaries or revolutionaries. His faith and hope lay with America and its people and those of the rest of the world rather than governments. In his open letter, he castigated America for preaching democracy at home but failing to practice it abroad, while he singled out Russia and China for preaching democracy abroad but failing to implement it at home. It is, however, no Jeremiad—naive, his comments might be, but Russell genuinely believed there are better ways for human beings to conduct their affairs. What is more, in calling into question the more bogus aspects of the current jazz scene, he was commenting from a position of stature and knowledge. That is why Shepp reacted as he did, and probably also why Feather latched onto Russell's choice of phrase. Among Russell's papers is a letter from critic and writer Martin Williams thanking him for writing the article, commenting, "and how much what it said needed saying."[22] Russell was certainly not alone in feeling as he did.

In fact, it seems unlikely that Shepp was indeed one of the musicians Russell was thinking of when he was interviewed by Morgenstern. The Norwegian saxophonist Jan Garbarek, who worked extensively with Russell in Scandinavia, was surprised at the suggestion that Russell might have directed his ire toward Shepp.

> I'm very puzzled by this information because I think he was a huge fan of Archie Shepp's. Because Archie Shepp was also for us one of the leaders and I certainly tried to comprehend as much as I could as a young man. I would say George was really behind that. He wanted to put that freedom into some larger form. It could be used alongside organized things, and then came his ideas about various strata in music and also different music going on at the same time. I think free playing was certainly one of these aspects. I'm sure he had a symbol for that kind of playing in his compositional tool kit.[23]

Today the debate may seem to have been a case of "spit and feathers," but it was clearly deadly serious at the time and prefigures the debate in America that grew in the 1990s around Wynton Marsalis and the views on the avant garde held by critics Stanley Crouch and Albert Murray. If history repeats itself, as Henry David Thoreau suggests, then, as Karl Marx added, the first time may be tragedy but the second is surely farce![24]

In terms of the pursuit of his musical goals, Russell certainly saw Europe as offering more fertile and productive ground for his ideas, as he explained in the article in *Avant* magazine in 1998.

> Musically I was very interested in the new music that was going on in Europe and so Stockhausen's *Momente* was very influential. Later pieces by Norwegian composer Kåre Kolberg, as well. He's not very well known but he is a fantastic composer and there was my need to free up the jazz score, free the musicians from the notes and also free up the tempos and stack tempos and aleatory writing. So, musically that was the reason. I felt choked in the USA because at the time I think there was what I would call a pretty conservative thing going on, that I didn't care for much. I thought Europe would give me freedom, which it did—Scandinavia particularly.[25]

There are a couple of points here that require elaboration. First, the regard between Russell and Scandinavia has always been a mutual one, and Russell has continued to be honored in Sweden, Norway, and Denmark. He expressed his gratitude to a group of journalists in an interview for Swedish Radio in 1995.

> I can say that America has given me a chance to develop my musical ideas, with Sweden . . . Sweden gave those musical ideas a chance to blossom when

I came here in 1965. I feel very much a part of the Swedish jazz cultural life because Sweden opened its doors very widely to me, and that was primarily due to the efforts of one of your really truly great jazz musicians, and that was Bosse Broberg, who at the time was director of jazz at the Swedish Radio and who had the good sense to hire Ulla Leksamda as his assistant. So, between them, I made out very well in Sweden.[26]

The second point concerns Stockhausen, and in particular his so-called moment form and specifically *Momente*, to which Russell referred in the *Avant* magazine interview. Malcolm Ball's discussion of the work, also in *Avant*, is not only instructive in itself but readers may detect certain parallels in Russell's own ideas and work.

The work that took "moment form" to its limits is *Momente* which Stockhausen worked on and off during the period 1961/70. The work uses three different kinds of "moments": K-moments (*klang*, sound or timbre), M-moments (melody) and D-moments (duration). Apparently it is no coincidence that these moments bear the initials of key people in Stockhausen's private life at the time where considerable personal conflict had arisen. D is Doris, Stockhausen's first wife and mother to four of his children, M is Mary Bauermeister, an artist who Stockhausen met in 1960 and resulted in a relationship developing with two more children, and K is obviously Karlheinz. (It is perhaps interesting to note that years later, the super-formula of *Licht* also is based around three characters: Eve, Michael and Lucifer.)

From 1963 through to 1970 Stockhausen began to give his performers less and less fixed musical notation using instead symbols such as plus, minus and equal signs, so the interpreter is to use his own musical skills to transform events using these signs and relating them to various parameters such as dynamic levels, duration, pitch etc. So plus (+) would be louder, higher, longer and minus (–) could be shorter, lower, slower, broadly speaking. This period also saw the introduction of live electronics in performance in works such as *Mixtur* for orchestra, sine-wave generators and ring modulators (1964), *Mikrophonie I and II* (1964/65), *Prozession* (1967) and *Kurzwellen* (1968). Throughout this period events in Stockhausen's life were taking dramatic changes and turns. One such event was his trip to Tokyo in 1966 and the realisation of *Telemusik* in the NHK studio. Stockhausen has said that he lived in a kind of dream world and was fascinated by all things Japanese and soon became "more Japanese than the Japanese."

His longest studio based work up to now (1965/67) was *Hymnen* for electronic and concrete sounds. That favourite musical "buzz" word of the 1980's "world music" really starts here with *Hymnen*. Here Stockhausen weaves about forty national anthems from all around the world with electronic sources discovered throughout his time at WDR and concrete sounds such as breathing and the sounds of short wave radio waves which adds an almost extra terrestrial quality to the near two hour long piece. *Hymnen* exists in three versions: 1. *Hymnen* Electronic and concrete music; 2. electronic and concrete music with soloists; and 3. *Hymnen* electronic music with orchestra (third region). Each of its four "regions" has key "centres": region 1 has the Internationale and Marseillaise as its centres, region 2 has West Germany and several African anthems, region 3 is centred around the American, Russian and Spanish anthems and the 4th region has two centres, one being the Swiss anthem and the other is a hymn associated with the Utopian realm of Hymunion in *Harmondie unter Pluramon*.[27]

Russell's decision to move to Sweden was fairly momentous (no pun intended), and it proved to be a life-changing one. Russell had made some remarkable music in America—pieces like "Cubano Be, Cubano Bop," "Jazz in the Space Age," and "All About Rosie" that still shock and surprise, and albums like *Jazz Workshop* that remain unparalleled in jazz. But Russell's music changed again in Scandinavia and he produced two of the finest extended works in jazz—*Othello Ballet Suite* and *Electronic Sonata for Souls Loved by Nature*—during his time in Sweden and Norway. Add to that the gigantic, sprawling oratorio *Listen to the Silence*, which was recorded two years after his return to America, and it is evident that this period of six or seven years was incredibly rejuvenating and revitalizing for the composer. All of Russell's subsequent work owes much to those years.

Critics, from America in particular, have misunderstood the importance of these years for Russell, seeing them as almost a holiday away from the main action Stateside.[28] Indeed, Russell's absence from the American scene goes some way to explain his ongoing difficulty in gaining acceptance with American jazz fans for his music. The sound quality of the records that resulted is not the best. They often sound muddy and with insufficient differentiation between the instruments. But somehow this detracts from neither the music itself nor the astonishing musicianship of the players. But more than that, Scandinavia offered access to facilities for Russell that America never had, as Russell explained to Ben Young,

> A young man who was head of jazz at the Swedish Radio, Bosse Broberg, commissioned everything I had ever written, recommissioned it for Swedish Radio broadcast. It was an experience, a very positive experience being there. They gave me all the time I needed to work in an electronic music studio to build the electronic tape foundation for *Electronic Sonata for Souls Loved by Nature*. I'd never worked with electronic music. They opened the doors for me. Miles Davis, bless his heart, in the pop music of the time, he saw a direction for jazz, and I saw it too. *Electronic Sonata* was an expression of what I saw.[29]

When Russell returned from his New York business trip in the spring of 1965 he was crippled with stomach pains. He arrived in Stockholm in a wheelchair and was again admitted to hospital. The Swedish surgeon removed a swab that his American counterpart had left in Russell's stomach after the earlier operation for ulcers and cleaned up the mess that had been left. Without this surgery, Russell might well have died. By the summer, however, he was well enough to tour Europe and Scandinavia.

It seems that Russell had two overlapping groups at the time—one with the personnel outlined in the *Down Beat* article, which prompted the spat with Archie Shepp, and another that had Americans Ray Pitts on tenor, Brian Trentham on trombone, Cameron Brown on bass, and Don Cherry joining Bertil Loewgren on trumpet. It was this group that made the recording at Stuttgart's Beethoven Hall in August 1965.

This recording, originally released against Russell's wishes as two separate LPs on the German MPS label, was released as a single edition on the CD reissue in 1998. It is an amazing group performance that deserves to be heard in its entirety. The first part of the concert—comprising the first LP—features a long suite built around Russell's compositions and Milt Jackson's "Bags Groove," Bird's "Confirmation," and Monk's "'Round Midnight," with Russell using the Lydian Concept to connect and unify the music. The second original LP includes "You Are My Sunshine," "Oh Jazz Po Jazz" (split over two sides of the record), and "Volupte." Produced by Joachim Berendt, this is one of the most "out" recordings Russell made.[30]

The opening track, "Freein' Up," contains some of Russell's finest piano playing, finding the composer occupying space somewhere between Thelonious Monk and Cecil Taylor, driving the piece through furious tempo changes and using some wonderfully rich tone clusters. The four horns create a constant internal dialogue within the music, and Russell's use of counterpoint and counter-rhythms is complex and masterful. But it is not just his arranging skill that integrates these themes into one whole. Rather it is, with no pun intended, his conceptual ability. Russell is able to bring the disparate and diverse together. The live version of "You Are My Sunshine" is a case in point. It is perhaps less breathtakingly challenging than the original with Sheila Jordan, and lacks the high drama of that performance. Yet it is almost as emotionally affecting. There is a delightful moment when Cherry finishes his solo in mid-cadenza where the audience reacts with laughter that conveys the humor and irony in Russell's use of the old warhorse, without detracting from its genuine sentiment. In several senses, this is Russell's master class in arranging, and many a student arranger could do much worse than start their studies here. "Oh Jazz Po Jazz," which always sounds like a title

Gershwin might have used, is beautifully played, with the musicians achieving a looseness in their performance that just slips by with a loping stride. Obviously, of the horns the great Don Cherry stands out, and as a longtime admirer Russell loved playing with him. But Pitts, Trentham, and Loewgren also acquit themselves well. However, it is the playing of the rhythm section that is perhaps the most striking aspect of the record. Heath and Brown work so well together in this context and leave Russell enormous scope to move between the horns and drums and bass. It is almost as if Russell has invented a new category of jazz, one that absorbs its history and projects its potential at the same time.

There are too many marvelous moments on the record to cover them in their entirety here. The opening brooding section of "Volupte," the almost New Orleans–like interlocking of the horns on Bird's "Confirmation" and elsewhere, the shock at the way Russell opens up still further Monk's "'Round Midnight," the wittiness of "Sunshine," and the liberties he takes with "Bags Groove"—these are a few such highlights. Sadly, this is the Russell album that is often overlooked. It certainly deserves better than *Down Beat*'s grudging three-and-a-half-star review, which argues that the record falls down in the final analysis due to "the unwillingness of his [Russell's] players to give themselves completely over to him—to his design." The reviewer's reaction is one thing; however, his ignorance of Russell's post-Brandeis music is another altogether. It is as if the reviewer lost all track with the composer's music after the late fifties.[31]

After Russell's group played the Stuttgart concert, they performed in Koblenz. When they began "Sunshine," some of the audience laughed, according to Berendt, good-naturedly. Then someone whistled. Russell stopped the performance, went to the microphone and said, with anger in his tone, "If you know it better, why don't you finish the concert?" Memories of Paris the previous year, or just Russell's occasional spikiness? Or maybe the tune and its origins simply meant a great deal to him.[32]

Prior to the German dates, Russell and his group played at Molde on July 29. Molde was to prove one of the most significant events of his time in Scandinavia—in more ways than one. The tenor player he was using for the date was Swede Lennert Åberg, who had met Russell the previous year when Russell had worked with the Emanon Big Band. It had been quite an occasion, with the leader of the sax section, Lennart Jansson, dead drunk, and the whole section fell apart during the faster numbers. Bernt Rosengren had left Russell's sextet, and the inexperienced Åberg was surprised to get the call.

We went to Molde to play at the festival there, July 1965. I was totally para-lysed by nervousness and at the airport in Oslo I succeeded with the impossible thing to just drop the saxophone on the floor. In Molde I checked it and the small round ring between the body and the bell was like an egg so I had to very carefully try to adjust it to be able to play it. I thought I almost did it, just a few millimetres left and I made a last effort and the Bell just was bent out in a nanosecond and the saxophone looked like a smoking pipe! The Bell did not point up but straight out! In Norway, they did not have any Selmer saxes, so one was sent for from Denmark! Meanwhile, we had to rehearse and I bor-rowed a sax from Booker Ervin but I could hardly get a sound out of it. I had heard the rumours about Don Byas having so hard reeds that only he could play it and so on so I thought this was something similar. G had always been nice to me but this time he lost his temper and screamed, "Blow Man Blow!" Maybe even, "Blow Motherfucker!" When the rehearsal was over and I unpacked the sax something fell out and it turned out that it was full of packages of cigarettes that Booker had smuggled! Probably some of them prepared too!

I thought the concert was a nightmare and I just wanted to disappear but G and "Tootie" Heath told me to follow to the control booth for the Norwegian TV to have a look at the result and I remember we looked at "'Round Mid-night" that was a feature for tenor sax and they both said, "Great!" and were very nice to me. Other musicians there were Donald Byrd and Dexter Gordon and G made a small speech for Dexter just before our concert. We also heard two very young unknown musicians from Oslo at a jam session, Jan Garbarek and Jon Christensen.[33]

Russell's ten or so months in Sweden had proved exceptionally eventful. He had married a young Swedish artist and had also had a child, his son Jock, by another young woman.[34] At Molde, he met Marit Jerstad, who had just separated from her husband. They soon became lovers and began a stormy relationship that lasted six years. Jerstad was involved with the Norwegian new music scene and its organization Ny Musikk, as well as with the theatre. She had developed what she describes as visual compositions to accompany music and would later create one of these for Russell's *Electronic Sonata*, which was performed with the piece at various festivals. Through her Rus-sell got to know most of the new composers on the Scandinavian scene, and they, along with Stockhausen, Ligeti, and Penderecki, were perhaps the last new influences on Russell's music.

After his concert at Molde, Russell went along to a session where a group of young Norwegian musicians were playing and sat in on piano. The group included a very young Jan Garbarek on tenor, Arild Andersen on bass, and Jon Christensen on drums. Andersen speaks for all of them when he recalls the event. "I remember he came up to a jazz club where we were playing with

Garbarek and Christensen, and I'm not sure if Terje was on that gig. George came up and sat in on piano and it was incredible. I still remember it. We played 'Just Friends,' and the energy just got up to the ceiling."[35]

It seems unlikely that guitarist Terje Rypdal was present, as he remembers meeting Russell for the first time on a later occasion.[36] More prosaically, Jan Christensen remembers how Russell was so taken with their playing, he immediately wanted to hire them.

> We played a concert at Molde Jazz Festival in the summer of 1965 with Jan Garbarek, and George Russell was sitting in at a jam session that evening and he liked very much what he heard, and so he invited me and Jan to come over to Stockholm, where he was living at the time. Jan was still at school but I was finished, so I could go and meet George in Sweden.[37]

As for Garbarek, he remembers the gig very well, both in terms of how it felt but also for the older musician's affirmation of what he and his peers were trying to create.

> I think I would have to go back to the very first meeting with George, because—I don't know if you are at all familiar with how that happened—it's enough to say that it was all about a release of energy. We had plenty of that, of course, being young free jazz musicians into everything like Coltrane and so on. So it was all about energy anyway. But George had a tremendous fire in him, and when he played with us, we seemed to reach yet another gear, another level. So it was opening up a freedom, and a freedom that was accepted by others at the time. It was a little bit difficult because we were the first generation in Norway that took up this really free-energy playing and this free-associative creation. But George was fully into it and he backed it and he was a part of it and he accepted it.[38]

Some fans and critics bemoan the absence in more recent times of artists and innovators of the stature of Louis Armstrong, Duke Ellington, Charlie Parker, Miles Davis, and John Coltrane. But such thinking results from nostalgia regarding their own first discovery of jazz and from the security that history can have when bestowing the mantle of greatness. There are at least a few who have changed the way the music sounds since then. One would be Keith Jarrett. Another would be John McLaughlin. Others might with justification argue on behalf of Wayne Shorter, Michael Brecker, and Pat Metheny, in which case Jan Garbarek would deserve more than a mention. He is not just an astonishing improviser with a huge, wide-ranging sonic palette, but the records he has made for ECM have defined a whole sound and genre. It is too easy to rely on the certainties of hindsight in making our judgments and critical evaluations.

Marit Jerstad, who was also present, saw something else. In all the interviews for this book—with men and women, colleagues and lovers—each
person has offered his or her own insights into Russell, his motivations, and
his character. However, it seems that it is often the women in his life who
have been most keen in their perceptions of him.

I came to a jam session after the concert and George was playing. And I got so
struck by his music. It struck me very deeply, and when I saw him sitting at the
piano, I felt very strongly his loneliness. We are all uniquely alone, and I felt
that very strongly about George—those two things, the man and his music.[39]

Her comments echo something that Sheila Jordan has said about Russell.

I watched him one time when he would come by and pick me up at my office
when we were still going together. And I was in the building and he was standing
outside the car—and I'll never forget that image—and he was standing there,
and there was an aura about him that was like he didn't even belong here. He
was displaced. He was standing there, but he looked like, "I don't belong here,"
and I'll never forget that look. I can't explain it but it was like a very lonesome
. . . I got a very lonely feeling when I saw him. I'll never forget that.[40]

Jerstad and Russell lived together for much of his time in Scandinavia,
and though they stopped being lovers in 1970, they remained friends. As Jerstad told Ian Carr, Russell had liaisons with other women, invariably white,
while they were together, and she had affairs as well. "When he had all his
affairs, I had some, which infuriated him."[41]

At the same time, they shared common interests in music, food, and philosophy—both had discovered the ideas of G. I. Gurdjieff. Jerstad told Carr
that Russell helped her develop more self-confidence, but it was certainly
a relationship characterized by its share of fights and arguments. Jerstad recalled that on one occasion in Italy, she threw a chair at Russell that missed
and went through a window. It seems, however, that it was an important
relationship for them both, not least in opening the world of Scandinavian
new music to the composer. They went to concerts together and socialized
with many of the musicians and composers involved in that world. It ended
when Russell had moved back to the States and when "he fell in love with
a mutual friend."[42]

Jerstad also noted that Russell arrived in Scandinavia with a certain sense
of bitterness and "a very strong rage" inside him.[43] These characteristics were
also part of the man and his music—and, however much age and maturity
may have impacted upon him, still are.

Just before he played at Molde and jammed with Garbarek, Andersen, and Christensen, Russell began writing a letter to his old friends Peggy and John Benson Brooks. The letter gives a strong insight into his thoughts and feelings at the time, not least in light of Jerstad's comments. It is an unusual letter that mixes the personal with Russell's political observations. When he began the letter, he was at Molde, due shortly on stage with his group. There is a slight discrepancy here over dates. Russell's letter is dated July 31, yet elsewhere the date of his performance was given as July 29. He notes that Dexter Gordon, Jimmy Cleveland, Booker Ervin, and Donald Byrd were also appearing at the festival, and that both Brian Trentham and Cameron "Cam" Brown were with the band: "Brian and Cam are here to stay—both would be fed to the Viet Nam meat grinder if they remained there. That shit is ridiculous."

Adding that Al "Tootie" Heath was on drums—Russell spells it "Tutti"— he writes that the "two Swedish cats" in the band on trumpet and tenor were "promising but just not up to the music we play or rather not up to the demands of the music." Russell then outlines his thoughts on America and its stance over Vietnam, contrasting America's sense of itself as the supporter of democracy and freedom while at the same time supporting some of the worst dictators on the planet: "[A]nd look at the 'anti-communist' mothers that have used our dough to degrade their own—Diem, Trujillo, Batista, Chiang [Kai-shek], Franco, Duvalier. We'll support any son of a bitch who says he's against godless communism."

Russell resumes the letter on September 2 and comments on what he felt was the way Down Beat had misrepresented his views (see above) and talks of the birth of his son, Jock. He then writes briefly about his recent German tour and the Stuttgart date with Don Cherry and mentions a concert the group was doing for German Radio and a big-band gig at the Konserthuset in Stockholm opposite Dexter Gordon. Then there is an interesting and amusing postscript: "Had an interview with AFN in Stuttgart [armed forces network] and expressed my views on Viet Nam. I was pretty stoned but I did get the impression that the interviewer was constantly try [sic] to change the subject."[44]

Unfortunately, it seems that any tape, if the interview was ever broadcast at all, no longer exists unless there is one in private hands. It would certainly be interesting to hear a "stoned," hip jazz musician bemoaning American foreign policy to a member of the U.S. armed forces. Russell has never been unwilling to speak his mind.

Essentially, Russell worked regularly throughout Sweden, Norway, and Denmark, with occasional forays into the rest of Europe, during the five years he spent in Scandinavia. He toured and recorded with a new sextet, but much of his work came from Swedish Radio and involved new works and recommissions of older material. As noted, Bosse Broberg was the person at Swedish Radio responsible for commissioning jazz projects. Broberg met Russell when he was working with the Emanon Big Band, a grouping that was beginning to explore areas outside more established lines of writing and arranging for large jazz ensembles. Russell's arrival in Scandinavia in 1964 proved very timely, as Broberg remembers.

> He sort of opened our minds to new ways of thinking with his theory of the Lydian scale as combining element or dimension. Also, he brought in philosophical ideas about music being a means of release. From early on he was making the case for synthesising different musical traditions, for example Afro-American with European (not to forget the tinge of Latin American).[45]

It was Russell's "audacious and unconventional writing techniques" that impressed Broberg, in particular the way Russell combined different sections of his groups and big bands in unpredictable ways. Broberg refers specifically and in detail to aspects of Russell's theories, for example, his distinction between vertical and horizontal forms. He notes Russell's role as a teacher in Scandinavia and describes him as, in effect, Swedish Radio's "composer-in-residence" during that period. As well as the records that resulted from Swedish Radio commissions, the radio station commissioned twenty-four performances by various Russell groupings between 1966 and 1983, of which fifteen performances took place between 1966 and 1969.[46]

In terms of Russell's impact on Swedish jazz, Broberg is unequivocal.

> Russell's ideas of anchoring improvisation with a scale or a central note over extended periods was of great importance. The method aims at opening the way for freer exploration. I regard this as important for the development of Swedish (then) contemporary jazz music. The study of his theoretical work in which he is discussing the relationship between vertical and horizontal forms and courses served as an inspiration for many practitioners—players as well as writers.[47]

By this point, Russell had begun to recruit the musicians he had jammed with at Molde and incorporate them into his sextet. As noted, Garbarek was just seventeen and needed to finish high school, so was not able to join immediately. Jon Christensen, who was four years older, joined Russell fairly immediately, and Arild Andersen came in as soon as he had completed his compulsory military service.

One of Christensen's first experiences with Russell was at a remarkable concert in Denmark in December 1965. It featured Russell with a big band, which appeared in the middle of two performances of Stockhausen's *Gruppen* for three orchestras.

> For me it was a learning process to be part of that thing, but there was one special concert in Copenhagen which was arranged by Danish Radio at the Tivoli Concert Hall featuring the music of George Russell and the classical composer Karlheinz Stockhausen. That was nice because Stockhausen had this famous composition where he used three bands on three different stages. We were there with the big band and George and Stockhausen were talking together, and it was nice to be part of a concert with him. He was very nice also. I think it was the late sixties. So many things happened.[48]

The way the music scene was set up at that time in Scandinavia must have been quite a pleasant surprise for Russell. There were many more opportunities for work and direct and indirect state sponsorship, both through public broadcasting stations and through organizations like Ny Musikk. Russell and his various groups performed at the Golden Circle in Stockholm, played at various schools, and performed two major concerts arranged by Ny Musikk at the University of Oslo in March 1966 and August 1967.[49]

At the time he had signed with the Swedish company Sonet Records, and much of the Scandinavian material came out first on that label. The actual recording sequence of the music released and dates when albums came out is rather complicated and is really a matter of interest only to jazz historians. The records actually released while Russell was in northern Europe, or in the process of returning to the United States, were *Othello Ballet* (which includes Russell's *Electronic Organ Sonata No. 1*), *Electronic Sonata for Souls Loved by Nature—1968* (the sextet version), and *The Essence of George Russell* (which contained the big-band version of *Electronic Sonata for Souls Loved by Nature*, *Now and Then*, and "Concerto for Self-Accompanied Guitar"). It makes sense—artistically and critically—to treat *Trip to Prillargui* from 1970 and *Listen to the Silence* from 1971 as being part of that same sequence of albums. Not only did they include much the same personnel, but they spring from the same source, both in terms of commissioning and inspiration.

The first piece Russell recorded in Sweden was *Now and Then*. It was premiered at Konserthuset, Stockholm, in autumn 1966 and was finally released on Sonet in 1970 along with a big-band performance of *Electronic Sonata for Souls Loved by Nature*, with sleeve notes by the Norwegian composer Kåre

Kolberg. It reveals clearly how far and how fast Russell's thinking about big-band composition had moved since *Jazz in the Space Age*.

There's a quote from Leonard Bernstein that seems very apt here: "We have reached that supra-level of musical semantics . . . where those apparently mismatched components can unite—tonal, non-tonal, electronic, serial, aleatory—all united in a magnificent new eclecticism."[50] Bernstein's words can fairly be applied to Russell, and "unity" is a word he uses often in conversation, particularly in terms of what he calls "chord-scale unity." One aspect of Russell's search has been to try to discover a point of shared origin for all music, in an emotional and philosophical rather than strictly historical sense. Another has been his desire to achieve a theoretical understanding that incorporates all music, Western and non-Western, composed and improvised. His ideas about tonality—or, as he puts it, "tonal gravity"—and of "time," in its musical and broader philosophical senses, provide places where these forms can be found, explained, and explored. His compositions are his research laboratories and the place where his theory is most articulately expounded. Arguably, *Now and Then* represents the first full flowering in sound of that theory. That is not to deride in any way what had gone before; rather it is to suggest that the music Russell began to make in Scandinavia epitomizes his mature output.

Famously, this was one of Jan Garbarek's first performances with a Russell band. Though Garbarek was still in school, Russell suggested that he might still be able to undertake some recordings in Stockholm.

> My reading wasn't that good, but he offered to send me the music a couple of months before, which he did. He sent me all the parts, I think, for tenor saxophone for his big-band music. That's how I learned to read music, basically, getting those parts and learning them for my trip to Stockholm, which went not brilliantly from my point of view, but I survived. I sat next to some of my real heroes, Swedish professional top musicians that I admired very much, and I was really in awe I would say of the whole situation. As I said, I barely survived, but I did survive. In a way that was a good thing for me.[51]

With his love of Shepp, Coltrane, and Albert Ayler, the young man must have felt in his element. This was a huge, Mingus-like piece in which different musical elements collide and combust. It's polyrhythmic, polytonal, and panstylistic, and Russell uses different musical strata working simultaneously and often pulling in completely different directions. In lesser hands, it would sound like chaos. In fact, ironically, it is the composer himself who seems to lose focus briefly at the end, when he continues playing after the band has finished. With Russell's skill as a musical architect, it embodies jazz past, present, and future. It is not Russell's greatest work, by any means, but certainly one that augurs in a new chapter in his music.

Stockhausen is certainly one of the influences that one begins to hear on *Now and Then* and also on *Othello Ballet*, which was Russell's next major work. "Influence" often feels too strong a word in such a context. At least during their earlier years, composers, if they are of any worth, constantly seek to incorporate new sounds, ideas, and approaches into their work. Russell is a musical explorer pursuing his own musical aims. The composer's voice that the listener hears is still Russell. It is just that his scope as a composer has expanded to incorporate what has been newly discovered. The word "parallel" often feels more useful, because it suggests a separate exploration of similar ideas and musical language. In that sense, the listener may hear Russell exploring similar territory to Ligeti, Penderecki, Stockhausen, and also Edgar Varèse.

Whether Varèse was a direct "influence" on Russell is a matter of conjecture. However, their music shares an explosive, canonlike quality, and Varèse was unusual as a classical composer in his strong interest in rhythm. He was also one of the first to experiment with the potential of electronics as a compositional tool.[52] Russell's range as a composer was now opening out in whole new directions. His early work might have drawn on Debussy, Ravel, Scriabin, and Stravinsky for inspiration. Now one has the sense that he has access to the whole world. He is beginning to draw on the African and North African ideas he is hearing. Listen to the Arabic feel that emerges on *Electronic Sonata* or the masterful percussive fiesta with which the second half of the piece commences. The tape he has put together for the piece uses snatches of music from different parts of the planet, and the feeling is now one of temporal distortion, of ideas imploding and emerging transformed.

By now Russell was using what was also the Jan Garbarek Quartet as part of his own sextet and as the core of the big-band work he was doing for Scandinavian radio. *Othello Ballet*, the next composition to be recorded, was written at the suggestion of Walter Nicks, the African American dancer and choreographer who was at the time a consultant at the University of Stockholm. One of the most successful dancers of his generation, it seems likely that Nicks had met Russell through Harry Belafonte, for whom Nicks had worked in the States. According to Max Harrison,[53] Russell did not collaborate closely with Nicks, and perhaps for that reason the music works very much on its own terms. The ballet, called *The Net*, was televised by various European TV stations during 1968. Recorded in November 1967, the music represents a step back from the freedom and experimentation with new forms that "*Now and Then*" represented. Russell's music had been used in a ballet before, in 1963, when the Warsaw Opera Ballet Company used the "Chromatic Universe" sections of *Jazz in the Space Age*.[54] *The Net* was, however, the only occasion when Russell wrote directly for the stage, as he explained to WKCR's Ben Young.

> That's the only experience I've ever had with doing music for ballet and I did the music . . . I mean, I had an idea of what the choreographer is wanting to bring out at certain places. *Othello*—it's pretty obvious that it's building up to a tension and the moods that it insinuates are pretty easy to follow. So I made mood my chief aim in the various areas of it because I know what's going to go on in those areas. Whether it's Othello getting a bit antsy because the antagonist was putting ideas in his head about his wife—Iago. So the moods were implied and I like to include mood in all my writing.[55]

A further comment Russell makes in the interview in relation to *Othello Ballet* and other extended works is also instructive.

> I write longer compositions because I consider a piece as a piece of theatre, really, and I think in terms of acts and events taking the listener on a trip down a . . . telling a story. Furthermore, I automatically rebel against this sort of unwritten law with most media that if you want to be heard you stay within a six-minute boundary. I'm never going to conform. If I want to write something six minutes I will, but I don't want to write it, so I'm trying to make the hit parade. So I feel like, as I said, that our music can represent music on a very high level and be a truly classical music and is in many instances, or was at least. Until this recent period when innovation became a bad word.[56]

He continues to stress that he is not suggesting that a profound piece of music cannot be written that is a few minutes long and popular, citing Ellington's "Sophisticated Lady" and Steely Dan's "Aja" as examples. He adds, "So that's a big challenge. But so is writing a forty-five minute work. Lots of people say that jazz composers can't write extended works. That made me mad."[57]

Othello Ballet comprises a series of events, and is perhaps Russell's first work using this approach. Despite its diversity and the shortness of some episodes and their abrupt endings, the coherence of the work is maintained throughout. What is more, Russell uses the full orchestra of twenty-three musicians to the fullest extent. The electronic instruments used—guitar, bass, organ, and possibly electric piano—add textures that could not be achieved any other way, and create contrasts with the acoustic instruments. Garbarek is again the dominant soloist. Though he might have struggled to read the parts, his instrument fashions blocks and sheets of sound that offset the finer detail that emerges from the ensemble. *Othello* is a dark, often brooding work, rich in emotion and mood. If it has parallels, these lie outside jazz. At times, Russell's themes and arrangements suggest Bernstein and the way in which he incorporated jazz elements into his work. However, the percussive quality of the work—the composer uses Christensen on kit drums plus three percussionists—and the way this combines with exclamatory brass choruses recalls the French American composer Edgar Varèse, to whom Russell and his confederates had listened in New York in the forties and fifties, along with Copland, Ives, and Milhaud.

When it was eventually released in the States, *Down Beat* gave *Othello Ballet* five stars, and the review's author wrote:

> *Othello* is a ballet in every sense of the word. It is danceable, with rhythms and polyrhythms playing against each other. Rather than being programmatic, Russell lets the dancers tell the story. His music is pure music that will stand alone, devoid of any associations with Shakespeare's tragic hero.[58]

The author singled out Garbarek for praise, describing him as "a complete gas." He was also impressed with Russell's *Electronic Organ Sonata No. 1*, which completes the LP, but saw it as the "work of a composer in transition," being Russell's first exercise within the form of electronic music. In fact it was not Russell's first such experiment, as he had for some time been working on the tape that would be used within the context of *Electronic Sonata for Souls Loved by Nature*.

There is actually an argument to be made that *Electronic Organ Sonata No. 1* is the distilled essence of George Russell. The recording, made at Grorud Church in Oslo on October 1, 1968, is essentially an improvisation by Russell; it was recorded by Bjornar Andresen and Kåre Kolberg, both avant garde composers in their own right. The recording was then taken into the electronic music studio of Radio Sweden, where engineer Gøte Nilsson worked with the tape. One hesitates to use the word "spontaneous" in this context, for Russell is clearly drawing heavily on the Lydian Concept here, and there is a lingering influence of Stockhausen about the whole project. What emerges with Russell's piece is something that has a certain fuguelike quality. Ideas are developed and returned to by the composer and then explored in a different way. There is little sense of linear progress, as is the case with much electronic music, but Russell creates an intense, controlled, and mood-laden work. These qualities are clearly further enhanced through its treatment in the studio. If only Russell had pursued this approach rather than leave it ostensibly behind him in Scandinavia. He has continued to use electronics in his music; however, the creation of a solo performance that was then treated electronically is not an experiment he has repeated.

That said, his brief dalliance with the form on *Electronic Sonata* is vital and exciting, and produced what Harrison notes was, aside from André Hodeir's *Jazz et Jazz*, "the first distinguished piece of electronic music in the jazz idiom."[59] Where Hodeir's piece is, however, less than four minutes in length, *Electronic Sonata* is a full hour in length, and the tape prepared in Radio Sweden's studios is used throughout.

It is not entirely clear exactly when Terje Rypdal joined Russell, but it was probably soon after the recording of *Othello Ballet*. As Rypdal remembers it, he was playing in a rock/jazz group called the Dream, with whom Garbarek had also played for a time.

> Then they asked me to join his new quartet. Arild had been in the military, and George was having these courses on the Lydian Concept in Oslo. So I started with Jan. I was desperate to learn anything that was more serious about improvisation. I had been improvising long before. I almost got fired from one band for not playing the same solo every night. So the interest was there. So I took this course and it was very important. It was a case of how you wanted to use the course, in a way. There were all sorts of possibilities.
>
> Then we started Jan's quartet and I was asked to join his [George's] sextet. I got the old valve trombone part from some recordings and it was so difficult. *(laughs)* So I spent several months rehearsing and trying to learn it, and it was probably one of the hardest things I have done [at] any time. We did quite a few gigs. A couple of gigs, like Prillargui, were recorded. So it was a real learning period. It was extremely important. Later on he got into this freer stuff, *Electronic Sonata*, that was very interesting. I could use some of the older rock things in that. I liked that time very much.[60]

The first recording of *Electronic Sonata for Souls Loved by Nature*—1968 was by Russell's sextet. The sense of temporal distortion is even more evident on this version than on its big-band sibling, recorded in 1970. With the blues-drenched playing of Garbarek and the way the electronic tape melds with and changes the group's performance, this is a genuinely spooky, otherworldly experience. These are the places that jazz-rock could have and should have gone. There is nothing quite like it in jazz. Yet the sense of continuity with Russell's early work remains. Russell has always liked to have the band drop out and leave the soloist alone. Here, not only does he do this to create dramatic tension or presage a change of mood or direction, but he uses the electronic tape to accompany and challenge the soloist. Arild Andersen's walking bass, Rypdal's Hendrix-inspired guitar, and Christensen's powerful drumming all combine to make this record a tour de force. As the music moves in and out of time, it is a summation of the stop-start rhythms and tempo changes Russell has used throughout his career. Arguably, this music is further out than even Miles Davis at that time. Yet at times straight-ahead passages hit a Cannonball Adderley/Horace Silver groove before slipping into a Monk-ish interlude, with some fine blues piano from Russell. This version more than complements its big-band sibling; it also shows how the composition can be refashioned and refocused.

The big-band *Electronic Sonata*, recorded in 1970, also features marvelous playing from Garbarek, but there is also some excellent Miles-ish trumpet from American exile Stanton Davis. Rypdal is an absolute asset to the piece throughout and his solo is quite stunning, while Jon Christensen and percussionist Sabu Martinez—echoing Chano Pozo—provide the music's heartbeat. Here the piece opens out into a massive outpouring of emotion that is truly exhilarating.

Both versions of *Electronic Sonata* came out in America quite a while after they were recorded, which lessened their impact. By that time Miles Davis had released both *In a Silent Way* and *Bitches Brew*, and Weather Report's first album had also been issued. Trumpeter Stanton Davis recalls hearing Miles's *Bitches Brew* and speaking to Russell about it.

> So we've done *Electronic Sonata*, it wasn't released pre-Miles *Bitches Brew* but it was pre-Miles Davis *Bitches Brew*. George knew that the universe and the world were going in that direction. When *Bitches Brew* came out, I was like calling George and saying "George, they're doing our stuff." He said, "I know. Miles knows what's going on," and just laughed.[61]

To place *Electronic Sonata* further in its rightful context, Davis notes the range of music and musicians he came into contact with through Russell while in Norway and confirms the kinds of influences that Russell was exploring.

> A lot of musicians I met through George, like Don Cherry and composers who were living in Scandinavia, they were writing very experimental kinds of things, aleatory types of things similar to Ligeti and Klaus Egge, who was a composer from Norway. I got involved in all those types of classicism that I probably would never have been connected with just playing jazz.[62]

Electronic Sonata is a remarkably coherent piece that seems to embrace musical styles from across the planet and exemplifies Russell's command of a variety of musical idioms. One section draws on North African music, another on Afro-Cuban and Latin music, and elements of the blues also surface.

Russell's palette is the whole world, but now it seems to want to include deep space as well. If his *Get Down with It* double album, recorded between 1970 and 1974, was "Miles' first attempt to make Ellington dance with Stockhausen,"[63] *Electronic Sonata* was Russell's, and it is arguably one of the finest attempts to merge jazz and contemporary music influences. Russell's grasp of harmony, and therefore of texture, is the key. He is forced to integrate sources and influences. He and Miles Davis have been among the few in jazz to grasp the rhythmic potential of Stockhausen's ideas. It is not just the elisions and abrupt changes of rhythmic emphasis or the collision of different rhythms; these were in large measure already present in Russell's music. But from now on, there is a much greater sense of how these can be used by the composer to create whole new shapes, textures and rhythms within the music and yet still, as he put it years before, *"You can retain the funk."*[64] The electronic tape Russell created in the Swedish Radio sound lab is never used just to color the work; the musicians improvise with it and respond to it. For example, one of the most dramatic sections of the big-band *Electronic Sonata* occurs when the African drumming on the tape is joined by the two drummers, Jon Christensen and Egil Johansen, and percussionist Sabu Martinez. Elsewhere, Garbarek responds directly to the electronic sounds in his improvisation. The tape changes the musicians' contributions, just as a written line might. This in itself is a hugely interesting development. There is music made in real time and, with the tape, music already created at a different point in time. In every sense, musical and philosophical, Russell is playing with time. If he chooses, he can change when the tape is used in the music and thereby change the composition and the way his musicians play it. Music from other times and places can be used to create a kind of temporal schism.

At one point the band members chant, "You can learn to live another way. Go inside and you'll awake anew someday. You can really change the world if only you believe it." The text is derived from Russell's involvement with the ideas of G. I. Gurdjieff, the Russian mystic who had taught extensively in France and Western Europe. Russell had been introduced to "The Work" in Norway in 1966 and had joined a "circle" there led by American expatriate Brenda Tripp. Gurdjieff, and even more so his follower Maurice Nicoll, had certain ideas about time that in an age of quantum physics seem now (slightly) less outlandish than might once have been the case. It is, however, to these ideas that Russell is making specific reference, and he is even illustrating them in the work itself by literally playing with time.

The tape also advances the composition and adds new levels of thematic coherence. This is incredibly complex music, but, on the big-band version, it is essayed by the orchestra with such skill, enthusiasm, and ease that it swings and drives with a Bacchanalian passion. With towering performances from Russell's core sextet, this is one of his greatest works and one of the few completely successful extended works in jazz. What is more, it has surely one of the greatest finales in jazz.

It is well worth contrasting the two sextet albums, *Electronic Sonata for Souls Loved by Nature—1968* and *Trip to Prillargui* from 1970. In some ways, *Prillargui* is the least satisfying of all these records. Recorded live at Estrad in Sweden in March 1970, it featured what had become Russell's core group of Jan Garbarek, Terje Rypdal, Arild Andersen, and Jon Christensen, along with the African American trumpeter Stanton Davis. Its shortcomings lie not in the performances or material but in the impression of incompleteness it leaves. It feels as if the listener has walked into a club halfway into the performance and has to leave before the end, never quite able to make sense of the whole. That said, it features powerful playing from Garbarek on his own "Theme," in practice a "head" arrangement, and Russell's "Souls," an extract from *Electronic Sonata*. With Russell's percussive piano in the background and some lovely guitar from Rypdal, these two tracks alone reveal what an exciting, visceral jazz-rock group this was—and what a pity it was that they did not record more together.

The performance then seems to lose some of its structure as it slips into a more abstract phase with Russell's "Event III" and Garbarek's "Vips." Again, the playing is fine—from the rhythm section and Garbarek, particularly so—and the rather retrospective, in this context, "Stratusphunk" has some very nice trumpet from Stanton Davis. Yet the dynamic built up by the first two numbers has been lost. The record recovers with Garbarek's loose, meandering "Esoteric Circle," with its Miles-ish trumpet solo from Davis, before launching into a powerful take on Ornette Coleman's "Man in the Moon," with some bravura guitar from Rypdal.[65] But again, the listener is left wanting more, as the track is phased out before the end. *Prillargui* remains an album with some fine moments but without a finale: a case of what might have been.

Electronic Sonata for Souls Loved by Nature—1968 and *Trip to Prillargui* certainly do give a sense of what the group was like live. Compared to Russell's earlier American bands, it was wilder, looser, and more spontaneous—occasionally guests like Don Cherry might sit in with the group. Russell continued to encourage his musicians to contribute to the band's book, just as he had with Dave Baker and Al Kiger. Perhaps the key difference, however, between this group and his earlier sextet lay in the use of electronic instruments and textures in the music. It is surprising that Russell himself did not use organ or Fender Rhodes in place of an acoustic piano, but then he has always been unduly modest about his abilities as a performer. And if Russell rejected free playing and atonality in jazz as an end in itself, it seems that with his Scandinavian sextet he found ways of incorporating such elements into his music. Garbarek remains proud of the group's prowess as a live act.

> Don Cherry was living in Scandinavia, and whenever he was around, if we played with George's big band or sextet, he would invite him on stage to play, which was a great boost as well. That was very free, what he did. We just opened up and let him go for as long as he wanted. Absolutely fantastic! Inspiring! So George was always open for leaving room for that sort of approach in his music. There was always room for anything there that he found valuable. It didn't have to be his own, but it created yet another "strata" [*sic*], you might say.[66]

Listen to the Silence was recorded two years after Russell returned to the States to commence what proved to be a long teaching career at the New England Conservatory. Its inspiration and commissioning lie within his Scandinavian period, and for these reasons, it should be considered within the context of the other recordings made in Sweden and Norway. Though this was not the only time Russell wrote for a choir, sadly, it was the only time his work in this area has been recorded and released. *Listen to the Silence* reveals a remarkable potential in this respect.

Commissioned by the Norwegian Cultural Fund for the 1971 Kongsberg Jazz Festival, *Listen to the Silence* was premiered on June 26 of that year. Not only had Russell composed and arranged the music, he had created the libretto, supplying both his own written material and also texts from Maurice Nicoll; Rainer Maria Rilke's *Duano Elegies*; Dee Brown's seminal lament for the Native American, *Bury My Heart at Wounded Knee*; and further texts from *Newsweek* and the *New York Times*. The orchestra comprised Russell's sextet from *Trip to Prillargui*, plus Bjornar Andresen on Fender bass (who had helped with the recording of the electronic tape for *Electronic Sonata*), Webster Lewis on organ, Bobo Stenson on electric piano, and Russell himself on timpani. The work also featured the chorus of the Musikk Konservatoriet of Oslo and eight additional singers from the New England Conservatory, including the exceptionally gifted Dan Windham as bass soloist. It is his voice that adds both great pathos and gravitas to the text.

Listen to the Silence owes its conception in part to the work of Ligeti, Boulez, and Stockhausen. Its use of prose extracts from newspapers, books, and like sources is not original to Russell—Boulez has used such material, as has Stockhausen. There are also parallels with Bernstein's *Mass* and Benjamin Britten's *Requiem Mass*. However, in a jazz context, Russell's work goes far beyond Ellington's *Black, Brown and Beige* and predates Anthony Davis's *X, The Life and Times of Malcolm X* by fifteen years.[67] It shares with both a didactic aspect. Russell's target is American imperialism, and in citing its treatment of the American Indian alongside its involvement in Vietnam, he draws parallels between American internal and external expansionism. Taken from a *Newsweek* review of Dee Brown's book, Russell quotes:

> The motive force for our theft of land and identity from the Indians was Manifest Destiny—the belief that white men were ordained to rule this continent.

And later:

> Manifest Destiny was a simple instrument to operate, once we got the hang of it.

Perhaps to avoid charges from right-wing critics that his concern about America's behavior ignores the crimes against freedom perpetrated by communist regimes, Russell also singles out Soviet use of psychiatric labels and institutionalization as a means of silencing its critics. Russell had been due to play the International Jazz Festival in Prague in 1968. The festival was cancelled because the country was invaded by several of its "allies." Russell kept the letter he received from the organizers apologizing for the cancellation. Given the circumstances, in which it was written, it is a masterpiece of calm understatement and quiet optimism, something Russell would understand and appreciate.[68]

Although determined to avoid exculpating the Soviet Union, in *Listen to the Silence* Russell directs his ire toward America, and his analysis is both trenchant and sophisticated, far more so than most artistic-political statements of the time. But Russell's didactic purposes with *Listen to the Silence* are not just political. His use of Maurice Nicoll's work *The Mark*, specifically in "Event IV," puts forward the concept of "Metanoia," or self-transformation through spiritual growth. Nicoll's book focuses on what he argues is the true message of the gospels and of Jesus Christ, namely, that it is about spiritual rebirth and the liberation of the unborn, latent person inside each of us. Nicoll's—and Russell's—message is that it is inside us that we can discover our essence. Russell is contrasting human potential that can be found inside us with the cruelties and destructiveness of goal-seeking, exploitative behavior.[69]

His conspiracy theories aside, Stanton Davis has a number of very valid points to make about *Listen to the Silence*.

> We did *Listen to the Silence*. What I really liked about it was that it had really classical and aleatory techniques of voice, which I thought was great, the

chanting and all that. There was a political reason that it wasn't released, because it had some antiwar statements in it and it was really a political message from that time. I guess coming up through the Vietnam War, I didn't think about it as being that serious, which is odd, but I guess some countries like the States, they stopped it so that record didn't come out too soon. When it did come out it opened up some doors about aleatory music again.[70]

Musically, Russell opts for quite a simple accompaniment for the voices at times. Sometimes, it is just percussion or Arild Andersen's bass. However, elsewhere the music is more complex. For example, in "Event I" a scored but free-sounding orchestra clashes with a chaos of voices. At times, some of the techniques that Russell uses recall Krysztof Penderecki's work, in particular *Threnody for the Victims of Hiroshima*, which, though scored for strings, creates highly vocalized effects.[71] Also, Penderecki's use of glissandi is mirrored in certain of the vocal techniques Russell uses, for example, the fade at the end of "Event II." *Listen to the Silence* also features one of Russell's most popular themes, and he has used it continually in concert and recorded it on three albums.[72] However, on this version, Stanton Davis's solo is one of the record's high points, revealing the trumpeter's wonderful grasp of the dramatic.

A comment from Bobo Stenson, who plays piano and keyboards on *Listen to the Silence*, is instructive and perhaps indicates why the Scandinavians took Russell so much to their hearts. Acknowledging Russell's influence on Scandinavian jazz, Stenson notes,

He opened up a new way of writing music and he involved a lot of people. He stayed there. He was there for quite some time. He had a sextet and different bands they put together and leading these big groups. He was busy there. He meant a lot to a lot of people. Also with Palle Mikkelborg in Denmark, who was one of his favorites, I guess. He meant a lot, especially in Norway and Sweden, I would say.

He continues, referring specifically to *Listen to the Silence*,

But that's what I'm saying. He opened up a new way of thinking and writing. When you write like that. I've always also been into classical music, and for me there was nothing strange about that. I like those kind[s] of things. He was very strong in those days. He had also the American tradition in the background. He had those heavy rhythms and bluesy phrases that can come in. As you say, it's kind of a mixture.[73]

Stenson suggests, with some justification, that it was the marriage of the blues and jazz, with a respect for and understanding of European art music, that defined Russell's approach and his appeal for northern Europeans, especially at a time when musicians in Europe were looking to develop their own ways of playing jazz.

While *Listen to the Silence* is not a completely successful work—specifically, in "Event III" its didactic purpose takes over from aesthetic considerations—it is a highly unusual and significant work to come from a jazz composer. Its strengths lie in the sense of mystery and otherness that its elements—voices, orchestra, and text—create for the listener. Again, there is simply nothing like it within jazz.

By this time, of course, Russell had returned to the United States and was living in Boston and teaching at the New England Conservatory. Talking to Ian Carr in 1992, Russell explained that despite his strong and positive feelings toward Scandinavia and the people who had befriended him, by 1969 it had become time to go home. He had come to feel that Swedish society, though less than that of Norway, was an emotionally inexpressive one.

> Then this feeling of being in an isolated, you know, in a culture that was emotionally mute, coupled with what was going on in America, and that was the kids like Alice [Russell's now wife] were coming up. They were protesting, you know. They were [protesting], and I think protesting about some very important things. Not just the Vietnam War but the way of life and the whole thing, you know. And, of course, many of them were not sincere, you know, because they ended up being on Wall Street and stuff and stockbrokers. But it seemed like a sincere movement—people going down South and the buses and things, and America was looking at itself, having a good look at itself, you know.[74]

Russell had worked consistently in Scandinavia, more so than at any time in his career. His group had played festivals and gigs in northern Europe. He had recorded for radio stations and was feted throughout the period he lived in Norway and Sweden. In an act of typical generosity, before he returned to America Russell helped Jan Garbarek record his first album with his own quartet, called *George Russell Presents The Esoteric Circle*. The title was obviously Russell's and is another reference to Gurdjieff. It is a marvelous debut, with impressive writing from Garbarek and playing from all four musicians—Rypdal, Andersen, Christensen, and Garbarek himself. Russell's assistance in the recording, which was made sometime in 1969, went far beyond mentorship, as Garbarek remembers.

> It was a quartet album, but George was kind enough to offer to pay for the recording expenses, which was done here at the museum of modern art. They have recording facilities. So he was sort of [the] behind-the-scenes guy there,

financially. So we had this master tape, which I tried to sell to ECM Records, which I later joined. They turned that down and said they would like to do their own recording. I think then George sold it to Flying Dutchman in the States. So George had no part in it in a musical sense. It was strictly our own material we were playing at time.[75]

The album was eventually released, as Garbarek correctly recalls, on the American Flying Dutchman label in 1971. Though Manfred Eicher of ECM did not take up the record—he has always had an executive preference for producing his artists himself—the futures of Garbarek, Rypdal, Andersen, and Christensen with the label were assured. In fact, it was at one of the Russell sextet gigs in 1969 in Bologna that Eicher first heard the group, and it was there that a series of very productive and creative partnerships were formed.

A comment about Russell's Scandinavia sojourn from Kåre Kolberg, the Norwegian composer who knew Russell well, is quite telling. As Kolberg points out, influence is often a two-way street.

To me, Scandinavian jazz and also Scandinavian contemporary music might have been important for him. It was absolutely important for us to meet him. I showed him what I had done and how I had made a system for one piece, and he said, "Well, it's okay, it's interesting, but it is as far from the Lydian Concept as it could come." It shows that he's open-minded and certainly not dogmatic. So he is [a] creative person and active and creative in finding new ways, but he also has a very strong theoretical background. He's a very systematic person. This combination may be rather radical for jazz musicians and for serious composers.[76]

It was not just Russell's music that developed while he was in Scandinavia, but also his theoretical ideas. Quite when, where, and how these new ideas came into play is unclear. For example, in the 1959 edition of *The Lydian Chromatic Concept of Tonal Organization*, Russell refers to horizontal and vertical polymodality, but does not use the terms "vertical tonal gravity," "horizontal tonal gravity," or "supra-vertical tonal gravity." It seems likely that it was in Scandinavia that Russell began to develop the new terminology to more accurately describe his theoretical ideas. He has certainly used these terms for several decades in his teaching at the New England Conservatory. However, volume 1 of the Lydian Concept deals at length only with vertical tonal gravity and indicates that the other two levels of tonal gravity are to be dealt with in the planned volume 2.[77]

The complexity of Russell's argument here deserves more space than is available here. These take us into the realms of musical theory as philosophy and draw on ideas regarding time that Russell derived from Maurice Nicoll. As briefly as possible, vertical tonal gravity (VTG) concerns what is happening in the moment "NOW" in a piece of music and loosely concerns the shortest (fractional) time duration of these three levels. Broadly speaking, the level of VTG is concerned with how melody is inferred, that is, derived from the scale ("parent scale," in Russell's terminology) that is determined by each chord. In jazz terms, we are talking about improvising over the chord changes. When the horizontal level is considered, we see musicians moving away from the individual chords of a piece and into more open modal areas centered on the "tonic stations" or cadence centers to which chords resolve (the "regional" level of melodic relating). The improvisational choices here offer more rhythmic flexibility than on the vertical level, and are often heard as longer lines or phrases that move over the chords. Russell uses the examples of melodies created by Lester Young (horizontal) versus Coleman Hawkins (vertical) to describe the differences between the two approaches. At the supra-vertical tonal gravity level, we are concerned with the totality of the musical piece or movement within it: that is, the improviser is focused—consciously or not—on the infinite resources of *one* Lydian Chromatic universe, that is, the overall key of the music.[78]

Ben Schwendener, a former student of Russell's, served as his primary assistant in classes from 1987 to 2003 and worked extensively on the editing and rewriting of both volumes of his Lydian Chromatic Concept. By all accounts, Russell referred to Schwendener in classes as "my right-hand man in the Lydian Chromatic Concept" and Schwendener inherited the teaching of the Concept at the New England Conservatory after Russell's retirement. Using Russell's analogy of "The River Trip," Schwendener explains it as follows:

So the vertically minded musician relates his or her melody to each "chordtown" along the river, asking: "What is the chord of the moment?" The horizontally minded musician, on the other hand, is centered on the larger tonic station "goals" within the harmonic stream. Here's the tonic station. These chords resolve to that tonic station. Horizontal melodic thinking involves looking ahead to tonic stations occurring in the music. You might think of the vertical musician as taking the "local" train or bus and the horizontal musician as taking the "express" to the larger towns or "tonic stations." On the level of supra-vertical tonal gravity, it's like you're navigating the tune in a rocket ship. You're just flowing over the whole thing in the overall key of the music, being ingoing, outgoing, whatever. Supra-vertical is the largest and freest state, which was really developed—the theoretical understanding of it, that is—after George heard Ornette in the late fifties and early sixties.[79]

Although Russell does not use the term "supra-vertical tonal gravity" in the 1959 edition of the Concept in discussing Ornette Coleman's approach, he notes that his improvisation derives from "The Chromatic Melody (parent Lydian Chromatic Scale) Inferred by the Over-all Tonic Station." He writes,

> However, the gravity of this over-all tonic is so broad that it allows Coleman to concentrate on other things like the meaning of the tune, or the idea suggested by a single tone, or the idea suggested by the preceding idea.[80]

It seems likely that Russell used his period in Scandinavia—and not least the teaching opportunities it provided—to refine his ideas in these respects. The other important development in his thinking concerns his concept of "vertical form" as an approach to composition. This will be discussed later at some length. Here it suffices to note that this was perhaps the final refinement in his oeuvre. Far from being a holiday from the main action Stateside, Russell had used his years in Sweden and Norway to produce some important works, but he had also revitalized and rejuvenated himself and his art.

Notes

1. Benoit Quersin, "Le Philosophe De Greenwich Village," *Jazz*, February 1963.
2. "The Playboy Panel: Jazz—Today and Tomorrow," *Playboy*, February 1964; "Tangents," *Down Beat*, June 18, 1964.
3. "George Russell Sends Call for More Blood Donors," *Down Beat*, October 22, 1964.
4. Interview with Garnett Brown, July 2004.
5. Interview with Barre Phillips, March 2007.
6. Ibid. See also Joe Boyd, *White Bicycles* (London: Serpent's Tail, 2006), p. 46. Boyd, the producer and sometime impresario, worked on the tour and recalls in his autobiography that the tour included Davis; Brubeck; the Charlie Parker All-Stars with Sonny Stitt, J.J. Johnson, and Howard McGhee; Roland Kirk; Sister Rosetta Tharpe; the Original Tuxedo Brass Band; the Coleman Hawkins/Harry Edison Swing All-Stars; and the George Russell Sextet—eight bands, six different itineraries, and four tour managers.
7. Interview with Phillips.
8. Boyd, *White Bicycles*, p. 53.
9. *George Russell Sextet, Live in Bremen and Paris*, Gambit Records 69293; *Chicago All Stars—George Russell Sextet—Uptown All Stars 1964 Live*, BJ036CD. It is unclear what the provenance of these two discs is or whether any payment will go to the musicians, who are still alive. I hesitate to recommend what may be a "bootleg" recording, but the Gambit disc features some truly fantastic playing from all

concerned—from saxophonist Joe Farrell and trumpeter Thad Jones in particular. It also contains some of the finest examples of Russell's talents as a pianist. What is more, the company have made a real effort to provide accurate information and reasonable sleeve notes. You pay your money and you take your choice.

10. Interview with Brown.

11. Interview with Phillips.

12. This story has acquired mythical status over the decades. It is probable that it was less Stravinsky's music that inspired the "riot" than other features of the performance by the Ballets Russes. Kevin Elyot, author of the television play Riot at the Rite, writing in the *Guardian* on March 2, 2006, suggests that it was Serge Diaghilev, the founder-manager of the Ballets Russes, who in part engineered the incident through provocative publicity and invitations to those he knew would detest the performance as well as those who would champion it. It was also arguably Vaslav Nijinsky's choreography and its sexual and barbaric subject matter that provoked the most outrage. Indeed, the performers could not hear the music above the din and Nijinsky resorted to standing on a chair in the wings, his coattails held by Stravinsky to stop him falling, shouting the calls to the dancers. It seems unlikely that the audience could actually hear the music either. Sometimes, interpretation is more important than historical fact.

13. Interview with Phillips.

14. William Peeples, "Top Jazzmen Move into Hinterlands," *Louisville Times*, April 6, 1960.

15. Ian Carr, interview with George Russell, June 1992.

16. Ian Carr, interview with Marit Jerstad for BBC Radio 3 broadcast *George Russell—The Invisible Guru*, July 1994.

17. Vivian Perlis, interview with George Russell, American Music Series, December 8, 1993, Oral History Project of American Music, sponsored and supported by the National Endowment for the Arts Special Jazz Projects.

18. Duncan Heining, "A Meeting with a Remarkable Man," *Avant* 7 (Summer 1998).

19. "Random Thoughts from George Russell," *Down Beat*, July 29, 1965.

20. Archie Shepp, "An Artist Speaks Bluntly," *Down Beat*, December 16, 1965.

21. George Russell, "Popular Delusions and the Madness of Crowds," *Down Beat*, April 7, 1966.

22. Martin Williams, letter to George Russell, March 25, 1966.

23. Interview with Jan Garbarek, July 2004.

24. Karl Marx, *The Eighteenth Brumaire of Louis Bonaparte* (Moscow: Progress, 1972), p. 5 "Hegel remarks somewhere that all great world-historic facts and personages appear, so to speak, twice. He forgot to add: the first time as tragedy, the second time as farce." For discussion of Jazz at Lincoln Center and related matters, see S. Nicholson, *Is Jazz Dead? Or Has It Moved to a New Address?* (Abingdon, UK: Routledge, 2005).

25. Heining, "A Meeting with a Remarkable Man."

26. Swedish Radio Panel interview with George Russell, 1995.

27. Malcolm Ball, "Licht aus Stockhausen," *Avant* 5 (Winter 1998): 6–11.

28. See, for example, Sy Johnson, "Interview: Bill Evans & George Russell," *Changes*, Spring 1972. For an alternative view on the same issue see Brian Priestley, Review of *The London Concerts Volumes 1 & 2* (Label Bleu LBLC65278), in *Gramophone Jazz Good CD Guide*, ed. K. Shadwick (Harrow, UK: Gramophone, 1995), p. 450; Max Harrison, "George Russell—Rational Anthems," *Wire* (1983): 19–21.

29. Ben Young, broadcast devoted to George Russell in celebration of his seventy-fourth birthday, WKCR Radio, New York, June 23, 1997.

30. Joachim Berendt was a renowned jazz critic and producer and wrote *The Jazz Book—From New Orleans to Jazz Now* (New York and Westport, CT: Lawrence Hill, 1974).

31. W. Russo, Review of *George Russell at Beethoven Hall* (Saba MPFS 15059), *Down Beat*, October 20, 1966.

32. Wolfram Knauer, sleeve notes to reissue of *George Russell Sextet at Beethoven Hall* (Complete Recordings), MPS 539084–2.

33. According to a letter from Russell to John Benson Brooks and his wife, Peggy, written between August and September 1965, he met Jock's journalist mother when she was visiting the States and just after his relationship with Wendy Brooks had ended. It seems that Jock might have been conceived in America rather than in Sweden.

34. E-mail interview with Lennart Åberg, July 2007.

35. Interview with Arild Andersen, November 2005.

36. Interview with Terje Rypdal, November 2005.

37. Interview with Jon Christensen, September 2005.

38. Interview with Garbarek.

39. Quote taken from Ian Carr's notebooks made from interviews for The Invisible Guru and Trailblazer programs for BBC Radio 3, broadcast July and August 1994.

40. Interview with Sheila Jordan, May 2004.

41. Carr, notebooks for The Invisible Guru and Trailblazer.

42. Ibid.

43. Ibid.

44. Letter from Russell to John Benson Brooks, July 1964.

45. E-mail interview with Bosse Broberg, May 2007.

46. Ibid. (See appendix B.)

47. Ibid.

48. Interview with Christensen.

49. Michael Tucker, *Jan Garbarek: Deep Song* (Hull, UK: East Note, 1998), p. 116.

50. Leonard Bernstein, *The Unanswered Question: Six Lectures at Harvard* (Cambridge, MA: Harvard University Press, 1976), pp. 421–22. I am indebted to Michael Tucker's *Jan Garbarek: Deep Song* for this insight and quote.

51. Interview with Garbarek.

52. See and hear Edgar Varèse, The Complete Works, Decca CD 475 487–2.

53. Interview with Rypdal.

54. Harrison, "Rational Anthems," pp. 19–21.

55. Ibid.

56. Young, broadcast devoted to George Russell.

57. Ibid.

58. J. Klee, Down Beat, April 29, 1971.

59. Harrison, "Rational Anthems."

60. Interview with Rypdal.

61. Interview with Stanton Davis, June 2003.

62. Ibid.

63. R. Cook and B. Morton, The Penguin Guide to Jazz on CD (Harmondsworth, UK: Penguin, 2000), p. 380. Davis was introduced to Stockhausen's music by the British cellist, composer, and conductor Paul Buckmaster. See Ian Carr, Miles Davis—The Definitive Biography (Hammersmith, UK: HarperCollins, 1999), p. 304; also Miles Davis with Q. Troup, Miles: The Autobiography (London: MacMillan, 1989), p. 312.

64. D. Cerulli, B. Korall, and M. Nasatir, The Jazz Word (New York: Ballantine, 1960), p. 191.

65. This tune was actually released as a 45 rpm single by Impulse, for which label Ornette was recording at the time, no doubt to coincide with the first manned space flight to the moon. Strangely, it did not chart. Pop fans preferred David Bowie's Space Oddity.

66. Interview with Garbarek.

67. Various versions of the Ellington piece are available. For the Anthony Davis this is available as Gramavision R2–79470.

68. Letter from management of the 5th International Jazz Festival, Prague, September 1968.

69. Maurice Nicoll, The Mark (Utrecht: Eureka Editions, 1998).

70. Interview with S. Davis.

71. See D. J. Grout and C. V. Palisca, A History of Western Music (New York: Norton, 1996), pp. 751–53.

72. George Russell and the Living Time Orchestra, The 80th Birthday Concert Concept; George Russell's Living Time Orchestra, The London Concert, Label Bleu LBLC 6527/8; George Russell—New York Big Band, Soul Note SN 1039.

73. Interview with Bobo Stenson, March 2007.

74. Carr, interview with G. Russell, June 1992.

75. Interview with Garbarek.

76. Ian Carr, interview with Kåre Kolberg for BBC Radio 3 broadcast George Russell—The Invisible Guru, July 1994.

77. See George Russell, Lydian Chromatic Concept of Tonal Organization (Brookline, MA: Concept, 2001), p. 197.

78. These comments draw both on ibid. and on George Russell, *The Lydian Chromatic Concept of Tonal Organization* (New York: Concept, 1959), See pp. xviii–xix in the 1959 edition.

79. Interview with Ben Schwendener, October 2003.

80. Russell, *The Lydian Chromatic Concept* (1959), p. xix.

CHAPTER NINE

∽

Living in an American Time Spiral

Gunther Schuller had already played an important part in George Russell's early career. He had commissioned Russell to write a piece for the Brandeis concert and hired him to teach his Lydian Concept at the Lenox School of Jazz. He had also been a friend and source of support throughout the fifties and sixties. The part that he would now play was, if anything, even more significant, because his offer of a post at the New England Conservatory was to shape the rest of Russell's working life.

The New England Conservatory, the oldest independent music school in the United States, was founded in 1867 by organist Eben Tourjée. Patterned on the European *conservatoire* model, the whole concept was quite revolutionary in America at that time and proved to be a significant success with budding classical musicians and singers. For many years the school grew and thrived, seeing the building of its prestigious and elegant Jordan Hall in 1903 and its community ties develop through its connections with the Boston Symphony Orchestra and the promotion of low-cost concerts open to all. However, by the time Schuller took over as president of the conservatory in 1967, the school was facing major difficulties. In recent times the school, once one of the top music colleges in North America, was in a state of financial and educational decline, as Schuller explains: "The enrollment, which is supposed to be around 250, was down to 75. This school was dying, and financially they had something like $78,000 left in the till when I arrived. I mean, the sheriff was about to put the padlock on the door."[1] Schuller had no idea how bad things were when he took the job, but set about transforming an institution mired in an earlier time and bringing it into the reality of the late twentieth century.

> It took a couple of years to get a grant from the Ford Foundation—$2.5 million, which we had to match then—but what I did was revolutionize the whole curriculum, and the first act of my presidency was to create the Jazz Department, in respect of which many on the board and the faculty were horrified, but I said to myself, there was no doubt in my mind, "1967? A major conservatory in the United States doesn't have a Jazz Department? The music that was created on this soil sixty, seventy years ago?" So to me, this was absolutely automatic that I would do that.[2]

Just as Schuller and John Lewis had created the whole notion of "jazz education" in America with the Lenox summer school, so his efforts have borne fruit in terms of college-based degrees in jazz. Other conservatories and schools soon followed suit, though at the time, as Schuller notes, many music educators considered his decision as little short of heresy. Schuller's connections in the jazz community were such that he was able to bring in some of the best and brightest minds in jazz, and although he left his post as president in 1977, his influence remains. Any school that can number among its staff over the years musicians of the caliber of Russell; pianist Jaki Byard; bassists Miroslav Vitous and Dave Holland; trombonist/arranger Bob Brookmeyer; saxophonists Jimmy Giuffre, Joe Maneri, Joe Allard, and Steve Lacy; and composer/pianist Ran Blake can be remarkably proud. But Schuller went even further by reaching out to the poorer, socially disadvantaged areas of Boston through offers of scholarships to pupils of ability.

> I had enough jazz connections, so I could bring in the best people as faculty, and the other thing I did was I went personally into the black communities here—Roxbury and Dorchester—and brought kids from there, who felt that the NEC was some white establishment they could never get into and they weren't welcome there. I went there and reached out and brought them in.[3]

Additionally, Schuller soon established the Third Stream Department, created the Ragtime Ensemble, the Duke Ellington Orchestra, a swing band, a country fiddle orchestra, and even a Klezmer ensemble. The New England Conservatory became a school that offered a fully rounded musical experience to its students with a curriculum that celebrated American music in its diverse forms.

But first Schuller needed a major jazz composer for his new department. There were two choices for Schuller. As he told Ian Carr in 1992, one of these was Charles Mingus. However, "Charles was still so busy playing bass and traveling around. George had more or less given up playing—he played the piano occasionally—but mostly he was composing, so that seemed to me the ideal choice."[4]

Russell not only offered his abilities as a composer and arranger; he was also jazz's leading—possibly only—theoretician and had been and was a bandleader of some stature.

> George was the one who was already composing in these new directions, and the uniqueness of George is that he then was able to formulate that into a theoretical concept which can be used both in a practical way as a way of performing and improvising but also as an intellectual concept. To this moment, I think he's the only one who's achieved that.[5]

This was a point he also discussed with Carr in 1992.

> He is one of the few composers who has managed and dared to write an hour-long ballet or some things that are almost like operas, gigantic suites that go beyond anything that Ellington did. So I admire him very much for taking up that particular cudgel, because that, to me, is still the one area where jazz has, by and large, not gone very far—in the extended form. Even Ellington did not achieve all that he might have in that area, and I think that Mingus and Russell are about the only two composers who really tackled that in a major way and have not gone outside of the jazz tradition, and I think that's the important way to do it.[6]

Asked how Russell fit in to the school, Schuller's comments tell us a lot about his own iconoclastic nature.

> Beautifully, because by that time he had already had his sextet and was also known as a performer and as a teacher to younger players and so on, with Dave Baker and all of those things with the Indiana University connection. He was famous enough as a composer and a performer and a theoretician that he was, I would have to say, he was rather readily accepted, except by some old diehards who thought this was pure heresy. They began with the idea that jazz shouldn't be allowed in the school. When I got here, the saxophone was not allowed as an instrument to be taught here—and I'm not even talking about jazz saxophone, even classical saxophone. That's how hostile it was.[7]

Schuller's perception of Russell as a teacher is not one that has been shared by all of his students, as will be seen. However, his comments are a fair assessment of Russell's character and Schuller's own experience of him.

As you know, he's a very quiet man. He does things by gentle persuasion rather than by presenting *pronunciamentos* or dicta, and I knew that about him, and it's true that some people went to his classes expecting to learn some kind of easy, tricky way to learn how to improvise or something like that, to get some kind of a formula for their careers, which of course is not the idea at all. They were disappointed and they couldn't connect up with George's way of presenting this material. This is a musical concept, and what it does, it puts into formal verbal intelligent, intellectual forms what is already happening, was already happening in jazz. Just as Rameau's theoretical teachings and other great theorists through the nineteenth century: They didn't invent, they simply quantified what had already been going on. That's what George did. Some people could deal with that, and maybe some of them relied too strictly that if they learned all those sort of concepts and rules George was sort of presenting . . . not that he was presenting them as rules, but just as a way to think and to hear . . . that this could make them instant stars or something. Of course that wasn't the idea at all, just as it isn't in classical theory. You can learn all that [but] it doesn't necessarily make you a great musician.[8]

As Marit Jerstad told Ian Carr, Schuller's offer was extremely important for Russell as an affirmation of his achievements.

George has always wanted to do everything himself—print it himself and distribute it. He felt very antagonistic toward big institutions—record companies and all that. All his life he's had a problematic relationship with the establishment. It was very important to him when he got the offer to be a teacher at the New England Conservatory. It meant a lot to him, and he's an excellent teacher because he has such a deep knowledge of music.[9]

Jerstad's assessment of Russell's abilities as a teacher is a fair one. However, no one who knows Russell well—or indeed at all—would describe him as an easy man. He has high expectations and standards, suffers those he sees as fools with difficulty, and has all the single-mindedness of a genius. However open he can be to new ideas or the suggestions and contributions of others, he can be stubborn when he has set his mind on a course of action and he will remain resolute about what he feels he has to offer, to the point of intractability. What you see is, with Russell, what you get, and that can be hard on those who struggle with those aspects of his character. Simply, one would feel for any shrinking violet who found himself in one of Russell's classes!

Carl Atkins, who conducted the orchestras for two albums Russell worked on—*Living Time* with Bill Evans and *Vertical Form VI*—was chair of the Jazz

Department for several years during Russell's long tenure. Atkins points out that Russell had his own way of doing things and was hard to shift.

> I remember we tried, when I was here, to get George to do other music, other than his own music, when he did the band. I would do the band one semester; George would do the band one semester, or Jaki Byard and George would split the band. And I would always do this wide array of things, and if I wrote a piece, I'd do that, but I'd do music by Thad Jones, I'd do "Aluminum Baby" by Jaki Byard. George would only do his music. So I said to George one time, "You know you've had such a wonderful experience with this music and you've known Dizzy and you've known Bird, you've known all of these people, it would be great if the kids could hear and could experience some other music with you, with the years of knowledge you've had about this music in general." His answer was pretty straightforward: "I don't do anybody else's music." That was the end of that conversation. To this day I don't think he's ever, at this institution in any of the times that I've played with him, done anybody else's music.[10]

Russell also avoided many of the petty departmental and interdepartmental political squabbles that went on in the New England Conservatory, as in any academic institution. This was probably a good thing, because Russell would probably have upset the applecart, unleashed a whirlwind, and destroyed the china shop had he got involved in such matters. According to Atkins, he and Schuller acted as a "buffer to keep George from having to deal with a lot of that." Russell's tendency to concentrate on "his stuff" created another difficulty for the administration, as did his colorful use of English, as Atkins notes.

> What happens at New England Conservatory, and it's unlike other schools, where a student comes in as a freshman and let's say he gets in the jazz band, and he plays one year with George Russell's concert group, and he may play a second year and George will do a second set of his music the second year. Well, by the third year George is starting to recycle stuff. So then you kind of have to say that this kid now has gone through that experience and you got to find another place for the kid. So it makes it a little bit of a logistic problem. You sort of generally only recycle freshmen and sophomores and first-year graduate students, but George wouldn't bend, and I heard stories when I came back here about how some of the bands had women in them who didn't like playing for George because George used language that sometimes certainly sounded misogynistic or didn't sound at least PC. One of his favorite sayings used to be, in the days when we had the band, was "Let's play the bitch." And he would say that to the kids. He'd say, "Let's play this bitch." Then there'd be a girl trumpet player standing there, and she'd kind of take umbrage at the use of

the word "bitch." George didn't mean anything by it. That ain't George. He's old-school on a lot of levels, but that's not him.[11]

Among the many students Russell has taught and affected at the New England Conservatory are musicians like Don Byron, Bill Urmson, Pat Hollenbeck, Marty Ehrlich, John Medeski, Ricky Ford, Marc Rossi, Andy Wasserman, Satoko Fujii, James Falzone, Gregory Burk, and Ben Schwendener, who, as noted, now teaches the Lydian Concept at the conservatory. Their comments are both intriguing and insightful.

Ingrid Monson, trumpeter and now Quincy Jones Professor of African American Music at Harvard, was a student at the New England Conservatory and is now a personal friend of George and Alice Russell. Her comments suggest a balanced assessment of Russell as a teacher.

It wasn't that people wanted to avoid the classes. They wanted to be a part of it, but they were afraid of being humiliated *(laughs)* and they were afraid of having George point to them to solo and have him say something negative. They were afraid that he wouldn't allow them to play solos in his band for one reason or another. I don't know if it was because I was a woman that I was outside whatever the kind of competitive thing among the guys was—they probably just didn't take me seriously at all. *(laughs)* So they were much more sensitive about whether they got called on to solo or corrected by George than I was. I figured I was going to take whatever criticism he has to say, and I found that he didn't have that much to say that was critical. I didn't find him this hypercritical person to be really scared of. It was, like, the late seventies, and I recall when he taught the course that he would sometimes say something off-color about sex, or something like that, that would make some people uncomfortable. It wasn't like he cursed a lot. I remember one time—and I just have to laugh thinking back on this—but we were sitting in the Lydian Chromatic Concept course and somehow he was talking about male and female principles, yin and yang, some Chinese stuff, active and submissive, and the women in the class, of course, we weren't buying this. At one point he mentioned something about *Hustler* magazine and everybody was shocked, and it was all part of George as this image of perhaps a rakish, sexually intimidating person perhaps. I think that it was kind of student lore. It's not like George did anything. It's like people are like nineteen, twenty years old. They're not real together with who they are in this dimension, and I never found anything he did . . . let me say that I had far more sexist experiences at the conservatory than from George. George was not real bad on that score in my opinion. As I got to know him at an older age, I think part of that sort of looking like a bad, tough guy is part of a kind of persona, of an exterior. In fact, George is a very sensitive guy, very thoughtful, warm, and I think Alice is a great woman.

I look back and I think about some of the discourse of that, and there was this extra nervousness about it was way beyond what was real, in my opinion. So he talked about maybe going out some times and maybe drinking too much or something. Big deal.[12]

Bill Urmson, now bassist with Russell's Living Time Orchestra, confirms that Russell taught and demanded high standards. "He definitely gave us the message that what was happening in New York was the standard. He was really proud of his time in New York, and he taught us a lot about how the New York standard was a very high ideal at the time." As he adds, "He definitely instilled that into us."[13]

Urmson appreciated and valued his studies with Russell, noting that it was clear in all his courses that the students were there to study the Concept and he was there to teach it. Not all students were comfortable with his approach, as Urmson explains.

At the time there were some issues—some students really felt that they wanted more of a personal touch with him. They wanted him to be more interested in what they were doing. But George was definitely there to explain his story, and if you were interested in that, it was a good situation. If you weren't, then you wouldn't get much out of the situation.[14]

That Russell could also be quite dogmatic, and that his expectations could appear to be paradoxical if not downright contradictory for some of his students, is evident from a story pianist Fred Hersch tells.

Certainly, we sort of came to blows over *All About Rosie*, where I deliberately did not listen to the original recording with its famous unaccompanied four choruses by Bill Evans. Because I didn't want to play it the same way. He got annoyed that I hadn't listened to the recording and that I wasn't playing that way, and I mouthed off. I said, "You want Bill Evans? Call him. I'm supposed to be here as a creative jazz musician. Here are the chord changes. I'm going to interpret them the way that I interpret them, and I would think that you would encourage me, as someone who talks a lot about freedom in music, to interpret them in a personal way." He didn't want to hear that. He got very angry.

At the same time, Hersch adds that he "sure enjoyed playing that music." Russell was, and remains, in his opinion, "a really significant composer."[15]

The clarinetist and composer Don Byron who was also one of Russell's students, remains a supporter of Russell, and acknowledges his own debt to him as a teacher in various ways. He makes two points, however, that reflect both his own self-awareness and his insight into how students in general, but in particular African American students, might have experienced Russell's classes.

> I couldn't say that I enjoyed the big class so much. There were a lot of other people around. I always felt that George was a little uncomfortable in front of the class. He was always kind of trying to prove things were right. There was a lot of pressure to answer a question exactly the way that he wanted a question answered. It was a bit like playing *Jeopardy*. So everybody was kind of on edge. It was kind of a feeling in the class of being on edge and being tested. It was not the greatest feeling. After I took it for a while, I wanted to interact with him in a different setting.[16]

The second-year class was much smaller and more intimate and clearly more comfortable, as Byron notes.

> It was different, because if you brought something in you could really get a sense of how he listened through the system that he'd devised, how he actually heard things. It was always interesting. At the time I saw him as someone who was a little cut off from developments that were happening. If you were interested in something and you brought that in he'd have some kind of analysis for that too, that would be surprising.[17]

As an African American student at the New England Conservatory, Byron recalls that "the atmosphere at the school—it wasn't very Afrocentric. There was about half a dozen of us black students who would be in the position to take his class at any one time, and he was the only person for a period that we could look up to."[18] Now a teacher himself, Byron's perspective has changed somewhat. Yet there is still a sense that his own contact with Russell was lacking for him at a personal level, and perhaps was more one-sided than he would have hoped.

> You know, he was the only black teacher at New England Conservatory a lot of the time that I was there. He was certainly the only black teacher in the Jazz Department or Third Stream. That's always incredible to me, but it happens a lot in academic settings. As a teacher now, I can see that when that happens and there are students of color around, they kind of look up to you in this kind of puppy-dog way. You try not to show too much favoritism in public. Yet you want them to do well, but you kind of get like "this is your bag/this is your stuff," and there's always this feeling that you should be better at it because you're black. You don't want to show favoritism. You're teaching for everybody. At the time I really didn't like him for it. Now I can see what the difficulty of the position is with my students.[19]

Clearly, as students, we experience our teachers in a variety of ways. We project our own aspirations, hopes, and fears onto them, just as much—if not more—than we make purely objective assessments of their capacity to help us to learn. The pupil-teacher relationship, even in adult education, is an ambiguous one that reawakens childhood anxieties and evokes quite primitive psychological defenses and responses. We rarely experience our teachers until much later as fully rounded human beings with human flaws as well as human virtues. A good teacher can help us reach our goals. A bad teacher will leave us despairing of our own inadequacy. The problem is that the individual who is "good" for one student may not be so marvelous for another. Urmson makes this point very well.

> I think George sizes you up pretty quick. When I first met him, he saw me as this kid. I remember that my bass had to be in for repair and I came to the first ensemble class and I didn't have an instrument. So I could tell he wasn't too happy with me, but when I came to the next class and he heard me play, he instantly warmed up because he really liked what he was hearing. He can be confrontational—I wouldn't say he has a lot of patience with students that are not . . . he really wanted to hear his music played well, even at a student level. . . . So if a student was really having a tough time I think it might not have been the most comfortable thing for the student. It may not have been a great thing for them to be there until they had it more together and could take on the challenge. So I think he could be . . . I've seen him be confrontational, but I've also seen him be very supportive. For me, he was very supportive in the beginning. I wasn't a virtuoso or anything, but I learned his music. I did the homework and I paid attention to it, so I didn't have any real confrontations in that sense. I think he was probably right in the middle. I could see him go both ways.[20]

He adds that Russell demanded a high level of commitment.

> He's sending a message that there's a very high level out there. I remember my first concert with him, he dedicated it to the level of excellence that John Coltrane had achieved. He was really trying to send the message that it was a serious business and we should be shooting for a higher level and not settle for the mediocrity that we see in the modern music around us every day.[21]

The woodwind virtuoso and multi-instrumentalist Marty Ehrlich remembers getting on well with Russell and recalls his enthusiasm.

> He was passionate about the Concept. It intrigued me from the start as a way to start getting a handle on the materials of music, one that I could readily use.

There seemed to always be a student or two who wanted to argue with George about how the Concept would help them play jazz. I think that they wanted to learn a style and the Concept doesn't teach a style, it teaches possibilities. Often though, George would take these arguments pretty personally.[22]

And the brilliant Japanese composer/pianist Satoko Fujii values the sense she got from Russell of her own potential. More than anyone else, she says, he taught her to compose.

I have learned I can do anything I want. There is nothing that we cannot do when we compose. He showed [how] to analyze all pieces we compose by Lydian Concept and this means we can do anything but we are still in a law of the cosmos. I was so released from everything by this class. Some other theory has many rules that we cannot do and [the] more we study [the] more we get the things we cannot do. But his concept is opposite. I felt good to try something I want to do. This idea help me a lot to be a musician including my big band writing.[23]

Ehrlich recalls one other incident that illustrated for him a rather unique perspective and an unusual lesson.

For some reason, George had sat in on the Afro-American Music History class taught by Carl Atkins. On that day, Carl does an interesting listening example. He plays two versions of "Amazing Grace" both sung in rural churches from the South, one black and one white. The white church is singing in what is called shape note singing. Carl asks us to define the difference. Students are descriptive but not much more. Finally, George joins in, and says emphatically, "The Blues Scale! The Black singers are using the Blues Scale!" Then Carl reads from the liner notes for the white shape note singers, how one listener, surely of a different class, called their singing "similar to the braying of asses." George gets clearly upset, and says in no uncertain terms to us, "This is ethnocentrism of the worst order." It was a defining artistic/moral lesson for me.[24]

And one last "testimonial," this time from pianist/composer John Medeski, perhaps serves to define a different possible response to Russell's demanding expectations.

He was really funny. He had lots of stories. He was a character, very feisty. I loved it. He had no problem breaking the balls of the students, which he did a lot. Look at the people he played with and worked with and the kinds of bands he had and records he made, then be at a school with these little punks? He definitely reminded us that we were punks. That was one of the things I loved about his big band [class]. It was hilarious to see him. He also knew how to rehearse a band—but the drummers! I felt so sorry for every drummer that ever played with him, because he was just brutal. That's how and what I learned from George. It was like picking up on his whole spirit, really respecting what he did and where he came from, and trying to just absorb everything I could from him.[25]

Russell's influence came both through his theoretical ideas and also through the sense that his students had of him as a musician and embodiment of jazz history. Another former student, clarinetist James Falzone, notes, "I think anyone at NEC came under George's influence, you know, even if not a direct student. His concepts float through there quite strongly."[26] And pianist Greg Burk comments, in similar fashion:

> George Russell the man certainly had as much if not more of an impact on me than the LCC. That is not to say that the Concept did not profoundly change the way I looked at harmony, melody and rhythm (and their inter-relationships). Through the four semesters of classes I had with George and the year of Big Band, I came to understand something fundamental about being a jazz musician. It is the depth of relationship between the creator and his creation, or the musician and his material in this case, that makes a master musician.

And he adds, "This kind of commitment was very inspiring to me as a student. George reminds me, in some ways, of a benevolent gunslinger from the old west, prepared to defend his territory, for which he has fought and rightfully owns."[27]

Russell had, after all, known Bird, Diz, Miles, Trane, Bill Evans, Dolphy, and Mingus. Some students may have found him intimidating, but others clearly gained a great deal from him.

A comment from bassist/composer Dave Holland, who taught at the school for a time when Russell was there and who is still a visiting lecturer, gives credit to both Russell's and Schuller's achievements there.

> I just want to say' how much I respect George's work and the fact that he's created. . . . He's done something which a lot of musicians aspire to, which is create a world of his own within the music. He defines it in his own way and so on, and he brought that idea into the school. One of the great things about New England Conservatory is that it's not a totally integrated curriculum where everybody's marching to the same step. It's a very independent attitude there, where each person that teaches there is given very much their own freedom to pursue their approach, so you get a wide diversity of concepts being presented within the program. Along with the normal staple kind of issues that need to be considered—of rhythm, harmony, and arranging, and things like

that, which are ongoing aspects of the program—the individual teachers are very much left to pursue their own method of teaching and their own concepts with the students that study with them, and I think that's a very good thing. In fact, in the last two years I've rejoined the faculty as an artist-in-residence. I go back to the conservatory one week each semester and present a weeklong series of workshops, a coaching ensemble, lectures, analysis, and so on, and it's been a very nice thing to be involved again. I enjoy it very much.[28]

If Russell avoided the political game playing of the school, he was nevertheless active as a teacher and in its program of concerts and events. Like all music schools, the New England Conservatory encourages its staff and students to give regular performances, many of which take place in Jordan Hall. Many of these performances have been recorded and can be heard in the school's sound archive. Perhaps the most significant of these concerts was *Time Line*, which Russell created and curated in 1992 to celebrate 125 years of the conservatory.

This huge three-hour collage was a musical depiction of American and world history from the Civil War through two world wars, economic depression, civil rights struggles, and anti-Vietnam protests. It took in Russell's own *Listen to the Silence, American Trilogy* (which was commissioned by the Glasgow Jazz Festival in 1990 and involved rearrangements of "Battle Hymn of the Republic," "You Are My Sunshine," and "Ballad of Hix Blewitt"), "Stratusphunk," *All About Rosie*, "Ezz-Thetic," and a new work, *Dialogue with Ornette*. To this were added American popular songs like "Brother, Can You Spare a Dime?" and "Oh, Susanna," songs and anthems from Europe and America, classic jazz pieces like "'Round Midnight," and popular and more obscure classical pieces from Beethoven's *Minuet in G* and Strauss's *Emperor Waltz* to Stravinsky's *Firebird* and Alban Berg's *Wozzeck*, along with carefully chosen narrative sections.

Dialogue with Ornette requires some elaboration. It came from a tape that Russell had made with Coleman in his apartment in New York in the sixties, just after the saxophonist had bought his first violin. Much later, Russell decided to use elements from the music they played together to produce a piece based on their improvised dialogue. It became both a small ensemble work and, orchestrated brilliantly by Pat Hollenbeck, a symphonic work.

Featuring at various times a full symphony orchestra and chorus, a big band and Klezmer ensemble, Russell layers *Time Line* with one piece fading into another, sometimes even using several pieces simultaneously. For example, one section involved three flautists: one improvising, another playing Ravel's *Bolero*, and a third Varèse's *Density 21.5*. It may sound like a mess, but in

Russell's hands the approach works. It is not surprising, therefore, that Russell also uses Charles Ives's "Country Band March," which Ives wrote in recollection of his bandmaster father. Ives Senior would have two or more marching bands playing different tunes parade around their hometown, to emerge in the town square because he liked the cacophony this would create.[29] Russell also uses works by Stockhausen and Cage (both fellow collagists), and draws upon Debussy's *Fêtes*, Schoenberg's *Pierrot Lunaire*, and Stravinsky's *Le Sacré Du Printemps*, all works that have affected and influenced him. Add to these "Ol' Man River," with its civil rights association with activist Paul Robeson, an African drum section, "Milestones" (his friend Miles Davis's first application of Russell's ideas), and a recording of the King Oliver Band, and the impression is that Russell is presenting the audience with a history of his own musical development. Even Penderecki's *Threnody* does not surprise, as it is suggested anyway by *Listen to the Silence*.

Over the concert's three hours, the performers and audience seemed to have a ball. It was truly a marvelous celebration of history and of music.[30]

Schuller had recruited Russell as a working composer/musician, and it was accepted that his career would continue alongside his teaching commitments. Of course, recordings and concert tours by faculty members serve to enhance the conservatory's reputation and attract new students. Russell continued to play in Scandinavia and elsewhere in Europe, and though performance opportunities became less common in the United States, his sextet performed at the prestigious Tanglewood concert series in the Berkshire Mountains in 1970, an appearance that was probably due to Schuller's support. Stanton Davis recalls that they had had problems there that contrasted with their experiences elsewhere.

> I remember one time we got back to town. We'd just done a great concert and got back to New York and then went to Tanglewood, and they didn't have the right equipment. They didn't have speakers big enough for *Electronic Sonata*. The guy who was talking to the engineer, he said, "Well, I don't really like this music anyway." So George was furious, but it was that kind of ignorance really.[31]

By contrast, two things happened in 1971–72 that had the potential to give a focus to Russell's profile in his home country. First, he received a Guggenheim Fellowship. Second, his old friend Bill Evans commissioned him to write an album-long suite for his second record for his new label, Columbia. The John Simon Guggenheim Memorial Foundation paid Russell a grant for $10,000 for "music composition" for twelve months from April 1972. In the same period, he also received a similar award from the National Endowment for the Arts. Explaining his reasons for returning to the United States, Russell told Ken Linden in a 1969 interview for *Jazz & Pop* magazine that with these two awards, "I felt like they finally said, 'Yes, George come on back.'"[32]

According to Evans's biographer, Peter Pettinger, signing with Columbia was, for Evans, "a childhood dream come true."[33] Clive Davis, the company's president, seemed keen to give the pianist every opportunity to explore new directions. As Davis told *Down Beat*, "Bill Evans—how do you get him out of what he's doing for the last few years and say, 'use your genius and start communicating to new audiences, get into exciting areas, use other instrumentation, bring your musical ideas to new people?' if the artist is not interested in doing that, then I'm not interested in having that artist record for us."[34] Russell's first album for Columbia, *The Bill Evans Album*, was a fairly straightforward trio set, though its troubled background and birth is detailed well by both Pettinger and Keith Shadwick.[35] Evans's second—and final—record for Columbia was to be everything Davis claimed he wanted, and more. This was, after all, now the label of electric Miles Davis, John McLaughlin, Weather Report, and Ornette Coleman.

Brian Hennessey, a friend of Evans and keeper of the Bill Evans Archive, questions whether the pianist actually initiated the recording of *Living Time*. Instead, he suggests the pressure came from the Columbia hierarchy. If Hennessey is right, then the company's handling of the album and its treatment of Evans and Russell's work is all the worse.

> I don't think he initiated it. *(laughs)* I don't think so. It was part of the pressure of trying to do something different rather than just carry on with a trio or even solo, but he'd been all through that. Solo, duo, trio, quintet, and he also needed the payments from the record companies, especially the down payments. So I don't think he really instigated that. I don't even think George did either.[36]

According to Hennessey's impression, Evans was not "particularly enamored with it": "I mean, he'd always be respectful of it, how much he respected the musicians that were on it and the composer, and all that sort of thing. He wouldn't say anything about how terrible it was. But he would dismiss it fairly quickly and get on with the next thing."[37]

Set against Hennessey's view are Evans and Russell's own comments in a two-part interview with arranger Sy Johnson for *Changes* magazine before the release of the record.[38] According to that article, Evans and Russell had spoken while Evans was doing some New York dates in 1971 about the possibility of doing a project together. Then Evans talked further with Columbia sales executives and was given the go-ahead for the project. It was to be a major undertaking—Russell planned an eight-movement, or event, suite featuring an enormous jazz orchestra. The band contained some of the finest musicians in America. As well as Evans's current trio of Eddie Gomez on bass and Marty Morrell on drums, the orchestra featured other rhythm players, with drums, percussion, guitar, electric bass, and two electronic keyboards alongside a full horn section. Tony Williams played drums, while Ron Carter and Stanley Clarke featured on Fender bass on several events. The woodwind section included Howard Johnson, Jimmy Giuffre, Joe Henderson, and Sam Rivers. Dave Baker, with a brief respite from the jaw problems that had brought a premature end to that aspect of his career, was in the trombone section with Garnett Brown and Dave Bargeron (then with Blood, Sweat & Tears), and Snooky Young, Richard Williams, Ernie Royal, and Stanton Davis were on trumpet. With Evans playing Fender Rhodes and acoustic piano, this should, by any standard, have been one of the greatest jazz summit meetings of the seventies.

What exactly went wrong is now unclear, but to quote Keith Shadwick, "If any major jazz album of the past 30 years or so needs a sympathetic remix, then this is the leading candidate."[39] Dave Bargeron, who has continued to work with Russell ever since, remembers that it was a truly groundbreaking experience, but one the musicians found hard to follow.

> As a jazz project and as a project to be done in a recording studio, this was revolutionary in the fact that there was George with essentially a double orchestra, two rhythm sections, Bill Evans as featured pianist, and this music organized in such a way that none of us had ever seen before, and the pieces separated into events with Roman numerals, subset of that, areas, subset of that, ABC within the areas. And coordinating all of these various functions for the very first time, George developing a technique of conducting this way, random events that would last a time span rather than a certain amount of measures. He had a little stopwatch with him or he had an assistant timing a section for him. It was an unbelievable experience, you know. It was a total immersion in George's genius from the get[-go]. And there I was and I enjoyed it so much. (laughs) It was so memorable, and the band we travel with now is called the Living Time Orchestra, and I'm very happy to be . . . I think I'm the only one that was involved on that first record from which the band's name comes from.[40]

According to Carl Atkins, Russell had decided to use his concept of vertical forms for the recording. Russell's approach to rehearsals has always been very exacting, and the musicians in the orchestra were struggling to understand his aims and expectations.

> What I remember was that I got a call from George or Helen Keene, who was the producer of Bill Evans, asking me if I could come to New York right away because they had had a session with George's music and it wasn't going very well. The musicians just didn't know quite what to make of all these cards that George was holding up with Roman numerals on it and cycles here and cycles there. If you remember that band, people like Ernie Royal, Joe Henderson, Sam Rivers, other trumpet players. He had a real mixture of veteran players and younger players and players who were out of a traditional playing bag and players like Sam Rivers, who were out of a more modern bag. So it was a real funny mixture of players, and so evidently they weren't taking to the music very well. They just didn't understand how to make it happen. I had done some things with George here with the school bands. I guess he remembered that we made some of those things work. So he asked me to come down and try to make this work. That's how I got the call. Then we did it and in two more sessions we put that album together.[41]

Atkins took on the role of conductor, and this enabled the session to be completed successfully. Atkins remembers that after that the only difficulty they had with the recording process concerned getting the musicians back from their breaks to continue the session. It was apparently not unlike herding cats of a different kind!

> So I asked Tony Williams if he had a whistle, a police whistle, in his kit. He said, "Yeah, I got one." I said, "Let me have it." I said, "What I'm going to do from now on, is I'm going to go outside the studio door on the street and I'm going to blow this whistle and wherever these cats are they'll hear the whistle." And that was the running joke. I'd go outside and blow the whistle and they'd come from all manner of places doing whatever they were doing.[42]

Atkins says that Evans was fully involved throughout.

> As we did the mix-downs, for example, he was very much involved in that and had some very good things to say about our ideas, and what I remember too after that was that he was very kind to me and had some very kind things to say about the things that we did, and about a week after the session he sent me a beautiful leather briefcase with just a little note in it, saying, "Thanks, Bill." I've still got the briefcase and I still got the note.[43]

Atkins says there was a marked difference between the record that Evans, Russell, and he finished and the one that was released. "When we did the mix-down, we left the product in one state, as I remember it. When the record came out it was in a different state. It was in a different acoustic state." Atkins puts this down to Columbia, who he believes made changes to put Evans out front in the mix and mask many of the things Russell had written. "I know when I've listened to it, and I haven't listened to it in a while, I've always said, 'That line didn't come through. Where is that line?'"[44]

Russell's third wife, Alice, however, offers a simpler explanation. "It was a terrible recording due in large part to substance abuse in those days by the people who were actually engineering the album. I'm afraid so. It seems so. The mix is appalling. You can't hear most of the horn parts on that record, and that's unfortunate because I think it's an amazing piece of music."[45]

The sound is very muddy. Russell's writing is quite dense anyway and benefits from the maximum possible separation available for analog technology. Russell rerecorded the piece in November 1995 with his Anglo-American Living Time Orchestra and additional musicians from various French *conservatoires* for Label Bleu. The clarity of the writing finally emerges, but also adds to the regret that the Bill Evans version had not fared better. In fairness, side 2 of the original LP sounds better than side 1, but so much detail has still been lost.

What remains is, by any standard, an astonishing record. There is some fabulous drumming from Tony Williams on "Event II" and "Event VI," along with a beautiful half-valve trumpet solo from Snooky Young. Elsewhere there are fine performances from Sam Rivers, a really outgoing solo on Event II and from Joe Henderson on Event V, set against Evans on electric piano. As for Evans, he performs some way outside his usual style, matching himself against the complex and multilayered orchestral environment Russell created for him. His playing on Event V is genuinely soulful and funky on Fender Rhodes, and he swings with a joyous freedom on acoustic piano. Keith Shadwick comments, "He plays with concision and force, often using phrases that are found nowhere else in his recorded output."[46] Evans had shown in all the projects he had undertaken with Russell an ability to adapt to the composer's harmonic idiom, and *Living Time* is no exception. This was the record Columbia had asked for—a modern Bill Evans record that took no prisoners and sat well alongside Miles Davis's *Bitches Brew*, Mahavishnu Orchestra, and Weather Report. As Max Harrison suggests, *Living Time*, like its peers, located its soloist or soloists wholly in the musical fabric: "Evans is not really a soloist: he is firmly embedded in the boiling complexity of, for instance, Events II and IV."[47]

Shadwick makes another telling point about the record's lack of success. "This is a terse and extreme harmonic idiom, especially in the jazz world—and perhaps this was the biggest reason for the piece's general failure to make a popular mark."[48] Not only did Bill Evans's fans stay away in droves, but, according to Alice Russell, "That's the one that lost Bill Evans so many fans. They were furious with him for playing that way. He got threats in the mail, 'If you ever, ever do anything like this again, I'll never buy another record.'"[49]

Columbia did little to promote the record and seems to have left Evans pretty much to his own devices, and then decided against renewing his contract. Evans was uncharacteristically forthright about the experience in an interview with Len Lyons some years later. "The stint I had with Columbia: I thought I'd finally arrived at a company that had the money and the interest. Clive Davis and I just didn't hit it off. I never even talked to the man, and he was already directing my career, making me 'creative,' 'communicative,' whatever." Maybe it is that which Brian Hennessey picked up from Evans."[50]

Like many on the jazz scene, Russell had stuck with Evans through his ten or more years of heroin addiction. Evans had finally kicked the habit thanks to methadone treatment. His life was on the up by this point, after years of quiet degradation. His long-term partner, Ellaine, was herself an addict and a fragile individual. In the spring of 1973 Evans met another woman while on tour on the West Coast and he told Ellaine of the affair. No sooner was Evans on his way back West when Ellaine threw herself under a subway train. Russell was one of the friends in whom Evans sought solace. Though Russell's recollection is hazy on some of the details, his account reveals their closeness as friends.

> About the saddest time with him was when the woman he married . . . I remember being in the house at the time, and she made a remark in front of Bill. She said, "I think if Bill left me I'd kill myself." Bill looked strangely surprised by that. Later on, he was going to St. Louis, I guess . . . I get a call that she jumped in front of a subway train. Bill was crying on the phone. He said, "Please come up." I go over to New York and to the church, he met me and gave me a hug, a tearful hug. I couldn't get that out of my mind for months and months and months. It seemed like such a horrible thing. He was on his way down. What a painful way for a beautiful man like that . . .[51]

In 1974 MCA reissued *Jazz in the Space Age* and *New York, N.Y.* as a twofer double package. Russell had often commented that he could not understand why the latter was out of the catalog, being a favorite work of his, so he was understandably happy when Leonard Feather wrote to him to advise of the reissue.[52] Bill Evans also appeared at Carnegie Hall with Russell for a performance of *Living Time* with a full band in 1974. Promoted by George Wein's organization, the event fared poorly in attendance, despite a double bill that also included Gary Burton performing music by Mike Gibbs. In his autobiography Wein uses the phrases "downright shameful" and "especially embarrassing" to describe the turnout—or, rather, lack thereof. It was, Wein noted, "a bold and terrific concert"—but one that only sold two hundred tickets.[53]

Surprisingly, the following year the performance was repeated, without Evans. Russell again played the hall, this time as part of the New York Jazz Repertory Company's series of concerts, on March 10, 1975, with pianists Alan Pasqua and Stanley Cowell and a band that included Tony Williams, Sam Rivers, Jimmy Giuffre, Stanton Davis, Howard Johnson, guitarist Sam Brown, bassist Herb Bushler, and John Clark on French horn, all of whom had been on the original session. Attendance seems to have been much better second time around.

Down Beat's Arnold Jay Smith, writing in the June 19 issue, complained about the poor sound and noted that "where *Living Time* made complete sense," the second half's performance of *Electronic Sonata* "made complete noise." And John S. Wilson in the *New York Times* was even more dismissive, writing, "The electronic sonata, which used a tape of swoops and chatters as an interlude between 'events' was filled with strong intense rhythms. But not even the spurts of excitement could entirely overcome the monotony of this long, meandering, repetitive work." It is quite possible that managing a reasonable sound balance in Carnegie Hall at that time for such a mix of instrumentation might have been beyond the capacity of the engineers. However, one is more tempted to comment that it is hardly surprising that Russell has spent so much of his career performing his music in the more open and sympathetic environments of European audiences.[54]

Gary Giddins took a very different view from Wilson and Smith in his "Weather Bird" column in the *Village Voice*. Contrasting an apparently bland performance of Michel Legrand the previous night, Giddins described Russell's first Carnegie Hall performance since "Cubano-Be, Cubano-Bop" in 1947 as "a personal triumph for the composer-theorist" but a flop in terms of public relations. Comparing Russell's "peripatetic career and the reluctance of major American labels to finance his recording projects" with that of film director Orson Welles, an inspired and apt comparison, Giddins mounted an assault on the conservatism of the jazz community. His analysis of Russell's theories and the music he heard provides an insightful response to both Smith and Wilson's narrow views and shortsighted criticisms.[55]

Following *Living Time*, the Carnegie Hall performance aside, Russell withdrew from performance and recording for a while and focused on his teaching commitments and his own further research into the Lydian Concept. It was in 1976 that Russell met Alice Norbury, who was director of the Midtown

School for the Arts in St. Louis, which was a legacy of the American community school movement. The New England Conservatory visited such projects across America each year to audition potential students. Russell came along on that particular visit and invited Norbury to dinner that first night. They spent the next year meeting in various cities where they both had business dealings, and at the end of the year, Russell asked her to move to Boston to live with him. They lived together for four years and married in 1981. Alice Norbury-Russell proved to be a major stabilizing influence on Russell's life but also has helped him organize and structure his working life in ways that have proved hugely beneficial. A former drama student, actress, model, and arts administrator, Alice has perhaps been able to bring both a business and an artistic focus to her husband's career. As she puts it, "My background melded well with George's in that we could speak a similar language."[56]

When Alice moved to Boston, she had intended to seek a position in the arts, but Russell asked if she would instead consider working with him.

George said, "It would be helpful if you would work with me because I have this idea of starting an orchestra again." Of course, he was at that time working on finishing volume 1 of this edition of the Concept. So I just gradually worked into doing what I do, which is basically acting as a sort of manager, tour manager, book publisher, CD producer, and also taking care of the business and secretarial side, which is a scream because of course I never learned to type because I never wanted to be anybody's secretary. *(laughs)*

She adds,

For a lot of couples, working together can be hellish, and it can be now and then with George and I, because we get on each other's nerves because I think we're both very much individuals and sort of loners, but for the most part I think it's been good. We've had an amazing life together and we've done some amazing projects when I look back on them.

Alice has helped Russell take things to a different level in the world of jazz, because, as she notes, "We never gave in to that sort of compelling mission that the jazz business has to make a musician feel like he's worthless—George never allowed that to happen to him." Russell, she says, has always insisted on doing things his way, "even when it was the wrong way, which wasn't often."[57]

To the lay jazz or classical music fan, the creation of a handful of new works over a period of twenty-five or thirty years may not seem that productive. The quality of Russell's output, however, speaks volumes, and is largely unmatched in the jazz world. Between 1976 and 1996, Russell produced eight major extended works—*Vertical Form VI* (1977); *Time Spiral* (1982); *African Game* (1983); *Uncommon Ground, Six Aesthetic Gravities, Centrifugue*, written for The Relâche Ensemble for New Music, and *La Folia: The Rocella Variations* (all 1989, the latter written together with Ben Schwendener); *American Trilogy* (1991); *Dialogue with Ornette* (1992); and *It's About Time* (1995).

As a rule, Russell writes when he has a record date, concert tour, or commission. Alice points out that when he does so, it is a painstaking and drawn-out process.

> George is not a prolific composer. Everything is written, even the things that sound improvised, as you know. He does a master plan for each composition, and that is where he determines what will happen in each measure for each instrument. The master plan is the thing that takes him the longest time. He can spend months on that, years on that if he's given that luxury. Thankfully he isn't, so he has to push on. Once the plan is in place, the actual writing of the composition is the easy part.[58]

After five years' absence from recording, Russell made *Vertical Form VI*, with Carl Atkins as "principal conductor" and a crack orchestra specially assembled by Swedish Radio for the commission. When it was eventually released in the States, John Diliberto in *Down Beat* gave it an encouraging four and a half stars, while Bob Blumenthal, writing in *Boston after Dark*, was also favorably impressed.[59] Describing the idea of "vertical forms" in the record's sleeve notes, Russell wrote,

> If you were standing in the middle of New York City on a typically busy day or night, focusing on all the patterns of sound around you, without attempting to identify their sources, you would be experiencing "vertical form"—layers or strata of divergent modes of rhythmic behavior. This one huge mass of sound is always there, holding linear time captive, and therefore going nowhere but up or down the scale of vertical density and complexity.[60]

Later, he used the analogy of the African choir. The music it creates is cyclic. Its level of intensity, density, and complexity may change, but it has no sense of forward movement. It is more as if it breathes, expands and contracts, and holds time suspended. This is a good description of the music on the record, and Russell went on to state that he considered *Now And Then* his first essay in vertical form, *Othello Ballet* his second, *Electronic Sonata* the third, *Listen to the Silence* the fourth, and *Living Time* the fifth.

The most remarkable aspect of *Vertical Form VI* is that, with the exception of a short interlude involving pianist Vlodek Gulgowski and Bertil Lövgren in Event IV, the entire piece is composed. This includes the apparently free improvisations in Events I and III. The writing is, like that in *Living Time*, dense and compressed. Its two most impressive aspects are its dark forests of concentrated rhythm and its impressive architecture. Within these the music flows smoothly and with, at its best, a filmic quality. It is a demanding work, but, with the exception of an all too brief finale and, arguably, Event II's rather repetitive closing section, it is a hugely rewarding piece. Perhaps best seen as an experiment or work in progress, as with so much of Russell's work, it is *sans pareil* in jazz.

As far as forming a big band was concerned, Russell got his wish. At club owner Max Gordon's suggestion, Russell began rehearsals for a series of dates at the Village Vanguard in New York scheduled for April 1978. As usual, Russell's expectations in preparing a band for performance was that the musicians would play his music as if they were on the stand, and as usual, he met a degree of understandable resistance from the band, and from the brass players in particular. Marty Ehrlich had not long finished his studies at the New England Conservatory when Russell asked him to play in his band.

> I was the youngest guy in the band, I believe, and I probably wasn't on that [same] page. I was in NYC to do exactly what he was doing. Even at NEC, George would get right up to you if he felt you weren't really playing hard on a part or a solo. It wasn't just accuracy; it was a vibe he was going for. This is something he shares with many composer/ensemble leaders I've had the fortune to work with. I tried my best to make the rehearsal have the intensity of a performance.[61]

In Russell's defense, his music is unusually difficult, and it is not enough for the players to read it and play it. He relies on them to make it breathe and come alive, to invest it with swing and movement.

Given Russell's difficulties in getting his music across in his home country and the debacle of his 1975 Carnegie performance, expectations of the New York dates were unusually high. Musicians, critics, and fans turned out in force, and the audience on one night included Donald Fagen and Walter Becker from Steely Dan. Critic Gary Giddins wrote a long piece in the *Village Voice* for his "Weather Bird" column,[62] and Stanley Crouch reviewed the gigs at length for the *Soho Weekly News*.[63] Russell presented a retrospective of his music for the engagement, which is captured in part by the *New York Big*

Band album on Soul Note, recorded four months later. Giddens comments that "his themes are luminescent, and they fully engage heart, mind and body. The orchestra played the music so forcefully and with such abandon that Russell actually did boogie." He continues, "The impact of his works depends on the exacting rhythmic and structural transitions; these reflect Russell's training as a drummer, but also the accomplishment of his musicians." He then singles out Stanton Davis and Terumasa Hino on trumpet, Janice Robinson on trombone, Ricky Ford and Roger Rosenberg on tenors (the article actually refers in error to Bob Handlin), Warren Smith on drums, Cameron Brown on bass, and the twin keyboards of Goetz Tangerding and Kikushi Masabumi for special mention.[64]

In the Stanley Crouch piece, the author bemoans a tendency among black musicians to ignore innovators from their own community because they are "sometimes so caught up in the hip convention of the moment." In so doing, they miss "a fresh aesthetic thrust—when it becomes hip—then attack the black artist with a new conception for using 'white boys.'" Crouch continues,

> The upshot of it all, though, is that much of Russell's recorded music suffers from a timbral dilution and a lack of rhythmic juiciness because so many of the players he used in the past, however, skilled at reading and execution or intellectually committed, lacked the *cultural* guts in their respective buckets to make the music stand up and shout the sophisticated folk message that is so central to Russell's art.[65]

A few lines further on he notes, "George Russell is, however, a man of great integrity and the integrated band he leads seems far above the kind of racial politics so many New York musicians work from at the behest of club owners, promoters and record companies. He has even been able somehow to inspire the notoriously tasteless Japanese trumpeter Hino to play fine Fats Navarro lines."[66]

As far as poor Hino is concerned, it is a case of damned if you do and damned if you don't. Crouch's comments succeed in proffering praise and taking it back in the same breath. In fairness, Crouch's article makes a number of interesting points, and he comes to praise Russell, not to bury him. One just wonders why he felt the need to bring the shovel.

Perhaps it is naive to expect otherwise. However, Russell's music does draw extensively on its African rhythmic heritage, but as a composer and artist he grasps the tradition of European art music with authority and confidence. Not only has he brought the complex harmonic vocabulary of twentieth-century classical music and aleatory techniques into jazz, but he has gifted the powerful, sophisticated rhythms of jazz to classical music. Crouch's piece has the inspirational title "From the Cottonfields to the Cosmos." A better description of Russell's music is hard to imagine. As an individual African American growing up in a racist society, he has more reason to feel aggrieved and bitter than many of his fellow citizens. Yet that is not how he experiences the world. His music is open to the whole earth and the cosmos, without bias. One feels that that is how one should write about his music.

Marty Ehrlich recalls, thirty years later, that various musicians were unhappy with Crouch's comments. "I recall only vague things about that review. I remember that it was intellectually dishonest and inconsistent as much of Crouch's writing was becoming and would become. (I was a fan of him in earlier years.) Yes, I remember certain players he singled out being hurt."[67]

The *New York Big Band* album gives a good representation of what the band must have sounded like, those nights in the Vanguard. It adds a fine version of "Cubano-Be, Cubano-Bop" from the Swedish session that produced *Vertical Form VI*, with Sabu Martinez on congas and strong trumpet from Bertil Lövgren and Americo Belotto. With modern production and recording, "Cubano-Be, Cubano-Bop" seems just as impressive, but now its true subtleties emerge. With no Janice Robinson or Kikushi Masabumi, only one keyboard, and Stanley Cowell on electric piano on the opening, "Living Time Event V," the studio band differs slightly from the live ensemble. However, with the exception of a strained vocal from Lee Genesis on "Big City Blues," this is a fine performance and an interesting retrospective of Russell's music. There is also a nice version of Billie Holiday's "God Bless the Child" and a sharp version of Stanton Davis's "Mystic Voices." Davis plays beautifully throughout, and particularly so on "Listen to the Silence," as do Roger Rosenberg on tenor and Gary Valente on trombone.

In 1980 Russell took a sextet to Italy that featured (in addition to himself on piano and organ) Lew Soloff on trumpet, Robert Moore on tenor and soprano, Victor Comer on guitar, the fine French bassist J. F. Jenny-Clark on bass, and Keith Copeland on drums. In the sleeve notes for the new version of *Electronic Sonata* the group recorded in the studios in Milan, Russell says that he had disbanded the New York Big Band "because most of our music was old music, although it wasn't old to the people who came to hear it." He then talks about his intention to form a new big band to do new material and considerably reworked versions of older tunes.[68]

Moore had studied with Russell and, as a little known musician even around Boston, was surprised to get the gig. It was a fairly short tour, but included performances at Tasso's Oak, Rome, and Venice. There was also a concert with the RAI Big Band that was to be broadcast, which Moore learned about only when they got to Italy.

> He was working with the RAI Big Band and some American musicians, and— let's see—there was Jean-Francois Jenny-Clark and Bobo Stenson and some other European people too, and so for that two-week period while we were in Rome rehearsing, I was doing both sextet and the big-band rehearsals, and after about two or three days and not being used to that kind of stuff my lips started blistering and bleeding. I really didn't know what to do, and what concerned me so much was that in the rehearsal with the big band, whenever it came time for me to solo, George wanted me to put 100 percent into it and I was just suffering. I remember in the midst of one solo I was just fumbling along trying to save myself, he came up to me and said, "Play like Trane! Play like Trane!" Oh my goodness, in fact there were several musicians who came up to me in the course of that tour—Ornette Coleman and some others—and they said, "Don't let George kill you, man!" *(laughs)* Somehow I made it through that and we did the record at the end, which I can't listen to anymore because all I can think of is the pain. I told a number of people that I remember reading a review of that recording, and one reviewer said, "Moore's solo is good . . ." and so forth and so on, " . . . but he climaxes too soon." *(laughs)* And I was thinking to myself that I wanted to climax at the start because it was so painful.[69]

Probably only the most devoted fan will check out this third version of Russell's opus, especially bearing in mind that it features on two later Russell records as well. That is unfortunate, because it is quite different from the Swedish sextet with Stanton Davis album. In a way, it is tighter and more inward looking, but the playing of Moore and Soloff is really quite beautiful, and both depart sonically and even timbrally from the approach of Davis and Garbarek. And Comer, Jenny-Clark, and Copeland contrast dramatically with Rypdal, Andersen, and Christensen. Even the way the electronic tape is used is changed from the original version. That said, it is probably for the most dedicated fans only.

It was the next project, however, that created the mold that would shape Russell's future career. In 1979 Russell had again been commissioned to write a piece by Swedish Radio. The piece, *Time Spiral*, provided the impetus for him to launch a new big band, though it was again called George Russell's New York Big Band. This band was, if anything, even better than its predecessor. *Time Spiral* was recorded in July 1982 at the Vanguard in New York for the Italian Soul Note label. It may not be from the top drawer of Russell's compositions, but it is a fine extended work, perhaps more traditional in structure and the greater degree of freedom it gives its soloists. The performance is a touch slow to get started, but from Marty Ehrlich's flute solo on, the band plays with a force and majesty that few records could match. With great piano from Jack Reilly and Mark Soskin, astonishing guitar from Jerome Harris, and ecstatic ensemble work, this is excellent big-band jazz. Side 2 of the LP features two versions of older tunes. Russell uses Jerry Coker's big-band arrangement of "Ezz-Thetic" for this version, while Goetz Tangerding, who played on *New York Big Band*, arranged "D.C. Divertimento." Ehrlich's alto really comes into its own on "Ezz-Thetic." As he explains, it was important to put the Dolphy version to one side and find his own way through the piece. "I wasn't thinking of Dolphy's solo so much as using this amazing melody as my jumping off point, more than the changes to "Love for Sale." It was a challenge I was only partly ready for at that age, as the tempo George took on the piece was fierce. I tried."[70]

As for the flute solo on *Time Spiral*, Ehrlich recalls, "I felt particularly good about the flute solo, and it might have been my idea to play flute there, one that George went for. I was glad to have a context to add some of the textural and sonic stuff I had been improvising with at that time into the context of George's music."[71]

Ehrlich also toured Europe that year with a Russell big band, with a memorable performance at the North Sea Festival in Holland, though two Italian dates had to be cancelled when Italy's soccer team made first the World Cup semifinal and then the final. "Italy won that year! Both concerts were cancelled, but I remember that George got paid and I think without a fight, as the promoters themselves said, "No one will come, not even us; the whole country will be watching these games!"[72]

Jack Reilly, who played keyboards on the session, notes that by the time of the recording, the band was really playing at its best.

> Well, it was done from live performances at the Vanguard. We had done three weeks of concerts, so it was really bedded down great. There was only one substitute; Ray Anderson came in on trombone and he was unbelievable. I couldn't believe what was coming out of the trombone. We played strong bebop stuff. It was just George took the tapes home and decided what to put out. It was a thrill to play with them. There were no talk-overs at the end of the night, where something wasn't working. He never did say much, either, at the initial rehearsals before the tour.[73]

Preparation had, as always, been demanding, but Reilly highlights another problem, which seems to recur with Russell bands and can even be traced back to the Chicago rehearsals with Earl Hines band.

He was upset when I couldn't read "D.C. Divertimento" right off. I said, "George you wanna read it?" It was the way he wrote it. I almost wanted to have it copied over for him. Boy, that was horrendous, and he had no patience with that. That was no excuse. I don't mean the musical part. No, the music was hard enough. Not really technically hard. It was just that the treble for the bass clef, the left-hand part was not lined up with the downbeat of the beats in the bar. The downbeat in the right hand was on the second and half the beat, and you knew it was supposed to go to the left hand, and vice versa. And it was in a terrible script. It was the script and the way it was lined up.[74]

Barry Galbraith, Russell's guitarist from the Jazz Workshop and other sessions, died on January 13, 1983. Galbraith had also taught at the conservatory with Russell and had been a close friend for almost forty years. Perhaps one of the most important things a person can do for a friend is to write his eulogy or obituary, something that defines him but also expresses personal loss. Russell was the obvious choice, and wrote in *NEC Notes* in the summer of 1983, "From 1950 to the late 1960s, I relied most heavily on Barry to make my music 'come off.' His guitar became a lead trumpet, or part of a saxophone section, or doubled in octaves with the bass and, at times, the whole orchestra. He was a professional in the true sense of the word." Russell continued, "In inestimable ways, he continues to color my life, as well as my music. It is, therefore, impossible for me to conceive of him as having departed."[75]

If the interest provoked in the United States by his 1978 Vanguard dates was encouraging, Russell must have been truly touched by the response his music was beginning to receive. It might not have been the second coming, but it certainly was not a case of "the prophet without honor." Several things seemed to happen in the space of a few months.

The first event was a concert in Russell's honor in March 1983 for the Boston Globe Jazz Festival at the Berklee Performance Center. Members of the New England Conservatory faculty and student body contributed, with a student ensemble led by Pat Hollenbeck and performers that included the original George Russell Sextet drummer Joe Hunt, trombonist Gary Valente, Ricky Ford, pianist Fred Hersch, and guitarist Mick Goodrick. Governor Michael Dukakis even proclaimed it "George Russell Day" in the Commonwealth of Massachusetts.[76] The second event was the commissioning by the Boston Jazz Coalition, from a grant from the Massachusetts Council on the Arts and Humanities, of a new work, *The African Game*, for a performance in Boston in the summer of 1983. The final event was that Blue Note label boss Bruce Lundval listened to the tape of the concert on a flight to the West Coast, and, liking what he heard, signed Russell as the first artist on the new Blue Note label. This was in 1984. This should have been the honor to match them all. If that did not turn out to be the case, it did lead to the most remarkable record Russell would ever make, and to a very good companion album from the same concert.

Recorded live at Emmanuel Church in Boston on June 18, 1983, and credited for the first time to George Russell and the Living Time Orchestra, *The African Game* is the record Russell was destined to make and the one that sums up man, music, and mind. As he told Francis Davis,

> People assume *The African Game* is about black evolution but it's not. It's about *human evolution* because we're all Africans at the core, when you trace these things back. It's ironic in a way that I'm playing the Afro-American Museum because there are so many white players in my band, it'll probably look like Buddy Rich's band to some people. But I've never bought that theory that says only black people have soul or essence of whatever—that does nobody any good. I don't care where a musician comes from or what he looks like. I listen for that electricity you get from certain players.[77]

Coming some five years later, this makes an entirely apt riposte to Stanley Crouch's *Soho Weekly News* piece.

The band at Emmanuel Church featured a mix of experienced and younger players. Among the older pros were the exceptional George Garzone on tenor and soprano and Keith Copeland, who had played with Russell in Italy in 1980 and 1982. The younger musicians included a very young Bill Urmson on electric bass, Mark Rossi on piano, and Mark White, now a professor at Berklee, on guitar. For Urmson in particular, it was a baptism by fire.

> I remember I was taking my last final exam at the conservatory, it was Jazz Studies, and Mark Harvey, a trumpet player in Boston, was the instructor, and I went to hand in my test and I was thinking, "That's it, I'm passing my last final. I'm done." And he says, "I've got to talk to you about something." He says, "George is doing this thing." So I'm literally hired. I was asked to play as I was handing in my final exam. What a segue. Right into George's band from class.[78]

Russell has always bridled at the oft-repeated suggestion that his music has suffered due to his reliance at times on student bands. Interviewed by Ben Young for WKCR, his response was quite acerbic to Young's innocent comment.

BY: It's a large list of players, mainly from the New England Conservatory or Boston area.
GR: They're mainly players from the Boston area but . . . they're . . . sometimes if you mention the term "students" it definitely tends to diminish any effort that

you're involved in. People forget that Miles was a student. He was a student at Juilliard, where he used to use the little practice rooms to work out what he'd learned with Bird the night before. George Garzone is a legend. He was a student at one time. We all were students. This is a pro band from the Boston area.[79]

It was one of Russell's first commissions in some time in the United States. For the work, Russell chose to compose nine events, each one representing a period in our evolution, giving each titles such as "Consciousness" (III), "African Empires" (VI), and "Cartesian Man" (VII). The remainder of the concert featured performances of *Time Spiral*; Russell's arrangement of Miles Davis's "So What," using Miles's own solo as the basis for the theme; Dave Baker's "War Gewesen"; and Carla Bley's "Rhymes." These four pieces were later issued by Blue Note under the album title *So What*.

Marc Rossi says the first thing he did when he was asked to do the gig was clear his week.

> So I could make sure I could practice my butt off. I wasn't going to take any chances on this. I saw some of the horn players at the rehearsals looking like they'd never looked at the part before. Not me, pal! My recollection of it was the amazing focus and the intensity of the music, putting this mammoth thing together with all these people, and the enormous sense of respect people had for George's music and the great joy of working at that very high level. It was absolutely one of the two or three most highest-level things I've ever had the privilege to do in my life. When you play with George, you go beyond yourself. You transcend.[80]

He found Russell inspiring to work with in this context. "George is very cool under all that fire. He's a lot of fun to work with. Very focused and very liberating at the same time. I think that everybody just plays at their best."[81]

There were some corrections to be made in the studio afterward due to leaks on some parts, but *The African Game* is essentially a very live recording. Rossi describes *The African Game* as one of Russell's two or three greatest works. He also did some U.S. dates with the Living Time Orchestra and says that Russell helped him manage his performance nerves. "You're not going to want to print this. George helped me get over some of my nerves. I remember asking him. He said, 'What are you nervous about?' I said, 'I'm afraid I might make mistakes and the audience will hear.' He goes, 'Fuck the audience! Play the music!'"[82] As Rossi explains it, it was one of those grow-up calls from a mentor to a pupil that changes an individual's thinking.

There are three very impressive things about *The African Game*. The first is Russell's vision for the piece and its inspiration in human evolution. The second is the architecture of the work. It is highly unusual and nonlinear in structure. It seems simultaneously episodic and yet it coheres over its forty minutes very successfully. There is a density and intensity to the writing, as always, and the different parts of the work shift constantly. Again, percussion and rhythm are key features in the architecture of the work, and Russell incorporated into the performance five Cuban Olu Bata drummers. Everything about *The African Game* is unexpected. The final aspect that impresses is the way the solos reflect Russell's ideas and yet are also so expressive. The listener is drawn to Mark Rossi's synthesizer solo on the final event, "The Future?" and Gary Joynes's tenor on "African Empires" (VI), and Mark White's guitar solo on "The Survival Game" (IV), which stand as models of how effectively writing and improvisation can combine in the right hands.

The African Game did not hit the stores until 1985. However, in October 1983 Russell embarked on what was, shockingly, his first ever American tour. The Living Time Orchestra were actually touring in support of *Live in an American Time Spiral*, but given the artistic success of *The African Game*, Russell devoted a large section of the concerts to the work. The tour took Russell's music to the San Diego Kool-Aid Festival; Tempe, Arizona; Albuquerque; Houston; and New York, among other places. On the whole the band was well received, though one review was quite dismissive of the soloing abilities of Russell's young musicians. Of the LTO's performance at the Entermedia Theatre in Greenwich Village, John Pareles wrote in the *New York Times*, "The band's soloists didn't add much to the music." He concluded, "Apparently, Mr. Russell is willing to pay that price in order to get his music played so precisely."[83] Whether this comment was justified or not is, without personal experience, hard to say, though Stanley Crouch reviewing a Sweet Basil performance in February 1984 suggested the band was "full of musicians who were full of more enthusiasm than authority." However, he was full of praise for Russell's music, and *The African Game* in particular, and granted that "Russell is far from trapped by the limitations of the players he can afford. In fact, by closing night the ensemble was showing impressive potential."[84]

Two things do seem to have really assisted Russell's career from the late seventies onward. The first of these, which has already been noted, concerns Alice Norbury-Russell's role as his business manager (or perhaps it should be "take-care-of-business manager"). The second was that Russell was taken on as a client by Marty Khan and Helene Cann and their agency, Outward Visions Inc. Having professional management and organization finally left Russell to work on his music and on the Concept, and let others take care of business.

Russell had been getting good press coverage in the States since his return. *Down Beat* had been particularly supportive, the occasional and inevitable nay-saying episode aside. Newspapers local to the New England Conservatory, such as the *Boston Globe* and the *Boston Phoenix*, were also in his corner, with Bob Blumenthal being a very strong advocate. In fact, it is unfair to be too critical of the media in terms of Russell's career. Certainly there seems to have been a rather chauvinistic downplaying of Russell's period in Scandinavia in some quarters.[85] However, it has to be said that the records Russell made in Europe were only haphazardly available until the early 1980s, when the Italian label Soul Note reissued these records and improved their distribution Stateside. *Down Beat* certainly did its bit from this point on. In its April 1982 issue, John Diliberto gave *Electronic Sonata for Souls Loved by Nature—1980* a fair four-star review, but gave *Vertical Form VI* four and a half. In December 1983 Bill Shoemaker, reviewing reissues of *Ezz-Thetics*, *The Essence of George Russell*, and *Live in an American Time Spiral*, awarded all three five stars and revealed a genuine appreciation of the continuities in Russell's work over time. He did, however, suggest that Jan Garbarek's work on the big-band *Electronic Sonata* represented the apex of his career. Here one merely notes the continuing quality of the saxophonist's music. *Down Beat* even gave Michael Cuscuna, the writer/producer/archivist who had worked extensively on the early eighties Blue Note reactivation, two pages to review the launch of Russell's own Concept label and the reissuing of *Othello Ballet*, *The Essence of George Russell*, *Electronic Sonata for Souls Loved by Nature—1968*, and *Listen to the Silence*.[86]

And Blue Note could not have asked for better press in response to the release in 1985 of *The African Game*. The *Houston Post* described it as "a vast, sprawling work that is also utterly compelling and thought-provoking." Robert Palmer called it "one of the most significant new album releases of the past several years," in a long *New York Times* piece entitled "A Jazz Visionary Eyes the Evolution of Life on Earth." J. D. Considine raved, "Masterpiece may be too modest an accolade" in the April 1985 issue of *Musician*, and the ever-reliable Bob Blumenthal wrote in another long article in the *Globe* that it was "the only new Blue Note we are likely to play over and over."[87]

However, more significantly in terms of the next phase of Russell's career, *The African Game* was beginning to cause ripples across the Atlantic.

Notes

1. Interview with Gunther Schuller, October 2003.
2. Ibid.

3. Ibid.

4. Ian Carr, interviw with Gunther Schuller for BBC Radio 3 broadcast *George Russell—The Invisible Guru*, July 1994.

5. Interview with Gunther Schuller.

6. Carr, interview with Schuller.

7. Interview with Gunther Schuller.

8. Ibid.

9. Ian Carr, interview with Marit Jerstad for BBC Radio 3 broadcast *George Russell—The Invisible Guru*, July 1994.

10. Interview with Carl Atkins, October 2003.

11. Ibid.

12. Interview with Ingrid Monson, November 2005.

13. Interview with Bill Urmson, June 2003.

14. Ibid.

15. Interview with Fred Hersch, January 2007.

16. Interview with Don Byron, July 2005.

17. Ibid.

18. Ibid.

19. Ibid.

20. Interview with Urmson.

21. Ibid.

22. E-mail interview with Marty Ehrlich, April 2005.

23. E-mail interview with Satoko Fujii, January 2005.

24. Interview with Ehrlich.

25. Interview with John Medeski, October 2003.

26. E-mail interview with James Falzone, April 2007.

27. E-mail interview with Greg Burk, April 2007.

28. Interview with Dave Holland, September 2006.

29. Charles Ives, Symphony No. 3, Naxos CD 8.559087

30. These observations derive from several sources, including a DVD and tape made by the New England Conservatory, program notes, a press release, and review data.

31. Interview with Stanton Davis, June 2003.

32. Ken Linden, "George Russell," *Jazz & Pop*, Autumn 1969.

33. Peter Pettinger, *How My Heart Sings* (New Haven: Yale University Press, 1998), pp. 203 and 212.

34. *Down Beat*, September 16, 1971.

35. Pettinger, *How My Heart Sings*; K. Shadwick, *Bill Evans: Everything Happens to Me—A Musical Biography* (San Francisco: Backbeat, 2002).

36. Interview with Brian Hennessy, April 2004.

37. Ibid.

38. Sy Johnson, "Interview: Bill Evans & George Russell," *Changes*, Spring 1972.

39. Shadwick, *Everything Happens to Me*, p. 154.

40. Ian Carr, interview with Dave Bargeron for BBC Radio 3 broadcast *George Russell—The Invisible Guru*, July 1994.

41. Interview with Atkins.

42. Ibid.

43. Ibid.

44. Ibid.

45. Ian Carr, interview with Alice Norbury-Russell for BBC Radio 3 broadcast *George Russell—The Invisible Guru*, July 1994.

46. Shadwick, *Everything Happens to Me*, p. 154.

47. Max Harrison, "George Russell—Rational Anthems (Phase 1, 2, 3)," *Wire* (Spring/Summer/Autumn 1983).

48. Shadwick, *Everything Happens to Me*, p.154.

49. Carr, interview with Norbury-Russell.

50. Quoted in L. Lyons, *The Great Jazz Pianists* (New York: Da Capo, 1983), p. 226.

51. Interview with George Russell, October 2003.

52. Leonard Feather, letter to George Russell, March 21, 1973. Not everyone feels as Russell does about New York, N.Y. Max Harrison has never liked it. See earlier citation.

53. G. Wein, *Myself Among Others* (Cambridge, MA: Da Capo, 2003), pp. 394–95.

54. Arnold Jay Smith, "The Music of George Russell," *Down Beat*, June 19, 1975; John S. Wilson, "Russell Presents His Episodic Jazz," *New York Times*, March 10, 1975.

55. Gary Giddins, "St. George and the Chord," *Village Voice*, March 24, 1975

56. Interview with Alice Norbury-Russell, October 2006.

57. Ibid.

58. Carr, interview with Norbury-Russell.

59. John Diliberto, Review of Electronic Sonata (SN1009) and Vertical Form VI (SN1019), *Down Beat*, April 1982.

60. George Russell, sleeve notes to Vertical Form VI, Soul Note 121019–1

61. Interview with Ehrlich.

62. Gary Giddins, "George Russell Boogies," *Village Voice*, April 17, 1978.

63. Stanley Crouch, "From the Cottonfields to the Cosmos," *Soho Weekly News*, April 20, 1978; the gigs were also reviewed by John S. Wilson (*New York Times*, May 4, 1978) and Don Nelsen (*Daily News* [New York], May 9, 1978). See also "Russell Storms the Vanguard," *Down Beat*, June 1, 1978.

64. Giddins, "George Russell Boogies."

65. Crouch, "From the Cottonfields to the Cosmos." My copy of the piece came via critic Ian Carr, who had written "Bullshit" by the quote.

66. Ibid. Again Carr has written "Rubbish" in the margins.

67. Interview with Ehrlich.

68. L. Jeske, sleeve notes to *Electronic Sonata for Souls Loved by Nature*—1980 Soul Note 121009–1.

69. Interview with Robert Moore, July 2004.

70. Interview with Ehrlich.

71. Ibid.

72. Ibid.

73. Interview with Jack Reilly, October 2003.

74. Ibid.

75. George Russell, "Barry Galbraith—Obituary," *NEC Notes*, Summer 1983.

76. See "By George," *Down Beat*, July 1983, p. 12; *Jazz Times*, June 1983; Bob Blumenthal, "A Tribute to a Local," *Boston Globe*, March 23, 1983.

77. Francis Davis, "George Russell: Intellect of the Heart," *Jazz Times*, December 1984.

78. Interview with Urmson.

79. Ben Young, broadcast devoted to George Russell in celebration of his seventy-fourth birthday, WKCR Radio, New York, June 23, 1997.

80. Interview with Marc Rossi, October 2004.

81. Ibid.

82. Ibid.

83. John Pareles, "Russell Big Band in Two Showpieces," *New York Times*, November 11, 1983.

84. Stanley Crouch, "George Russell's Victory," *Village Voice*, February 21, 1984.

85. Sy Johnson's comment is the most extreme example. In general, it is mentioned en passant or not at all.

86. Diliberto, Review; Bill Shoemaker, Review of Ezz-thetics (Riverside Original Jazz Classic OJC-070), The Essence of George Russell (Soul Note 1044/5), and Live in an American Time Spiral (Soul Note 1049), *Down Beat*, December 1983; Michael Cuscuna, Spotlight review of reissues of Othello Ballet, The Essence of George Russell, Electronic Sonata 1968, and Listen to the Silence, Down Beat, February 13, 1975.

87. Bob Claypool, Review of *The African Game, Houston Post*, June 4, 1985; Robert Palmer, "A Jazz Visionary Eyes the Evolution of Life on Earth," *New York Times*, April 28, 1985; J. D. Considine, Review of *The African Game, Musician*, April 1985; Bob Blumenthal, "Captured by the Game," *Boston Phoenix*, May 14, 1985. See also *Down Beat*, October 1985 for review of Sweet Basil residency.

CHAPTER TEN

~

It's About Time

John Cumming, director of British independent producers Serious, had worked on a number of projects for the Arts Council of Britain's Contemporary Music Network. CMN promotes and helps fund tours by important British, European, and American artists and composers, mainly from jazz and new music. Cumming had recently managed a Carla Bley tour and had worked with Gil Evans, Steve Reich, and others, as well as organizing the Camden Jazz Festival. In 1985 Annette Morreau, the founder of CMN, contacted him with the suggestion of a UK tour with George Russell.

> I said, George Russell would be fantastic, but the problem is you've got to find a way of doing it, because trying to bring a full band over from the States, and I was aware that the last band I'd seen—I'd never met George—but I knew it was an unhappy experience. It was a touring band that I'd bumped into when I was tour-managing Carla Bley's band. I bumped into them at a couple of festivals here, there, and everywhere, and I knew some of the guys in the band, and it was clearly not a happy experience, partly because the business side was being very badly handled in Europe and partly because it was a pickup band, really, and there were some people that he trusted and others that he didn't get on with. And I said, I think you've got to be really careful, because apart from the fact that it's going to be an expensive operation, maybe the thing to do is to talk to George in a different way. Let's find out what he wants to do. Let's find out if he's interested in forming a band that takes players that he does trust from America and build British artists around it, select some of the young musicians that are coming through that will respond well, that might give something back to the music, so that there'll be a real dialogue.[1]

Cumming had used this approach with other artists, and, on a business trip Stateside, approached Russell.

> George came and picked me up and took me to Anthony's Pier 9, which is a famous seafood restaurant full of pictures of Mafiosi on the wall. There's all these pictures of Frank Sinatra with dodgy Italians, and we sat and talked and drank, not getting pissed or anything, but we sat and drank wine for about two hours and talked about the scene in general and what might happen. Then he drove me to the airport, because I had to fly on somewhere else. So he drove me to the airport and we continued to talk on the way, and that's really how it started. He was really interested in the idea, told me what he needed for rehearsal time, told me the kind of players he wanted to have in the band, and we worked it from there.[2]

Russell's first UK tour took place in February and March 1986, and the Anglo-American Living Time Orchestra played ten dates covering virtually the whole of England. Of the players who made that tour, one or two proved with hindsight to be wrong for the music, and while saxophonist Courtney Pine had proved an excellent choice, his own career was just taking off and he was unable to play with Russell again. Russell brought with him keyboardist Brad Hatfield, bassist Bill Urmson, and drummer Keith Copeland. Serious's success in selecting the right players is illustrated by the fact that a fair number of those chosen would play on Russell's subsequent European tours. Trumpeter Stuart Brooks, saxophonists Pete Hurt and Chris Biscoe, and Danish trumpeter Palle Mikkelborg would all continue their association with Russell into the twenty-first century. Trombonist Pete Burchill would also play on Russell's next European tour in 1989, while bass trombonist Ashley Slater played with Russell on two further tours.

The experience of playing with Russell was to prove particularly important to the young Courtney Pine. He describes it as a marvelous apprenticeship that taught him a lot about being a bandleader, like how to rehearse a band, how to get the best out of his musicians, how to conduct, and how to relate to an audience. As he says, "At that time it was just what I needed."

As well as his own band, Pine had been instrumental in forming and directing the Jazz Warriors big band.

> We had some really deep conversations, and out of that the things that were played by the Jazz Warriors came out of that whole experience. He's got this Lydian Chromatic Concept that Steve Williamson showed me first, and I got a copy of it and read it inside out and played it inside out, but just checking his scores, I based my writing for the Jazz Warriors on that experience. All the

African cross-rhythms, where you get three or four drums playing, he's not just done that, but put it on brass instruments, so you get that kind of cross-rhythm thing happening. So when I looked down the score and saw how George did it, I thought, "That's exactly what I'm going to do," and I did.

And he adds, "Yeah, a lot of those tunes are George Russell inspired."[3]

Chris Biscoe had heard, via trombonist Rick Taylor, who was helping Serious put the band together, that the tour was happening. Biscoe was a fan of Russell's sixties sextet records, in particular *The Outer View*, and asked Taylor to consider him for the tour. "I said, I'd be really interested in that because I really liked the music. I really love that format of the sextet, because you can get very interesting colors and a bit of orchestration, but you still get the sort of small-band feel with it as well."[4]

Rehearsals were exacting, as Biscoe recalls, and it was not easy for the players new to Russell's music. "The first rehearsal, we did an enormous amount of material in three days. It was very hard material and it was very intense—in physical circumstances that were extremely difficult, because it was extremely cold and rather dank in the place we were rehearsing in. It was pretty tough because he's quite a hard taskmaster."[5]

As a relative newcomer, Pine was surprised by the amount of written material that they were to cover. "I remember loads of sheet music and turning loads of pages over and thinking, 'Is this right?' I'd never seen so much music for a jazz gig. I mean, I'd done other big bands, but there were just reams and reams of stuff. And it was very complex music." Pine says Russell used his arrangement of "So What" as "a way of finding out who in the band could do what and to bring the American rhythm section he'd brought from the States and the British horn players together."

"He wanted to get the feel right first," Pine remembers, and though the band struggled through the piece at first, it became easier from there on. "After that I realized that this guy wasn't just wanting us to play what was on the paper. He was after something special."[6]

Pine's comments are important. What he is saying is that musicians who have played with Russell over protracted periods may not have studied with him, but they still absorbed much of what he has to say musically and theoretically.

Pete Hurt played baritone and bass clarinet on Russell's first tour and on subsequent tours. He was primarily a tenor and soprano player, and it was his reputation as a musician that got him the gig, and he played the initial rehearsals on borrowed instruments. He was using Courtney Pine's rather ancient bass clarinet and a baritone borrowed from a friend.

So George can look a bit fearsome sometimes, and he'd never heard us play before, and we started playing and I thought, "Oh, God. He hates us." But after a bit he seemed to think to himself, "Actually, they're not too bad," and everyone began to relax a bit. But personally, I was very nervous, but after the first rehearsal I started to enjoy it. Playing most of George's music, you have to rehearse fairly intensely. You need a road map really. Apart from some of the earlier things, which are quite straightforward, you can't just sit down, it's not like someone counts in and you're off. I've done Carla Bley's big band and that's a lot more straightforward. I think George's music is, in the end, more rewarding because you have to work a lot harder at it and you get more out of it.[7]

Hurt explains further:

Some of his music is fairly straightforward, but some of it is like, "What on earth do I do here?" because he has such a unique way of writing. He may have one rhythm going, say, in the rhythm section, and he has a group of instruments, not necessarily written sections, like a saxophone, a keyboard, and a trombone who do something completely against the rhythm. It might be completely out of tempo, and there might be several other groups of instruments doing other completely different things, and you've got to try and coordinate all this. If you're playing out-of-tempo lines against a fixed rhythm, trying to ride that can be very difficult. Sometimes the parts can be a little confusing, and it takes a lot of rehearsal to coordinate all these different layers going on.[8]

British-based Canadian trumpeter Kenny Wheeler was also on that tour and remembers Russell's stagecraft and skill at communicating with both band and audience.

We played some of the old pieces, like "All About Rosie." I must admit that I liked them much better than the newer pieces. The newer pieces kind of had a lot of different things happening at once, so much so that when I played my part I didn't feel it was all that important somehow. But I did like his actual compositions. They were very good. As for the audience, I think they loved the music. As I said, George was very good at communicating to an audience, and to the band also, but the audiences seemed to like it very much.[9]

Bearing in mind that Russell had not toured Britain before, the tour was a major success. Cumming was particularly pleased, and was determined to continue what had proved a very successful partnership with George and Alice Russell. "We had a lot of fun on the tour, as you do when you start to feel comfortable with people. You get away from that sort of thing where it's, 'Oh, god, I hope that's all going to work.' You get to the point where you can see the tour growing night by night and the music growing night by night."[10]

Reviewing the opening date of the tour at London's Logan Hall, John Fordham's piece in the *Guardian* confirmed a mixture of first night nerves and bravura playing. "For a pick-up band," wrote Fordham, "it was a spectacular first night with some of the most demanding compositions in Jazz."[11] Richard Williams in the *Times* was quietly enthusiastic about the gig and seemed to enjoy the first set's back catalog of "Cubano-Be, Cubano-Bop," *All About Rosie*, and *Electronic Sonata* more than set two's *The African Game*. He noted in respect of the latter, "Between bouts of therapeutic rowdiness, several memorable events occurred."[12] By the time the tour hit Southampton's Mountbatten Hall, however, Derek Eaton's review in the *Southern Evening Echo* began with the words, "Electrifying, riveting, immaculate" and ended, "The hall reverberated to incredible gargantuan sounds."[13] In fact, the tour went so well overall that Russell was back the following year to play festivals in France and Austria, and also the Bracknell Festival in the UK.

Russell had worked well with both his audiences and his musicians, who appreciated his democratic style, as Chris Biscoe notes.

> In fact, in a way it's surprising and not surprising, in view of what I said about him being a taskmaster. I think he's a very nice person, and, for instance, he always travels with the band. We've done some terribly tough schedules for someone his age, because he's not a young man. I thought he would certainly have been justified in saying, "I want a limo" or "Put me on a plane," instead of going on the coach with the other people or something like that. He wants to travel with the band—and I've seen other examples of that—not to have special treatment. In the way he treats people, he's a very sort of democratic person.[14]

The warmth of the response Russell had received in the UK was reflected in an article by Stan Woolley. Woolley produced a full and detailed profile of Russell for British magazine *Jazz Journal* that proved the beginning of a love affair between the British jazz press and the composer.[15]

In autumn of 1987 and back in America, Russell played a prestigious concert at Washington's Baird Auditorium in the Museum of Natural History. The concert, one of a series of avant garde big-band performances promoted by the District Curators and Smithsonian Resident Associates, was preceded by a long feature from Howard Mandel in the *Washington Post*.[16] The program featured *The African Game*, *Electronic Sonata*, and "Cubano-Be, Cubano-Bop," which included a tape recording of Sabu Martinez's 1977 performance in Stockholm. As Geoffrey Himes wrote in the *Post*, "Not only were the harmonics, melodic and dynamic shifts in the extended suites often astonishing but the rollicking, joyful rhythms often tempted one to flout the Smithsonian's decorum and get up in the aisles and dance."[17]

That November, Russell toured the United States with a sextet that included Russell on piano, Mingus alumnus John Stubblefield on saxes, Graham Haynes on trumpet, Brad Hatfield on keyboards, Bill Urmson on bass, and Keith Copeland on drums. Compared to the difficult experiences of the sixties, Russell was, in comparison, having some success in getting his music out there to the American public.

The following spring Russell was invited to play in Japan for the first time at the end of the 4th Tokyo Music Joy Festival, with a version of the Living Time Orchestra that featured a number of Japanese musicians. Kuniharu Akiyama, reviewing the concert in *Komei Shimbun*, commented, "Responding to the prism of emotions, we, the audience, feel the throbbing in our hearts, and enjoy a feeling of being musically satiated; this was the effect of Russell's performance that night." The concert was recorded and released as *New York—Live in Tokyo* in Japan on Electric Bird, with strong performances of "Cubano-Be, Cubano-Bop," *All About Rosie, Electronic Sonata*, and "Pan-Daddy" (from *The Stratus Seekers*), as well as extracts from *Listen to the Silence* and *New York, N.Y.* A video was also made of the performance and issued in Japan, although both remain very hard to obtain.[18]

In fact, Russell's visit provoked a lot of interest in Japan, not only in his music but in his Lydian Concept. Japanese composer Toru Takemitsu had already expressed his admiration for the work, and as a result of the TMJ concert Russell was invited back in 1993 to give a two-day seminar at the Epicurus Studio in Tokyo. William Penn Montgomery, writing in the *Japan Times*, noted, "Russell was pleased with the turnout and said that it was encouraging to see his work taken seriously in Japan. The price tag of ¥20000 for the clinic and ¥13000 for the Japanese version of the book was worth the chance to spend two days studying with the master."[19]

Back in Boston, Russell premiered another new piece on March 18, 1988, at the New England Conservatory's Jordan Hall as part of the Boston Globe Jazz Festival. Intriguingly, *Six Aesthetic Gravities* was commissioned by Boston Musica Viva, an ensemble devoted to twentieth-century composition, and was Russell's first commission by a "classical" music group. According to *Down Beat*, Russell's piece stole the show from Kurt Weill's one-act opera *War Play*, and "manifested Russell's typically vivid textures and dance-like momentum."[20] Then, at the end of June, another Russell work, *Centrifugue*, was given its first and only performance in Philadelphia as part of the Freedom Week celebrations. Performed by the contemporary music ensemble Relâche and commissioned by Bell Atlantic, Daniel Webster of the *Philadelphia Inquirer* raved about the piece and Relâche's "purpose and authority" in its execution.[21]

Such varied opportunities to compose and perform must have seemed very encouraging. Yet, though hardly overnight, a gradual shift had begun around 1988 that would see a change in Russell's area of operation. Russell again toured Europe in the spring of 1988 and was now becoming a regular feature on the European jazz scene. The relationship with John Cumming and his team became increasingly important, while gigs in his homeland became less frequent. Without the kinds of packages of support, funding, and organization offered by a company such as Serious, the economics of touring a big band was prohibitive. Nor at that time in the States was there a network of producers capable of piecing together a realistic tour schedule.

Apart from a three-date concert series in 1999 and a number of one-time appearances, Russell was to make his last major U.S. tour in 1988, though the full Anglo-American Living Time Orchestra would play four East Coast dates in 1999. Sponsored by the New England Foundation for the Arts, the Living Time Orchestra visited five New England states, playing ten colleges and universities, including Wesleyan, Lowell, and Dartmouth. Russell had also been commissioned by New England Presenters to write a new work, which he called *Uncommon Ground*.

Around this point, work prospects for big bands became increasingly bleak in the United States. American jazz artists, including those writing for and leading large ensembles, looked more and more to Europe for gigs, and a process began where Europe's festivals became dominated by American performers. It was not that Russell stopped being honored and acknowledged in America. Ironically, just before embarking on one European tour, Russell was contacted by Kenneth Hope of the John D. and Catherine T. MacArthur Foundation and told that he had been awarded a fellowship. The sum involved was $375,000, paid over five years, and followed a similar award to Russell's friend and New England Conservatory colleague Ran Blake. The press statement from the foundation noted that *The Lydian Chromatic Concept of Tonal Organization* was "one of the first major theoretical contributions by a jazz musician. It stands as a pioneer work in the investigation of contemporary modal harmony."[22]

Russell's 1989 Living Time Orchestra included Brad Hatfield, Bill Urmson, Chris Biscoe, Stuart Brooks, Pete Hurt, Pete Burchill, and Ashley Slater, who had toured with him in 1986. Russell had been very sorry to lose Courtney Pine, but accepted that Pine had to avail himself of the chances that were coming his way. His replacement, who had joined the Living Time Orchestra in 1987, could not have been better. Andy Sheppard had begun his playing career with a group called Sphere featuring Geoff Williams on piano, Pete Maxfield on bass, and Tony Orrell on drums, with Trevor Taylor occasionally depping for Orrell. Signed by Island Records alongside Pine in the mid-eighties, Sheppard is the only British musician to have played with the "Big Three" American big-band leaders—Gil Evans, Carla Bley, and George Russell. He had played with Russell's band in Japan in 1988 and had also been introduced to Bley by Steve Swallow, who had recommended him along the lines: "You're going to love this tenor player. He doesn't sound like anyone else."[23] Sheppard recalls his first rehearsal with Russell very clearly indeed. He had already listened to *The African Game*, but when he got to the first rehearsal,

> All the stuff I thought was improvised was all written. It was just a nightmare. I was really struggling. So I knew George was into scales, and the music had a scale written on it from the previous sax player. It's my tenor solo, so I'm sticking on this scale, thinking that's what he wants, just to improvise using these notes. Anyway, he came over, and he's a bugger, is George, and he says, "It's no good just playing a blues scale, man!" but really heavy! So I thought, there's two ways here. Either leave and don't come back or say, "Fuck you!" and I just went mad when I played and got the gig![24]

Also joining the Living Time Orchestra in 1988 was pianist Steve Lodder. Lodder replaced Django Bates, who was unable to make that year's tour and who, with hindsight, was perhaps not the best choice in the first place. Bates's approach is not only distinctive but idiosyncratic, or even eccentric, characteristics that are not easily accommodated in Russell's music world. Lodder was, however, an excellent replacement. As it was for Sheppard and others before them, the first rehearsal in a basement in Clerkenwell was a mindblower. Not only was the noise deafening, but the bigger problem was the adjustment required by Russell's music.

> There was no looking at it beforehand and of having to get into this man's way of thinking. Just sitting there, reading and reading. You can't really do that. I remember going home after the first day, thinking that this was the tiredest I'd ever felt, simply because there was so much information being chucked at me because the music is so dense, so you're trying to find your way around aurally and trying to find your way around on the page, which is hard. Not an easy day.[25]

Making aural sense of things is itself a problem initially, as Lodder explains. This is partly because of the way Russell organizes the music: in cycles that compete and interlock in different ways at different times. However, it is also because of the way the internal arrangement of musicians into pairs, trios, and quartets within the whole varies within and between numbers.

> [It's] partly organizationally, because of all the cycles and the way it's orga-nized, jumping from one thing to another, but with other people, so it's not the same people all the time. So you'll be taking a cue from somebody from across the other side of the band. Playing something with them against maybe four other things happening. Again, they're going to be independent. You have to find who you're with, where you are on the page, and who your allies are, because some people might help you. Rehearsals can be tricky as well, because he knows exactly what he wants; if he's not hearing it, you can spend a long, long, long time trying to get [him] to hear it. So it can be a drum pattern or particular synth sound or anything that—if it's not as he's heard it in his head or heard it before in performance—the rehearsal will just stop, and it could be twenty minutes, and that's a very uncomfortable twenty minutes if you're the person on the receiving end not coming up with the goods for some reason or because you don't understand or it's not possible or whatever.[26]

Nor is it easy for a keyboard player in the band working with three other chordal instruments—perhaps a synth, guitar, and vibes—especially when you are not merely doubling a part, as Lodder notes. "The keyboard's very much there for colors and power and harmonic complexity, because he likes that. There'll be two internal areas sometimes going on in the keyboards, and another one in the vibes. Then the guitar will take a line over the top."[27]

If it sounds like a recipe for chaos, it rarely is, and Lodder points out that this is due to Russell's grasp of harmony. "I think because he's got a really good understanding of the way things stack up harmonically, with things on top of other things. So that what for somebody is a full conventional jazz chord, that's kind of the starting point for George, and then other things just get put on top."[28]

Others joining the band in 1989 included trumpeter, author, and broad-caster Ian Carr, who would later make two BBC Radio 3 documentaries on Russell—*The Trailblazer* and *The Invisible Guru*. Steve Johns had by now replaced Keith Copeland on drums, and the other important arrival was gui-tarist David Fiuczynski. Russell has always had a strong affinity for guitarists from Barry Galbraith onward, and was immediately taken with Fiuczynski's guitar playing.

The band played dates in the UK that included the Brecon and Edinburgh festivals, The Maltings in Aldeburgh (the venue associated with Benjamin Britten), and four nights at Ronnie Scott's Club, where the band recorded a two CD album for the French Label Bleu. They also played dates in Belgium, Germany, Luxembourg, and Portugal. Press coverage was excellent, with features in the *Guardian*, *Times*, *Sunday Times*, *International Herald Tribune*, and *Time Out*.[29]

The London Concert was recorded August 28–31 at Ronnie Scott's Club. Recording at the club is not easy, as the control booth itself is—or at least was—located in another building a few doors along Frith Street. Though the album is essentially a live recording, the difficulty of some of the material coupled with the usual problems involved in obtaining a good sound balance of a large ensemble in a small club meant that some parts were recorded or overdubbed during the day. Keyboardist Brad Hatfield remembers it as an amusing but challenging experience. Those pieces that had been played extensively on the road were working really well, but some others needed additional rehearsal.

> So it took its toll, on the horn players especially. Also, being in that club and the band being at the dynamic level we were, we had horns at the back, so the rhythm section's in front, which we do because that keeps the rhythm section from getting too much into the horn mikes, but it doesn't keep the horns from blasting in to the overheads of the drum mikes. So it was an engineering nightmare, further confounded by the fact that the control booth was down the street. So you actually had to leave the club, walk down a couple of buildings, go up a couple of staircases, through somebody's office, and finally you arrive at the control room. So going and checking out playbacks and communicating with the engineer in a normal fashion was ridiculous. So we had a lot of telephone conversations. *(laughs)*[30]

Russell had recognized the talent of guitarist David Fiuczynski when he was a student at the New England Conservatory.

> I just started hearing stories about him, what an awkward character he was in terms of his music and personally. Actually my first experience was, I couldn't take his ensemble class because I had tendonitis. I couldn't even play that much my first year at the conservatory. I was rehearsing with a trio, and he came down to the room where we were rehearsing, and he had a locker there and was putting some music away. He heard us playing and he started listening. We were all really intimidated but kept on playing until he was like, "Wow! Where have you been hiding?" *(imitates Russell)* He invited us to play a piece at his annual concert at the school, and I think that's probably one of the few times he's ever had someone do a piece that wasn't his music. A great introduction. We were scared when he left. We were scared when we played. It was great. From then on I started taking his classes. He was really supportive.

Fiuczynski's comments about Russell as a teacher and bandleader provide a real insight into the composer's priorities. Acknowledging that he still uses Russell's perspective on, and distinction between, the vertical and horizontal approaches to improvisation and composition in his own work, Fiuczynski sees Russell's personality and charisma as being highly significant in terms of his ability to communicate his ideas and expectations.

> Besides the fact, he was just a very inspiring person and there was just so much there as soon as he walked into the room, and just by being there and being with him and interacting. Even though he's a no-bullshit kind of guy, he didn't have any patience if you didn't do your homework, but he didn't have any patience if you did all your homework and weren't saying anything. He didn't have any time for that either. He didn't care about correct notes. He wanted flavor, groove, soul, happiness, pain, lyricism. That was very important to him.

Now a teacher at Berklee, Fiuczynski understands Russell's impatience in this respect only too well. While still at NEC, Fiuczynski began playing in the Living Time Orchestra. The Ronnie Scott's Club gigs and recording were the highlight of his involvement with Russell.

> It was intense. It was, like, my first really big thing. We'd played the music inside and out, but even if you know the music, it's work—great work, if you can get it—but it's a lot of concentration and focus. There was also a lot of pressure to get it done. We'd record during the day, do a couple of shows at night, and record again during the day. It must've been really hard on the lead trumpet players.

Beginning, as usual, with three days of intense rehearsal, the demands were certainly severe, but as Fiuczynski reveals, there are clear reasons why Russell's musicians are prepared to put up with his demands.

> As much as he wanted from you, you received twice back, if not more. Just in terms of the support or the criticism you would get. It was always there for you to grow. And when he gave you a spot to do your thing, he always wanted you to shine. He encouraged you to speak in your own voice. It was always very exciting for him to hear something creative, new, and different. The last thing he wanted to hear was something that had already been done. He could be very hard if something was played incorrectly, but I'll never forget that when we were playing things correctly and he was frustrated, he was like, "You've got the notes together. Screw the notes. I can care less about the notes. You have to say something."[31]

Brad Hatfield was very much involved in remixing the record back in Boston, and the sound on *The London Concert* is quite exceptional given the problems its making involved. Ian Carr had been asked to do the tour in the absence of Japanese trumpeter Tiger Okoshi. He was not playing that much at the time, concentrating instead on his writing and broadcasting. One of Britain's finest musicians, Carr began the tour struggling with his embouchure.

The tour had taken the Living Time Orchestra to Italy, where Carr was quite well known due to his work with Nucleus and with the pan-European United Jazz and Rock Ensemble. Before one of the Italian dates, he was recognized by some Italian fans on the street. "I was with the trumpets and we were just getting ready and three Italians came 'round the corner, and one said, in a very loud voice, 'That's the legendary Ian Carr.' And the other trumpeters looked at me in complete disbelief." Disbelief turned to dismay later, however.

> I'd been writing a lot right up to the time we were there, and my chops were no good, and on the first day, I could see these young guys saying, "God, this is the 'great' Ian Carr. What the hell's going [on]?" So in the interval, I went up to George and said, "George, would you really rather like me to drop out and get somebody else?" He said, "No, no. I want you." So I stayed, and of course by the third rehearsal my chops were really strong, and so it was okay. But I really liked him for that. I would have gone, you know, because he could have got several other trumpet players.[32]

Carr was in fine form by the time they got to Ronnie's and plays beautifully on *The London Concert*'s versions of "So What" and "Electronic Sonata," which also features the 'rap' Russell had added on a previous tour. Amusingly, Carr had been banned from Ronnie's following a disagreement with its other owner, Pete King, eighteen years before. Fortunately, bygones were allowed to be bygones and Carr's ban was lifted.

As Andy Sheppard remembers, the band was really hot by the time they played Ronnie's. "It was a good band actually; the balance of personalities, I thought, were really strong—Chris Biscoe, they [the rest of the band] really kind of rose to the occasion. I think that's what George liked about the British band was that they all wanted to get it right and play the music and give it that 100 percent."[33]

The London Concert features fine performances of "So What" and *Electronic Sonata*, but it is also very much a new record. It contains the only recordings of Russell's two 1988 commissions, *Six Aesthetic Gravities* and *Uncommon Ground*. The band also performs "Struggle of the Magicians," by sometime Living Time Orchestra member Mark White, and "La Folia: The Rocella Variations," a joint composition with Ben Schwendener, Russell's assistant/deputy. *Uncommon Ground* is a highly dramatic piece, with dense electronic synth passages and with powerful bass lines from Bill Urmson. Soloists emerge from the sound and punctuate the music briefly rather than dominate it with extended choruses. "La Folia," on the other hand, is one of the more atypical pieces in Russell's repertoire, suggesting that Schwendener's influence on the piece was quite significant. Its opening has an almost madrigal feel to it, but it opens out beautifully, with strong playing from Andy Sheppard and David Fiuczynski, into what might be described as "funky baroque." But perhaps the most important piece on the double CD is "*Six Aesthetic Gravities*," which betrays its origins as a piece for a non-jazz ensemble, its sections fitting together subtly but perfectly building its structure, section by section. Though it has its moments of drama and release, the impression it leaves is one of quiet intensity. An excellent record, *The London Concert* makes a good place for the Russell novitiate to begin.

On both sides of the Atlantic, 1990 proved to be a good year for Russell. Back home in Boston in January, Russell was one of the three recipients of a Jazz Master Fellowship awarded by the National Endowment for the Arts. The other recipients were Cecil Taylor and trumpeter/composer Gerald Wilson. The award of $20,000 was again given without strings.[34] Then, in July in Britain, the Living Time Orchestra was in Glasgow for its International Jazz Festival. In fact, Russell was composer-in-residence for the week, which he and the band spent working with school and college students, as well as performing a concert at the Theatre Royal on Friday, July 6. There were a few changes in the band from 1989. Tiger Okoshi was back, Teese Gohl took over briefly from Steve Lodder, Pat Hollenbeck made his first European trip with Russell, and David Mann (who had been in Japan with Russell) and John Purcell were in for Chris Biscoe and Pete Hurt. Russell was also commissioned to write a new work for the festival. In fact, he produced something quite exceptional. In *American Trilogy*, he took two earlier pieces, "You Are My Sunshine" and "The Ballad of Hix Blewitt," and added to them "The Battle Hymn of the Republic" to create a three-movement work. The piece has been a concert favorite since then.[35]

The Glasgow concert was broadcast on November 5, 1990, on BBC Radio 3. Derek Drescher, then a producer at the BBC and a tireless supporter of jazz throughout his period at the station, was the architect behind the program and also behind Ian Carr's two documentaries on Russell. It is perhaps hard for music fans in countries without a well-established and well-funded public service broadcasting network to appreciate how essential this is for minority interest music to get exposure and access to audiences. Radio 3 is a jewel in the UK's media. Its support for classical music, new music, world music, and jazz is *sans pareil*, and has been so for decades. There is simply nothing to touch it anywhere in the world.

Introduced by veteran broadcaster Charles Fox, the program also featured a long interview with Andy Sheppard about his experiences working with Russell. The band plays *Listen to the Silence*, *American Trilogy*, and *Uncommon Ground*, closing, as always, with "So What."

Russell returned with the Living Time Orchestra in 1991 to play the Town & Country Club in London as part of the Camden Jazz Festival. There had been good pre-gig publicity. Martin Gayford had written a good piece in the *Telegraph* prior to the festival, and even Tower Records was plugging the concert.[36]

Reviewing the gig in the *Financial Times*, Garry Booth was full of praise for both Russell and Jimmy Giuffre, who had played the Jazz Café with Paul Bley and Steve Swallow as part of the festival. His review carried mixed encouragement for the Jazz Warriors, noting that they only really came alive when American trombonist Craig Harris joined them, and he all but ignored Cassandra Wilson's support slot for the Living Time Orchestra gig. Booth wrote, "The sight and sound of the Living Time Orchestra is far removed from the image of Russell as jazz theorist and provides the best possible opening to the 'outdoor' season ahead and close to a Camden fest of mixed blessings."[37]

By way of complete contrast, Roland Ramanan's review in the *Wire* put the opposite case. The Warriors' performance, he wrote, "clearly demonstrated the potential that can be unleashed from the Jazz Warriors if they only had a strong conductor and a writer with imagination and courage." Cassandra Wilson, however, "bewitched and beguiled with her marvellous voice." The Living Time Orchestra, on the other hand, got short shrift. Ramanan refers to Russell's "over-stuffed rhythm section," which "came equipped with concrete over-shoes," and described "Uncommon Ground" as "fairly typical: simple motifs being added to, layer by layer, until I was being pushed back by the wave of sound." He concludes, "I was grooved but not moved."[38]

The May 1991 European release of *The London Concert* from the band's 1989 Scott Club residency brought, however, a glowing review from the *Guardian*'s John Fordham:

> The recording catches Russell's characteristic mix of mid-tempo rockers, baroque classicisms that turn into funk, misty abstract passages illuminated by sudden flares, wry outbursts of jazz tempo. The sheer quantity of musical

events behind the solos (slabs of ensemble horn sounds colliding, slewing guitar effects, percussion cross-rhythms) makes Russell's band an ensemble of compelling intensity and depth whilst sustaining a rock group's rhythmic earthiness.[39]

There was a further spring date in Paris that year, plus a couple of gigs in France and Belgium that autumn. By contrast, 1992 seems to have been a comparatively quiet year for Russell, with just one gig for the Living Time Orchestra in Virginia. There was also quite a delay between the European release and the American release on Stash Records, and it was not until March 1993 that Gary Giddens reviewed the album in the *Voice*. Giddins's only complaint was that Stash issued *The London Concert* as two separate discs. Otherwise, it was a "stunning entertainment, brash and vigorous and swinging, sometimes eerily beautiful, frequently ebullient."[40] A couple of months after the U.S. release, Russell was elected to the Hall of Fame in *Down Beat*'s 2nd Annual Achievement Awards for Jazz Education. Bearing in mind that Russell was now seventy and had been teaching at the New England Conservatory for a quarter century, it was an honor richly deserved. MacArthur Fellowships, Guggenheim Awards, NEA Awards—no one could suggest that Russell was without honor at home. Periods of public neglect aside, however, the most sorry occurrence in Russell's long and distinguished career took place between the spring of 1992 and August 1993.

It all began with a casual lunch between Marty Khan, Russell's American manager, and Rob Gibson, director of the Lincoln Center's jazz program. There are differing accounts of what did and did not happen and of what was and was not said. Because of these differences, it has never really been put to bed. It went on to become the focus of disagreement within New York's jazz community and indirectly produced one of its strangest tales.

Khan remembers that Gibson at one point mentioned that "he was tired of trying to tell his children that all of the great jazz musicians were dead and that there were no living great jazz musicians." Khan asked him, "What about George Russell? That's certainly one of the giants of modern music, not just jazz. What about him? He'll be turning seventy years old shortly and I think he'll be an ideal person." According to Khan, Gibson agreed and suggested that they put the prospect of a Russell concert at the Lincoln Center in motion. A meeting followed between Alice Russell, Helene Cann, and Gibson, which seemed to indicate a strong intent on the part of the Lincoln Center team to go ahead with the project. A fax from Alice Russell to John Cumming dated March 26, 1992, notes that the meeting took place the previous week. Her fax confirms her strong impression that Gibson was committed to the idea. She even notes two sets of dates offered—"August 4 through August 14 for a week of rehearsal and a concert," and later another date in the following March. Alice then expresses concern that the latter would be better due to plans to tour Europe in August 1993. Again according to Khan, from June 1992 onward he and Cann tried to contact Gibson by phone to follow up the suggested concert, but were not able to speak with the director. By the tone of Khan's fax to Gibson dated December 23, 1992, Khan was not only justifiably frustrated but had also been quite rudely treated by some junior Lincoln Center staff.[41]

Gibson's letter dated January 4, 1993, is conciliatory and apologetic. While one could not conclude from it that anyone was getting cold feet about the project, one sentence seems, with hindsight, prophetic, if not indicative in that respect. Noting that the Center had not completed its planning for the forthcoming season of concerts by the time intended, Gibson writes, "While we understand that we may have missed out on an opportunity to produce some programs because of our delays, this is something we must accept."[42] The rest of his comments certainly indicate an intention to continue to try to promote Russell at the Center. Further attempts to achieve any progress with this on the part of Outward Visions foundered. The concert never went ahead and the Russells remain entirely unclear about why this proved the case.

In such circumstances, rumor and supposition often fill in the gaps. According to Marty Khan, he was contacted in the summer of 1993 by a New York journalist who had been at a meeting with a number of other journalists and Lincoln Center staff at Gibson's home. It transpired that this had taken place on July 13, 1993, and the purpose was to try to improve relations between the Lincoln Center and the New York and jazz press. A report of the meeting appeared in the *Village Voice* more than a year later in the context of a longer article by Richard B. Woodward about "the missteps that have dogged jazz at Lincoln Center."[43] Titled "Jazz Wars: A Tale of Age, Rage and Hash Brownies," the article included the allegation that the journalists were fed brownies for dessert laced with hashish. This was, of course, vehemently denied by Rob Gibson.

> We invited eight to ten guys over just to talk. I actually thought it was a nice dinner and I thought we had a good time. But at the end of the night the publicist at Jazz at Lincoln Center (Marilyn Laverty), who had made dessert, served brownies. Somebody said, "What'd you put in the brownies?" She said, "Wouldn't you like to know!" Two weeks later a cover story appeared in the *Village Voice* called "A Rage Supreme" where they claimed we had put hash in the brownies—hashish in the brownies—which was of course a total and utter lie . . . this is the kind of stuff that goes on.[44]

Russell's connection with the discussions was a small one, but has, in the context of the debacle, assumed more prominence. Khan states that the journalist who contacted him told him that "one of the things that was brought up was the issue of what had happened to the George Russell event that was supposed to occur." Khan continued, "At that time, Stanley Crouch told them that the reason why George was not . . . why the date was not going to happen is that after numerous phone conversations between Stanley and George, George adamantly refused to use an acoustic rhythm section for the performance of his earlier works like *All About Rosie* and the classic works that he had done in the early fifties."[45]

In a way, this all sounds like a case of "he said, she said," but the fact that the Russells have been left unclear why the planned or proposed concert did not go forward results from the fact that they have never received a clear response from the Lincoln Center. Certainly, as far as they are concerned, no such conversations between Russell and Crouch ever took place. The reason the Russells, Khan, band members, friends, colleagues, and associates believe the concert discussed did not go ahead was Russell's use of electric instrumentation. The outcome is that Russell was unable in later life—and indeed during what has been his most active and successful period as a performer—to perform his music at the Lincoln Center, which has become one of the most prestigious in America in presenting jazz to the public.

In September 1998 the *New York Times* ran its own story on Jazz at Lincoln Center. The author covers much of the areas of dispute, and quoted Russell at one point: "They've done a lot to take the essence of jazz and distort it; they've put a damper on the main ingredient of jazz, which is innovation. I think that whatever happens at Lincoln Center, history will have to correct it because it does need correcting terribly."[46] In fairness to all concerned, this a measured and dignified comment, especially in light of Russell's own experiences.

A while later, after Gibson left Lincoln Center, Alice Russell received a further approach regarding a possible concert at the venue around Russell's eightieth birthday in 2003. Money was apparently discussed, but according to Khan and Alice Russell, the sums involved would have seen the Russells partly funding the concert. Russell himself decided that, in any event, he was unwilling to have anything to do with Jazz at Lincoln Center, and the proposal went no further.[47]

As a codicil to the Lincoln Center saga, Russell did get to play New York with his Anglo-American Living Time Orchestra in 1999. The band played in Boston, Washington, and New York. The Washington gig at the Smithsonian was high profile with a good fee, and this allowed a certain amount of flexibility for the New York date. Sadly, the venue was less prestigious than Russell deserved. It was also very poorly publicized by the firm the Russells were using, which resulted in Khan and Cann taking over late in the day to try and improve the situation. Ben Ratliff of the *New York Times* provided a generally favorable review, though he was not overawed by the sound of the synths, which he deemed "jazzanachronisms."[48] That said, the concert on May 8 at the Tribeca Arts Center garnered a fine review from John Szwed in the *Village Voice*.

As Szwed wrote in a highly perceptive conclusion about a program that featured *American Trilogy, It's About Time, All About Rosie,* and the Gil Evans arrangement of "Stratusphunk,"

> It's also obvious now that those reassuring rock rhythms make Russell's compositions seem more innocent than they really are: underneath lie shifting moods and tone centers, overlapping contrapuntal figures and riffs which skip across the beat and erode tonality. Even deeper yet, there are his serpentine, rumbling 5/2 bass lines: perhaps subsonic representations of a musical world to which jazz—whatever that is—is still afraid to commit.[49]

Writing on his Web site three years later, Marty Khan commented:

> In 1999, we had the wonderful opportunity to hear George's *real* Living Time Orchestra (the one that Europeans have had the benefits of hearing for years) in its first (!?!) American appearance. We traveled from Tucson just to be at these concerts in New York City and at the Smithsonian in Washington, D.C.[50]

Russell's problems in sustaining a consistent audience for his music in America seem to have little to do with either proper acknowledgment of his talents or of his contribution to jazz, the Lincoln Center debacle aside. Although his ability to tour regularly with musicians of his choice at appropriate recompense certainly resulted in a switch of focus of operations to Europe, Russell played quite a number of concerts in the United States following his return from Scandinavia. While these were less frequent than they might have been, Russell is not the only jazz artist of stature who has found work in Europe easier to come by from the eighties to the present. The problem for Russell seems in part the costs of touring a big band coupled with lack of funding support, and what might be seen as the innate conservatism of American audiences. If the latter remark seems a little unfair, American readers might ask themselves why many of their more adventurous jazz musicians have found Europe more welcoming of their talents from the fifties to the present.[51]

In 1993 Russell toured Europe once again, playing in France, Italy, and at London's Jazz Café. The Paris date at the Banlieues Bleues Festival included a performance with students from the Conservatoire National Supérieur de Musique et de Danse de Paris in what would prove an interesting and new development for Russell. The concert at the Jazz Café, though well received, was perhaps less successful in terms of the size of its audience.

Though John Cumming remembers that the problem really had more to do with the size of the venue and the expanded stage that was required for the band, Andy Sheppard recalls being disappointed on Russell's behalf. He had experienced similarly small audiences elsewhere in Europe when on tour with Russell, and he compared this with touring with Gil Evans.

> Gil certainly had this kind of charisma in himself and was . . . he was kind of successful when I was touring with him. In Italy especially, places would be packed and I toured with George and there would be very few people. I remember doing a gig in the Jazz Café, which was a fantastic gig, and there was, like, a handful of people, and I just couldn't understand that. Here was this major figure in twentieth-century music, and most people just couldn't get up to speed with it. People who were there really loved it because, of course, it is a challenging and full-on experience or it was with that band.[52]

However, Russell himself seems to have taken all this in his stride, as if he does not expect anything else. He invariably refers to the Concept and points out that this is, for him, the most important thing in his life and his major contribution to jazz and music in general. Yet at the same time, his response to an audience is invariably warm and open, especially when people react positively to him and his music.

In 1994 Russell played the Umbria Jazz Festival for the first time and also the North Sea Jazz Festival in the Hague, as well as gigs in Newcastle and Pori in Finland. Guy Barker, one of Britain's brightest and charismatic young musicians, and veteran Henry Lowther, who had played at Woodstock with the Keef Hartley Band, had come in on trumpets to replace Ian Carr and Tiger Okoshi. Guitarist Dave Fiuczynski had also left, and though Adam Rogers had filled in during 1993, there was a need to find a long-term and serious replacement. Thanks once again to John Cumming, Mike Walker, the musician chosen to fill Fiuczynski's shoes, proved perfect for the band. As Cumming puts it, "George loves Mike Walker and with good reason. He's dead right for George because George likes to hear a screaming Rock guitar in there."[53]

The following year, Swedish saxophonist Lennart Åberg and John Cumming of Serious jointly commissioned Russell to write a new piece, *It's About*

Time, with funds from the Swedish Rikskoncerter and the Arts Council of England. Prior to its performance in Stockholm in November, Russell and the Living Time Orchestra were able to present the work, complete with a small symphony orchestra drawn from various French music schools at La Cité de la Musique as part of the Paris Banlieues Bleues Festival. This project had been painstakingly put together with the help of Serious and had been orchestrated by Living Time Orchestra member Pat Hollenbeck. In fact, later that year Russell was able to record the new work for the French company Label Bleu, along with a new version of the work he had written for Bill Evans, *Living Time*.

Russell again toured the United Kingdom in November 1995, once more with Arts Council support, playing a date at London's Queen Elizabeth Hall as part of the London Jazz Festival and another in Huddersfield for its Contemporary Music Festival. As John Cumming recalls, Russell was invited to give a lecture at Huddersfield as part of the festival program, something he had done at other festivals during the later phase of his career. "I mean, I once heard him do a lecture on the Lydian Concept in Huddersfield where you could hear the sound of jaws dropping on the floor as he managed to combine the African Diaspora and the Ottoman Empire in one sentence as part of the touching points of the Lydian Concept."[54] Russell liked to shock, though never as an end in itself.

A few dates in France, including one at La Maison de la Culture in Amiens, were sandwiched in the middle, and the band was able to record both *It's About Time* and *Living Time* for Label Bleu in a local studio. The band was a powerful mix of the tried and trusted. The tour went exceptionally well, with good pretour publicity encouraged in Serious's usual efficient fashion. Ronald Atkins wrote in the *Saturday Guardian Guide*, "It took us long enough to get George Russell over here. Now, his Living Time Orchestra has become a welcome fixture." It is a fair description of the reception that greeted Russell when he and his band came to Europe. Phil Johnson's comments in his review of the Bath leg of the tour in the *Independent* were typical, beautifully capturing the power and internal dynamism that the band had developed: "George Russell gave his musicians their heads, pointing at soloists, as if lighting the blue touch paper and then standing well back."[55]

It's About Time was released on Label Bleu in Europe in March 1997. John Fordham made the record his jazz CD of the week in the *Guardian*, while the Scottish newspaper the *Herald* noted that *It's About Time* was "Russell at his most mobile and punchy." The album was not, however, issued until May 1999 in the States. This did at least coincide with the three-date Living Time Orchestra tour of the East Coast that year, and John Szwed drew the public's attention to it in his *Village Voice* review of the Tribeca gig.[56]

This is a record that grows in stature over time. *It's About Time* is a fine latter-day Russell work. Its interlocking parts slide together like a well-oiled machine. At times, some of the synth sounds do sound a bit like they were left over from the previous decade, but it is the way that Russell builds sounds, textures, and rhythms upon each other, and yet is still able to afford his soloists remarkable degrees of freedom, that surprises. In fact, Stanton Davis, Mike Walker, and Andy Sheppard are all given incredible latitude within a piece that is so clearly and carefully structured. There is also some fine playing from Dave Bargeron and Brad Hatfield, but it is the magnificent edifice Russell creates—or has his orchestra create—that really impresses. The power and energy that is released in the second section of the piece is quite staggering. What is more, the version of *Living Time* is everything the Bill Evans version was not allowed to be. Young French pianist Paul-Christian Staicu takes many of the solos Evans covered on the Columbia release. Staicu is not Evans, obviously; however, there is a quality to his performance and something about his pianistic touch on the keys that is hugely effective and affecting. His lines are crystalline and beautifully defined. Bargeron, his second time around on this one, gets a lot of room on Event V and has that tailgate sound that truly grabs the gut, and Stanton Davis constantly surpasses expectation. Mike Walker, Andy Sheppard, and Brad Hatfield provide some of the work's finest moments of tension and release. The sound on the record is excellent, with the strings and other horns clearly audible in the mix. Again, Russell's vertical form structure is the defining feature: It seems constantly on the verge of either exploding or imploding, and yet it really swings and rocks and sounds as if the musicians are genuinely having a great time. All things considered, Russell has succeeded in continuing the modern big-band work that had begun with *Now and Then* in 1966 and has developed and honed his writing into an intricately balanced world of melody and countermelody, rhythm and counter-rhythm, all emerging from some of the widest and richest harmonic textures in jazz.

By now Russell was seventy-four years old, but he was far from resting on his laurels. He enjoyed the companionship of musicians, as he always had, and had, if anything, become more enthusiastic about being on the road with his music, at least for part of the year. Teaching commitments at the New England Conservatory continued, and, as ever, he was working on a new edition of *The Lydian Chromatic Concept of Tonal Organization*, which would be published in 2001, though a second volume Russell had planned has yet to appear. In early spring 1998, Russell and Serious embarked on their most ambitious project to date. In fact, outside the confines of the New England Conservatory, it is hard to imagine the idea coming to anything at all Stateside.

At one point, John Cumming was pushing for a performance of *Time Line*, Russell's three-hour celebration that premiered at the New England Conservatory in 1992. In reality, this proved impractical even on an abridged basis, much to Alice Russell's relief.[57] The project that replaced it was, however, almost as ambitious and almost as difficult to realize.

As well as other European dates, the plan was for Russell and the Living Time Orchestra to perform concerts in both Paris and London, using musicians, jazz and classical, from the Paris Conservatoire and the London Guildhall School of Music and Drama. The program was to feature three sets. The first would present *Stratusphunk*, *All About Rosie*, and *Dialogue with Ornette*, the latter performed in an extended version by the student classical players conducted by Pat Hollenbeck. The second set featured the whole of *Vertical Form VI*, using professional and student jazz players as well as various classical students. Finally, the Living Time Orchestra performed *American Trilogy* and an extract from *It's About Time*, closing, as always, with "So What." The British program notes list Pat Hollenbeck and Hiroaki Honshuku as assistant musical directors, which fairly describes the roles that both, and Hollenbeck in particular, were now taking on. Hollenbeck works on orchestration in the film industry, with actor/director Clint Eastwood and others, as well as being percussionist for the Boston Pops. His assistance to Russell since joining the band has been immeasurable, according to Steve Lodder.

> Pat [has] been an incredible addition in terms of the orchestration side and also in terms of the rehearsal side. He takes a lot of work off George. Pat's used to rehearsing Hollywood Bowl orchestras, so he's immediately comfortable with a large party of musicians and complexity as well. It doesn't faze him at all. He's got incredible ears. In fact, he'll often pick up something that George might not in terms of wrong notes or whatever.[58]

Hollenbeck had been very active in working on the *It's About Time* recording, and he was carrying much of the load for this project as well. The French rehearsals and performance went quite smoothly, despite the fact that some seventy people, many of them musicians, were involved. Generally, organizing musicians is never easy. However, it was not until the circus arrived in London and began rehearsals at the Guildhall that problems really began. Essentially, it seems that a combination of obstruction on the part of some teaching staff at the Guildhall and what can only be described as an absence of any efficient administration system dedicated to the project was to blame. Even the list of the names of students from the Guildhall traveling to France did not arrive till very late in the proceedings, while the French had their end tied up well in advance. There had been plans to use singers from the Guildhall but, in John Cumming's words, "we had to drop the choir at one stage because they didn't get it together—nobody could quite work out why." As Cumming continues,

> We were finding that students weren't turning up when we thought they were. They were being fitted around rehearsals of other things. There was a big problem internally at Guildhall attached to this between the Jazz Department and the Classical Department, as it were. One senior member of staff at the Guildhall who had basically helped to set the project up and who was the enthusiast left it because George had a go at him.[59]

It was clearly far from a happy or satisfactory situation, as was evident when I was interviewing Russell for a magazine article during a break in rehearsals. Russell was, frankly, furious. Cumming acknowledges this:

> Within all that there was a lot of tension. We were having to move rehearsal rooms into unsuitable spaces, and students were actually coming up to people throughout that project saying, "We wish we'd known more about this because actually we're doing an opera in the evening. We're not actually able to devote the time we should be to this, but this is much more interesting music." Some of this is quite boring, but it doesn't help; it meant that George felt that he'd been undervalued actually.[60]

Of course, this cannot and should not be compared with the events five years earlier (and again circa 2001–2002) involving Jazz at Lincoln Center. This was simply a case of chronic inefficiency rather than bad manners. Fortunately, for once, the series of communication and other failures that dogged the London end did not affect the final performance at the Barbican in London. It was a triumph, and both the Living Time Orchestra and the students from both sides of the channel rose boldly to the challenge. Cumming's view of events prior to the performance has not changed, but he is clear that what happened that night at the Barbican made it worthwhile.

> I think, to be honest, there are two things or three about that project. The first thing is that despite all the problems, we came out with a triumph, I have to say. I think we've all listened to the music, one way or another, of it, and people who were there, the critics who were there—it actually was remarkable. I think that sometimes out of complicated practical issues the art comes shining through at the end of the day.[61]

John Fordham, who had written a long piece in the *Guardian* prior to the concert,[62] wrote, without exaggeration:

> In a storm of sound that lasted almost three hours, the mix of American, British and French musicians resembled a vast Rock n' Roll band, a Moroccan Folk ensemble, a symphonic band playing a hoe-down, a Free-Jazz group, a jostling crowd of Dixieland street-stompers, a scholarly Schoenbergian tone-row outfit whose drinks had been spiked and plenty more besides.[63]

It really was that good and, though sadly it remains unreleased, the symphony orchestra's performance of *Dialogue* is simply wonderful.

As late as 2002–2003, Russell's passion remained undiminished, though his energy could not always keep pace with his enthusiasm. In 2002 he took up an offer from Umbria Jazz to carry its *'Round Midnight* slot at the Teatro Morlacchi for the week. Unfortunately, some key players were unavailable. Andy Sheppard was touring with the Carla Bley Very Big Band, and Chris Biscoe was unable to make the tour. George Garzone and Steve Slagle took their places. Despite the fact that he was now less than a year from his eightieth birthday, Russell was keen to use the residency to cover his entire catalog, as Steve Lodder recalls.

> George was charged for it, no doubt about it, and the list of music that he wanted to play over that week went back across his career, including things this band has never looked at. He came up with all this music and he wanted to play it all. He wanted to play a different set every night. There were actually things that mitigated that, because there were different saxophone players, as Andy and Chris couldn't make it. They were having trouble enough with the regular material, let alone stuff the band hadn't looked at before. George's energy, even though he is amazing, completely amazing, it's fallible. So in the end the list got whittled down, but, yeah, he came with very high expectations of what we would do that week, which in the end we didn't get anywhere near. But we did a slightly different gig most nights.[64]

One of the finest gigs was the band's early evening show on Monday, July 15, again at the Teatro Morlacchi. The atmosphere in the rococo, eighteenth-century theatre was electric. It was thundery, humid weather, and the hall has no air-conditioning, but something happened that night: a release of music that brought band and audience together. Looking around the theatre, even in the boxes, people were leaning forward, willing the band on, and, finding it hard to be still with excitement, desperate for release. The Living

Time Orchestra delivered on every count. Lodder remembers that this night felt special.

> **SL:** I think the real feeling that night . . . and I remember that particular night . . . of wanting to play for George because he was struggling . . .
> **DH:** In what sense?
> **SL:** In the sense of he was struggling with the idea that we wouldn't be able to get through all the material he wanted to get through. He was looking . . . the phrase "retrospective" comes to mind. I think he was looking on it as a sort of retrospective, but obviously very present, but wanting to trawl back to hear things that he hadn't heard for a long time. Then, when that wasn't happening, the frustration about it, and then that built a bit before we got that release.[65]

It was evident nonetheless that it was getting harder for Russell to make these transatlantic trips, let alone play week-long residencies 'round midnight. Although he missed these dates, Andy Sheppard was in Perugia for some of the concerts and recalls that band members were concerned for Russell.

> I thought that was a tough gig for George, because he's seventy-nine, he flies over from the States, he rehearses the band as George is wont to do, and, of course, instead of concentrating on six pieces of music, he'll want to play his entire back catalog. So things get half rehearsed, and all the guys in the band were exhausted in the restaurant at eight o'clock, as they'd been rehearsing all day, and then they'd be on stage at midnight. I just thought this is a really tough gig for a man of that age.[66]

In fact, at the end of the week, Russell and the band had to travel to the other end of Italy for one more concert. This was exhausting for the younger, fitter members of the band, but for Russell, often determined to be there with his musicians, sharing their company, it can take weeks to recover. It was also a colossal strain on his wife, Alice. It was clear that week in Perugia that there would not be many more tours.

There was, however, one more shake of the tail to be had. It came about once again with the assistance of John Cumming, and, as tour manager, Martel Ollerenshaw. Russell celebrated his eightieth birthday with concerts at the Moers Festival, Royal Northern College of Music in Manchester, and the Barbican. For several band members, the Moers gig was one of the best they had experienced with the orchestra. This was despite the fact that there was little time between their arrival and the evening show. For Pat Hollenbeck, it was a defining moment, despite the presence of a new drummer, Richie

Morales. His comments also explain something essential about this band and jazz in general.

> **PH:** It was just that everything was right. The audience was with us the whole time. The sound was good for both the band and the audience, and everything just seemed to be right. This was an interesting experience, because this is a new drummer and that was his first concert with the band. The band is really affected by any changes in personnel, because all of a sudden that person's personality and their playing makes it different. It's fascinating actually.
>
> **DH:** It's like a family, people have said.
>
> **PH:** It's a scary thing when there's a new adopted child in there, but when you get a great musician and plug them in they bring a special something and it's really excellent. We're unlike a classical or symphonic orchestra; if you change a violinist or somebody in another section you're not going to really know the difference. But here everybody has a key part in this, so it's not a situation like that, where certain people are like the rank-and-file people just playing their parts. It really affects the whole thing.[67]

Palle Mikkelborg was also back in the band, and Russell noted with almost fatherly approval that trumpeter Stanton Davis was in no way put out by the Danish musician's presence and was genuinely welcoming. Again, there was a feeling within the band of "doing it for George." Even new member Richie Morales could sense it, and felt he had gelled fine within the band.

> I mean, if I did something that was totally out of the realm of possibility, they'd let me know. *(laughs)* But we had a concert in Germany on Monday, and they—Alice and George—were very complimentary and said that they felt it was one of the better, if not the best, performances the band had done. I don't know how much of that is just trying to make me feel comfortable, but it felt really good, and you can tell when the band gets the right groove and the atmosphere is right, then everybody plays better and the whole band levitates, because with an ensemble this size—most of my background is in small-group work—it's the difference between driving a sports car and a bus in terms of performance. It can get very unwieldy and awkward if things aren't synced up.[68]

Manchester was also a fine performance, albeit with a poor turnout due to an almost total absence of pre-concert publicity. In fact, the band and Russell had worked earlier in the day with some students from the college, and the tour's sound engineer made a point of getting them free tickets for the gig, much to the apparent annoyance of box office staff. There were moments of great drama, with Palle Mikkelborg's entrance playing the theme from *Listen to the Silence*, followed shortly after by Russell. There were fine performances of *Electronic Sonata, It's About Time*, and "So What," and an unusual small-group arrangement of "Dialogue with Ornette" featuring a guest appearance by violist Christopher Jenkins. But the meat of the evening came from a staggering performance of *The African Game*. Mike Walker on guitar seemed to be on fire, and Andy Sheppard in particular seemed to pick up on his energy, while Mikkelborg, Bargeron, Biscoe, and Lodder seemed determined to seize every opportunity they were given as well.

The Barbican gig was even better, and fortunately the Russells and Cumming had the foresight to ensure it was recorded for posterity. The lengthy applause at the end says everything. There was a sense across the auditorium that the band had given everything and that this was probably the last time the audience would see this jazz legend—one of the last remaining links to Bird, Diz, Gil, Miles, and Mulligan—on a British stage. As Alice Russell says, "We wondered about letting the applause go on that long at the end of the record. But then I said, 'Oh, hell! Why not?'"[69]

If, as seems likely, *The 80th Birthday Concert* is Russell's last record, then it is a fine valediction. In the absence of the Blue Note version of *The African Game*, it puts a very significant musical work back in the catalog, and in a form that is the equal of—though in places quite different from—the original. Most importantly, it features a great big band playing music that matters to them personally with the utmost commitment. But one writer felt otherwise. Paul DeBarros found it "pompous" and "melodramatic," noting that "Russell favors structure over lyricism, a liability he shares with modern architecture."[70] I would disagree with DeBarros about modern architecture as well.

Music and work had to continue. Russell prepared the New England Conservatory big band for a special concert to celebrate one hundred years of the Jordan Hall in October 2003. He continued teaching until he took a sabbatical in 2004, after which, at age eighty-two, he retired. The honors continued. There were trips to Stockholm and Copenhagen for concerts of his music. For the latter, he was able to take Brad Hatfield, Stuart Brooks, Richie Morales, and Pat Hollenbeck with him, though it certainly was not "touring" like in the old days. Then, on March 5, 2007, Russell was one of thirty-four jazz legends honored at the Kennedy Center in Washington. His peers included Dave Brubeck, Clark Terry, Chick Corea, Gerald Wilson, Phil Woods, Marion McPartland, Toshiko Akyoshi, Curtis Fuller, and Freddie Hubbard. Closer to home for Russell and his own history in the music, Buddy DeFranco, Jon Hendricks, Dave Baker, Ornette, and Benny Golson, who played on *New York, N.Y.*, were also being honored at the gala.[71] If only Miles, Gil, and Trane could have been there.

Notes

1. Interview with John Cumming, May 2003.

2. Ibid.

3. Interview with Courtney Pine, May 2005.

4. Interview with Chris Biscoe, February 2006.

5. Ibid.

6. Interview with Pine.

7. Interview with Pete Hurt, June 2003.

8. Ibid.

9. Interview with Kenny Wheeler, August 2004.

10. Interview with Cumming.

11. John Fordham, "George and the Geometry," *Guardian* (Manchester), February 28, 1986.

12. Richard Williams, "Patterns of Relish," *Times* (London), February 28, 1986.

13. Derek Eaton, "Band Strikes High Note," *Southern Evening Echo* (Southampton), March 3, 1986.

14. Interview with Biscoe.

15. Stan Woolley, "George Russell," *Jazz Journal* 39, no. 10 (October 1986).

16. Howard Mandel, "The Mathematical Musician," *Washington Post*, September 27, 1987.

17. Geoffrey Himes, "Russell: In the Mood for Modes," *Washington Post*, October 3, 1987.

18. Kuniharu Akiyama, reviewing the concert in *Komei Shimbun*, March 5, 1988; George Russell and the Living Time Orchestra—New York—Live in Tokyo, Electric Bird 6488/89.

19. William Penn Montgomery, "Theorist Proposes a Scale Harmonious with All Music," *Japan Times*, August 6, 1993.

20. Fred Bouchard, Review of Boston Musica Viva performance of Six Aesthetic Gravities, *Down Beat*, June 1988.

21. Daniel Webster, "Relâche Presents Flashes of Americana," *Philadelphia Inquirer*, July 1, 1989.

22. F. Gonzalez, "Russell Will Finish My Life's Work," *Boston Globe*, July 19, 1989.

23. Duncan Heining, "Carla Bley," *Independent* (London), November 16, 1999.

24. Duncan Heining, "Learning to Wave," *Avant* 9 (Autumn 1998).

25. Interview with Steve Lodder, February 2003.

26. Ibid.

27. Ibid.

28. Ibid.

29. C. Davis, "The Week Ahead (Preview of Brecon Jazz Festival," *Times* (London), August 12, 1989; R. Cook, "Old Hand Who Gets a Kick out of the Big Band," *Sunday Times* (London), August 27, 1989; J. Fordham, "King George's Gold Blend," *Guardian* (Manchester), September 1, 1989; P. Urpeth, "George Russell (Preview of

LTO at Ronnie Scott's Club, London," *Time Out*, August 30–September 6, 1989; M. Zwerin, "Probing the Dialectics of Chords," *International Herald Tribune*, August 10, 1989.

30. Interview with Brad Hatfield, June 2003.

31. Interview with David Fiuczynski, February 2006.

32. Interview with Ian Carr, April 2003.

33. Interview with Andy Sheppard, April 2003.

34. J. P. Kahn, "Names and Faces: Russell Named Jazz Master," *Boston Globe*, January 2, 1990.

35. K. Mathieson, program notes for Glasgow International Jazz Festival; Press release for GIJF, June 1989.

36. Martin Gayford, "Ignoring the Sirens," *Weekend Telegraph* (London), March 16, 1991; N. Hadsley, "George Russell: Don't Kick Sand at This Theory with Muscle," *TOP*, February 1991.

37. Garry Booth, Review of Camden Jazz Festival, *Financial Times*, March 26, 1991.

38. Roland Ramanan, Concert review of Cassandra Wilson, George Russell at Town & Country Club; Jazz Warriors, Tony Remy at Shaw Theatre, *Wire*, May 1991, pp. 18–20. As a general rule, I avoid commenting on other writers' work. This deserves some response, however. Sadly, it is an example of an inexperienced journalist masking his own lack of knowledge and understanding with slick and gratuitous comment. Myth debunking and icon smashing are often seen by young writers as ways of building a reputation, while the insertion of the odd clever phrase or mot juste is believed to be a substitute for critical insight. The jazz community should expect better.

39. John Fordham, "Lazy Rocking Russell," *Guardian Weekly* (Manchester), May 12, 1991.

40. Gary Giddins, "Making It New," *Village Voice*, March 30, 1993.

41. Interview with Marty Khan, February 2004; Alice Russell, fax to John Cumming, March 26, 1992; Marty Khan, fax to Rob Gibson, December 23, 1992.

42. Rob Gibson letter to Marty Khan, January 4, 1993.

43. Richard B. Woodward, "Jazz Wars: A Tale of Age, Rage and Hash Brownies," *Village Voice*, August 9, 1994.

44. Quoted in S. Nicholson, *Is Jazz Dead? Or Has It Moved To A New Address?* (New York: Routledge, 2005), p. 60. Nicholson provides a very complete and thorough discussion of issues involving Jazz at Lincoln Center.

45. Interview with Marty Khan, February 2004.

46. P. Applebome, "A Jazz Success Story with a Ting of the Blues," *New York Times*, September 22, 1998.

47. E-mail correspondence between Marty Khan and Lincoln Center.

48. Ben Ratliff, "Rock, Funk and Electronics in a Splashy 80s Sound," *New York Times*, May 12, 1999. According to Marty Khan, the representative of the *Times* asked for the volume to be turned down! Interview with Khan.

49. J. Szwed, "Still on His Own Page," *Village Voice*, May 25, 1999.

50. Marty Khan [writing as George Lane], "George Russell & Anglo-American Living Time Orchestra Perform in USA for First Time," GMN.com, 7.12.02.

51. Readers wishing to accuse me of Eurocentrism might wish to note Francis Davis's comments in "George Russell: Intellect of the Heart," *Jazz Times*, December 12, 1984: "If as robust and stimulating work as The African Game fails to arouse jazz listeners, one will be forced to share its composer's concern for the survival of jazz. But one will also be forced to conclude that it is the complacency of the Jazz faithful, rather than the indifference of the mass media, that may ultimately plant the seeds of destruction."

52. Interview with Sheppard.

53. Interview with Cumming.

54. Ibid.

55. Ronald Atkins, "The Guide—Preview of LTO at Queen Elizabeth Hall," *Guardian* (Manchester), November 11, 1995; Phil Johnson, "Music—Review of Russell & LTO at the Forum in Bath," *Independent* (London), November 21, 1995.

56. John Fordham, "A Time to Live," *Guardian* (Manchester), March 21, 1997; *Herald* (Glasgow), March 15, 1997.

57. Fax correspondence between Alice Russell and John Cumming.

58. Interview with Lodder.

59. Interview with Cumming.

60. Ibid.

61. Ibid.

62. J. Fordham, "Send Off the Clones," *Guardian* (Manchester), March 5, 1998. See also A. Shipton, "Play What You Mean," *Jazzwise*, March 1998; S. Oliver, "George Russell," *Jazz Express*, February 1998; Phil Johnson, "Lydian Modes and All That Jazz," *Independent* (London), March 7, 1998.

63. J. Fordham, "Stars in the Eye of a Storming Sound," *Guardian* (Manchester), March 9, 1998.

64. Interview with Lodder.

65. Ibid.

66. Interview with Sheppard.

67. Interview with Pat Hollenbeck, June 2003.

68. Interview with Richie Morales, June 2003.

69. Interview with Alice Norbury-Russell, October 2006.

70. Paul DeBarros, Review of The 80th Birthday Concert (Concept), *Down Beat*, November 2005.

71. W. Jenkins, "Living History," *Jazz Times*, May 2007.

CHAPTER ELEVEN

~

On Conceptual Thinking

The circumstances leading to George Russell's "discovery"[1] of the Lydian Concept have been described already. Those events provide a context for Russell's research and even furnish and people his social and cultural milieu. To recap very briefly, Russell learned from his friend Harold Gaston the "rudiments of musical theory" while both were in hospital with tuberculosis. This gave him a sufficient understanding and knowledge to begin to write and arrange music. Working as a drummer with Benny Carter's orchestra, he was replaced by Max Roach. In turn, he sold his first composition ("New World") to Carter, and from there worked with and composed for Earl Hines in Chicago.

On moving to New York, he was introduced into the group that met at Gil Evans's 55th Street apartment by Max Roach. He seems to have been accepted quite readily into that group, which included several composer-arrangers who had already achieved a fair measure of success, such as Gil Evans, John Lewis, Gunther Schuller, and Gerry Mulligan. A meeting with Miles Davis, himself the rising star of the group, prompted Russell to begin questioning the relationship in traditional Western music between scales and chords. A further period of hospitalization allowed him to develop his ideas in greater depth and, while recovering with Max Roach and his family, to begin their elaboration.

Essentially consistent with the known facts, this is the story Russell has told in interviews since the mid-fifties. Its details fulfill certain functions. The period in the sanatorium with Gaston explains how Russell went from a level of (comparative) ignorance of musical theory to a sufficient level of competency that he was able to begin composing and arranging. The introduction from Roach to the 55th Street set provides an entrée to that group. The meeting with Davis raised the question that would lead to George Russell's life's work. It explains history and to an extent validates the explanation by its references to key, even seminal, personalities.

The possibility that the influence of Professor Eileen Terry, his music teacher at Wilberforce University, was greater than Russell later acknowledged need not imply that he is being in any way disingenuous in his account. We all tend to identify influences upon us retrospectively, with the benefit and coloring provided by history and we are not always the best judges of the significance of certain life events against others. We all like to see ourselves as self-determining in our own lives. As an African American adolescent in Cincinnati, Russell had friendships that sustained him in the face of educational experiences that scarred him. It seems highly likely that Gaston's "teaching" felt greatly more significant to Russell than the formal tuition of Terry. And his desire, in turn, to be positive about his own direction and choices following his damning encounters with a white-dominated school system and society may have overridden any incentive to examine other possible determining factors in his life.

Though he has always played down his own early period of musical activity, by the time he arrived in New York he was hardly a neophyte. He had drummed with the renowned Wilberforce Collegians. We also know from his friend Nadi Qamar that he had begun writing, arranging, and even leading his own groups in Cincinnati by his late teens. He had played with Benny Carter, one of the leading bandleaders of the day, and composed and, probably, arranged for him. He had composed and arranged for Earl Hines and rehearsed his band. That is quite a résumé for a twenty-two-year-old. In fact, it is hardly the career trajectory one would predict for a sixteen-year-old high school dropout!

We have noted that there is something in the story that George Russell tells that bears comparison with similar tales of other discoverers of strange new truths. Sigmund Freud always portrayed the early years of his "discovery" of psychoanalysis as a struggle against an academic establishment unwilling to accept his ideas. The reality was that psychoanalysis was met with a remarkable degree of interest, despite its radical nature.[2] Likewise, much is made of the discovery of the theory of relativity by a lowly Swiss patent clerk recently refused promotion. And one of the most influential economists of the mid-twentieth century failed to achieve his desired post in the UK Treasury because he finished second in the 1906 Civil Service examinations. Of course, Albert Einstein's theories revolutionized physics and John Maynard Keynes's view of economics had an impact on American society through Theodore Roosevelt and the New Deal, on postwar Europe through the Marshall Plan, and through J. K. Galbraith on the Kennedy and Johnson administrations.[3]

It is not a matter of questioning the truth of their biographies. It is the way such biographical (or autobiographical) facts are interpreted and retold that creates myth. Is there an element of self-mythologizing in Russell's case? Have those who have written articles about him helped create elements of myth in their retellings of his story? The answer to the latter is certainly yes, when one considers the weight given by many critics to the biological father Russell never knew in his development as an artist.

The desire individuals have to see themselves as self-determining was, if anything, heightened in Russell by the fact of his adoption. His roots lie in relationships rather than in biological ties. Perhaps the story that his natural father was a professor of music gave him something to aspire to, but it is through knowing our parents, siblings, grandparents, uncles, aunts, and cousins that we understand or define our place in the physical world. These are ties of blood that root us in the natural world. In Russell's case, the absence of such ties seems to have been quite liberating and allowed him a positive sense that he was able to, in effect, create himself. To whatever extent that is so, as Karl Marx noted, "Men make their own history. They do not do so in circumstances of their own choosing."[4]

For Russell, it seems to be music that rooted him in the natural world, in the natural order. It is surely not accidental that he describes the Lydian Chromatic Concept of Tonal Organization as "the science of tonal gravity." In making music a part of nature and in emphasizing this as the heart of his claim for his theory, he roots himself physically and biologically in the world. That does not mean he is wrong; simply that what we seek, we find, and how we describe it owes something to our own biography.

If that conversation with Miles Davis provided the germ of an idea, the context in which the Lydian Concept was discovered is at least, if not more, important. Perhaps it took time for bebop to extend its grasp outside New York and other metropolitan centers. However, in New York in 1946–1947, it was the hottest ticket in town, and Russell found himself right there at the center of it all. It was not just a bunch of musicians trying something new. It was a context as intellectually and culturally challenging as any new artistic movement. When Gunther Schuller recalls hearing Scriabin coming from Russell's apartment just before they met, it was an immediate shared reference point. When Russell remembers watching Hindemith or Stravinsky's assistant rehearsing the orchestra at the Lincoln Center, it indicates his and the group's hunger for new ideas. It was a circle that recognized like minds and encouraged and mutually supported those who were changing jazz. And those like minds gave him a home when he came out of the sanatorium, in the case of Max Roach; gave him a concert stage for his first major composition, in the case of Dizzy Gillespie; gave him academic validation for his ideas in providing him with the opportunity to teach other musicians through the Lenox School of Jazz, in the case of John Lewis and Gunther Schuller; and took his ideas to a world audience, in the case of Miles Davis and John Coltrane.

It is a point that Andy Wassermann, a former student and friend of Russell's, expresses beautifully.

> It always seemed to be his neighbors and his friends were Dizzy Gillespie and Max Roach and Gil Evans and Bill Evans . . . it was all camaraderie and all community. There wasn't any conservatory. It wasn't about money. It wasn't, "Oh, I'm going to make friends with Max Roach so I can make money." They were all basically poor. You hear about the prejudice. They were doing this because of where they were at that point in time. All of that is the conjunction of him as a theoretician and the Lydian Chromatic Concept is based on his life in the culture of jazz.[5]

These are the comparatively recent origins of the Concept. But Russell has always stressed that he discovered it, in the sense that "it" was already and always there. In a way, by his account, he "rediscovered" it. In this sense, the Concept can be traced back to ancient Greece and the musical and mathematical ideas of Pythagoras. In "An Historical Perspective of the Lydian and Major Scales,"[6] Reed Gratz suggests that the origins of modes predate 500 BCE Greece and lie in ancient China and India. While this seems highly possible, Pythagoras is a convenient starting point. For the ancient Greeks, music was inseparable from numbers. Musical sounds and rhythms were ordered and "exemplified the harmony of the cosmos and corresponded to it."[7] It was Pythagoras who seems to have identified the ratios of the fourth, the fifth (most important for our purposes), and the octave—in legend, according to Boethius—by listening to the tones emitted by different hammers in a blacksmith's workshop. For other Greek thinkers such as Ptolemy, music was similarly connected with astronomy, and the planets shared with music the same mathematical laws to the extent that certain modes were believed to correspond to certain planets and their movements. Five centuries earlier, Plato had poetically elaborated the notion of the "music of the spheres," heavenly sounds made by the planets as they spun and moved through the sky. Mythology and poetics aside,[8] Pythagoras and other Greek thinkers were simply but articulately defining musical notation in terms of mathematical relationships. One note was so many steps or such an interval away from another. At the same time, they were expanding a set of scientific laws that governed the art of music.

It is no accident, therefore, that in *The Lydian Chromatic Concept of Tonal Organization*, George Russell draws on correspondences between Pythagoras's "spiral of fifths,"[9] the Lydian scale, and the overtone series. Certainly, Russell and his students see the Concept as a return to more ancient musical theories and a departure from the dominance of the major and minor scales of Western music. As Russell himself says, "The Pythagorean spiral of fifths was the basis for a tuning system which governed Western music from antiquity to the mid-15th century."[10]

It is worth suggesting that Russell is in fact being conservative in his dating. Certainly the replacement of the old church modes occurred after the Council of Trent (1545–1563), and their use continued after the council's closure. Though the Council of Trent is often held responsible for the increasing dominance of the major and minor scales—or at least their application in the services of the Catholic Church—this is not historically the case. Though the church was probably an influence in the adoption of the major and minor scales, the period during which this took place was much longer than sometimes credited. What is more, the church was merely one force in that process, and quite possibly not the main one. Although this may sound an arcane point, it is one worth noting, as several internet Web sites hold the council responsible for all manner of musical crimes, including the proscribing of the so-called Devil's Interval or Devil's Tri-Tone.[11] As these Web sites draw on a similar understanding of modal theory to the Lydian Concept, a clear distinction needs to be made. In practice, the council's pronouncements on the issue of modes was incredibly vague, and it makes no mention of the "Devil's Interval/Chord/TriTone" or indeed, to give it its Latin name, the *diabolus musica*.[12] In fact, this conspiratorial thesis is a conflation of three separate issues—the influence of the Council of Trent; the use of accidentals in plainsong and Gregorian chant to camouflage the difficult tri-tone interval, which was known as the *diabolus musica*; and the development of the major and minor scales and the decline of the old church modes. In fact, Russell refers to this very clearly and without confusion in his book.[13]

There are issues relating to the correspondence or not between the Greek modes, or *tonoi*, and the church modes, to which Greek names were given in the Middle Ages. It is also open to question how far the *tonoi* can be regarded as modes in any more modern sense. In one way, they were more like regional accents or ways of pitching according to approximate scales. Nor in the Middle Ages were the church modes necessarily fixed in terms of pitch.[14] This is not to suggest that George Russell's thesis is in any way invalidated by such considerations. First, the notion of a ladder of fifths seems well grounded in Pythagoras's musical ideas and in later musical developments. Additionally, similar scalar intervals are found in a variety of ethnic musical forms. Sir James Jeans, in his groundbreaking *Science and Music*, noted the discovery of two flutes in Egypt dating from approximately 2000 BCE that gave a seven-note scale identical with that of the "Synto-lydian scale of Ancient Greece."[15] Donald Grout, in *A History of Western Music*, notes both the prevalence of a Lydian raised fourth in Polish folk music and Chopin's use of it in his compositions.[16] Finally, G. H. Ranade, in *Hindusthani Music: An Outline of Its Physics and Aesthetics*, points out the importance in Indian music of obtaining the various notes of the scale through a chain of successive fifths. He dates this practice back to 300 BCE in India.[17] Furthermore, as a "theory as method," which is the Concept's core function, its efficacy as an aid to teaching improvisation, improvising, and as a compositional tool is its primary justification. Historical grounding for the theory or its applicability across a range of ethnic forms is not essential to it. Nevertheless, additional research to ground the Concept historically would certainly strengthen the claims of Russell and others for it.

When it comes to how the major and minor scales came to dominate Western music, *The Lydian Chromatic Concept of Tonal Organization* is quite comprehensive in its explanation, at least in musical terms. Russell refers to the "Ionian major and Aeolian minor scales" becoming "the fundamental tonality for Western music." He lists six reasons for this, from the acceptance of an additional four church modes, including the Ionian mode, as outlined by Glareanus (1547), the renumbering by Zarlino in 1558 of the modes and his placing the Ionian mode first, the Council of Trent, and the growing popularity of the Ionian mode. More vaguely and with less documentary evidence, Russell suggests that economic, political, and religious changes at a societal level contributed to a different set of cultural requirements of music. Specifically, the non- or less goal-oriented modes needed to be replaced by more goal-directed, resolution-seeking, even martial forms.[18]

It is unfortunate that this point is not developed at greater length, because it encapsulates a number of issues and locates cultural superstructural changes against an infrastructure that was moving from an agrarian economy through mercantilism toward an industrial model. It is worth suggesting here that the industrial model itself, with its highly stratified class structure and increasingly streamlined means of production, transformed the demand for music from one rooted in the past and present to one constantly moving forward. Ironically, given the emphasis on progress, such a model would require fixed points in terms of pitch, scales, instrumentation, harmony, and rhythm to enable effective and repetitive (re)production, that is, on an industrial model. Again, further research in this area would assist claims on behalf of Russell's theory.

With regard to musical/historical influences on Russell as a theorist/composer, he is not alone in recognizing the crucial function of a scale or octave based on the interval of fifths. Karlheinz Stockhausen, for example, is quoted at length on the subject in *The Lydian Chromatic Concept of Tonal Organisation*.[19] There are some, however, who question the usefulness of Russell's seeking to establish such precedents for his ideas in, for example, the work of Bach, Debussy, and Ravel.[20] However, this seems rather unfair. First, as we have argued, the theory actually requires a more extensive historical grounding. Second, precedents help establish a broader context for debate and are theoretically useful for that reason alone. Third, although a distinction can be made between "Russell the Theorist" and "Russell the Composer," once again ironically, this search for precedent serves to locate him in both regards as a modernist in theory and practice. In the former respect, he is an heir to Messiaen, Schoenberg, and Webern. In the latter, Russell's writing of music seems to owe as much of a debt to a lineage that includes Debussy, Stravinsky, Scriabin, Schoenberg, and Stockhausen as it does to Ellington, Strayhorn, Mulligan, and Gil Evans. In fact, along with John Lewis, Russell is perhaps one of the most obviously "Third Stream" composers to come out of jazz.

This is not to suggest that it is easy to hear in George Russell's compositions the influences of such other composers. It is easier to see the impact of earlier theorists on the Concept. However, the issues are similar and focus much more on shared concerns. Russell's capacity to make connections between a diverse range of sources and ability to fashion an effective and eventful synthesis of these ideas and influences is an essential feature of his genius and his contribution to jazz and music generally. Three or so examples should illustrate this point.

For a musician, composer, or theorist of the last three hundred plus years to claim Bach as an influence hardly astounds. In all respects, Bach seems omnipresent as an influence across epochs and styles. In Russell's case, Bach is cited in terms of his use of the old church modes as well as the major and minor scales, which the Baroque era brought to prominence. Bach's Fugue No. 24 in B Minor is analyzed as an example of vertical tonal gravity from the perspective of the Lydian Chromatic Concept, as is the Prelude No. 1.

Here, Russell is not just seeking to show precedent for the Concept. He is emphasizing that these were, up to that point, at least, established and accepted as a basis for the creation of musical works. It was not just theory but "theory in use," or praxis.[21]

If we look at Russell the composer and teacher, we find an ongoing influence from Bach on his work. Andy Wassermann recalls his studies in composition with George Russell:

> The very first thing he said was, "Man, I don't care what you write . . ." —because I would write pieces and bring them in and he would critique them—the only thing he ever said was, "Funky fugues, man. I don't care what you do. I want it to be a funky fugue." And when you listen to his music, that's what it is.[22]

It is a comment that does not apply across the board to George's work as a whole, any more than it would in Bach's case. And the fugue form did not originate with Bach, as pianist Balint Vazsonyi notes:

> He [Bach] did not invent the fugue, that most rule-governed device in music which requires the weaving of simultaneous melodic strands unfolding so they coincide in legitimate harmonies without losing their independence, all conforming to stringent structural patterns. Nothing is more prone to becoming a mind game. Nothing proved Bach's unique genius more conclusively than the sheer musical beauty he achieved in his fugues, so that intellectual appreciation of their inimitable mastery remains an optional extra.[23]

However, if the term "funky fugue" would not describe programmatic works like *The African Game* or *Listen to the Silence* or *Living Time*, it could be a description of Russell compositions from the Jazz Workshop sessions through *Vertical Forms VI* to *Six Aesthetic Gravities* and certainly to *It's About Time*, as well as small-group works like "Stratusphunk." For Russell, the fugue has that cyclical quality he enjoys. It is not seeking resolution. It grows upward in ever-ascending spirals. Several of these works are also strongly contrapuntal, another feature of the form and particularly of Bach's writing. They are also rich in unusual harmonies. However, to these Russell adds elements that are much more modern in origin.

The cyclical form of the fugue and rondo are, after all, quite suited to jazz improvisation and composition, as Jacques Loussier, John Lewis, and Dave Brubeck have shown. The greater problem in jazz is that of extended form. On the whole, longer pieces in jazz have relied on a series of solos in place of thematic development. Russell the composer uses, in addition to the jazz solo, a number of other devices. The first of these is a complex layering of rhythmic patterns using a range of instruments, not just drums and bass. These polyrhythms interweave like an African drum choir, and on a piece like *Living Time Event II*, the effect is like that of swirling winds in a vortex. The second derives from the creation of harmonies across the orchestra. As Andy Sheppard notes:

> George's music is very dense, so that a lot of the written stuff is very hard to play, and he'll have different rhythms happening at the same time, where the bass player's "one" is different to the drummer's "one," which is different to my "one" when you're reading the part. So that time cycles are happening simultaneously and the band will be playing in different keys, and then there's the whole Lydian Concept. It's a very dense, intricate world.[24]

When Sheppard prepared himself to play with George Russell the first time, he listened to *The African Game*. "I thought the whole first section sounded fairly improvised to me. It sounds like the band are pretty free there." When he sat down at the rehearsal and saw the music, however, "All the stuff I thought was pretty free and improvised was actually written, and the system of cues is incredibly complex." Add the fact that what he as the tenor player was playing at a given point could be "wildly different to what the saxophone player next to you is playing. . . . It makes you question the music you play. You think am I right here?"[25]

Some players and composers question the amount Russell writes. Keyboardist Masabumi Kikuchi, who played briefly with Russell but more extensively with Gil Evans, contrasted the two experiences for Stephanie Stein Crease: "After the first night, I couldn't do it. His [Russell's] music is all very scored and you can't do anything else." With Gil Evans, "He wanted the orchestra to play beyond notation." After being with Russell, "I realized how much freedom Gil gave me," he explained to Evans's biographer.[26]

And the British composer and bandleader Graham Collier makes a similar point. Despite acknowledging Russell's significance in expanding the potential for the big band, Collier says, "I'm not an enormous fan of George's work, and, like a lot of people, I find he writes too much. He has a tendency for that." He tells a story about Gil Evans to explain the kind of model he prefers.

> I'll tell you a funny story. Do you know John Ellson [director of Serious Music]? He told me he went to pick up Gil from the airport for some London Festival commission and he said to Gil, "Have you finished the piece yet? Is it all done?" Gil said, "Yeah, I've got it in here somewhere." And he pulled out this scrap of paper and that was it. Yet they made a magnificent concert out of it.[27]

Yet comparing and contrasting these two composers is less about idle preference and much more about how their styles derive from similar interests in the music of the late nineteenth and early twentieth centuries. Both are highly chromatic in their use of tones and textures. From his period with Thornhill onward, Evans used the horns, in particular the lower range brass instruments, to create soft, vibrating colors. Later, in his own bands, those same colors became less definite and more impressionistic as they emerged from the pastel washes of electric instruments and percussion. Ravel and Debussy, in particular Debussy's *Prelude de l'aprèsmidi d'un faun*, are significant influences here.[28] Musical time hangs suspended, and there is no definite tonal center anchoring the music. Yet time, according to the principles of tonal gravity—or, to use Russell's own favored philosophical metaphor, Living Time[29]—is more important in Russell's music. Time is about rhythm, dance, pulse, energy—essential ingredients in Russell's art. His colors are those of abstraction as opposed to impressionism: harder, brighter, and more explicit. And where Evans learned from Debussy and Ravel that coloration could derive from minimizing writing, Russell took the message that you could actually produce these effects through notation. Same source, different—but equally justifiable—conclusions.

The Russian composer Alexander Scriabin is another acknowledged influence on the Concept and on Russell's music. Again, there is the issue of color and chromaticism, and Scriabin seems to have been something of a synesthete, associating notes and tones with specific colors and emotions. Arguably, Scriabin was one of the first composers to utilize serial techniques. Well-known authority George Perle said of Scriabin, "He was the first to exploit serial procedures systematically as a means of compensating for the loss of traditional tonal functions." Of most significance here, however, is that Scriabin based his own "theoretical association of music and color on the circle of fifths that lies at the basis of traditional harmony, a circle of nearly related chords and keys proceeding upwards in fifths in a clockwise direction and downwards anticlockwise in descending fifths."[30] The sound of *Prometheus, The Poem of Fire*, which Gunther Schuller heard coming from Russell's apartment that day, was, it seems, a purposeful rather than merely aesthetic choice.

However, despite his studies with Stefan Wolpe, who studied with Schoenberg's pupil Webern, Russell never embraced atonality. He has always favored polytonal or tonal approaches as a composer, and indeed this sits more easily with the Concept's notion of chord-scale unity. Russell was very clear on what he learned from the composer in his contribution to Austin Clarkson's *On the Music of Stefan Wolpe*.

The two things that impressed me, that caused me to think in a new way, were his theory of the rate of chromatic circulation as a means of destroying any tonical integrity and the principle of the thirdless sound. I thought that was incredible. . . . The rate of chromatic circulation and the thirdless sound were big ideas. The works that would show that are on an RCA Victor album, *The Jazz Workshop, George Russell* (1956). Other works are "Lydian M-1" and *All About Rosie*, written for small chamber orchestra.[31]

Russell was clearly already being highly selective in what he was taking from different sources. Even back in the forties, his focus was on tones (the overtone series in particular), color, and fifths, but also on ways of suggesting several tonal centers simultaneously in his music. This does not mean Russell's music sounds like any of these other composers. One of his strengths as a writer is a lack of such self-consciousness or artifice. What is more, Russell comes to these ideas from his roots in jazz. It is constant searching that led him to ask how the questions that Schoenberg, Webern, Stravinsky, Messiaen, and others were seeking to address might apply to jazz. His music might have its origins in the music of his childhood, heard in the churches, on the riverboats, and through the doorways of clubs, and might remain true to the spirit of improvisation. However, this is why his music, more than that of any other composer, deserves the epithet "Third Stream."

One hears the dilemma of the twentieth-century post-romantic composer—including George Russell—when one reads of Schoenberg:

Wagner's last works and his own early music, he [Schoenberg] argued, had expanded tonality so far that it was possible to introduce into any given key any note foreign to that key. If a key can be expressed as well by other notes as by those proper to it, can it be said to exist? To talk of any notes as being foreign to the key is nonsensical, for harmony is simply a sounding together of tones.[32]

Predicting the jazz of the future in 1959, Russell wrote:

Specifically, it's going to be a pan-rhythmic, pan-tonal age. I think jazz will bypass atonality because jazz actually has its roots in Folk Music and Folk Music is scale-based music; and atonality negates the scale. I think jazz will be intensely chromatic and not be atonal.[33]

Russell might have been wrong on a number of his predictions, and the rigid distinction between chromaticism and atonality perhaps does not hold up. However, it emphasizes the continuity of his concerns and a peculiarly jazz solution to the composer's dilemma of the twentieth century. He goes on to note,

> But there is another realm between this and the very tonal music such as Mozart and the classicists wrote. This is called "pan-tonality," where the basic folk nature of the scales is preserved, and yet, because you can use any number of scales or you can be in any number of tonalities at once, and/or sequentially, it also creates a very chromatic kind of feeling, so that it's sort of like being atonal with a Big Bill Broonzy sound. *You can retain the funk.*[34]

This clearly indicates Russell's conscious drawing together of these two different traditions. In bringing jazz, as a folk-based music, together with European art music, with its post-Baroque place in the Academy, he is in a way doing something akin to other modern composers who drew on folk forms. One thinks of Igor Stravinsky, Béla Bartók, Sergei Prokofiev, Aaron Copland, Percy Grainger, Benjamin Britten, and, of course, Vaughan Williams.

Though one should not pigeonhole Russell's music, it does seem that his sojourn in Scandinavia opened up his music to the ideas of twelve-tone music. His association with Ny Musikk, the Norwegian branch of the International Society for Contemporary Music, certainly seemed to be paralleled by a new experimentalism, and one that led into the areas of both jazz-rock and serialism several years ahead of Miles Davis's explorations of such ideas. His sleeve notes for *Electronic Sonata for Souls Loved by Nature—1968* bear striking witness to his intentions.

> The essential concepts which inspired the creation of the *Electronic Sonata for Souls Loved by Nature* lay in philosophical and socio/musical areas. Its socio/musical objective was to create a pan-stylistic electronic tape; a tape consisting of fragments of many different styles of music, avant-garde jazz, ragas, blues, rock, serial music etc. treated electronically. And to have this tape serve as a palate upon which non-electronic musical statements of a pan-stylistic nature could be projected. The wedding of non-electronic pan-stylism to electronic pan-stylism was meant to convey the cultural implosion occurring among the earth's population, their coming together. Also it is meant to suggest that man, in the face of encroaching technology, must confront technology and attempt to humanize it.[35]

Russell seems to have relished the respect given him in Norway and Sweden. In turn, some of those influences began to emerge in his writing. Stockhausen's influence on composition, and, more importantly, on the appreciation of the range of options facing the composer, was perhaps the most obvious force acting on modern European music at that point. It is unsurprising that some of those same concerns began to appear in Russell's work as a composer, though not perhaps so much as a theorist. If similar ideas had already informed his theorizing, it is more the case that the Concept can and does accommodate Stockhausen without needing to make specific room for him or his approach.[36] In terms of music, perhaps the most clear examples of Stockhausen's influence on Russell are heard in *Living Time*, the abrupt elisions in the hugely underrated *Othello Ballet Suite* and, in perhaps Russell's finest work, *The African Game*, and inevitably in *Electronic Organ Sonata No. 1.*

It is clear, therefore, that however much of a distinction one might make between Russell as theorist and as composer, similar concerns, trends, and ideas inform his work in both respects.

So far we have examined the context in which George Russell's "discovery" of the Lydian Concept took place. We have discussed its origins and questioned the adequacy of its historical grounding, suggesting that this is a flaw to be addressed by research rather than anything more fundamental. We have also looked at the influences on his work and ideas within the worlds of classical music and European art music. In this respect, Russell has been described both as a twentieth-century composer sharing the concerns of that epoch and as a Third Stream composer. Neither description is, of course, exclusive. In addition, we have noted those who question Russell's search for precedent and his "overemphasis" (within a jazz context) on composed music.

So how has the Concept changed through its three editions? Primarily, it has perhaps become more—though still perhaps inadequately—grounded in more general musical history and more successfully rooted in musical theory. For one thing, more examples are provided from a broader range of stylistic sources. However, its essential origin as "theory as methodology" has continued. In this, its purpose and value lie in its potential to allow the student to create himself as a musician. It is essentially, though not only, a tool for improvisers, and for composers as well. It should therefore have considerable potential for teaching jazz.

There is a view among some musicians, fans, and critics that sees the whole notion of jazz education as somewhat controversial. At risk of caricature, that view argues that the roots of jazz lie in spontaneity and improvisation and therefore belie the possibility it can be taught to any degree. Rather it can be learned only through the combination of "woodshedding" and live performance, through which the most fortunate eventually find their own true voice. Accordingly, teaching jazz merely leads to the creation of clones of the heroes of jazz and ties the music to a vision that serves to perpetuate the past.[37] This is a perspective that idealizes and rarefies the learning process in jazz and stereotypes jazz education. In fact, such ideas can be traced far beyond the origins of jazz, let alone jazz education, and their source lies in confused notions of the *tabula rasa*, the "idiot savant," and Rousseauvian and Enlightenment beliefs about nature and the natural order.[38] It also idealizes the way ideas are transmitted in jazz. Few musicians ever develop an original voice that is anything more than the sum of their influences. That doesn't automatically invalidate their work or ability to reframe or recontextualize the ideas of others.

There is much that can be taught in jazz. The question is "how," not "whether" it is done. At its best, education (in general) does much more than teach facts, theories, and processes. It seeks to develop in the student an inquiring mind, as well as a level of understanding and the creative ability to apply ideas and place facts in historical or theoretical contexts. It is the inquiring mind that establishes new relationships between different aspects of knowledge and promotes new learning and ideas. The motto of the Jesuits, "Give me the child until he is seven and I will give you the man," does not necessarily have a sinister aspect.

The permissive and motivational character of Russell's Concept is an aspect stressed by British pianist Howard Riley, who studied with Dave Baker in Indiana after the trombonist left Russell's group.

> What I got out of it was that it made me think a lot about the notes you can use against chords. I had just begun to play a lot of music that was without chord sequences, and it opened my ears for that as well because I realized the kind of harmony you can get in a nonfunctional harmonic situation. In other words, the kind of notes you can put against chords where the harmony isn't functional. I seem to remember that George Russell stresses that it's not a system but more a philosophy of tonality, and everybody can find their own identity via that, and that's exactly what happened with me because through reading it, it made me think about different things, and eventually it got translated into my playing and it freed up a lot of my note choices when I was playing, so I did actually get further toward my own identity. I mean I realized before I read the Concept that with chord changes that there are limitless combinations of notes—you could put any note against any chord and make it work—but I think the Lydian Concept just took me one step further down that road, and then it was down to my ear and what I thought when I was playing. I think that did loosen things up for me.

This is something Riley now seeks to communicate to his own pupils in order to help them expand their own range of note choices in relation to the chords they are playing. "I try to get over to my students that there are limitless possibilities, as long as you're hearing it and you know what you're doing, it can only add to the interest of your playing. That's the long-term thing I got out of the Concept." And he notes, "It could get to be a real doctrinaire thing, but Dave, and George Russell as well, they're not doctrinaire about it. They just hope it will help you get toward your own identity, which indeed it did help me at that time."[39]

Randy Brecker is another musician who illustrates the value of education in jazz. Brecker studied jazz and the Lydian Concept with David Baker privately and at Indiana University. He had also had quite a bit of experience on the bandstand prior to these studies. Brecker draws on Russell's ideas both as an improviser and composer.

> They're very closely connected, and I think everyone has adapted modality and the Lydian Concept that George has mapped out so well into their playing. It goes without saying that it's part of the jazz repertoire and vocabulary that one needs to know. Particularly when, around that time, Miles's *Kind of Blue* had really exposed that modal way of playing to the wider public. I think a lot of what I play is based on those teachings. The book is hard to get through. I had to take it very slowly, I remember, at the time, because a lot of it was over my head. But I still go back and refer to it.

Brecker continues, emphasizing the value of formal study in jazz as a lifelong process:

> Also, just the fact that I've continued to kind of educate myself, because other than studying with David at Indiana they didn't have a full-fledged jazz department yet. So pretty much I had to pick up everything on my own, and I still kind of study out of books to shorten the gaps in my own education and I still used [it], and particularly in my writing back then, unbeknownst to me, because I didn't know how to codify things. I quite often used minor modality, and I'd play a triad with one hand and a bass note with the other hand and then move the bass note with the same triad and notice that it changed the tension, but I didn't know how to connect the two. Now I do, and it's all still based on modes, still based on a lot of things that George discussed in his book, melodic minor modes.[40]

The method of the Lydian Concept does not eradicate the "hit-and-miss" of trial and error or the surprise of serendipity. It teaches the student about musical relationships in a new way and provides a map for their exploration and elaboration. It doesn't prescribe how to travel from A to B or G or from Do to Re or Ti. As Andy Wassermann suggests:

> Like, here's a map. You want to go from Cincinnati to West Stockbridge. You can go via Florida or Senegal, West Africa. You can take a rowboat. You can

walk. You can take a moped. You can take a jet plane. You can go up via Montreal. You can take a rocket ship, orbit the earth a few times, and then come down to West Stockbridge. He says, "All of those ways I'm going to show you are possible, but however you want to go from Cincinnati to West Stockbridge, that's up to you."[41]

The nonprescriptive aspect of the Concept is something George Russell stresses. "I think the Concept tells me that music has a living, natural organization that is totally objective and noninvasive with small laws and that tonal organization is based on the principle of tonal gravity."[42] And elsewhere: "It's not a theory that demands that you go from the two to the five to one. It's a theory that opens up choice for musicians. There are no rules but there are laws, but [because] the laws are big, there are very few laws."[43]

The contrast in terms of "traditional" musical education, in relation to jazz or other styles, is in part a question of this permissiveness. Though the Concept is a "system," reflecting in turn a methodology, it is not rigid or—and this is crucial—deterministic but instead based upon the development of an understanding of how musical elements are organized. As Ben Schwendener, now teacher of the Lydian Concept at the New England Conservatory, notes:

> My understanding is that, when learning music theory in the traditional Western way, you are taught to write in many different styles using the "rules" or accepted conventions of whatever style or period you're trying to be in. For instance, a sonata or fugue, or eighteenth/nineteenth-century counterpoint, or even when in jazz theory you learn about II, V, I progressions and transcribe and learn solos on your instrument and learn about different chord substitution techniques and ways jazz musicians have traditionally used to navigate through the changes [chord progression] of a piece.

By contrast,

> The Concept is not a "paint by numbers" sort of concept. It ultimately puts 100 percent responsibility for creativity on you. That's not to say that analysis of what's already been done doesn't play an important role in learning the Concept—it's that conceptual analysis uncovers the tonal resources a composer/improviser employed in his or her work and how tonal gravity is being manifested. Any system can be identified, if one chooses, after that. All systems and methodologies, within equal temperament, are embraced in the Lydian Chromatic Concept. The Concept simply offers an objective organization of all the tonal resources (melodic and harmonic) available. It's up to the musician to arrange or combine any selection from these elements in a way

that fulfils the creative aim of whatever music is trying to be created. You can either choose from a methodology, or you choose from natural elements and create your own "methodology" or "system." Choosing from natural elements and their "modes of behavior," as George puts it, allows for direct access to your own essence. George mentions "essence" a lot. I think what he's referring to is that unified core of your being that expresses one's individuality.[44]

The issue of gravity and its relationship to tones, and, in turn, music's relationship to nature, are all points that we will return to later. For now, it serves to note the permissive character of the Lydian Concept. Again, it is no accident that for a person for whom relationships, personal and musical, are so important, the musical system he should create is one concerned primarily with the relationships between tones. Furthermore, given his experiences in childhood and adolescence of racism and oppression, it is unsurprising that his system should be one based on possibility and openness rather than prescription. The maplike quality of the Concept allows exploration within a framework, and that framework is to an extent defined by the tuning system of equal temperament with which we are familiar. Two points need to be made here. The first is that for George Russell, the central position of the major scale is replaced by the Lydian scale, or, as he describes it, the "parent" scale of all other scales. Without any irony, he avoids terms such as "dominant" and "subdominant." To quote Schwendener again, "Seventh chords are often called 'dominant,' but George doesn't like that term. That term is prejudicial."[45]

How far this is about nuance and language may be a matter of dispute. To an extent, all music is about relationships, as is everything in life. Replacing one set of words with another is as likely to create confusion as enlightenment. One can argue that the experiences of an individual, however significant or traumatic, cannot provide a rationale for the creation of an alternative musical system. Finally, one may suggest that the "innovation" of replacing the F of the major scale with a raised fourth is a small advance, whatever the claims for its closer approximation sonically to the preceding and following notes in the order. It may, in fact, be that the "proof" or disproof of George's claims for the Concept will lie outside the arena of music and more certainly in those of science, perhaps in physics but more probably in the area of neurology. To an extent, with the Lydian Concept, as with most things, "you pays your money, you takes your choice."

Russell's departure from traditional terminology is an issue for some students. Marc Rossi, a former student and now a teacher of the Concept, recalls other students struggling with this aspect of Russell's ideas. "A lot of kids in the class were always, 'What do we need the Lydian scale for? What's wrong with the major scale?' Always trying to say, 'Well, what is good about this?' But for me, a new way of looking and a new way of thinking was very comfortable."[46]

And Schwendener acknowledges that some students do struggle as well with the language and with the defining of music as a science, here as the science of tonal gravity.

> I think it's because George redefined what he felt music theory should be, which is a science—as he puts it—"the Art and Science of Tonal Gravity." Understanding music should first and foremost be accessing the natural objective elements that are available. It has nothing to do with how people feel about it—good or bad, right or wrong, happy or sad, or a methodology or a stylistic consideration. It has simply to do with how tonal gravity behaves.[47]

Pianist and composer Jack Reilly goes further. Having studied with Russell in the fifties, he found that the Concept made more sense when he translated some of the terminology back into traditional theoretical terms. In particular, he found Russell's use of the term "chordmode" confusing. His comments were made without animosity.

> Yes, the Concept made more sense when I related, or, better yet, translated the terminology back into traditional theoretical teachings. To recap and give one example simplifying the above: Traditional theory says the V chord is always a dominant seventh of any major scale and of any ascending minor scale. The Lydian Chromatic Concept of Tonal Organization says the II is a dominant seventh of any Lydian scale. To reiterate, by using the same Roman numeral symbols to name his chordmodes, George clashes head on with traditional classical theory. Solution? Don't study classical theory, if you want to really understand and apply the Lydian Chromatic Concept of Tonal Organization to your jazz playing! Or do what I did; apply George's seven principal scales to your jazz playing, omitting the chordmode theory. Only then I was able to dialectically fuse and conflate his theory with my classical theoretical training!

Reilly, though broadly supportive of Russell's ideas and aims, is clearly questioning how far such new terms mask ideas that can be accommodated within more traditional musical theory.[48]

Darius Brubeck, in "1959: The Beginning of Beyond,"[49] suggests that jazz changed dramatically in that year. Within the article, he builds a case that four highly influential records—Miles Davis's *Kind of Blue*, John Coltrane's *Giant Steps*, his father's *Time Out*, and Ornette Coleman's *Shape of Jazz to*

Come—provided a series of portents for where jazz could go. But he also noted the significance of the Lenox School of Jazz, Gunther Schuller and John Lewis's pioneering of the notion of Third Stream music, and George Russell's Lydian Chromatic Concept. For Brubeck, the importance of these ideas lay in their influence on musicians who encountered them directly at Lenox and indirectly through these four classic albums.

Brubeck's assessment of Russell the composer is balanced and respectful. He describes him thus: "As an academically trained composer he added unusual technical skill at manipulating structure, harmony and balance, affecting the usual concerns of jazz composition, which are the interplay of improvised solos and ensemble passages. He was a daring and rigorous experimentalist as a composer (see for example, "All About Rosie" and "Living Time"). Perhaps because he did not project himself enough as a performer (on piano) his music is little known to the public, but it remains controversial, influential and respected within professional circles."[50] One can forgive the "academically trained composer" line, which seems to arise from George's studies with Stefan Wolpe (not "Stephen," as misspelled in the piece). This is a fair and concise summary of Russell's music and importance.

When Brubeck looks at Russell's book, *The Lydian Chromatic Concept of Tonal Organization*, he is less complimentary. "Unfortunately, his attempt to present and prove such an audaciously comprehensive theory sometimes resulted in unreadably turgid discourse burdened with jargon, yet the work's influence has spread far beyond those who have actually read it."[51]

If, however, as Russell suggests, the Concept does offer something outside that provided within the major and minor scales and the way we have come to understand the theory of music in the West, then old terms may fail to convey adequately the points George Russell wants to make. He prefers, for example, the word "chordmode" to "chord." For Russell, the new word conveys the idea that a chord contains within it its own scale or mode, with which it is in unity. Perhaps better than "contains" would be the word "predicts," which has a specific scientific application. Either way, it seems that Russell is making a point that could not be made by the more traditional term. Likewise, if one accepts Russell's assertion that the Concept and the laws on which it is based are present in nature, then his desire to find language that is not judgmental or prejudicial is more than a whim; it is, rather, an appropriate attempt to assert the "naturalness" of such elements without ascribing value to them individually. They then become merely aspects of musical behavior to be chosen and used by the composer or improviser.

Even more crucially, Russell's departure from the use of words such as "free" and "freedom" (both with strong positive and negative associations), "atonal," and "dissonant" and their replacement with terms like "ingoing," "semi-ingoing," "semi-outgoing," and "outgoing" does more than restate existing and philosophical positions. He is actually redefining those positions in terms of the continuing relationship of tones to a fixed musical point. In turn, using his schema, it becomes easier or even simply possible for musicians to remain cognizant of where they are in the musical firmament, how they got there, how they can return to their point of origin or where to go next, regardless of how far they have migrated from their starting point. If Russell is talking about a musical map, then it is a vastly complex one. To return to Wassermann's analogy, one wonders if a road map covers the point adequately. Perhaps we are better using the comparison of a map of the heavens, where points move predictably, though not entirely so. This parallel perhaps conveys more comprehensively the dynamic quality of the Concept.

But Brubeck's article, sometimes seen as considerably critical of Russell and the Concept, also credits Russell with a valuable insight into why we have a major scale with a perfect fourth rather than a Lydian scale and its derivatives, and quotes Russell from the 1959 edition of the Concept:

> The major scale probably emerged as the predominating scale of Western music, because within its seven tones lies the most fundamental harmonic progression of the classical era . . . the tonic major chord on C . . . the sub-dominant major chord on F . . . the dominant seventh chord on G—thus, the major scale *resolves* to its tonic major chord. The Lydian scale *is* the sound of its tonic major chord.[52]

As Brubeck rightly suggests, "This is original, brilliant, even self-evident, but no one had quite said it before. The practical implications are indeed far-reaching and amount to a theory that works for playing and teaching jazz."[53] Given Brubeck's own status as an important jazz educator, this last point is praise indeed. Essentially, Russell redefined the basis of jazz improvisation, shifting it from chords to chord-scalar relationships. Brubeck questions Russell's "special terminology," citing the terms "vertical polymodality" and "auxiliary diminished scale" specifically. For him, Russell's "justifications, precedents and far-reaching claims" for the Concept "complicate rather than clarify." Although other musicians go much further in their support, Brubeck's dispassionate and objective survey and final assessment would seem in itself to justify and validate Russell's work and contribution to jazz. There is almost an acknowledgment in his next words that the Concept has offered something fresh and vital to jazz, when he writes, "but the Lydian Chromatic Concept meant liberation from the obsolete concerns and dictates of 'legit' academic theory which is based on a different tradition of tonal organisation."[54]

Another critic, Barry Kernfeld, in correspondence with Brubeck, questions the validity of both the Lydian Concept and Ornette Coleman's Harmolodics, but notes that they have their uses.

> [T]he theoretical underpinnings of harmolodic theory are extremely suspect, even more so than those of George Russell's Lydian Chromatic Concept, but there is no question that these sorts of casual, home-made approaches to jazz theory have been of great value to performers and educators, helping them to capture, or to communicate, through inferential or emotive means, some of the processes involved in Jazz improvisation.[55]

Faint praise or backhanded compliment, perhaps. However, Kernfeld and Brubeck recognize the usefulness of theorizing about jazz improvisation and moving the theoretical debate outside the parameters of the more traditional music theory approaches associated with European art music. It is an acknowledgment that the latter cannot adequately encompass the syncretic nature of jazz, with its roots in Western classical, Northern Hemisphere folk and church music, Arabic and West African influences and origins, and in its ongoing relationship with popular music.[56]

Of course, not all musicians accept the value or need for such theorizing. Chuck Israels, who played on "Stratusphunk," adopted such a position in an e-mail interview.

> George's theories seem to me to result in complex ways of looking at things that have been understood in simpler ways for hundreds of years. It's more obfuscation than revelation to musicians who are well educated in traditional analysis—like going from London to Paris by way of Buenos Aires. You can make the trip, but it's not the most efficient route. In the nine-year history of the National Jazz Ensemble, only one composition provoked criticism from the band members. When we played All About Rosie, Greg Herbert (the great saxophonist who had worked with Thad and Mel, and Woody Herman) said that it was the only thing in our entire repertoire that rang false to him. He felt it was full of what he called "fake blues licks."[57]

As with many discussions of ideas and theories, we reach an impasse. There are those who reject it entirely, those who question but recognize some aspects as significant, and there are the active proponents. However, the very wide-reaching claims Russell makes for the Lydian Chromatic Concept of Tonal Organization actually demand a greater justification than that. In asserting that the basis of the Lydian Chromatic Concept of Tonal Organization lies in "the science of tonal gravity" and that this provides a scientific basis for the Concept, a much higher standard of proof is required.

There have been attempts to assess and evaluate Russell's ideas theoretically. Mark S. Haywood, in the *Annual Review of Jazz Studies* in 1991, has suggested that Russell's theories need updating to account for new developments in jazz, in particular what Haywood calls "melody-based harmony," in other words, that harmony is implied by the melody line rather than by the chord or tonic station.[58] While this may be a point worthy of further study, it does seem that Haywood might just be putting the cart before the horse and that, in most instances at least, the melody line has already been suggested by preexisting harmony in some form. Others might also suggest that this notion was accommodated anyway by Russell's vertical-horizontal tonal gravity distinction between melody and harmony.

In *Jazzforschung—Jazz Research*, the journal of the Graz Institute of Jazz, Alfona Michael Dauer provides a very thorough analysis of Russell's work that is satisfyingly free of jargon.[59] And in 2002, in *Contemporary Music Review*, Peter Burt provides a similarly intriguing assessment of Russell's influence on the Japanese composer Toru Takemitsu. Noting the latter's frequent references to his reading in 1961 of the 1959 edition of the Concept, Burt explores in detail, albeit tentatively, similarities in their harmonic practices.[60] Both articles are broadly supportive of Russell's ideas. However, André Jeanquartier's article in *Jazzforschung* offers perhaps the most thorough critique of Russell's theories. The points he makes are beyond the scope of this book (or my own grasp of musical theory). Briefly, however, Jeanquartier argues that Russell fails to prove the dominance of the Lydian scale or its value against the major scale. Its only advantage, according to the author, might be within the realms of modal jazz. In his opinion, it is otherwise too static and undynamic as a means of accommodating most modern music. He adds that there are significant deficiencies in the formation of Russell's scales, which he says are unbalanced, inconsistent, and arbitrary in their use of non-Lydian scales. Most significantly, Jeanquartier argues that there is nothing in Russell's system or in his scales that could not have been produced within the traditional system of major-minor tonality.[61] It is an article of depth and substance that is well researched and argued. This is the article to which Russell's students and pupils must apply themselves, for its conclusions are, if unanswered, quite damning.

It is, however, not without flaw, and some brief points may be made here. First, within any system, musical or otherwise, one's starting point is important. How the universe will look and be experienced is greatly affected by things like perspective and trajectory. All systems are accommodations with reality. It seems unfair to criticize Russell in this regard without exploring the universe from his point of origin. If Russell's system does not sustain its own logic, then so be it, but it should also be evaluated on its own terms. That said, in claiming that his ideas take in the whole world of equally tempered music, Russell clearly invites challenges such as those of Jeanquartier. A second issue relates to whether Russell's system can better accommodate ethnic, non-Western music. This is not a simple point. To claim that Western musical ideas can best or even adequately account for music as diverse as that of Islam, the blues, gamelan, and so forth, smacks of ethnocentrism. Third, there is the issue of what kind of theory the Lydian Concept actually is. Russell's claims for it aside, it sits most easily within the terms of "practice theory," "praxis," or "theory for use," that is, theory that guides and informs action. In these terms, Russell's ideas also need to be judged in terms of their utility. In fairness, Jeanquartier does credit Russell in terms of the way his ideas have opened up our understanding of the relationship between chords and scales, and also credits him with influencing the development of both modal and free jazz. In the latter respects, some of his attributions are questionable. For example, he cites Ornette Coleman, Bill Evans, and Lee Konitz as musicians influenced by Russell, yet, as has been seen, this is an oversimplification. This point clearly does not undermine Jeanquartier's academic argument, though it raises issues about the quality of his scholarship. Either way, his article deserves to be read by proponents and opponents of Russell's ideas.

In a 2004 interview, Russell illustrated his own perception of the relationship between his ideas and science. "For one thing, it tells me that gravity does exist in music and is the groundwork of music. It's based on gravity. All the sounds you hear come from gravity." He continued, "My intention is to show that gravity is the basis of harmony and music and that it is a science therefore."[62]

As far as I have discovered, no critic has taken issue with Russell's claim for an objective scientific basis for the Concept. His argument is that gravity affects all things in the universe, and music and tones must therefore be similarly subject to the laws of physics. This is the meaning of his term "tonal gravity." Perhaps other critics see this claim as an irrelevance or outside their purview. In fact, it is the weakest aspect of the theory. Tones, as sounds, are not affected by gravity at all. Two tones emitted from the same source and location but at different high and low frequencies may sound different yet occupy the same area in space. Water or air or other media, which allow sound to cross distances, are affected by gravity, and the speed of sound is therefore not a constant. However, sound itself remains entirely unaffected by the force of gravity. In space, no one can hear you scream. As a place without gravity, there is no medium for the vibrations to compress and thereby to create audible noise. Sadly for the Lydian Chromatic Concept of Tonal Organization, the term "tonal gravity" is either an oxymoron or a misnomer.[63] At best, it works as convenient metaphor.

For obvious reasons, Russell sought to locate his ideas within the field of physics. First, the study of sound and acoustics clearly comes within the scope of that discipline, and Russell, albeit as an autodidact, would have been aware of that, not least through his contact with his friend George Endrey. Secondly, physics was, during that period, the dominant field of scientific research. Developments in neuropsychology, which may well be of more relevance to Russell's theories, did not begin to emerge until the 1990s.

And yet, if Russell's understanding of "tonal gravity" as a physical fact is flawed, there is a sense in which such a notion can be sustained as a theoretical concept with a certain explanatory power. This in turn has parallels in various academic disciplines. We might call such conceptual approaches "theory as metaphor."

In the field of ecology and biology, the independent scientist James Lovelock has put forward the highly influential Gaia hypothesis, which posits that the planet is a "living organism." While many of his followers accept this as a literal truth, Lovelock uses this term in a more restricted scientific sense of the "earth as a self-regulating system." The idea is both theory and metaphor. Marx's theory of "dialectical materialism," of class conflict providing the dynamic in human economic and social evolution, has survived numerous adaptations by later theorists. It too has descriptive and explanatory power without necessarily achieving the levels of proof required in the physical sciences. In the field of psychology, Freud's view of the personality as comprising three parts (id, ego, and superego) that interact in a dynamic fashion according to deep-seated drives and motivations, would also fit our definition of "metaphorical theory." Jung's notion of the "collective unconscious" is a further example from psychology. Considered in this light, perhaps we should not be so quick to dismiss the notion of "tonal gravity" out of hand. However, proponents of the Concept do need to engage in this debate at this kind of theoretical level; otherwise, "tonal gravity" could be unfairly marginalized as an arcane or even occult notion.

At the same time, in relation to Russell's "scientific" claims for his theory, certain more favorable comments can be made in terms of the approach he adopted and applied to the development of the Lydian Concept. For example, Russell has answered the oft-asked question "Why the 'C' Lydian scale?" on many occasions. He has explained that he was intrigued that musicians like Parker and Gillespie often ended their solos on the raised fourth rather than resolve to the tonic.[64] His description of his methodology given, for example, to Ian Carr, Vivien Perlis, and Ben Young, could sound like a crude process of trial and error, with the outcome the result of serendipity. To me, it appears to be a quite scientific procedure of empirical research based on inductive reasoning. This method moves from specific observations and measures, begins to detect patterns and regularities, formulates some tentative hypotheses that can be explored, and finally ends up developing some general conclusions or theories. Of course, within the context of "pure" scientific research, researchers record each experiment, observation, and measurement. Clearly, Russell did not do so. Nevertheless, his research is broadly "replicable," given that he has described how he explored notes, scales, and chords in terms of their relationships. The actual practice involved playing notes against scales or chords against scales. In addition, he was focusing on listening to the overtone series. Finally, as Russell has noted, his approach was not to accept his "discovery" at face value; rather, he consciously sought to test it. The process, known in the philosophy of science as "falsification,"[65] seems very apt in this context. Recognizing that any new theory would immediately meet resistance, Russell told Kirk Silsbee in an interview for *Cadence*, "So I became its chief challenger and tried to destroy the logic of it and what stood up, I then built on that. In fact, I think that's the only way theories should really be tested. I don't think a theory should be released or let go of or enforced on other people until it's been through that process."[66] It should be clear from the above that I certainly do not dismiss entirely Russell's "scientific" claims for his ideas.

Some critics, musicians, and students may wonder whether these issues need amount to a hill of beans as far as they are concerned. To them, we would suggest that this shortcoming of the Concept is actually quite destructive for its claims of universality, demonstrability, and objectivity, prerequisites for the status of law. If it is not law, then it is opinion—or, better, hypothesis. If it is the latter, then the question arises whether its propositions are verifiable or if it is even framed in terms that allow its propositions to be tested by means that are themselves replicable. This is the burden of proof science requires of its theories and laws, and its rigorous approach to evidential claims indeed underpins theorizing within the social sciences and arts.[67] That is why this point is so critical.

The Concept, certainly according to George Russell himself and to some of its advocates, seems to seek to say something about the natural order of things. Among the difficulties Russell's theory presents is that it claims both "scientific" status as law, but also that it draws on metaphysics and mysticism as sources of inspiration, as explanation, and as revealed truth. For unbelievers, these are clearly religious, ethical, and philosophical concerns rather than scientific or other objective issues for debate. This is clear from the references to P. D. Ouspensky and G. I. Gurdjieff[68] and to comments that appear at various points in the text of his book. For example, Russell writes, "Duality and its side effects, they [philosophers such as Gurdjieff] claim are the chief causes of suffering on Earth."[69] And even more so, in the last paragraph of the 2001 edition, "I hope this knowledge will light your way, inspiring and empowering your essence to express its truest, most unique self—not only musically, but also daring to venture into music's womb, that unseen philo-spiritual world which is music's seminal source and foundation connecting it—and you—to the stars."[70]

Expressed in this way, it appears a highly ecological theory that relates the principles of music and its fundamental building blocks back to nature and the fabric of the universe, from musical relationships to human relations and to our relationship to the world. However, here it has moved into the realm of belief system, requiring faith as its touchstone. It might be fine and even helpful to think in these terms about music. It is surely better that we, as a species, put our trust in our connectedness with all living things and all matter in our universe than continue to exploit our world and space for our own greedy, rapacious ends. However, such ideas are spiritual and/or political, not scientific. Ingrid Monson has discussed Russell's spiritual beliefs and in particular how they derive from Gurdjieff's ideas about nature, gravity, harmony, and unity. As she points out, Russell's theory is "essentialist" in its most exact meaning.[71] That is, it is about essence and the individual's goal of enlightenment in allowing full expression of his or her essence. It does not matter that Russell did not discover Gurdjieff until he was living in Scandinavia, by which time *The Lydian Chromatic Concept of Tonal Organization* had reached its second edition. Like many "seekers" after universal truths, when he found Gurdjieff it was for him the realization of a search, and 'The Work' made sense in terms of his own existing artistic and spiritual goals.

As he wrote to me on the subject,

> I would avoid Americans in Europe when I could, but one day I met an American musician who I had seen around Stockholm. I tried to ignore him, but he approached me, and said, "Man, you have to read this book," and shoved it between my arm and sensing my coldness, said, "It's about all and everything in life," while walking away. I never saw him again, and I don't recall his name, but I hope we meet again on this or whatever planet, so I can tell him how

grateful I am that he introduced me to Gurdjieff. He's always there when you need him; he always has answers for whatever situation or puzzlement you find yourself in. His is the only philosophy/practice, which has ever seemed to me to be objective. I have read and reread his books, as well as the books of Dr. Maurice Nicoll, whom I believe worked with Jung until he "discovered" Gurdjieff. In any event, whatever road leads to a psychological pathway for one's life is the right one.[72]

Expressed in this way, George Russell is functioning intellectually according to a different definition of science, that of "science as knowledge." In the terms that he is concerned with, that knowledge base can include Platonic, Pythagorean, Buddhist, Hindu, mystical-Christian, or indeed any philosophical belief system. The test of those beliefs owes little to Western "scientific" models of proof, but lies instead in the existential and experiential. It is necessary to understand this to fully appreciate George Russell's philosophical position rather than simply dismiss it out of hand.

Ingrid Monson adopts, in her discussion of Russell and Coltrane's spiritual beliefs and their relationship to the music they created, a systemic and therefore dynamic model of causality.[73] Though with such a model it is rarely possible to be too specific about the influence or importance of different variables or factors within the system, it is possible to map very effectively relationships within the system. It also allows different theories to be applied, depending on the level of the system being analyzed. For example, intrapsychic aspects may require a different theoretical approach from those existing at the level of group interaction. In addition, it is possible to draw on competing theoretical explanations and allow these to coexist in a state of tension without resolution, thereby offering a richer and deeper appreciation of the issues involved. Finally, a systems approach to causality addresses cause and the creation of meaning in a nonlinear, non-time-bound fashion. "Causes" are not necessarily fixed insofar as they may be constantly reevaluated and understood according to changes in thinking. Meaning is something that human beings endow upon events.

Nevertheless, in claiming "scientific" validity for his theory, he also opens it to legitimate challenge or analysis from the perspective of modern scientific thinking. In that regard, the theory is severely lacking. At the same time, and in light of Monson's highly articulate evaluation of Russell's and Coltrane's spiritual grounding for their musical ideas and their application in music, those ideas and their operation to different, nonscientific standards of proof should remain an additional consideration in any analysis.

Two questions arise, however. The first of these is whether or not George Russell's theories can potentially be grounded in science. Its corollary is then "How?" And second, whether without such theoretical grounding the Lydian Chromatic Concept has any value in its distinction between three different levels of "tonal gravity"—vertical tonal gravity, horizontal tonal gravity, and super-vertical tonal gravity.

The answers to the first question may well lie not in physics but in neurology and the research that has advanced so rapidly in the 1990s and early twenty-first century. The branch of psychiatry known as neuropsychiatry has made huge strides in understanding how the brain processes and integrates sensory information to such an extent that the distinction between the "brain" of science and the "mind" of philosophy has become increasingly blurred.[74]

Research into the brain and what we loosely call "the mind," has advanced to a point where neuroscientists are able to identify which sections of the brain are associated with which functions, how thought and feelings interact, how moral decisions and aesthetic judgments might be made, and how and why art, music, and belief form part of our world. It has become not only concerned with the stuff that was outside the parameters of science but rather has taken that as its most important subject matter.

As the pianist and academic Lady Natasha Spender has noted,

> Music has existed in all human cultures, as far as we know, and all scale systems are based on the octave, which suggests a neurological factor. This suggestion is supported by the fact that animals conditioned to respond to a certain pitch will do so almost equally to its octave, whereas the intervening notes will evoke either much less response or none at all.[75]

Spender goes on to point out how a neuropsychological theory might explain how listeners make sense of music. The model she seems to prefer is necessarily complex and dynamic. How else would it be possible to explain both the octave of "Western" equal temperament and the Indian octave of twenty-two semitones or different individual responses to music? The approach Spender explores acknowledges three dominant approaches—music as a set of arbitrary conventions (based on David Hilbert's view of mathematics), as a Platonic description of an existing reality, and as a property of the mind (based on Noam Chomsky's theory of language). Of these, George Russell's view is obviously closest to the second. Their potential interrelationship could be briefly described in the following way. Music appears to be an objective and natural phenomenon produced by human beings to satisfy physiological and psychological need. Key elements of its form—rhythm, melody, harmony, and tones—occur across epochs and cultures to the extent that its structure and elements appear to be both ingrained and culturally determined. In the latter respect, its more constant elements may be neurologically determined. The capacity to process the sensory information contained in music is dependant on human biology—the sensitivity of the ear and its ability to transfer information to the brain, and the capacity of the body to respond physiologically to that information—and on neurology—the brain's capacity to organize and process that sensory information and to initiate certain responses through the release of certain adrenalines. In turn, the capacity of the brain to process sensory information necessitates at least two elements. First, hardwiring in the brain similar to that suggested by Chomsky for language and grammar; second, a vocabulary of conventions.[76]

In many ways, neuropsychology has moved on considerably since Spender wrote the article, and her lengthy discussion of aesthetics would now be encompassed by that discipline. The neurologist V. S. Ramachandran points out that while culture plays an enormous role in the development of different artistic styles, art is not entirely arbitrary or idiosyncratic.

> The solution to the problem of aesthetics, I believe, lies in a more thorough understanding of the connections between the thirty visual centres in your brain and the emotional limbic structures. And once we have achieved a clear understanding of these connections, we will be closer to bridging the huge gulf that separates C. P. Snow's two cultures—science on the one hand and arts, philosophy and humanities on the other.[77]

Ramachandran goes on to suggest that "human artists through trial and error, through intuition, through genius have discovered the figural primitives of our perceptual grammar." Using the example of synesthesia, he explains how this capacity is located in the brain and indeed that this condition runs in families and is more heavily represented among artists, poets, novelists, and musicians. The common feature here seems to be the capacity to make creative, counterintuitive leaps in the form of metaphor.[78] This does not mean that all artists have this condition. Rather, it serves as an example of the extent of our knowledge of the brain and how far we are now able to locate such traits in specific areas of neural function. It is surely within this field that the scientific test for George Russell's theory must lie, and not in physics, as he proposes.

Readers may well be aware that despite critiquing Russell's theory in terms of its scientific claims, we have certainly not lost sight of those claims and ideas. We have used words like "nonlinear," "non-time-bound," "tension," "nonresolution," and "dynamic," which Russell could and indeed does use in relation to the Concept. Additionally, we are acknowledging and accounting for what Russell understands as the spiritual dimension of the Lydian Concept.

Scientists, including psychologists, are trying to understand as material events things that would previously have been consigned to the realms of fringe religion and New Age philosophy. One such area concerns the use of music as a source of healing. In *The Healing Drum—African Wisdom Teaching*, Yaya Diallo and Mitchell Hall describe the involvement of musicians of the Minianka in Mali in healing psychological disturbance.[79] Based on knowledge, observation, and insight, the musician selects particular rituals involving dance and specifically chosen rhythms appropriate to the healing process. With a patient in severe distress or in a manic state, the high slap tones of the *djembe* drum might be avoided, and slower, more calming rhythms deployed. By contrast, with patients who are depressed or withdrawn, more enervating rhythms and tones would be used. The key is that the ritual, music, rhythms, and any additional medicines should be specifically selected for that patient and his or her illness.

To the hardened rationalist this may sound like "mumbo jumbo," itself a derogatory term employed by colonialists wishing to impose their own religious ideas on poor benighted savages. Surprisingly, it does seem to work. As Diallo and Hall suggest,

> How music can facilitate psychological therapy is perhaps ultimately a mystery. Since psychologically disturbed individuals are rhythmically disturbed as well, the use of the healing drum for sustained periods of time at a steady rhythm that suits the patient is a potent remedy or body-mind healing. Through the ears, the entire nervous system is affected. Sound energy is transformed into biochemical nervous energy. As the brain waves and rhythms of internal organs are stabilised, the person functions as a more synchronous whole. What is healing if not making whole?[80]

A quick comparison with the use of medication is instructive. The drug Stemetil, or prochlorperazine, is used in high doses to treat both schizophrenia and acute mania and in lower doses to treat nausea, vomiting, morning sickness, and severe vertigo or Ménière's disease, which is a disorder of the inner ear. The interesting thing to consider is: What do such different conditions have in common that they might be effectively treated by the same drug? In fact, all these conditions share a number of similar problems. One of these is the overproduction of dopamine. A second is that the patients' capacity to process and integrate sensory information has become affected by their respective conditions. The third—and this is in part intended as a facetious comment—is that they have all become "unbalanced." The most obvious therapeutic effect Diallo and Hall are describing is that this drum-ming helps restore the individual's capacity to integrate sensory information or it helps restore "balance."

Occupational therapist and Ph.D. student Carla van Heerden has been researching the relationship of rhythms that are unique to individuals in terms of how these may affect their ability to process and integrate sensory infor-mation. Her research relates to the work of child psychiatrist John Bowlby on attachment and separation and also that of Allan Schore.[81] Part of van Heerden's hypothesis concerns rhythms of the mother's heartbeat that the fe-tus will have experienced and internalized at some primal level. In that sense, she is examining unique, rather than more general, species-wide questions. Additionally, her research goal is to address issues regarding how therapeutic interventions may redress or compensate for sensory processing deficits. At the same time, her work is part of a continuum of research that connects hu-man beings, sounds, and rhythms in terms of biology and neurology.

> The issue is that some individuals lack the capacity to respond appropriately to certain situations or the tasks that arise in them. It appears that what has failed in their case is not in the area of behavioral learning but is something much more fundamental. It is, and my research focuses upon, a question of how they are able or unable to process sensory information effectively. It seems that the neural pathways that would allow them to do this have not been wired properly.[82]

How this relates to the questions raised by the Concept is quite simple. It indicates that it is possible to help individuals overcome this sensory process-ing deficit and even enable the creation of new neural pathways in the brain. Doing this may even involve something as simple and fundamental as one the most basic of sounds: the drumbeat that replicates the human heart. But, as van Heerden points out, the key is that the rhythm is not the same for every individual, probably because the rhythm the fetus hears in the womb differs. When the individual finds that rhythm on the drums and learns to replicate it in "its purest form," it becomes possible to promote more effective sensory integration and more effective adaptive responses.

Van Heerden also has an interesting point to make about Russell's three levels of tonal gravity.

Putting that in my theoretical framework would read a bit like this. At the level of vertical tonal gravity the musicians are working at the "immediate" level in terms of the sensory information they are processing. At what you describe as horizontal tonal gravity, they are drawing extensively on their sensory memory. Finally, at the level of supra-vertical tonal gravity they are engaging in a highly complex sensory integration of the whole.[83]

It is also worth noting the work of Allan Schore in the area of what he calls "prosody." His concern in this respect is with the therapeutic effects of tone of voice, which he in turn relates to the infant's earliest experiences of the human voice—namely, or at least most commonly, that of the mother or primary caregiver.[84]

Several points arise from this. First, it emphasizes the importance for the Concept of relating its findings in music to the developing science of neuropsychology. Second, Russell's description of the three levels of "tonal gravity" may well have its parallels or even roots in the ways human beings process sensory information. In this regard, his ideas may make sense beyond the realm of metaphor. Third, Russell's decision to block through his estate any future editions of *The Lydian Chromatic Concept of Tonal Organization* becomes all the more unfortunate. The need for more research both scientific and historic implies that its future must lie in the hands of its most gifted students.

We are finally ready to evaluate Russell's contribution to jazz and music in general. The Concept presents teachers and students with a map of chords and their modes that allows improvisers and composers to explore complex harmonic, melodic, and chromatic ideas while remaining aware of their place in that musical universe. Terms such as "ingoing," "semi-ingoing," "semi-outgoing," and "outgoing" make as much sense as those such as "free," "in," or "out," and are just as accurate as those like "atonality." By relating even the most "outgoing" sounds to an original tonal center or centers, these terms have greater potential usefulness in helping students of music to explore the wider possibilities of tone and color. The issue of "new" terminology, in the broader sense, and charges of obfuscation really hang on how far Russell is genuinely saying something "new." On this, the jury is perhaps still out.

In terms of his influence on jazz as a theorist, Russell is the only musician-composer to have produced a written and original body of ideas. Those ideas have had an impact on the development of modal jazz and on musicians from Miles Davis, John Coltrane, Eric Dolphy, Art Farmer, Dave Baker, Oliver Nelson, Steve Swallow, and others. Subsequent generations carry that influence forward in the continuing and extensive use of modes in the music. But Russell's importance continues through younger players and composers—musicians such as Randy and Michael Brecker, John Medeski, Don Byron, Courtney Pine, Ricky Ford, Jan Garbarek, Terje Rypdal, Jon Christensen, Satoko Fujii, and Marty Ehrlich. His influence is seen in jazz-rock and in what seems to be a growing body of Third Stream music from America, Europe, and Asia. In both these respects, he is not the only force to be recognized. Gil Evans, Gunther Schuller, and even Duke Ellington are significant in the latter regard, while Joe Zawinul, Wayne Shorter, John McLaughlin, Gary Burton, Mike Gibbs, and Herbie Hancock are truly seminal figures in terms of jazz-rock—though even here, Russell's influence, directly or indirectly, on these musicians can be traced.

It may be that Russell as both theorist and composer will become more significant as jazz composers (and some, such as Mark Anthony Turnage and Gavin Bryars, from classical music) continue to develop a *lingua franca* that extends the combination of improvisation and composition in the music. The signs are there in the work of Satoko Fujii, Jon Balke, Colin Towns, Christian Wallumrod, Tim Berne, mathias rüegg, and Keith Tippett that extended form is now the territory for jazz to conquer. In this case, George Russell can surely look down from his pinnacle, smile, and reflect on his own pioneering days. Works from *All About Rosie* and *Jazz in the Space Age*, through *Electronic Sonata for Souls Loved by Nature* and *Living Time*, to *The African Game*, *Six Aesthetic Gravities*, *Uncommon Ground*, and *It's About Time* provide a marvelous, rich legacy and library for younger explorers.

Anyone who remains to be convinced should simply listen to Russell's sixties sextet records. Whether it is *Jazz Workshop*, *Ezz-Thetics*, or *Stratusphunk*, this is as good as small-group jazz gets. What more is there to say? George Russell has been a jazz composer, Third Stream composer, theorist, drummer, pianist, bandleader, teacher, innovator, and pioneer. Many of the best and brightest of several generations of jazz musicians owe him a greater or lesser debt. Let's hope that wherever he goes next, he takes the sounds of that last standing ovation from the Barbican with him, ringing in his ears.

Notes

1. The quotes merely serve to emphasize George Russell's way of describing the beginnings of the Lydian Concept in his work.

2. See F. J. Sulloway, *Freud—Biologist of the Mind* (Bungay, Suffolk: Fontana, 1980).

3. John Maynard Keynes was placed second of the ten who were accepted that year. The top person had first choice of which department to enter and chose to enter

the treasury (which Keynes would have done had he come top). Keynes, with the next choice, entered the India Office. Keynes was very unhappy when he received detailed results of the examination. He came top in logic, psychology, and the essay, while his worst subjects were mathematics and economics. He expressed disbelief at both the mathematics and economics results, and commented, probably accurately, that he knew more about economics than his examiners. This tale is, nevertheless, the stuff that myths are made of. I have heard other versions of this story, including one where Keynes only achieved a third-class degree at Cambridge. See J. J. O'Connor and E. F. Robertson, "John Maynard Keynes," JOC/EFR, October 2003, www-history.mcs.st-andrews.ac.uk/Mathematicians/Keynes.html.

4. Karl Marx, *The Eighteenth Brumaire of Louis Bonaparte* (Moscow: Progress, 1972).

5. Interview with Andy Wassermann, June 2004.

6. Reed Gratz, "An Historical Perspective of the Lydian and Major Scales," appendix 1 in *Lydian Chromatic Concept of Tonal Organization*, by George Russell (Brookline, MA: Concept, 2001).

7. D. J. Grout and C. V. Palisca, *A History of Western Music* (New York: Norton, 1996).

8. However much we might separate these from musical theory, such notions were broadly incomprehensible to the ancient Greeks. See ibid., chap. 1.

9. George Russell, *Lydian Chromatic Concept of Tonal Organization* (Brookline, MA: Concept, 2001), p. 234.

10. Ibid.

11. See, for example, Greg Malcangi, quoted at http://www.recording.org/ftopict-8561.html, August 9, 2001 6:51 a.m.: "Arguably one of the most interesting chords is the Tri-Tone. A chord made up of three notes with a minor third interval between each. In the 1530's (if I remember correctly) there was a big meeting of the catholic church called the Council of Trent. Because of its nastiness, the tri-tone was known at that time as the 'Devil's Chord.' The Council of Trent outlawed the tri-tone. Any composer using a tri-tone in their music would be excommunicated, which at that time almost certainly meant death. I don't know if this law was ever repealed or whether it is just ignored. So a warning to any Christian composers out there, only use a tri-tone if you're absolutely sure that none of your family or friends are likely to stone you to death! By this I mean the use of small rocks, not an overdose of grass!"

12. See J. Waterworth, ed./trans., *The Canons and Decrees of the Sacred and Œcumenical Council of Trent* (London: Dolman, 1848).

13. George Russell, *Lydian Chromatic Concept of Tonal Organization* (Brookline, MA: Concept 2001), p. 227.

14. Grout and Palisca, *A History of Western Music*, pp. 10–13, 56.

15. J. Jeans, *Science and Music* (Cambridge: MacMillan, 1937).

16. D. J. Grout, *A History of Western Music* (London: Dent, 1973).

17. G. H. Ranade, *Hindusthani Music: An Outline of Its Physics and Aesthetics* (Poona, India: Ranade, 1951).

18. George Russell, *Lydian Chromatic Concept of Tonal Organization*, pp. 226–28.

19. Ibid., p. 229–30. Quote taken from J. Cott, *Stockhausen: Conversations with the Composer* (New York: Simon & Schuster, 1973).

20. Darius Brubeck, "1959: The Beginning of Beyond," in *The Cambridge Companion to Jazz*, ed. M. Cooke and D. Horn (Cambridge: Cambridge University Press, 2002).

21. George Russell, *Lydian Chromatic Concept of Tonal Organization*, pp.152–54, 205–208. See also H. Rosenwald, "The Chorale—Artistic Weapon of the Lutheran Church," in *The Musical Heritage of the Lutheran Church, Volume I* (Valparaiso, IN: Valparaiso University, 1945).

22. Interview with Andy Wassermann.

23. Balint Vazsonyi, quoted in *Washington Times*, August 22, 2000.

24. Interview with Andy Sheppard, March 2003.

25. Ibid.

26. Stephanie Stein Crease, *Gil Evans—Out of the Cool* (Chicago: A Cappella, 2002), pp. 279–80.

27. Interview with Graham Collier, November 2004.

28. Stein Crease, *Out of the Cool*, pp. 17 and 180.

29. See Maurice Nicoll, *Living Time and the Integration of Life* (Bristol, UK: Stuart, 1952).

30. See K. Anderson, sleeve notes to Scriabin Piano Concerto, Prometheus, The Poem of Fire, Naxos CD 8.550818. See also Grout and Palisca, *A History of Western Music*, p. 672. Incidentally, Shostakovich acknowledges Scriabin (and Chopin) in his use of the cycle of fifths in his 24 Preludes and Fugues Op. 87. The ideas contained in certain of these pieces actually sound more "jazz-like" than those expressed in the composer's Jazz Suite Nos. 1 & 2.

31. Austin Clarkson, ed., *On the Music of Stefan Wolpe—Essays and Recollections* (New York: Pendragon, 2003).

32. W. Mellers, *Man & His Music—Romanticism and the Twentieth Century* (London: Barrie & Rockliff, 1969), p. 182. It is also worth noting that Schoenberg preferred the term "non-tonality" to that of "atonality," which perhaps suggests a greater correspondence between his ideas and Russell's. See K. Haas, *Inside Music* (New York: Anchor, 1991), p. 347.

33. George Russell, "Where Do We Go From Here?" in *The Jazz Word*, ed. D. Cerulli, B. Korall, and M. Nasatir (London: Ballantine, 1960), p. 190.

34. Ibid.

35. George Russell, sleeve notes to *Electronic Sonata for Souls Loved by Nature—1968*. Soulnote 121034–2.

36. George Russell, *Lydian Chromatic Concept of Tonal Organization*, p. 39.

37. Comparison of the mind to a blank writing tablet occurs in Aristotle's *De anima* (fourth century BC), as well as the Stoics. During the Enlightenment, a new and revolutionary emphasis on the tabula rasa occurred, when the English empiricist John Locke, in his *Essay Concerning Human Understanding* (1690), argued for the

mind's initial resemblance to "white paper, void of all characters," with "all the materials of reason and knowledge" derived from experience. Though Locke himself fell back on "reflection" as a power of the mind for the exploitation of the given "materials," his championship of the tabula rasa signaled even more radical positions by later philosophers.

38. With regard to Rousseau, see *Discours sur l'origine de l'inegalité (Discourse on the Origin of Inequality*, 1755). Rousseau argues that natural man is good and then traces the successive stages by which man has descended from primitive innocence to corrupt sophistication. The political anarchist and philosopher William Godwin was influenced by Rousseau, and Godwin in turn influenced the Romantic poets such as Wordsworth, Byron, Shelley, and Coleridge. See, for example, Wordsworth's poem "The Prelude." It's probably to the Romantic movement that we owe the belief that schooling and education undermine rather than foster naturalness and authenticity. Alternatively, we may concur with Doris Day when she says to Clark Gable's hard-bitten newshound in the film *Teacher's Pet* (1958), "Education teaches us how to spell experience."

39. Interview with Howard Riley, December 2005.

40. Interview with Randy Brecker, August 2006.

41. Interview with Wassermann.

42. Interview with George Russell, June 2004.

43. Interview with George Russell, March 2003.

44. Interview with Ben Schwendener, October 2003.

45. Ibid.

46. Interview with Marc Rossi, October 2004.

47. Interview with Schwendener.

48. Interview with Jack Reilly, September 2005.

49. Brubeck, "The Beginning of Beyond," pp. 190–91.

50. Ibid., p. 191.

51. Ibid., p. 192.

52. George Russell, in ibid., p. 192.

53. Brubeck, "The Beginning of Beyond," p. 193.

54. Ibid.

55. Barry Kernfeld, in ibid., p. 193.

56. M. Westbrook, "The Credibility Gap," *Jazz on CD* 17 (August 1995): 16–18. Also interview with Westbrook March 1996; P. Thomas, "The Myth of Jazz, Parts I & II," *Avant* (Winter 1998): 32–33 and (Spring 1999): 32–33.

57. E-mail interview with Chuck Israels, August 2004.

58. Mark S. Haywood, "The Harmonic Role of Melody in Vertical and Horizontal Jazz," *Annual Review of Jazz Studies* 5 (1991).

59. Alfona M. Dauer, "Das Lydisch-Chromatische Tonsystem Von George Russell Und Seine Anwendung," *Jazzforschung/Jazz Research* 14 (1982).

60. Peter Burt, "Takemitsu and the Lydian Chromatic Concept of George Russell," *Contemporary Music Review* 21, no. 4 (2002).

61. André Jeanquartier, "Kritische Anmerkungen Zum 'Lydian Chromatic Concept,'" *Jazzforschung/Jazz Research* 16 (1984).

62. Interview with G. Russell, June 2004.

63. M. Nelkon, *Principles of Physics* (Harlow, UK: Longman, 1981), chaps. 22 and 23; I. S. Grant and W. R. Phillips, *The Elements of Physics* (Oxford: Oxford University Press, 2001), pp. 245–72. The difference between "sound" waves and electromagnetic wave phenomenon, such as light and radio waves, relates to mass. Sound has no mass upon which gravity can act. This is why sound requires another medium, such as air or water, through which it can travel. Unlike light waves, which consist of tiny particles called photons, sound cannot travel where there is no atmosphere. By contrast, light and radio waves can travel through space. See also J. Gribbin, *Get a Grip on the New Physics* (London: Weidenfeld & Nicholson, 1999), pp. 82–90.

64. See, for example, Bob Blumenthal, "George Russell—Stratus Seeker," *Down Beat*, October 1983; P. Wilson, "George Russell's Constant Quest," *Down Beat*, March 17, 1972; O. Jones, "George Russell—A New Theory for Jazz," *Black Perspective in Music*, Winter 1973.

65. See, for example, R. G. A. Dolby, "The Sociology of Knowledge in Natural Science," *Science Studies* 1, no. 1 (1971); and K. Popper, *The Logic of Scientific Discovery* (New York: Basic, 1959).

66. Kirk Silsbee, "George Russell," *Cadence*, June 1996.

67. Dolby, "The Sociology of Knowledge in Natural Science"; Popper, "The Logic of Scientific Discovery."

68. George Russell, *Lydian Chromatic Concept of Tonal Organization*, pp. 213–14.

69. Ibid., pp. 214, 236.

70. Ibid., p. 237.

71. Ingrid Monson, "Oh Freedom—George Russell, John Coltrane and Modal Jazz," in *In the Course of Performance*, ed. B. Nettle and M. Russell (London: University of Chicago Press, 1998).

72. George Russell, e-mail to the author, April 12, 2005.

73. Monson, "Oh Freedom."

74. V. S. Ramachandran, Reith Lectures, 2003, BBC Radio 4; A. R. Damasio, *Descartes' Error—Emotion, Reason and the Human Brain* (New York: Quill, 2000).

75. Natasha Spender, "Psychology of Music," in *Oxford Companion to the Mind*, ed. R. L. Gregory (Oxford: Oxford University Press, 1987), p. 499. See also A. Storr, *Music & the Mind* (London: HarperCollins, 1992); chapter 2—"Music, Brain and Body"—is of particular interest and relevance. Finally, Daniel J. Levitin's *This Is Your Brain on Music* (New York: Penguin, 2006) offers a recent and enthusiastic contribution to the issue. See pages 99–107 and his final chapter—"My Favorite Things"—for some valuable insights and intriguing speculations.

76. Spender, "Psychology of Music."

77. Ramachandran, Reith Lectures, lecture 3: "The Artful Brain."

78. Ibid.

79. Yaya Diallo and Mitchell Hall, *The Healing Drum—African Wisdom Teachings* (Rochester, VT: Destiny Books, 1989), p. 161.

80. Ibid.

81. John Bowlby, *Attachment and Loss*, vols. 1–3 (London: Pimlico, 1997); with regard to Allan Schore, see, for example, Allan N. Schore, *Affect Dysregulation and Disorders of the Self* (New York: Norton, 2003).

82. Interview with Carla van Heerden, September 2005.

83. Ibid.

84. See Allan N. Schore, "A Neuropsychoanalytic Viewpoint—Commentary on Paper by Steven H. Knoblauch," *Psychoanalytic Dialogues* 15, no. 6 (2005): 829–54.

~

Postscript

George Russell and the Living Time Orchestra had one more outing. On September 20, 2008, at the new Institute for Contemporary Art, Pat Hollenbeck and Alice Russell brought a version of the LTO together for what proved to be their last concert with Russell at the helm. Performing as part of the Ditson Concert Series, British guitarist Mike Walker and pianist Steve Lodder joined a number of Boston-based musicians to pay tribute to George Russell and celebrate his eighty-fifth birthday. Joining them on stage for "You Are My Sunshine" was, of course, the great Sheila Jordan.

Lloyd Schwartz reviewed the concerts for the *Boston Phoenix* on September 25 and said of the LTO's performance,

> The most roof-raising was the evening with the George Russell Living Time Orchestra. Perhaps the festival's most poignant moment came when the legendary master of avant-garde jazz, now 85, got up from his first row seat and, a bit shaky, began to dance and conduct extended sections of his 1983 through-composed *The African Game*, which alternates sounds of the jungle (lion-roaring trombones) with the cacophony of modern technology, and his love letter to his wife, Alice, the ballad *It's About Time*. Jazz singer Sheila Jordan wailing *You Are My Sunshine* created another sensation.[1]

I would have given a great deal to have been there.

Finally, after a long illness, on Monday, July 27, 2009, at around 9 p.m. Eastern Standard Time, with his wife Alice, his son Jock, and one or two close friends at his bedside at Mass General, George Russell left us. As always, the plaudits have followed. Some of these came from critics like John Fordham, who knew Russell's music well and who championed it. From others, the words rang less true and their eulogies mixed half-remembered anecdotes and all too hastily checked details. It often seems that we forget people when they are alive but fall over ourselves to acknowledge their passing.

Perhaps none of this truly matters because, as Alice Russell once said to me, "People can dismiss George's ideas all they want but the evidence is there in the music." Russell had a wonderfully rich, full life packed with great achievements and success. Having known the man, I think he will rest content with the legacy he leaves behind.

Note

1. Lloyd Schwartz, *Boston Phoenix*, September 25, 2008.

APPENDIX A

∿

Recordings

George Russell—1950s Recordings

The Jazz Workshop
"Ezz-Thetic," "Jack's Blues," "Ye Hypocrite, Ye Beelzebub," "Livingstone, I Presume"
Personnel—Art Farmer (t), Hal McKusick (as, f), Barry Galbraith (g), Bill Evans (p), Milt Hinton (b), Joe Harris (d)
Rec. March 31, 1956.
"Round Johnny Rondo," "Night Sound," "Concerto for Billy the Kid," "Concerto for Billy the Kid (alt version)," "Witch Hunt"
Personnel—Art Farmer (t), Hal McKusick (as, f), Barry Galbraith (g), Bill Evans (p), Milt Hinton (b), Paul Motian (d)
Rec. October 17, 1956.
"Fellow Delegates," "Ballad of Hix Blewitt," "Ballad of Hix Blewitt (alt. version)," "Knights of the Steamtable," "The Sad Sergeant"
Personnel—Art Farmer (t), Hal McKusick (as, f), Barry Galbraith (g), Bill Evans (p), Teddy Kotick (b), Osie Johnson (d). (Russell plays boobams on "Fellow Delegates")
Rec. December 21, 1956.
Reissued as George Russell, *The Complete Bluebird Recordings*, Lonehill LHJ10177. Released originally RCA Victor LPM1372.

New York, N.Y.
"Manhattan" (Richard Rodgers–Lorenz Hart)
Personnel— Art Farmer, Doc Severinsen, Ernie Royal (t), Bob Brookmeyer, Frank Rehak, Tom Mitchell (tb), Hal McKusick (as), John Coltrane (ts), Sol Schlinger (bs), Barry Galbraith (g), Bill Evans (p), Milt Hinton (b), Charlie Persip (d), Jon Hendricks (narr)
Rec. September 12, 1958.
"A Helluva Town," "Manhattan-rico"
Personnel—Art Farmer, Ernie Royal, Joe Wilder (t), Bob Brookmeyer, Jimmy Cleveland, Tom Mitchell (tb), Phil Woods, Hal McKusick (as), Al Cohn (ts), Gene Allen (bs), Barry Galbraith (g), Bill Evans (p), George Duvivier (b), Max Roach (d—"A Helluva Town" only), Don La-mond (d—"Manhattan-rico" only), Al Epstein (bgo—"Manhattan-rico" only), George Russell (chromatic drum—"Manhattan-rico" only), Jon Hendricks (narr)
Rec. November 24, 1958.
"Big City Blues," "East Side Medley," "Autumn in New York" (Vernon Duke), "How About You" (Burton Lane–Ralph Freed)
Personnel—Art Farmer, Joe Wilder, Joe Ferrante (t), Bob Brookmeyer, Frank Rehak, Tom Mitchell (tb), Phil Woods, Hal McKusick (as), Benny Golson (ts), Sol Schlinger (bs), Barry Galbraith (g), Bill Evans (p), Milt Hinton (b), Charlie Persip (d), Jon Hendricks (narr)
Rec. March 25, 1959.
Released originally as Decca DL9216.

Jazz in the Space Age
"Chromatic Universe (pts 1–3)," "The Lydiot"
Personnel—Al Kiger, Ernie Royal (t), Dave Baker, Frank Rehak (tb), Jimmy Buffington (frhn), Walt Levinsky (as), Dave Young (ts), Sol Schlinger (bs), Barry Galbraith or Howard Collins (g), Bill Evans, Paul Bley (p), Milt Hinton (b), Don Lamond (d)
Rec. December 29, 1959.
"Waltz from Outer Space," "Dimensions"
Al Kiger, Ernie Royal, Marky Markowitz (t), Dave Baker, Frank Rehak, Bob Brookmeyer (tb), Hal McKusick (as), Dave Young (ts), Sol Schlinger (bs), Barry Galbraith (g), Bill Evans, Paul Bley (p), Milt Hinton (b), Charlie Persip (d)
Rec. January 27, 1960.
Released originally as Decca DL9219.

At the Five Spot

"Sippin' at Bells" (Miles Davis), "Dance Class" (Carla Bley), "Swingdom Come" (Russell), "121 Bank Street" (Dave Baker), "Beast Blues" (Carla Bley), "Moment's Notice" (John Coltrane)

Personnel—Al Kiger (t), Dave Baker (tb), Dave Young (ts), George Russell (p), Chuck Israel (b), Joe Hunt (d)

Rec. September 20, 1960.

Released originally as Decca DL9220.

Stratusphunk

"Stratusphunk" (Russell), "New Donna" (Russell), "Bent Eagle" (Carla Bley), "Kentucky Oysters" (Dave Baker), "Lambskins" (Russell), "Things New" (Russell)

Personnel—Al Kiger (t), Dave Baker (tb), Dave Young (ts), George Russell (p), Chuck Israel (b), Joe Hunt (d)

Rec. October 18, 1960.

Released originally as Riverside RLP-341.

George Russell Sextet in Kansas City

"War Gewesen" (Dave Baker), "Rhymes" (Carla Bley), "Lunacy" (Dave Baker), "Sandu" (Clifford Brown), "Tune Up" (Miles Davis), "Theme" (Russell)

"Mardi Gras," "Vamp" also recorded but unissued

Personnel—Don Ellis (t), Dave Baker (tb), Dave Young (ts), George Russell (p), Chuck Israel (b), Joe Hunt (d)

Rec. Feburary 23, 1961.

Released originally as Decca DL4183.

Ezz-Thetics

"Ezz-Thetic" (Russell), "Nardis" (Miles Davis), "Lydiot" (Russell), "Thoughts" (Russell), "Honesty" (Dave Baker), "'Round Midnight" (Monk-Williams)

Personnel—Don Ellis (t), Dave Baker (tb), Eric Dolphy (as, bcl), George Russell (p), Steve Swallow (b), Joe Hunt (d)

Rec. May 8, 1961.

Released originally as Riverside RLP-375.

The Stratus Seekers

"Pan-Daddy" (Russell), "The Stratus Seekers" (Russell), "The Stratus Seekers" (alt. version not issued), "Kige's Tune" (Al Kiger), "Blues in Orbit" (Russell), "A Lonely Place" (Russell), "Stereophrenic" (Dave Baker)

Personnel—Don Ellis (t), Dave Baker (tb), John Pierce (as), Paul Plummer (ts), George Russell (p), Steve Swallow (b), Joe Hunt (d)
Rec. January 31, 1962.
Released originally as Riverside RLP-412.

The Outer View
"Au Privave" (Charlie Parker), "Zig-Zag" (Carla Bley), "The Outer View" (Russell), "You Are My Sunshine" (Jimmie H. Davis), "D.C. Divertimento" (Russell)
Personnel—Don Ellis (t), Garnett Brown (tb), John Pierce (as), Paul Plummer (ts), George Russell (p), Steve Swallow (b), Pete LaRoca (d), Sheila Jordan (v—"You Are My Sunshine" only)
Rec. August 27, 1962.
Released originally as Riverside RLP-440.

Live in Bremen and Paris
"'Round Midnight" (Monk), "You Are My Sunshine" (Jimmy Burns), "D.C. Divertimento" (Russell), "Sippin' at Bells" (Davis)
Rec. Bremen, September 1964.
"The Outer View" (Russell), "Volupté (Russell), "You Are My Sunshine" (Jimmy Burns), "D.C. Divertimento" (Russell)
Rec. Salle Pleyel, Paris, October 1, 1964.
Personnel—Thad Jones (tp, c), Garnett Brown (tb), Joe Farrell (ts), George Russell (p), Bare Phillips (b), Albert Heath (d)

At Beethoven Hall Vol 1
"Freein' Up" (Russell), "Lydia and Her Friends: Lydia in Bags' Groove/Lydia's Confirmation/Lydia Round Midnight/Takin' Lydia Home" (Russell)
Personnel—Don Cherry (cnt), Bertil Loewgren (t), Brian Trentham (tb), Ray Pitts (ts), George Russell (p), Cameron Brown (b), Albert Heath (d)
Rec. August 31, 1965.
Released originally as Saba (G)SB15059ST.

At Beethoven Hall Vol 2
"You Are My Sunshine" (Jimmie H. Davis), "Oh Jazz, Po Jazz" (Russell), "Volupte" (Russell)
Personnel and date as above.
Released originally as Saba (G)SB15060ST.

George Russell—Swedish Recordings and After

Now and Then

Personnel—Palle Mikkelborg, Bertil Lövgren, Palle Boldtvig, Jan Allan (t), George Vernon, Gunnar Medberg (tb), Runo Ericksson (btb), Christer Boustedt, Claes Rosendahl (as), Bernt Rosengren, Jan Garbarek (ts), Erik Nilsson (bs), George Russell (p), Rune Gustafsson (el g), Roman Dylag (b), Jon Christensen (d), Rupert Clemendore (congas)

Rec. Stockholm, September 16, 1966.

Released originally on *The Essence of George Russell* Sonet SLP1411/2.

Othello Ballet Suite

Personnel—Rolf Ericson, Bertil Lövgren, Lars Samuelsson, Weine Renliden (t), Gunnar Wennberg (frhn), George Vernon, Olle Lind, Christer Torge (tb), Walter Arlind, Aldo Johansson (tba), Bengt Christianson (f), Arne Domnerus (as), Bernt Rosengren, Jan Garbarek (ts), Rune Falk (bs), Knud Jorgensen, Lars Sjosten (p), Nicke Wohrman (g), Lars Blomberg (clo), Roman Dylag (b), Kjell Mattison (el-b), Jon Christensen (d), Rupert Clemendore, Janos Kajlinger, Thore Swanerud (perc), George Russell (cond, org)

Rec. Stockholm, November 3 and 4, 1967.

Electronic Organ Sonata No. 1

George Russell (org).

Rec. Grorud Church, Oslo, October 1, 1968.

Both released originally as *Othello Ballet Suite* Sonet SLP1409.

Electronic Sonata for Souls Loved by Nature—1968

Personnel—Manfred Schoof (t), Jan Garbarek (ts), Terje Rypdal (el g), George Russell (p), Red Mitchell (b), Jon Christensen (d)

Rec. Sonjia Henie/Niels Onstad Center For The Arts, Høvikodden, Oslo, April 28, 1969.

Released originally as Strata East SES-1976/1.

Trip to Prillargui

"Theme," "Souls," "Event III," "Vips," "Stratusphunk," "Esoteric Circle," "Man on the Moon"

Personnel—Stanton Davis (t), Jan Garbarek (ts), Terje Rypdal (el g), George Russell (p), Arild Andersen (b), Jon Christensen (d)

Rec. Estrad, Sweden, March 1970.
Released originally as Soul Note SN1029.

Electronic Sonata for Souls Loved by Nature
Personnel—Stanton Davis, Jan Allan, Bertil Lövgren, Maffay Falay, Lars Samuelsson (t), Olle Lind (btb), Arne Domnerus (as, cl), Jan Garbarek (ts), Claes Rosendahl (ts, as, ss, f), Lennart Aberg (ts, ss, f), Erik Nilsson (bs, bcl), Rune Gustafsson, Terje Rypdal (el g), George Russell (p, cond), Bengt Hallberg (p), Berndt Egerbladh (vib, xy), Georg Riedel, Arild Andersen (b), Jon Christensen, Egil Johansen (d), Sabu Martinez (congas)
Rec. Stockholm, October 6, 1970.
Released originally on *The Essence of George Russell* Sonet SLP1411/2.

Listen to the Silence
Personnel—Stanton Davis (t), Jan Garbarek (ts), Terje Rypdal (g), Bobo Stenson (el p), Webster Lewis (org), Arild Andersen (b), Bjornar Andresen (Fender b), Jon Christensen (perc), George Russell (tym), Sue Auclair, Gailanne Cummings, Joyce Gippo, Kay Dunlap, David Dusing, Ray Hardin, Don Kendrick, Don Hovey, Dan Windham (voices)
Rec. Kongsberg Church, Kongsberg, Norway, June 26, 1971.
Released originally as Concept CR002.

Vertical Form VI
Personnel—Lars Olofsson, Bengt Edvarsson, Jörgen Johansson (tb), Sven Larsson (btb, tba), Ivar Olsen (frhn), Jan Allan (t, frhn), Håken Nyquist (t, flhn, frhn), Americo Bellotto, Bertil Lövgren (t, flhn), Arne Domnerus (as, ss, cl), Ian Uling (as, ts, f), Lennart Åberg, (as, ts, ss, f), Bernt Rosengren (as, ts, ss, f), Erik Nilsson (bs, bcl, f), Rune Gustafsson (g), Bjorn Lind (el p), Vlodek Gulgowski (el p, syn), Monica Dominique (el, p, clavinet, cel, org), Stefan Brolund (el b), Bronislav Suchanek, Lars-Urban Helje (acc b), Lars Beijbon, Leroy Lowe (d), Sabu Martinez (congas)
Rec. Estrad, Sweden, March 10, 1977.
Released originally as Soul Note SN1019.

Cubano Be, Cubano Bop
Personnel—Lars Olofsson, Bengt Edvarsson, Jörgen Johansson (tb), Sven Larsson (btb), Jan Allan, Håken Nyquist, Americo Bellotto, Bertil Lövgren (t), Arne Domnerus, Ian Uling (as), Lennart Åberg, Bernt Rosengren (ts), Erik Nilsson (bs), Rune Gustafsson (g), Vlodek Gulgowski (el p, syn), Lars-Urban Helje (acc b), Lars Beijbon (d), Sabu Martinez (congas, v)

Rec. Estrad, Sweden, March 10, 1977.
Released originally on *New York Big Band* Soul NoteSN1039.

George Russell, *New York Big Band*, Soul Note SN1039
"Living Time Event V," "Big City Blues," "Listen to the Silence Pt 1 and
Pt 2," "Mystic Voices" (Stanton Davis), "God Bless The Child" (Billie
Holiday–Al Herzog, arr. Ernie Wilkins)
Personnel—Gary Valente (tb), Dave Taylor (btb), Stanton Davis, Terumasa
Hino (t), Lew Soloff (t, flhn), John Clark (frhn), Ricky Ford, Roger
Rosenberg (ts), Marty Ehrlich (as), Carl Atkins (bs, bcl), Mark Slifstein
(g), Stanley Cowell (p—"Living Time Event V" only), Ricky Martinez
(el p, org), Cameron Brown (b), Warren Smith (d), Babafumi Akunyon
(congas), Lee Genesis (v—"Big City Blues" only)
Rec. Village Vanguard, August 16, 1978.
Released originally on *New York Big Band* Soul Note SN1039.

Electronic Sonata for Souls Loved by Nature 1980
Personnel—Lew Soloff (t), Robert Moore (ts, ss), Victor Comer (g), George
Russell (p, org), J.F. Jenny Clark (b), Keith Copeland (d)
Rec. Milan, June 9 and 10, 1980.
Released originally as Soul Note SN1009.

Live in an American Time Spiral
"Time Spiral," Ezz-thetic," "D.C. Divertimento"
Personnel—Ron Tooley, Stanton Davis, Brian Leach, Tom Harrell (t), Ray
Anderson, Earl McIntyre (tb), Marty Ehrlich (as, f), Doug Miller (ts, f),
Bob Hanlon (bs), Jerome Harris (g), Jack Reilly (acc p), Mark Soskin
(ky), Ron McLure (b), Victor Lewis (d)
Rec. New York, July 30 and 31, 1982.
Released originally as Soul Note SN1049.

The African Game
Personnel—Mike Peipman, Chris Passin, Roy Okutani, Mark Harvey (t),
Peter Cirelli, Chip Kaner (tb), Jeff Marsankas (btb), Marshall Sealy
(Frhn), George Garzone (ts, ss), Gary Joynes (ts, ss, f), Dave Mann (as,
ss, f), Janus Steprans (as, ss, f), Brad Jones (bs, bcl, f), Mark White (g),
Mark Rossi, Bruce Barth (ky), Bob Nieske (acc b), Bill Urmson (Fender
b), Keith Copeland (d), Dave Hagedorn (perc), Olu Bata—Joe Galeota,
Lazarro Perez, Kuto Perez, Amaro Laria, Enrique Cardenas
Rec. Boston, June 18, 1983.
Released originally as Blue Note BT85103.

So What

"So What" (Miles Davis, arr. Russell), "Time Spiral"

Personnel—Mike Peipman, Chris Passin, Roy Okutani, Mark Harvey (t), Peter Cirelli, Chip Kaner (tb), Jeff Marsankas (btb), Marshall Sealy (Frhn), George Garzone (ts, ss), Gary Joynes (ts, ss, f), Dave Mann (as, ss, f), Janus Steprans (as, ss, f), Brad Jones (bs, bcl, f), Mark White (g), Mark Rossi, Bruce Barth (ky), Bob Nieske (acc b), Bill Urmson (Fender b), Keith Copeland (d), Dave Hagedorn (perc), Joe Galeota (congas)

"Rhymes" (Bley), "War Gewesen" (Baker)

Personnel—Mark Harvey (t), Chip Kaner (tb), Janus Steprans (as), Gary Joynes (ts), Mark White (g), Mark Rossi (ky), Bill Urmson (Fender b), Keith Copeland (d)

Rec. Boston, June 18, 1983.

Released originally as Blue Note BT85132.

Live in Tokyo

"Listen to the Silence," "Cubano-Be, Cubano-Bop," "All About Rosie," "Manhattan" (Rogers-Hart), "Autumn in New York" (Duke), "Pan-Daddy," "Electronic Sonata for Souls Loved by Nature"

Personnel—Lew Soloff, Palle Mikkelborg, Shin Kazuhara, Nubuo Katoh (t), Ray Anderson, Osamu Matsumoto (tb), Sumio Okada (btb), Andy Sheppard, Kohsuke Mine (ts, ss), David Mann (as, f), Kazutoki Umezu (bs, bcl), Mark White (g), Brad Hatfield, Sohichi Noriki (ky), Bill Urmson (b), Keith Copeland (d), Pat Hollenbeck (perc)

Rec. Gotanda Kan-i Hoken Hall, Tokyo, February 28, 1988.

Released originally in Japan only as Electric Bird 6488/89. Also issued as video in Japan.

The London Concert

"La Folia: The Rocella Variations" (Schwendener/Russell), "Uncommon Ground," "Electronic Sonata for Souls Loved by Nature—Events XI–XV," "Listen to the Silence," "Struggle of the Magicians" (Mark White), "ix Aesthetic Gravities," "So What" (Davis, arr. Russell)

Personnel—Ian Carr, Stuart Brooks, Mark Chandler (t), Pete Beachill (tb), Ashley Slater (btb), Andy Sheppard (ts, ss), Chris Biscoe (as, ss, cl), Pete Hurt (bs, ts, bcl, f), Brad Hatfield, Steve Lodder (ky), David Fiuczynski (g), Bill Urmson (b), Steve Johns (d), Dave Adams (perc)

Rec. Ronnie Scott's Club, London, August 28–31, 1989.

Released originally as Stash STCD560/1. (USA), Label Bleu 65278 (Europe).

It's About Time
"It's About Time," "Living Time"
Personnel—Stanton Davis, Tiger Okoshi, Stuart Brooks (t), Dave Bargeron
(tb), Richard Henry (btb), Andy Sheppard (ts, ss), Chris Biscoe (as, ss,
cl), Pete Hurt (bs, ts, bcl, f), Brad Hatfield, Steve Lodder (ky), Mike
Walker (g), Bill Urmson (b), Billy Ward (d), Pat Hollenbeck (perc).
Orchestral musicians: Paul-Christian Staicu (p), Régis Huby, Laetitia
Bellanger, Maria Castro Balbi, Frédéric Norel, Johan Renard, Vanessa
Urgarte, Cédric Allali, Antoine Ferreyra, Nicolas Maiofiss, Yuri Bessiere
(vn), Etienne Cardoze, Grégory Lacour (clo), Nicolas Folmer (t), Laurent
Lair (tb), Benoit Fourreau (tba), Lionel Surin (cor anglais), Thomas Savy
(ts), Marie Poulanges, Stéphane Ramanantsitohaina, Claire Bobij (as),
Cécile Daroux (f), Luc Isenmann (perc)
Rec. Amiens, France, November 1995.
Released originally as Label Bleu LBLC6527/8.

The 80th Birthday Concert
"Listen to the Silence," "Electronic Sonata for Souls Loved by Nature," "The
African Game," "It's About Time," "So What" (Davis, arr. Russell)
Personnel—Stanton Davis, Palle Mikkelborg, Stuart Brooks (t), Dave
Bargeron (tb), Richard Henry (btb), Andy Sheppard (ts, ss), Chris Biscoe
(as, ss, cl), Pete Hurt (bs, bcl), Hiro Honshuku (f, elec) Brad Hatfield,
Steve Lodder (ky), Mike Walker (g), Bill Urmson (b), Richie Morales
(d), Pat Hollenbeck (perc)
Rec. London, June 13, 2003.
Released originally Concept 2005.

Associated Recordings

Charlie Parker and Dizzy Gillespie, *Diz 'N Bird at Carnegie Hall*, Blue Note
CDP 7243
"Cubano-Be, Cubano-Bop" (Russell-Dizzy Gillespie-Chano Pozo), "Relaxin'
at Camarillo" (Charlie Parker; arr. Russell)
Dizzy Gillespie, Dave Burns, Elmon Wright, Raymond Orr, Matthew McKay
(t), Taswell Baird, William Shepherd (tb), Howard E. Johnson, John
Brown (as), James Moody, Joe Gayles (ts), Cecil Payne (bs), Milt Jackson
(vib), John Lewis (p), Al McKibbon (b), Joe Harris (d), Chano Pozo (v,
conga), Lorenzo Salan (bongos)
Rec. September 29, 1947.

Dizzy Gillespie and his Orchestra, *The Complete RCA Victor Recordings 1937–1949*, RCA
"Cubano-Be, Cubano-Bop" (Russell-Gillespie-Pozo)
Personnel—Dizzy Gillespie, Benny Bailey, Dave Burns, Elmon Wright, Lamar Wright Jr. (t), Ted Kelly, William Shepherd (tb), Howard E. Johnson, John Brown (as), Joe Gayles, George Nicholas (ts), Cecil Payne (bs), John Lewis (p), Al McKibbon (b), Kenny Clarke (d), Chano Pozo (v, conga)
Rec. December 22, 1947.

Buddy DeFranco and His Orchestra, *1949–52 Studio Performances*, Hep CD77
"A Bird in Igor's Yard" (Russell)
Personnel—Buddy DeFranco (cl, ldr), Bernie Glow, Paul Cohen, Jimmy Pupa, Jack Eagle (t), Ollie Wilson, Earl Swope, Bart Varsalona (tb), Lee Konitz, Frank Socolow (as), Al Cohn, Jerry Sanfina (ts), Serge Chaloff (bs), Gene DiNovi (p), Oscar Pettiford (b), Irv Kluger (d)
Rec. April 23, 1949.
Released originally as Buddy DeFranco, *Crosscurrents*, Capitol M-11060.

Charlie Ventura, *Blue Prelude*, Membran 222489-444 (4-CD set)
"Caravan" (Juan Tizol-Irving Mills- Duke Ellington; arr. Russell)
Personnel—Stan Fishelson, Johnny Mandel, Dale Pierce, Red Rodney (t), Mort Bullman, Benny Green, Bart Varsalona (tb), Bill Barber (tba), Ray Beckenstein, Frank Socolow (as), Charlie Ventura (ts, bs, ss), Al Cohn, Al Epstein (Young) (ts), Manny Albam (bs), Barry Galbraith (g), Lou Stein (p), Curly Russell (b), Ed Shaughnessy (d), George Russell (tamb)
Rec. December 28, 1949.
Released originally as 78rpm Charlie Ventura and His Orchestra, "Caravan" c/w? EP A659.

Artie Shaw and His Bop Band, *The Artistry of*, Fresh Sound FSR CD397
"Similau" (Russell)
Personnel—Artie Shaw (cl, ldr), Don Paladino, Don Fagerquist, Dale Pierce, Vic Ford (t), Sonny Russo, Fred Zito, Ange Callea, Porky Cohen (tb), Herb Steward, Frank Socolow (as), Al Cohn, Zoot Sims (ts), Danny Bank (bs), Jimmy Raney (g), Gil Barrios (p), Dick Niveson (b), Irv Kluger (d)
Rec. January 1950.

Lee Konitz, *Same*, Modern Jazz Archive 221950-306
"Ezz-Thetic," "Odjenar" (Russell)

Personnel—Miles Davis (t), Lee Konitz (as), Billy Bauer (g), Sal Mosca (p), Arnold Fishkin (b), Max Roach (d)

Rec. March 8, 1951.

Released originally as 78rpm Lee Konitz, "Indian Summer" c/w "Odjenar," New Jazz 853; Prestige 753; and Lee Konitz, "Ezz-Thetic" c/w "Hi-Beck," New Jazz 843; Prestige 743.

Teddy Charles Tentet, *Same*, COL 6161

"Lydian M-1" (Russell)

Personnel—Teddy Charles (vib), Art Farmer (listed as "Peter Urban") (t), Don Butterfield (tba), Gigi Gryce (as), J.R. Monterose (ts), Sol Schlinger (bs), Jimmy Raney (g), Mal Waldron (p), Teddy Kotick (b), Joe Harris (d)

Rec. Jan 17, 1956.

Originally released on Teddy Charles Tentet, *Same*, Atlantic 1229.

Hal McKusick, *Jazz Workshop* (See George Russell, *The Complete Bluebird Recordings*, Lonehill LHJ10177.)

"Lydian Lullaby" (comp/arr. Russell)

Personnel—Hal McKusick (as, f), Barry Galbraith (g), Milt Hinton (b), Osie Johnson (d)

Rec. March 3, 1956.

"The Day John Brown Was Hanged" (comp/arr. Russell)

Personnel—Hal McKusick (as, f), Barry Galbraith (g), Milt Hinton (b), Osie Johnson, George Russell (d)

Rec. March 3, 1956.

"Miss Clara" (comp/arr. Russell)

Personnel—Hal McKusick (as, f), Art Farmer (t), Jimmy Cleveland (tb), Sol Schlinger (bs), Barry Galbraith (g), Milt Hinton (b), Osie Johnson (d)

Rec. April 4, 1956.

Released originally as Hal McKusick, *Jazz Workshop*, RCA 1366.

Hal McKusick Quartet, *The Complete Barry Galbraith, Milt Hinton, Osie Johnson Recordings*, Lonehill LHJ10176

"Give 'Em Hal" (Manny Albam), "When the Sun Comes Out" (Ted Koehler–Howard Arlen), "Can't Get Out of This Mood" (Jimmy McHugh–Frank Loesser), "These Foolish Things" (Jack Strachey–Holt Marvell–Harry Link), "Out of This World" (Harold Arlen–Johnny Mercer), "This Is New" (Kurt Weill–Ira Gershwin), "Over The Rainbow" (Harold Arlen–Yip Harburg), "Serenade In Blue" (Harry Warren–Mack Gordon),

"Prelude to a Kiss" (Irving Gordon–Irving Mills–Duke Ellington), "Irresistible You" (Don Raye–Gene De Paul)
Personnel—Hal McKusick (as, f), Barry Galbraith (g), Milt Hinton (b), Osie Johnson (d), George Russell (arr)
Rec. November 3, 1956.
Released originally as Hal McKusick Quartet *Jazz at the Academy* Coral 57116.

Max Roach Quintet, + 4, EmArcy 822 673-2
"Ezz-Thetic" (Russell)—Max Roach (d), Kenny Dorham (t), Sonny Rollins (ts), Ray Bryant (p), George Morrow (b)
Rec. September 19, 1956.
Originally released as Max Roach Quintet, + 4, EmArcy MG36098.

Marilyn Moore, *Moody Marilyn Moore*, Bethlehem LP BCP-73
"Born to Blow the Blues" (George Russell—Jack Segal)

Lucy Reed, *This Is Lucy Reed*, Fantasy OJCCD 1943-2
"In The Wee Small Hours of the Morning" (Dave Mann–Bob Hilliard; arr. Russell), "This is New" (Kurt Weill–Ira Gershwin; arr. Russell), "Born to Blow the Blues" (comp. Russell–Jack Segal)
Personnel—Art Farmer (t), Romeo Penque (Ehn, f), Sol Schlinger (bs, bcl), Barry Galbraith (g), Don Abney (p), Milt Hinton (d), George Russell (d)
Rec. January 1957.
"There He Goes" (Jack English; arr. English), "Love for Sale" (Cole Porter; arr. Gil Evans), "A Trout No Doubt" (Philip Kadison-Dan Howell; arr. Evans), "No Moon at All" (Redd Evans–Dave Mann; arr. Evans)
Personnel—Jimmy Cleveland (tba), Tommy Mitchell (btb), Romeo Penque (Ehn, fl), David Kurtzer (bsn), Harry Lookofsky (vn), Gil Evans (p), Bill Pemberton (b), George Russell (d)
Rec. January 1957.
Released originally as Lucy Reed, *This is Lucy Reed*, Fantasy F-3243.

The Birth of the Third Stream
"All About Rosie"
Personnel—Louis Mucci, Art Farmer (t), Jimmy Knepper (tb), Jim Buffington (Frhn), John LaPorta (as), Hal McKusick (ts), Robert DiDomenica (f), Manuel Zegler (bsn), Barry Galbraith (g), Bill Evans (p), Teddy Charles (vib), Joe Benjamin (b), Teddy Sommer (d), Margaret Ross (hp)
Rec. June 10 and 20, 1957.
Last CD issue Sony 1996 485103-2.
Released originally as *Modern Jazz Concert*, Columbia WL127.

Hal McKusick Quintet, *Cross Section Saxes*, Decca DL 9209
"Stratusphunk" (Russell), "The End of a Love Affair" (Edward C. Redding; arr. Russell), "You"re My Thrill" (Jay Gorney-Sidney Clare; arr. Russell)
Personnel—Hal McKusick (bcl, as), Art Farmer (t), Barry Galbraith (g), Bill Evans (p), Milt Hinton (b), Charlie Persip (d)
Rec. April 7, 1958.
Available as Hal McKusick, *Now's The Time*, Decca GRD -651.
Released originally as Hal McKusick, *Cross Section Saxes*, Decca DL 9209.

Art Farmer, *Portrait*, Contemporary C3554
"Nita" (Russell)
Personnel—Art Farmer (t), Hank Jones (p), Addison Farmer (b), Roy Haynes (d)
Rec. April 19 and May 1, 1958.

The Gil Evans Orchestra, *Out of the Cool*, Impulse IMPD 186
"Stratusphunk" (Russell)
Personnel—Gil Evans (p, leader, arr.), John Coles, Phil Sunkel (t), Jimmy Knepper, Keg Johnson (tb), Tony Studd (btb), Bill Barber (tba), Eddie Caine (as, f, picc), Budd Johnson (ts, ss), Bob Tricario (bsn, f, picc), Ray Crawford (g), Ron Carter (b), Elvin Jones, Charlie Persip (perc)
Rec. November 18, 1960.

Gerry Mulligan and the Concert Jazz Band, *A Concert in Jazz*, Verve MGV 8415
"All About Rosie" (Russell; arr. Brookmeyer)
Personnel—Gerry Mulligan (bs, p), Nick Travis, Doc Severinsen, Don Ferrara (t), Bob Brookmeyer, Willie Dennis, Allan Ralph (tb), Gene Quill (as, cl), Bob Donovan (as, f), Jim Reider (ts), Gene Allen (bs, bcl), Bill Crow (b), Mel Lewis (d)
Rec. July 10 and 11, 1961.
Released originally as V/V6-8415.

J. J. Johnson, *The Dynamic Sound of J.J. Johnson*, RCA 3350
"Stratusphunk" (Russell)
Personnel—J.J. Johnson (tb), Thad Jones, Clark Terry, Ernie Royal, Jimmy Maxwell, Joe Wilder (t), Jimmy Cleveland (tb), Tony Studd (btb), Bill Stanley (tuba), Jim Buffington (Frhn), Harvey Estrin, Jerome Richardson, Jerry Dodgion, Bud Johnson,, Oliver Nelson, Raymond Beckenstein (reeds), Hank Jones (p), Bob Cranshaw (b), Grady Tate (d)

Rec. December 7–9, 1964.
Released originally as RCA Victor LSP-3350.

The Gil Evans Orchestra, *Blues in Orbit*, Enja 3069
"Blues in Orbit" (Russell)
Personnel—Gil Evans (p, el p, ldr, arr), Ernie Royal, Johnny Joles (t), Garnett Brown, Jimmy Cleveland (tb), Julius Watkins, Ray Alonge (Frhn), George Marge (f, ss), Billy Harper (ts, f), Howard Johnson (bs, tba), Joe Beck (g), Herb Bushler (b), Alphonse Mouzon (d), Donald McDonald (perc)
Rec. 1971.

Bill Evans & the George Russell Orchestra, *Living Time*, Columbia KC31490
Personnel—Bill Evans (p), George Russell (comp, cond), Carl Atkins (cond), Snooky Young, Ernie Royal, Richard Williams, Stanton Davis (t), Snooky Young, Ernie Royal, Richard Williams, Howard Johnson (flhn), Dave Bargeron, Dave Baker, Garnett Brown (tb), John Clark (Frhn), Howard Johnson, Dave Bargeron (Tba), Jimmy Giuffre, Joe Henderson, Sam Rivers (ts), Jimmy Giuffre, Sam Rivers (f), Sam Rivers (ob), Jimmy Giuffre (cl), Howard Johnson (bcl), Ted Saunders, Webster Lewis (ky), Sam Brown (el g), Eddie Gomez (b), Ron Carter, Stanley Clarke, Herb Bushier, Sam Brown (el B), Tony Williams, Mary Morell (d), Marc Belair (perc)
Rec. New York, May 1972.

Gil Evans, *Svengali*, Atlantic SD1643
"Blues in Orbit" (Russell)
Personnel—Gil Evans (p, el p, ldr, arr), Tex Allen, Richard Williams (t), Joseph Daley (tb, tba), Howard Johnson (tba, bs, flhn), Peter Levin, Sharon Freeman (Frhn), Dave Sanborn (as), Billy Harper (ts, f), Trevor Koehler (bs, ss, f), Ted Dunbar (g), David Horowitz (syn), Herb Bushler (el b), Bruce Ditmas (d), Susan Evans (perc)
Rec. May 30, 1973.

Brecker, Evans, Watts & Turrentine, *Select Live Sax Workshop*, Polydor Japan J00J20351
"Stratusphunk" (Russell)
Personnel—Michael Brecker, Stanley Turrentine (ts) Bill Evans (ts, ss) Ernie Watts (ts, as) Don Grolnick (p, arr) Yoshio Suzuki (b) Adam Nussbaum (d)
Rec. July 29, 1989.

~

Tour Dates, 1982–2005

All performances are by George Russell and the Living Time Orchestra, unless otherwise noted.

1982

George Russell New York Big Band
July 2: Commacchio Ravenna Jazz, Italy; Milan; Bologna; New Morning Clubs, Geneva and Paris; July 17 and 18: North Sea Jazz Festival; The Pori Jazz Festival, Finland (other venues, exact dates unknown)

George Russell New York Big Band
July 26–August 1: The Village Vanguard, New York, New York
Musicians: Stanton Davis, Tom Harrell, Ron Tooley (t), John Clark (frhn), Earl McIntyre (btb), Marty Ehrlich, Doug Miller, Bob Hanlon (saxes), Jerome Harris (g), Ron McClure (elb), Jack Reilly, Mark Soskin (ky), Victor Lewis (d), Lee Genesis (v)

George Russell New York Big Band
Sept 2: Chicago Kool Jazz Festival, Grant Park, Chicago, Illinois
Musicians: Lew Soloff, Stanton Davis, Tom Harrell, Ron Tooley (t), John Clark (frhn), Earl McIntyre (btb), Marty Ehrlich, Doug Miller, Bob Hanlon (saxes), Jerome Harris (g), Ron McClure (el b), Jack Reilly, Mark Soskin (ky), Ronnie Burrage (d), Lee Genesis (v)

1983

George Russell and the Jazz Orchestra
June 18: The Emmanuel Church, Boston, Massachusetts
Musicians: Mike Peipman, Chris Passin, Roy Okutani, Mark Harvey (t), Peter Cirelli, Chip Kaner (tb), Jeff Marsankas (btb), Marshall Sealy (frhn), George Garzone (ts, ss), Gary Joynes (ts, ss, f), Dave Mann (as, ss, f), Janus Steprans (as, ss, f), Brad Jones (bs, bcl, f), Mark White (g), Mark Rossi, Bruce Barth (ky), Bob Nieske (acc b), Bill Urmson (Fender b), Keith Copeland (d), Dave Hagedorn (perc), Olu Bata—Joe Galeota, Lazarro Perez, Kuto Perez, Amaro Laria, Enrique Cardenas

George Russell and the Swedish Radio Jazz Orchestra
May 20: Kulturhuset, Stockholm, Sweden
Musicians: Americo Bellotto, Håkan Nyqvist, Gustavo Bergalli, Ulf Adaker (t), Lars Olofsson, Nils Landgren, Sven Larsson (tb), Krister Andersson, Lennart Aberg, Erik Nilsson, David Wilczewksi (saxes), Henrik Janson (g), Bobo Stenson, Lars Janson (ky), Palle Danielsson (ac b), Teddy Walter (el b), Örjan Fahlström (cond), Lars Beijbom (d), Okay Temiz (p)

Oct 3: San Diego Kool Jazz Festival, San Diego, California; Oct. 6: Gammage Auditorium, Arizona State University, Tempe, Arizona; October 7: New Mexico Jazz Workshop, Kimo Theatre, Albuquerque, New Mexico; Oct. 8: Lawndale Art Annex, Houston, Texas; October 13: New Mexico Jazz Workshop, Kimo Theatre, Albuquerque, New Mexico; November 12: Police Athletic League, Bronx, New York and Entermedia Theater, New York, New York
Musicians: Mike Peipman, Roy Okutani, Stanton Davis (t), Chip Kaner, Howard Prince (tb), George Garzone, Gary Joynes, Dave Mann (saxes), Mark White (g), Bill Urmson (Fender b), Brad Hatfield, Rick Martinez (ky), Dave Hagedorn (p), Graham Gullian (d)

1984

February 7 to February 12: Sweet Basil, New York, New York
Musicians: Tiger Okoshi, Mike Peipman, Ken Cervenka, Stanton Davis (t), Chip Kaner, Howard Prince (tb), George Garzone, Dave Mann, Dave Finucane (saxes) Mark White (g), Bill Urmson (Fender b), Brad Hatfield, Rick Martinez (ky), Graham Gullian (d), Dave Hagedorn (perc)

June 22: "Jazz Live," Afro-American Historical and Cultural Museum, Washington, D.C.; June 23: Kool Jazz Festival, Philadelphia, Pennsylvania; June 30: Kool Jazz Festival, Saratoga Performing Arts Center, Saratoga, New York
Musicians: Tiger Okoshi, Mike Peipman, Ken Cervenka (t), Chip Kaner, Howard Prince (tb), Bill Barron, George Garzone, Dave Mann (saxes) Mark White (g), Brad Hatfield, Rick Martinez (ky), Bill Urmson (Fender b), Graham Gullian (d), Dave Hagedorn (perc)

1985

May 22: The Bottom Line, New York, New York; May 23, Walker Art Center, Minneapolis, Minnesota; June 23: DeCordova Museum & Sculpture Park, Lincoln, Massachusetts
Musicians: Stanton Davis, Ken Cervenka, Mike Peipman (t), Chip Kaner, Howard Prince (tb), George Garzone, Dave Mann, Gary Joynes (saxes), Mark White (g), Bill Urmson (Fender b), Brad Hatfield, Rick Martinez (ky), Keith Copeland (d), Pat Hollenbeck (Ed Uribe replaces Pat Hollenbeck for June 23)

July 9 to July 14: Sweet Basil, New York, New York
Musicians: Sonny Fortune, Jimmy Giuffre (saxes—guest artists), Stanton Davis, Mike Peipman, Ken Cervenka (t), Chip Kaner, Howard Prince (tb), George Garzone, Dave Mann, Dave Finucane (saxes), Brad Hatfield, Rick Martinez (ky), Bill Urmson (Fender b), Mark White (g), Keith Copeland (d), Pat Hollenbeck (perc)

September 11: The Boston Arts Festival, The Hatch Shell, Boston, Massachusetts
Musicians: Stanton Davis, Mike Peipman, Ken Cervenka (t), Chip Kaner, Howard Prince (tb), George Garzone, Dave Mann, Dave Hubbard (saxes), Brad Hatfield, Rick Martinez (ky), Bill Urmson (Fender b), Mark White (g), Keith Copeland (d), Pat Hollenbeck (perc)

1986

Feb. 26: Logan Hall, London, UK; Feb. 27: Mountbatten Theatre, Southampton, UK; Feb. 28: Concert Hall, Royal Northern College of Music, Manchester, UK; March 1: Triangle Arts Centre, Birmingham, UK; March 2: Haymarket Theatre, Leicester, UK; March 3: Warwick University Arts

Centre Hall, Coventry, UK; March 5: Leadmill, Sheffield, UK; March 8: Arts Centre, Southport, UK; March 9: Civic Theatre, Leeds, UK; March 12: People's Theatre, Newcastle upon Tyne, UK
Musicians: Stuart Brooks, Kenny Wheeler, Palle Mikkelborg (t) Pete Beachill (tb), Ashley Slater (btb) Chris Biscoe, Pete Hurt, Courtney Pine (saxes), Brad Hatfield, Django Bates (ky), Chris Watson (g), Bill Urmson (Fender b), Keith Copeland (d), Dave Adams (perc)

George Russell and the Scandanavian Jazzensemble
May 25 & 26: The Bergen International Festival, Bergen, Norway
Musicians: Palle Mikkelborg, Bertil Lövgren, Nils Petter Molvaer (t), Eje Thelin (tb), Olle Holmqvist (btb), Knut Riisnaes (ts), John Tchicai (as), Vidar Johansen (bs), Terje Rypdal (g), Bobo Stenson, John Balke (ky), Arild Andersen (ac b), Bo Stief (elb), Alex Riel (d), Marilyn Mazur (perc)

1987

July 2: Jazz à Vienne, France; July 4: Bracknell Festival, UK; July 5: Weisen Jazz Festival, Austria; Schwatz, Austria; Stadtgarten, Cologne, Germany; Balzano, Italy; Veneto Jazz, Padua, Italy; North Sea Jazz Festival, The Hague, Netherlands (exact dates unknown)
Musicians: Stuart Brooks, Dave de Fries, Palle Mikkelborg, Kenny Wheeler (t), Pete Beachill (tb), Ashley Slater (btb), Andy Sheppard (ts, ss), Chris Biscoe (as, ss, cl) Pete Hurt (bs, ts, bcl), Brad Hatfield, Django Bates (ky), Chris Watson (g), Bill Urmson (Fender b), Keith Copeland (d), Dave Adams (perc)

Oct. 2: Baird Auditorium, Smithsonian Museum of Natural History, Washington, D.C.; October 3: Port of History Theatre, Philadelphia, Pennsylvania
Musicians: Mike Peipman, Ken Cervenka, Tiger Okoshi (t) Chip Kaner (tb), Howard Prince (btb), Rob Scheps (ts), Dave Mann (as), Dave Finucane (bs), Brad Hatfield, Marc Rossi (ky), Bill Urmson (Fender b), Mark White (g), Keith Copeland (d), Pat Hollenbeck (perc)

George Russell Sextet
Nov. 7: Grinnell College, Grinnell, Iowa; Nov. 9: Kuumbwa Jazz Center, Santa Cruz, California; Nov. 10: Great American Music Hall, San Francisco, California; Nov. 14: Kimo Theatre, Albuquerque, New Mexico; Nov. 15: Memorial Auditorium, Ohio University, Athens, Ohio; Nov. 17–22: Sweet Basil, New York, New York

Musicians: George Russell (p), John Stubblefield (sax), Graham Haynes (t), Brad Hatfield (ky), Bill Urmson (Fender b), Keith Copeland (d)

1988

February 28: Tokyo Music Joy, U-Port Hall, Tokyo, Japan
Musicians: Palle Mikkelborg, Lew Soloff, Shin Kazuhara, Nubuo Katoh (t), Ray Anderson, Osamu Matsumoto (tb), Sumio Okada (btb), Andy Sheppard, Kohsuke Mine (ts), Dave Mann, (as), Kazutoki Umezu (bs), Brad Hatfield, Sohichi Noriki (ky), Bill Urmson (Fender b), Mark White (g), Keith Copeland (d), Pat Hollenbeck (perc)

May 7: Newcastle Jazz Festival, Playhouse Theatre, Newcastle upon Tyne, UK; May 9: The 100 Club, London, UK; May 10: New Morning Club, Paris, France; May 11: Coutances Festival, Theatre Municipale, Coutances, France; May 12: Angouleme Festival, France; May 13: Grand Theatre, Maison de la Culture, Amiens, France; May 14: The Bimhuis, Amsterdam, Netherlands
Musicians: Palle Mikkelborg, Stuart Brooks, Dave des Fries (t), Pete Beachill (tb), Ashley Slater (btb), Andy Sheppard (ts, ss), Chris Biscoe (as, ss, cl) Pete Hurt (bs, ts, bcl), Brad Hatfield, Steve Lodder (ky), Bill Urmson (Fender b), Chris Watson (g), Keith Copeland (d), Dave Adams (perc)

August 6: Real Art Ways, Trinity College, Hartford, Connecticut
Musicians: Stanton Davis, Tiger Okoshi, Ken Dunbar (t), Chip Kaner, Peter Cirelli (tb), George Garzone, Dave Mann, Dave Finucane (saxes), Dave Fiuczynski (g), Brad Hatfield, Teese Gohl (kb), Bill Urmson (Fender b), Steve Johns (d), John Hollenbeck (perc)

Oct. 15: Portland Performing Arts Center, Portland, Maine; Oct. 21: Mertens Theater, University of Bridgeport, Bridgeport, Connecticut; Oct. 23; Ira Allen Chapel, University of Vermont, Burlington, Vermont; Oct. 25: Arts Center on Brickyard Pond, Keene State College, Keene, New Hampshire; Oct. 28: Maine Center for the Arts, University of Maine, Orono, Maine; Oct. 29: Center for the Performing and Visual Arts, University of Lowell, Lowell, Massachusetts; October 30: Cambridge Multicultural Arts Center, Cambridge, Massachusetts; Nov. 1: Spaulding Auditorium, Dartmouth College, Dartmouth, New Hampshire; Nov. 3: Jorgensen Auditorium, University of Connecticut, Storrs, Connecticut; Nov. 4: Crowell Concert Hall, Wesleyan University, Middletown, Connecticut; Nov. 5: Palmer Auditorium, Connecticut College, New London, Connecticut

Musicians: Mike Peipman, Ken Cervenka, Tiger Okoshi, Andy Gravish (t), Chip Kaner (tb), Bill Lowe, Peter Cirelli (btb) Dave Mann (as), Rob Scheps (ts), Dave Finucane (bs), Teese Gohl, Marc Rossi, Brad Hatfield (ky), Dave Fiuczynski (g), Bill Urmson (Fender b), Steve Johns (d), Pat Hollenbeck, Doug Lippincott (perc)

1989

Aug. 12: Internationales Jazz Fest, Festhalle, Viersen, Germany; Aug: 13: Game Festival, Rossijnol, Belgium; Aug. 15: Middelheim Park, Antwerp, Belgium; Aug. 18: Snape Maltings, Concert Hall, Saxmunden, UK; Aug. 19: Brecon Jazz Festival, Market Hall, Wales; Aug 20: Queen's Hall, Edinburgh, Scotland; Aug. 23 and 24: Amphitheatre, Jazz in August, Lisbon, Portugal; 28–31: Ronnie Scott's, London, UK; September 2: IX Festival Internazionale del Jazz, Roccella Jonica, Italy
Musicians: Stuart Brooks, Ian Carr, Mark Chandler (t), Pete Beachill (tb), Ashley Slater (btb), Andy Sheppard (ts, ss), Chris Biscoe (as, ss, cl) Pete Hurt (bs, ts, bcl), Dave Fiuczynski (g), Brad Hatfield, Steve Lodder (ky), Bill Urmson (Fender b), Steve Johns (d), Dave Adams (perc)

1990

May 20: New Music America, Annenberg Center, Philadelphia, Pennsylvania: May 22: Hartford Festival of Jazz, Bushnell Park, Hartford, Connecticut
Musicians: Tiger Okoshi, Mike Peipman, Ken Cervenka (t), Chip Kaner, Bill Lowe (tb), Rob Scheps, Dave Mann, Anthony Paquette (saxes), Dave Fiuczynski (g), Marc Rossi, Brad Hatfield (ky), Bill Urmson (Fender b), Steve Johns (d), Pat Hollenbeck (perc)

July 6: Theatre Royal, Glasgow International Jazz Festival, Glasgow, Scotland; July 9: Amsterdam Jazz Festival, Amsterdam, Netherlands; July 10–15: Umbria Jazz Festival, Perugia, Italy
Musicians: Tiger Okoshi, Stuart Brooks, Tim Hagans (t), Dave Bargeron (tb), Ashley Slater (btb), Andy Sheppard, Dave Mann, John Purcell (saxes), Dave Fiuczynski (g), Brad Hatfield, Teese Gohl (ky), Bill Urmson (Fender b), Steve Johns (d), Pat Hollenbeck (perc)

1991

March 18: Teatro Metropolitan, Catania, Italy; March 19: Teatro Communale, L'Aquila, Italy; March 20: Teatro Rasi, Ravenna, Italy; March 21: Auditorium

Santa Chiara, Trento, Italy; March 23: Teatro Ariosto, Reggio Emilia, Italy; March 24: Camden Jazz Festival, Town and Country, London, UK
Musicians: Tiger Okoshi, Stuart Brooks, Ian Carr (t), Dave Bargeron (tb), Ashley Slater (btb), Andy Sheppard (ts, ss), Chris Biscoe (as, ss, cl) Pete Hurt (bs, ts, bcl), Adam Rogers (g), Brad Hatfield, Steve Lodder (ky), Bill Urmson (Fender b), Steve Johns (d), Pat Hollenbeck (perc)

April 16: Maison de la Culture, Salle Gil Evans, Amiens, France
Musicians: Tiger Okoshi, Stuart Brooks, Ian Carr (t), Dave Bargeron (tb), Ashley Slater (btb), Andy Sheppard (ts, ss), Chris Biscoe (as, ss, cl) Pete Hurt (bs, ts, bcl), Dave Fiuczynski (g), Brad Hatfield, Steve Lodder (ky), Bill Urmson (Fender b), Steve Johns (d), Dave Adams (perc)

Oct. 28: Theatre 140, Brussels, Belgium; October 29: Festival d'Automne à Paris, Théâtre des Champs Elysées, Paris, France
Musicians: Ian Carr, Tiger Okoshi, Henry Lowther (t), Dave Bargeron (tb), Rick Taylor (btb), Andy Sheppard (ts, ss), Chris Biscoe (as, ss, cl) Pete Hurt (bs, ts, bcl), Dave Fiuczynski (g), Brad Hatfield, Steve Lodder (ky), Bill Urmson (Fender b), Steve Johns (d), Dave Adams, Pat Hollenbeck (perc)

1992

June 27: Filene Center, Wolf Trap, Vienna, Virginia
Musicians: Tiger Okoshi, Takuya Nakamura, Mike Peipman (t), Dave Bargeron (tb), Bill Lowe (btb) Rob Scheps (ts), Kathy Halverson (bs), Jim Odgren (bs) Dave Fiuczynski (g), Brad Hatfield, Marc Rossi (ky), Bill Urmson (Fender b), Steve Johns (d), Doug Lippincott, (p)

1993

March 31: The Arsenal, Metz, France; April 6: Teatro Tenda, Florence, Italy; April 8: Roccella Jonica, Italy; April 10: Banlieues Bleues Festival, Maison de la Culture, Bodigny, France; April 11: The Jazz Cafe, London, UK
Musicians: Stuart Brooks, Ian Carr, Tiger Okoshi (t), Malcolm Griffiths (tb), Ashley Slater (btb), Andy Sheppard (ts, ss), Chris Biscoe (as, ss, cl) Pete Hurt (bs, ts, bcl), Adam Rogers (g), Brad Hatfield, Steve Lodder (ky), Bill Urmson (Fender b), Steve Johns (d), Pat Hollenbeck (perc), with students from the Conservatoire National Supérieur de Musique et de Danse de Paris (Bodigny and Metz only)

1994

July 8 and 9: Umbria Jazz Festival, Perugia, Italy; July 10: North Sea Jazz Festival, The Hague, Netherlands; July 13: Newcastle Jazz Festival, Newcastle upon Tyne, UK; July 24: Pori Jazz Festival, Pori, Finland
Musicians: Guy Barker, Henry Lowther, Stuart Brooks (t), Dave Bargeron (tb), Richard Edwards (btb), Andy Sheppard (ts, ss), Chris Biscoe (as, ss, cl) Pete Hurt (bs, ts, bcl), Mike Walker (g), Brad Hatfield, Steve Lodder (ky), Bill Urmson (Fender b), Billy Ward (d), Pat Hollenbeck (perc)

1995

April 2: Festival Banlieues Bleues, Cite de la Musique, Paris, France
Musicians: Tiger Okoshi, Stuart Brooks, Guy Barker (t), Dave Bargeron (tb), Richard Edwards (btb), Andy Sheppard (ts, ss), Chris Biscoe (as, ss, cl) Pete Hurt (bs, ts, bcl), Mike Walker (g), Brad Hatfield, Steve Lodder (ky), Bill Urmson (Fender b), Billy Ward (d), Pat Hollenbeck (perc), with additional musicians from the Conservatoire National Supérieur de Musique et de Danse de Paris, Le Conservatoire national de Région d'Aubervilliers-La Courneuve, L'Ecole nationale de musique et de danse de Montreuil, and L'Ecole nationale de musique de Romainville

George Russell and the Swedish Radiojazzgruppen
Nov. 4: Berwald Hall, Stockholm, Sweden
Musicians: Palle Mikkelborg, Bertil Lövgren, Magnus Broo, Peter Asplund, Fredrik Norén, Hans Dyvik (t), Olle Holmqvist, Nils Landgren, Bertil Strandberg, Anders Wiborg (tb), Rolf Nyqvist (horn) Johan Hörlén, Ronny Stensson (as), Lennart Aberg, David Wilczewski (ts), Alberto Pinton, (bs), Johan Norberg (g) Brad Hatfield, Esbjorn Svensson, Bengt Hallberg (ky), Teddy Walter, (b) Jukkis Uotila (d), Pat Hollenbeck, Rene Martinez (perc) Coltrane Magnum Price (v)

Nov. 10: The Maltings, Farnham, UK; Nov. 11: London International Jazz Festival, Queen Elizabeth Hall, London, UK; Nov. 15: Maison de la Culture, Amiens, France, Nov. 17: Turner Sims Hall, Southampton, UK; Nov. 18: The Forum, Bath, UK; Nov. 19: Town Hall, Birmingham, UK; Nov. 20: Lawrence Batley Theatre, Huddersfield Contemporary Music Festival, Huddersfield, UK; Nov. 22: Maison de la Culture, Nevers, France
Musicians: Stanton Davis, Tiger Okoshi, Stuart Brooks (t), Dave Bargeron (tb), Richard Henry (btb), Andy Sheppard (ts, ss), Chris Biscoe (as, ss, cl) Pete

Hurt (bs, ts, bcl), Hiro Honshuku (f), Mike Walker (g), Brad Hatfield, Steve Lodder (ky), Bill Urmson (Fender b), Billy Ward (d), Pat Hollenbeck (perc)

1998

March 7: Barbican Hall, London, UK; March 8: Cite de la Musique, Paris, France.
Musicians: Stanton Davis, Stuart Brooks, Guy Barker (t), Dave Bargeron (tb), Richard Henry (btb), Andy Sheppard (ts, ss), Chris Biscoe (as, ss, cl) Pete Hurt (bs, ts, bcl), Hiro Honshuku (f), Mike Walker (g), Brad Hatfield, Steve Lodder (ky), Bill Urmson (Fender b), Billy Ward (d), Pat Hollenbeck (perc), with additional musicians from Guildhall School of Music and Drama and Conservatoire de Paris

May 29: The Moers Festival, Moers, Germany; May 30: Verona Jazz 1998, Teatro Romano, Verona, Italy
Musicians: Stanton Davis, Tiger Okoshi, Stuart Brooks (t), Dave Bargeron (tb), Richard Henry (btb), Andy Sheppard (ts, ss), Chris Biscoe (as, ss, cl) Pete Hurt (bs, ts, bcl), Mike Walker (g), Brad Hatfield, Steve Lodder (ky), Bill Urmson (Fender b), Billy Ward (d), Pat Hollenbeck (perc)

1999

May 6 and 7: Scullers Jazz Club, Cambridge, Massachusetts; May 8: The Five Spot Jazz Series of Lost Jazz Shrines, Tribeca Art Center, New York, New York; May 10: The Library of Congress, Coolidge Auditorium, Washington, D.C.
Musicians: Tiger Okoshi, Stanton Davis, Stuart Brooks, Scott Aruda (t, Boston only), Dave Bargeron (tb), Richard Henry (btb), Andy Sheppard (ts, ss), Pete Hurt (bs, ts, bcl), Jason Hunter (as), Hiro Honshuku (f, elec), Mike Walker (g), Brad Hatfield, Steve Lodder (ky), Bill Urmson (Fender b), Billy Ward (d), Pat Hollenbeck (perc)

2002

July 15–20: Umbria Jazz Festival, Perugia, Italy; July 21: Pescara Jazz Festival, Pescara, Italy
Musicians: Stanton Davis, Tiger Okoshi, Stuart Brooks (t), Dave Bargeron (tb), Richard Edwards (btb), George Garzone (ts), Steve Slagle (as), Pete Hurt (bs, ts, bcl), Hiro Honshuku (f, elec), Mike Walker (g), Brad Hatfield,

Steve Lodder (ky), Bill Urmson (Fender b), Billy Ward (d), Pat Hollenbeck (perc)

2003

June 9: The Moers Festival, Moers, Germany, June 12: Manchester Royal Northern College of Music, Manchester, UK; June 13: Barbican Hall, London, UK
Musicians: Stanton Davis, Palle Mikkelborg, Stuart Brooks (t), Dave Bargeron (tb), Richard Henry (btb), Andy Sheppard (ts, ss), Chris Biscoe (as, ss, cl) Pete Hurt (bs, ts, bcl), Hiro Honshuku (f), Mike Walker (g), Brad Hatfield, Steve Lodder (ky), Bill Urmson (Fender b), Richie Morales (d), Pat Hollenbeck (perc), with Christopher Jenkins (vla, UK concerts only)

2005

George Russell's Living Time Orchestra
October 29: Musikhost 2005, Odense, Denmark
Musicians: Palle Mikkelborg, Stuart Brooks (t), Brad Hatfield (ky), Bo Stief (b) Richie Morales (d), Pat Hollenbeck (perc), with students from Det Fynske Musikkonservatorium

Bibliography

"Adventuring with George Russell." *Jazz Today*, June 1957.

"Afterhours—A Jazz Discussion with Clark Terry, Don Ellis, Bob Brookmeyer, George Russell." *Down Beat*, November 9, 1961.

Akiyama, K. "The Joy of Listening to Music—The George Russell Performance," *Komei Shimbun*, March 5, 1988.

Albertson, C. Sleeve notes to *Stratusphunk*. Riverside RLP 9341.

Anderson, K. Sleeve notes for Debussy, *La Mer, Nocturnes*, Naxos CD 8.550262.

———. Sleeve notes to Scriabin, *Piano Concerto, Prometheus, The Poem of Fire*. Naxos CD 8.550818.

Applebome, P. "A Jazz Success Story with a Tinge of the Blues." *New York Times*, September 22, 1998.

Atkins, Ronald. "The Guide—Preview of LTO at Queen Elizabeth Hall." *Guardian* (Manchester), November 11, 1995.

Baillie, M. Sleeve notes to *The Artistry of Artie Shaw*. Fresh Sound FSR-CD397.

Baker, D. "Jazz: The Academy's Neglected Stepchild." *Down Beat*, September 23, 1965.

Baker, D., L. B. Baker, and H. Hudson. *The Black Composer Speaks*. Metuchen, NJ: Scarecrow Press, 1978.

Ball, M. "Licht aus Stockhausen." *Avant* 5 (Winter 1998).

Balliett, Whitney. Review of George Russell Sextet, Jazz in the Garden, MoMA, New York. "Musical Events—Jazz Concerts." *New Yorker*, July 1960.

———. Review of George Russell—*New York, N.Y.* (Decca DL9216). *New Yorker*, December 1959.

Becker, H. S. *The Outsiders Studies in Sociology of Deviance*. New York: MacMillan, 1966.

Benade, A. H. *Fundamentals of Musical Acoustics*. New York: Dover, 1990.

Benson Brooks, John. "George Russell." *Jazz Review*, February 1960.

Berendt, Joachim. *The Jazz Book—From New Orleans to Jazz Now*. New York and Westport, CT: Lawrence Hill, 1974.

Berger, P., and T. Luckmann. *The Social Construction of Reality*. Harmondsworth, UK: Penguin, 1981.

Bernstein, Leonard. *The Unanswered Question: Six Lectures at Harvard*. Cambridge, MA: Harvard University Press, 1976.

Blangger, T. "George Russell." *Coda*, December 1990/January 1991.

"The Blindfold Test—André Previn." *Down Beat*, October 26, 1961.

"The Blindfold Test—George Russell." *Down Beat*, January 5, 1961.

Blumenthal, Bob. "A Tribute to a Local." *Boston Globe*, March 23, 1983.

———. "Captured by the Game." *Boston Phoenix*, May 14, 1985.

———. "George Russell—Stratus Seeker." *Down Beat*, October 1983.

———. "George Russell Finds Music's Missing Link." *Boston Phoenix*, April 24, 1973.

Booth, Garry. Review of Camden Jazz Festival. *Financial Times*, March 26, 1991.

Bouchard, Fred. Review of Boston Musica Viva performance of *Six Aesthetic Gravities*. *Down Beat*, June 1988.

Bowlby, John. *Attachment and Loss*. Vols. 1–3. London: Pimlico, 1997.

Boyd, Joe. *White Bicycles*. London: Serpent's Tail, 2006.

Britt, Stan. Sleeve notes for Affinity reissue of *Jazz in the Space Age* AFF152.

Brubeck, Darius. "1959: The Beginning of Beyond." In *The Cambridge Companion to Jazz*, edited by M. Cooke and D. Horn. Cambridge: Cambridge University Press, 2002.

Bud, R. *Penicillin—Triumph and Tragedy*. Oxford: Oxford University Press, 2007.

Burt, Peter. "Takemitsu and the Lydian Chromatic Concept of George Russell." *Contemporary Music Review* 21, no. 4 (2002).

Burton, Nelson. *My Life in Jazz*. Cincinnati, OH: Clifton Hills Press, 2000.

"By George." *Down Beat*, July 1983.

Campbell, Joseph. *The Hero with a Thousand Faces*. London: Fontana, 1993.

Carr, Ian. Program notes for a Contemporary Music Network tour (1992).

———. Interview with George Russell for BBC Radio 3 broadcast *Invisible Guru*.

———. Interview with George Russell for BBC Radio 3 broadcast *The Trailblazer—George Russell*.

———. *Miles Davis—The Definitive Biography*. Hammersmith, UK: HarperCollins, 1999.

———. Notebooks for BBC Radio 3 Broadcasts *Invisible Guru* and *Trailblazer*, broadcast July and August 1994.

Cerulli, Dom. "George Russell." *Down Beat*, May 29, 1958.

Cerulli, D., B. Korall, and M. Nasatir. *The Jazz Word*. New York: Ballantine, 1960.

Chilton, J. *Song of the Hawk*. London: Quartet, 1990.

"Chords and Discords." *Down Beat*, June 26, 1958.

Cincinnati City Directory, 1923.

Clark, K. B., and M. P. Clark. "Racial Identification and Preferences in Negro Children." In *Reading in Social Psychology*, edited by Maccoby, Newcomb, and Hartley. New York: Holt, Rinehart & Winston, 1958.

Clarkson, Austin., ed. *On the Music of Stefan Wolpe—Essays and Recollections*. New York: Pendragon, 2003.

Claypool, Bob. "Blazing the Fusion Trail." *Houston Post*, October 8, 1983.

———. Review of *The African Game. Houston Post*, June 4, 1985.

Cochran, Polly. "Workshop Creates Learned Jazz." *Indianapolis Star*, August 4, 1957.

Considine, J. D. Review of *The African Game. Musician*, April 1985.

Cook, Richard. "Old Hand Who Gets a Kick out of the Big Band." *Sunday Times* (London), August 27, 1989.

Cook, R., and Brian Morton. *The Penguin Guide to Jazz On CD*. Harmondsworth, UK: Penguin, 2000.

Cosgrove, Stuart. "The Zoot-Suit and Style Warfare." *History Workshop Journal* 18 (Autumn 1984).

Cott, J. *Stockhausen: Conversations with the Composer*. New York: Simon & Schuster, 1973.

"Critics Poll Results." *Down Beat*, July 18, 1963.

Crouch, Stanley. "George Russell's Victory." *Village Voice*, February 21, 1984.

———. "From the Cottonfields to the Cosmos." *Soho Weekly News*, April 20, 1978.

Cuscuna, Michael. "Spotlight Review of Reissues of *Othello Ballet, The Essence of George Russell, Electronic Sonata 1968*, and *Listen to the Silence*." *Down Beat*, February 13, 1975.

Dabney, Wendell P. *Cincinnati's Colored Citizens*. Cincinnati, OH: Dabney Publishing, 1926.

Damasio, A. R. *Descartes' Error—Emotion, Reason and the Human Brain*. New York: Quill, 2000.

Dauer, Alfons M. "Das Lydisch-Chromatische Tonsystem Von George Russell Und Seine Anwendung." *Jazzforschung/Jazz Research* 14 (1982).

Davis, C. "Structuralist of Free Form." *Times* (London), November 10, 1995.

———. "The Week Ahead (Preview of Brecon Jazz Festival)." *Times* (London), August 12, 1989.

Davis, Francis. "George Russell: The Intellect of the Heart." *Jazz Times*, December 12, 1984.

———. *Jazz and Its Discontents*. Cambridge, MA: Da Capo, 2004.

———. *Tonight, A Rare Treat in Music. Philadelphia Inquirer*, June 22, 1984.

Davis, Miles, with Q. Troup. *Miles: The Autobiography*. London: MacMillan, 1989.

DeBarros, Paul. "Review of *The 80th Birthday Concert* (Concept)." *Down Beat*, November 2005.

DeMichael, Dom. "Newport Report." *Down Beat*, August 13, 1964.

———. "Spotlight Review of *Jazz in the Space Age* (Decca9219) and *George Russell Sextet at the Five Spot* (Decca9220)." *Down Beat*, June 8, 1961.

———. "Vortex: The Dave Baker Story." *Down Beat*, December 17, 1964.

Diallo, Yaya, and Mitchell Hall. *The Healing Drum—African Wisdom Teachings.* Rochester, VT: Destiny Books, 1989.

Diliberto, John. Review of *Electronic Sonata* (SN1009) and *Vertical Form VI* (SN1019). *Down Beat*, April 1982.

DiNardo, R. "Jazz Prophet." *Boston Globe Sunday Magazine*, June 12, 1983.

Dolby, R. G. A. "The Sociology of Knowledge in Natural Science." *Science Studies* 1, no. 1 (1971).

Drago, C. "Boston Globe Festival—Safe but Sound." *Jazz Times*, June 1983.

Driggs, Frank. Liner notes in *The Fletcher Henderson Story*. (Columbia CL419).

"Drummer to Composer." *Cincinnati Post*. July 13, 1957.

Dylan, Bob. *Chronicles, Volume One.* London: Simon & Schuster, 2004.

Eaton, Derek. "Band Strikes High Note." *Southern Evening Echo* (Southampton), March 3, 1986.

"1199er Wins Acclaim as Jazz Composer." *RWDSU Record*, September 15, 1957.

Elyot, K. "Riot at the Rite." *Guardian* (Manchester), March 2, 2006.

Fanon, F. *Toward the African Revolution.* Harmondsworth, UK: Penguin, 1970.

———. *The Wretched of the Earth.* Harmondsworth, UK: Penguin, 1969.

Feather, Leonard. "Dance Biz Needs Younger Leaders: DeFranco." *Down Beat*, March 9, 1951.

———. Letter to George Russell. March 21, 1973.

———. Review of *Moody Marilyn Moore*, Bethlehem LP BCP-73. *Down Beat*, March 6, 1957.

———. Review of *The RCA Jazz Workshop—George Russell and his Smalltet* (RCA Victor LPM1372) *Down Beat*, August 7, 1957.

———. Sleeve notes to *George Russell Sextet Live in Kansas City* (Decca DL4183).

Fitzgerald, M. "The Lenox School of Jazz." JazzDiscography.com, November 1, 1993. www.jazzdiscography.com/Lenox/lenhome.htm.

Fordham, John. "George and the Geometry." *Guardian* (Manchester), February 28, 1986.

———. "King George's Gold Blend." *Guardian* (Manchester), September 1, 1989.

———. "Lazy Rocking Russell." *Guardian Weekly* (Manchester), May 12, 1991.

———. "Send Off the Clones." *Guardian* (Manchester), March 5, 1998.

———. "A Time to Live." *Guardian* (Manchester), March 21, 1997.

———. "Stars in the Eye of a Storming Sound." *Guardian* (Manchester), March 9, 1998.

Gamble, P. "George Russell the Lydian Pioneer Takes Stock with Peter Gamble." *Jazz Journal*, July 1992.

Garrigues, C. H. Reviews of *The RCA Jazz Workshop—George Russell and His Smalltet* (RCA LPM 1372) and *The RCA Jazz Workshop—Hal McKusick* (RCA LPM 1366). *San Francisco Examiner*, August 25, 1957.

Gayford, Martin. "Ignoring the Sirens." *Weekend Telegraph* (London), March 16, 1991.

George Russell—A Jazz Portrait. WGBH Radio, Boston.

"George Russell, Le Retour D'Un Grand Du Jazz." *Le Courier Picard*, November 13, 1995.

"George Russell Sends Call for More Blood Donors." *Down Beat*, October 22, 1964.

Gibson, Rob. Letter to Marty Khan. January 4, 1993.

Giddins, Gary. "George Russell Boogies." *Village Voice*, April 17, 1978.

———. "Making It New." *Village Voice*, March 30, 1993.

———. "St. George and the Chord." *Village Voice*, March 24, 1975.

Giglierano, Geoffrey J., and Deborah A. Overmyer, with Frederic L. Propas. *The Bicentennial Guide to Greater Cincinnati: A Portrait of Two Hundred Years.* Cincinnati, OH: Cincinnati Historical Society, 1998.

Gleason, Ralph J. "An Album That Couldn't Have Been Made At All Ten Years Ago." *San Francisco Chronicle*, July 13, 1958.

Goffman, E. *Stigma.* Harmondsworth, UK: Penguin, 1968.

Gold, D. "Aaron Copland: The Well-Known American Composer Finds Virtues and Flaws in Jazz." *Down Beat*, May 1, 1958.

Gonzalez, F. "From Blue Note, a George Russell Tone Poem." *Boston Globe*, May 3, 1985.

———. "Russell Will Finish My Life's Work." *Boston Globe*, July 19, 1989.

Grant, I. S., and W. R. Phillips. *The Elements of Physics.* Oxford: Oxford University Press, 2001.

Gratz, R. "An Historical Perspective of the Lydian and Major Scales." Appendix 1 in *Lydian Chromatic Concept of Tonal Organization*, by George Russell. Brookline, MA: Concept, 2001.

Gribbin, J. *Get a Grip on the New Physics.* London: Weidenfeld & Nicholson, 1999.

Grout, D. J. *A History of Western Music.* London: Dent, 1973.

Grout, D. J., and C. V. Palisca. *A History of Western Music.* New York: Norton, 1996.

Guralnik, P. *Searching for Robert Johnson.* London: Pimlico, 1998.

Haas, K. *Inside Music.* New York: Anchor, 1991.

Hadsley, N. "George Russell: Don't Kick Sand at This Theory with Muscle." *TOP*, February 1991.

Hal McKusick Quartet—The Complete Barry Galbraith, Milt Hinton and Osie Johnson Recordings. Sleeve notes. Lonehill LHJ10176.

Harper, C. *Dazzling Stranger: Bert Jansch and the British Folk and Blues Revival.* London: Bloomsbury, 2001.

Harrison, Max. "George Russell—Rational Anthems (Phase 1, 2, 3)." *Wire*, Spring/Summer/Autumn 1983.

———. "Gerry Mulligan." In *These Jazzmen of Our Time*, edited by R. Horrocks. London: Jazz Book Club, 1959.

———. Reviews of *The RCA Jazz Workshop—George Russell and His Smalltet* (RCA LPM1372) and *George Russell—New York, N.Y.* (Decca DL9216). *Jazz Review*, November 1960.

———, ed. *Modern Jazz: The Essential Records*. London: Hanover Press, 1975.

Haywood, Mark S. "The Harmonic Role of Melody in Vertical and Horizontal Jazz." *Annual Review of Jazz Studies* 5 (1991).

Hazell, Ed. *Berklee: The First Fifty Years*. Boston: Berklee Press, 1995.

Heckman, Don. "The Changing Face of the Large Jazz Group." *Down Beat*, April 25, 1963.

Heckman, D. Review of *Modern Jazz Concert: Six Compositions Commissioned by the 1957 Brandeis University Festival of the Arts* (Columbia WL127). *Jazz Review*, November 1959.

———. "Review In Depth—George Russell." *Metronome*, November 1961.

———. "Sheila." *Down Beat*, May 9, 1963.

Heining, Duncan. "Bley's Way." *Jazzwise*, September 2007.

———. "Carla Bley." *Independent* (London), November 16, 1999.

———. "Learning to Wave." *Avant* 9 (Autumn 1998).

———. "A Meeting with a Remarkable Man." *Avant* 7 (Summer 1998).

Hendler, M. "Gedanken Zum 'Lydischen Konzept' Von George Russell." *Jazzforschung/Jazz Research* 16 (1984).

Hentoff, Nat. "An Afternoon with Miles Davis." *Jazz Review*, December 1958.

———. "The Birth of THE COOL." *Down Beat*, May 2, 1957.

———. "George Russell." *Broadcast Music Inc.*, 1960.

———. "George Russell: Emergence of a Jazz Composer," *HiFi Stereo Review*, October 1962.

———. "Introducing Bill Evans." *Jazz Review*, October 1959.

———. Review of *The RCA Jazz Workshop—Hal McKusick* (RCA 1366). *Down Beat*, May 16, 1957.

———. "The Jazz Mainstream." *Saturday Review*, June 29, 1957.

———. "Jazz's Third Stream." *Down Beat*, May 29, 1958.

———. "Way Out Front with George Russell." *Hi Fi/Stereo Review*, October 1963.

Himes, Geoffrey. "Russell: In the Mood for Modes." *Washington Post*, October 3, 1987.

Hinton, M., and D. Berger. *Bass Line: The Stories and Photographs of Milt Hinton* Philadelphia: Temple University Press, 1988.

Hoefer, George. "Caught in the Act (Review of *George Russell Sextet at the Five Spot*)." *Down Beat*, September 15, 1960.

Huddersfield Contemporary Music Festival Program Notes. November 1995.

Hultin, Randi. Review of Kongsberg Festival—performance of *Listen to the Silence*. *Down Beat*, September 16, 1971.

"Jazz School's First Session at Lenox." *Down Beat*, March 6, 1957.

Jeanquartier, André. "Kritische Anmerkungen Zum 'Lydian Chromatic Concept.'" *Jazzforschung/Jazz Research* 16 (1984).

Jeans, J. *Science and Music*. Cambridge: Macmillan, 1937.

Jenkins, W. "Living History." *Jazz Times*, May 2007.

Jeske, L. Sleeve notes to *Electronic Sonata for Souls Loved by Nature—1980*. Soul Note 121009–1.

John, G., and D. Humphrey. *Because They're Black*. Harmondsworth, UK: Penguin, 1971.

Johnson, Phil. "Lydian Modes and All That Jazz." *Independent* (London), March 7, 1998.

———. "Music—Review of Russell & LTO at the Forum in Bath." *Independent* (London), November 21, 1995.

Johnson, Sy. "Interview: Bill Evans & George Russell." *Changes*, Spring 1972.

Jones, O. "George Russell—A New Theory for Jazz." *Black Perspective in Music*, Winter 1973.

Kahn, Ashley. *A Kind of Blue*. London: Granta, 2000.

Kahn, J. P. "Names and Faces: Russell Named Jazz Master." *Boston Globe*, January 2, 1990.

Katz, L. "All That Jazz Theory." *Boston Herald*, May 5, 1999.

Katz, Richard. "Music Festival at Brandeis University." *Jazz Today*, August 1957.

Khan, Marty. Fax to Rob Gibson. December 23, 1992.

——— [writing as George Lane]. "George Russell & Anglo-American Living Time Orchestra Perform in USA for first Time." GMN.com, 7.12.02.

Klee, J. Review of *Othello Ballet Suite and Electronic Organ Sonata No.1* (Flying Dutchman FDS-122). *Down Beat*, April 29, 1971.

Knauer, Wolfram. Sleeve notes to reissue of *George Russell Sextet at Beethoven Hall (Complete Recordings)*. MPS 539084–2.

Kofsky, Frank. Review of *Ezz-thetics* (Riverside 375). *Down Beat*, November 9, 1961.

Konitz, Lee. "Blind Date." *Down Beat*, July 11, 1958.

Korall, Burt. Original sleeve notes to *Jazz in the Space Age*. Decca DL-9219.

———. "Who Is George Russell?" *Down Beat*, February 16, 1961.

———. "Where Do We Go from Here?" In *The Jazz Word*, edited by D. Cerulli, B. Korall, and M. Nasatir. New York: Ballantine, 1960.

Kramer, A. Sleeve notes to *George Russell—The Complete Bluebird Recordings*. Lonehill LHJ10177.

Laing, R. D. *The Divided Self*. Harmondsworth, UK: Penguin, 1971.

———. *Self and Others*. Harmondsworth, UK: Penguin, 1975.

Lawless Jones, Bill. "Diggin' That Joyous Jazz." *NIP*, March 1990.

———. Sleeve notes to *Cincinnati Jazz Collection Volume I* (1998). J Curve Records J71098.

———. Sleeve notes to *Cincinnati Jazz Collection Volume II* (1999). J Curve Records J7005.

Levin, Michael. "Despite Bad Acoustics, Gillespie Concert Offers Some Excellent Music." *Chicago Tribune*, October 22, 1947.

Levitin, Daniel J. *This Is Your Brain on Music*. New York: Penguin, 2006.

Lincoln Collier, James. *The Making of Jazz—A Comprehensive History*. Basingstoke, UK: Papermac, 1981.

Linden, Ken. "George Russell." *Jazz & Pop*, Autumn 1969.

Lyons, L. *The Great Jazz Pianists*. New York: Da Capo, 1983.

MacDonald, R. "Writing the Galton Case." In *On Crime Writing*. Santa Barbara, CA: Capra Press, 1973.

Macero, Teo. "Blindfold Test." *Down Beat*, March 6, 1957.

———. Review of Teddy Charles Tentet, *Same* (Atlantic 1229). *Metronome*, June 1956.

Management of the 5th International Jazz Festival, Prague. Letter to George Russell. September 1968.

Mandel, Howard. "The Mathematical Musician." *Washington Post*, September 27, 1987.

Marcus, G. *Mystery Train*. London: Omnibus, 1977.

Marmande, F. "George Russell, celui qui a change la notion de jazz." *Le Monde*, April 1, 1995.

Marx, Karl. *The Eighteenth Brumaire of Louis Bonaparte*. Moscow: Progress, 1972.

Mathieson, K. *Cookin'—Hard Bop and Soul Jazz 1954–65*. Edinburgh: Canongate, 2002.

———. Program notes for Glasgow International Jazz Festival.

McIver, Don L. "Hal McKusick's Performance Is Good, But—." *Fort Lauderdale Sunday News*, April 28, 1957.

Meehan, N. *Time Will Tell—Conversations with Paul Bley*. Berkeley, CA: Berkeley Hills Books, 2003.

Mellers, W. *Man & His Music—Romanticism and the Twentieth Century*. London: Barrie & Rockliff, 1969.

Memphis Commercial Appeal, July 21, 1957.

Miles Davis—The Complete Birth of the Cool. Sleeve notes. Capitol 724349455023.

Monson, Ingrid. "George Russell." In *International Dictionary of Black Composers*, edited by S. A. Floyd Jr. Chicago: Fitzroy Dearborn, 1999.

———. "Oh Freedom—George Russell, John Coltrane and Modal Jazz." In *In the Course of Performance*, edited by B. Nettle and M. Russell. London: University of Chicago Press, 1998.

Montgomery, William Penn. "Theorist Proposes a Scale Harmonious with All Music." *Japan Times*, August 6, 1993.

Moore, Robert E. "George Alan Russell: Jazz's First Theorist." *Trotter Institute Review* 2 (Summer 1988).

Morgenstern, Dan. "The Art of Playing." *Down Beat*, October 22, 1964.

Nelkon, M. *Principles of Physics*. Harlow, UK: Longman, 1981.

Nelsen, D. *Daily News* (New York), May 9, 1978.

Niccoli, R. A. "Stearns Conducts Jazz Panel Series." *Down Beat*, September 7, 1951.

Nicholson, S. *Is Jazz Dead? Or Has It Moved to a New Address?* Abingdon, UK: Routledge, 2005.

Nicoll, Maurice. *Living Time and the Integration of Life*. Bristol, UK: Stuart, 1952.

———. *The Mark*. Utrecht: Eureka Editions, 1998.

"9th Jazz International Critics Poll." *Down Beat*, August 3, 1961.

Nisenson, Eric. "George Russell." *Music Sound Output*, July 1964.

———. "Modes and Modalities." *Jazziz*, April 1994.

———. *Round about Midnight—A Portrait of Miles Davis*. New York: Da Capo, 1996.

Notes to *New York, N.Y*. CD reissue Impulse IMP 12782.

O'Brien, J. *Panache* 18, no. 5.

O'Conner, Norman J. "Jazz at Brandeis—Some New Areas Are Opened for Jazz by the Work of a Noted Institute of Culture and Learning." *Down Beat*, July 25, 1957.

O'Connor, J. J., and E. F. Robertson. "John Maynard Keynes." JOC/EFR, October 2003. www-history.mcs.st-andrews.ac.uk/Mathematicians/Keynes.html.

Oliver, S. "George Russell." *Jazz Express*, February 1998.

Oliver, W. "Black Males and Social Problems: Prevention through Afro-Centric Socialization." *Journal of Black Studies* 20, no. 1 (1989).

Palmer, Robert. "A Jazz Visionary Eyes the Evolution of Life on Earth." *New York Times*, April 28, 1985.

———. "Some Timeless Music by George Russell Band." *New York Times*, February 8, 1984.

Pareles, John. "Russell Big Band in Two Showpieces." *New York Times*, November 11, 1983.

Peeples, William. "Top Jazzmen Move into Hinterlands." *Louisville Times*, April 6, 1960.

Perlis, Vivian. Interview with George Russell, American Music Series, December 8, 1993. Oral History Project of American Music, sponsored and supported by the National Endowment for the Arts Special Jazz Projects.

Pettinger, Peter. *How My Heart Sings*. New Haven, CT: Yale University Press, 1998.

"The Playboy Panel: Jazz—Today and Tomorrow." *Playboy*, February 1964.

Popper, K. *The Logic of Scientific Discovery*. New York: BasicBooks, 1959.

Porter, Lewis. "The Atlantic Years." In *John Coltrane Companion*, edited by C. Woideck. New York: Shirmer, 1998.

Priestley, B. Review of *The London Concerts Volumes 1 & 2* (Label Bleu LBLC6527/8). In *Gramophone Jazz Good CD Guide*, edited by K. Shadwick. Harrow, UK: Gramophone, 1995.

Quersin, Benoit. "La Passe Dangereuse." In *John Coltrane Companion*, edited by C. Woideck. New York: Shirmer, 1998.

———. "Le Philosophe De Greenwich Village." *Jazz*, February 1963.

Ramachandran, V. S. Reith Lectures, 2003. BBC Radio 4.

Ramanan, Roland. Concert review of Cassandra Wilson, George Russell at Town & Country Club; Jazz Warriors, Tony Remy at Shaw Theatre. *Wire*, May 1991.

Ranade, G. H. *Hindusthani Music: An Outline of Its Physics and Aesthetics*. Poona, India: Ranade, 1951.

"Random Thoughts from George Russell." *Down Beat*, July 29, 1965.

Ratliff, Ben. "Rock, Funk and Electronics in a Splashy 80's Sound." *New York Times*, May 12, 1999.

Reisner, Bob. "Jazz Composition." *Village Voice*, July 10, 1957.

"Report on Lenox." *Down Beat*, October 15, 1959.

Review of George Russell—*Jazz in the Space Age* (Decca DL9219). *Metronome*, June 1961.

Review of George Russell Sextet—*Ezzthetics* (Riverside 375). "Record Notes." *Reporter*, September 28, 1961.

Review of George Russell Sextet—*The Outer View* (RLP440). *Time*, May 22, 1964.

Review of *The Outer View* (Riverside 440). *Down Beat*, July 18, 1963.

Review of *The RCA Jazz Workshop—George Russell and His Smalltet* (RCA Victor LPM1372). *Cash Box*, June 15, 1957.

Review of *The RCA Jazz Workshop—George Russell and His Smalltet* (RCA Victor LPM1372). *Hi-Fi Low-Down*, October 1957.

Review of *The RCA Jazz Workshop—George Russell and His Smalltet* (RCA Victor LPM1372). *Jazz Today*, September 1957.

Review of *The RCA Jazz Workshop—Hal McKusick*. *Metronome*, June 1957.

Review of Teddy Charles Tentet, *Same* (Atlantic 1229). *Time*, May 21, 1956.

Rilke, R. M. *Duino Elegies*. London: Chatto & Windus, 1981.

Rosenwald, H. *The Chorale—Artistic Weapon of the Lutheran Church*, in *The Musical Heritage of the Lutheran Church, Volume I*. Valparaiso, IN: Valparaiso University Press, 1945.

Rousseau, J. J. *Discourse upon the Origins of Inequality*. Mineola, NY: Dover, 2004.

"Russell Storms the Vanguard." *Down Beat*, June 1, 1978.

"Russell Writing for Victor Jazz." *Down Beat*, March 21, 1956.

Russell, Alice. Fax to John Cumming, March 26, 1992.

Russell, B. O. Letter to Mr. B. H. Heard, Wilberforce College, March 3, 1941.

Russell, George. "Barry Galbraith—Obituary." *NEC Notes*, Summer 1983.

———. *The Lydian Chromatic Concept of Tonal Organization*. New York: Concept, 1959.

———. *Lydian Chromatic Concept of Tonal Organization*. Brookline, MA: Concept, 2001.

———. "Popular Delusions and the Madness of Crowds." *Down Beat*, April 7, 1966.

———. Review of Jimmy Giuffre 3—*Travelin' Light* (Atlantic 1282). *Jazz Review*, November 1958.

———. Reviews of Johnny Mandel—*I Want to Live* (UAL4005) and Henry Mancini—*The Music from Peter Gunn* (RCA LPM1956). *Jazz Review*, June 1959.

———. Sleeve notes to *Electronic Sonata for Souls Loved by Nature—1968*. Soulnote 121034-2.

———. Sleeve notes to *Vertical Form VI*. Soul Note 121019-1.

———. "Where Do We Go from Here?" In *The Jazz Word*, edited by D. Cerulli, B. Korall, and M. Nasatir. London: Ballantine, 1960.

Russell, R. *Bird Lives*. Aylesbury, UK: Quartet, 1988.

Russo, W. Review of *George Russell at Beethoven Hall* (Saba MPFS 15059). *Down Beat*, October 20, 1966.

Sampson, Paul. Review of *The RCA Jazz Workshop—Hal McKusick*. *Washington Post*, May 5, 1957

"The School at Lenox." *Down Beat*, November 10, 1960.

"The School of Jazz." *Down Beat*, October 3, 1957.

Schore, Allan N. *Affect Dysregulation and Disorders of the Self*. New York: Norton, 2003.

———. "A Neuropsychoanalytic Viewpoint—Commentary on Paper by Steven H. Knoblauch." *Psychoanalytic Dialogues* 15, no. 6 (2005).

Schuller, G. "The Future of Form in Jazz." *Saturday Review*, January 12, 1957.

———. *The Swing Era*. Oxford: Oxford University Press, 1989.

Schwartz, Lloyd. *Boston Phoenix*, September 25, 2008.

Scumach, Murray. Review of *The RCA Jazz Workshop—Hal McKusick* and McKusick *Jazz at the Academy*. *High Fidelity*, November 1957.

Shackel, R. G. *Heat, Light and Sound*. London: Longmans, 1944.

Shadwick, Keith. *Bill Evans: Everything Happens to Me—A Musical Biography*. San Francisco: Backbeat, 2002.

Shepp, Archie. "An Artist Speaks Bluntly." *Down Beat*, December 16, 1965.

Sherman, Fred. "McKusick Album Is Best Thing to Come out of Jazz Workshop." *Miami Herald*, June 23, 1957.

Shipton, A. *A New History of Jazz*. London: Continuum, 2001.

———. "Play What You Mean." *Jazzwise*, March 1998.

Shoemaker, Bill. Review of *Ezz-thetics* (Riverside Original Jazz Classic OJC-070), *The Essence of George Russell* (Soul Note 1044/5), and *Live in an American Time Spiral* (Soul Note 1049). *Down Beat*, December 1983.

Siclier, S. "Le triomphe de George Russell à la Cité de la musique." *Le Monde*, April 4, 1995.

Silsbee, Kirk. "George Russell." *Cadence*, June 1996.

———. Sleeve notes to reissue of *George Russell Sextet at the Five Spot* (2000). Verve 088112287-2.

"Six Works of Jazz Commissioned by Brandeis University." *Down Beat*, April 4, 1957.

Smith, Arnold Jay. "The Music of George Russell," *Down Beat*, June 19, 1975.

Spender, Natasha. "Psychology of Music." In *Oxford Companion to the Mind*, edited by R. L. Gregory. Oxford: Oxford University Press, 1987.

Stein Crease, Stephanie. *Gil Evans—Out of the Cool*. Chicago: A Cappella, 2002.

Stone, I. F. "The United States as Three Nations, Not One." *I.F. Stone's Weekly*, October 7, 1957. In *The Best of I.F. Stone's Weekly*, edited by N. Middleton. Harmondsworth, UK: Penguin, 1973.

Storr, A. *Music & the Mind*. London: HarperCollins, 1992.

Sulloway, Frank J. *Freud, Biologist of the Mind*. Bungay, Suffolk: Fontana, 1980.

Swedish Radio Panel interview with George Russell, 1995.

Szwed, J. "Still on His Own Page." *Village Voice*, May 25, 1999.

"Tangents." *Down Beat*, June 18, 1964.

Thomas, P. "The Myth of Jazz, Parts I & II." *Avant* (Winter 1998/Spring 1999).

T. K. Blue Official Web Site. www.tkblue.com.

Tucker, Michael. *Jan Garbarek: Deep Song*. Hull, UK: East Note, 1998.

Ullman, M. "George Russell's Mode of Jazz," *Boston Review*, February 1986.

Urpeth, P. "George Russell (Preview of LTO at Ronnie Scott's Club, London)." *Time Out*, August 30—September 6, 1989.

Vann Woodward, C. *The Strange Career of Jim Crow*. New York: Oxford University Press, 1966.

Walters, John L. "Jazz, the Art of Harmony." *Independent* (London), March 9, 1998.

Waterworth, J., ed./trans. *The Canons and Secrees of the Sacred and Œcumenical Council of Trent*. London: Dolman, 1848.

Webster, Daniel. "Relâche Presents Flashes of Americana." *Philadelphia Inquirer*, July 1, 1989.

Wein, G. *Myself Among Others*. Cambridge, MA: Da Capo, 2003.

Westbrook, M. "The Credibility Gap." *Jazz on CD* 17 (August 1995).

Williams, M. Letter to George Russell. March 25, 1966.

Williams, Richard. "Patterns of Relish." *Times* (London), February 28, 1986.

Wilson, John S. Review of George Russell Sextet—*Stratusphunk* (Riverside RLP-341). *Down Beat*, March 2, 1961.

———. "George Russell: His Big Band and His Big Theory." *New York Times*, November 10, 1983.

———. "Jazz: George Russell." *New York Times*, May 4, 1978.

———. "Russell Presents His Episodic Jazz." *New York Times*, March 10, 1975.

———. Sleeve notes to *Hal McKusick—Jazz Workshop*. RCA Victor LPM1366.

Wilson, P. "George Russell's Constant Quest." *Down Beat*, March 17, 1972.

Withrow High School yearbook, 1939.

Woodward, Richard B. "Jazz Wars: A Tale of Age, Rage and Hash Brownies." *Village Voice*, August 9, 1994.

Woolley, Stan. "George Russell." *Jazz Journal* 39, no. 10 (October 1986).

Wordsworth, W. *The Collected Poems*. Ware, Hertsfordshire, UK: Wordsworth Poetry Library, 1994.

Wykoff Zapoleon, Marguerite. "Cincinnati Citizens: Elizabeth Campbell (1862–1945) and M. Edith Campbell (1875–1962)." *Queen City Heritage* 43, no. 4 (Winter 1985).

Young, Ben. Broadcast devoted to George Russell in celebration of his seventy-fourth birthday. WKCR Radio, New York, June 23, 1997.

Young, Ben. Interview with Nadi Qamar. WKCR Radio, New York, 1998.

Zwerin, M. "Probing the Dialectics of Chords." *International Herald Tribune*, August 10, 1989.

Interviews

Åberg, Lennart. E-mail, July 2007.
Anderson, Arild. November 2005.
Atkins, Carl. October 2003.
Baker, Dave. April 2004.
Biscoe, Chris. February 2006.
Blake, Ran. October 2003.
Bley, Carla. February 2004.
Bley, Paul. June 2007.
Brecker, Randy. August 2006.
Broberg, Bosse. E-mail, May 2007.
Brookmeyer, Bob. October 2003.
Brown, Garnett. July 2004.
Burk, Greg. E-mail, April 2007.
Byron, Don. July 2005.
Carr, Ian. April 2003.
Charles, Teddy. E-mail, October 2007.
Christensen, Jon. September 2005.
Coleman, Ornette. July 2005.
Collier, Graham. November 2004.
Cumming, John. May 2003.
———. May 2007.
Davis, Stanton. June 2003.
Davis, William. August 2004.
Ehrlich, Marty. E-mail, April 2005.
Falzone, James. E-mail, April 2007.
Fiuczynski, David. February 2006.
Ford, Ricky. October 2003.
Fujii, Satoko. E-mail, January 2005.
Garbarek, Jan. July 2004.
Gibbs, Mike. June 2005.
Giuffre, Juanita. June 2004.
Guard, Tom. May 2005.
Hatfield, Brad. June 2003.
Hendricks, Jon. April 2006.
Hennessy, Brian. April 2004.
Hersch, Fred. January 2007.
Holland, Dave. September 2006.
Hollenbeck, Pat. June 2003.
Hunt, Joe. June 2004.
Hurt, Pete. June 2003.
Israels, Chuck. E-mail, August 2004.

Jordan, Sheila. May 2004.
Khan, Marty. February 2004.
Konitz, Lee. April 2004.
Lodder, Steve. February 2003.
Mikkelborg, Palle. June 2003.
McPheeters, Dwight. June 2004.
Medeski, John. October 2003.
Monson, Ingrid. November 2005.
Moore, Robert. July 2004.
Morales, Richie. June 2003.
Motian, Paul. June 2006.
Norbury-Russell, Alice. November 2004.
———. October 2006.
Phillips, Barre. March 2007.
Pine, Courtney. May 2005.
Reilly, Jack. October 2003.
———. September 2005.
Riley, Howard. December 2005.
Rivers, Sam. November 2005.
Rossi, Marc. October 2004.
Russell, George. March 2003.
———. April 2003.
———. June 2003.
———. October 2003.
———. December 2003.
———. June 2004.
Rypdal, Terje. November 2005.
Schuller, George. E-mail, May 2006.
Schuller, Gunther. October 2003.
Schwendener, Ben. October 2003.
Sheppard, Andy. April 2003.
Stenson, Bobo. March 2007.
Swallow, Steve. February 2004.
Urmson, Bill. June 2003.
van Heerden, Carla. September 2005.
Wassermann, Andy. June 2004.
Wheeler, Kenny. August 2004.
Young, Dave. January 2007.

The author is also indebted to Ian Carr, who furnished his handwritten transcripts of interviews with Jimmy Giuffre, Juanita Giuffre, John Lewis, Art Farmer, Carla Bley, Steve Swallow, Ran Blake, Sheila Jordan, Steve Ellman, Don Byron, Gunther

Schuller, Mark Harvey, Jan Garbarek, Jon Christensen, Kåre Kolberg, Marit Jerstad, Alice Russell, Bill Urmson, Dave Bargeron, Tiger Okoshi, Brad Hatfield, and Robert Moore. Ian also supplied transcripts of his own interviews with George Russell. Even though not all of the above have been quoted, their comments have helped inform this biography.

Index

~

About the Author

Duncan Heining has been writing about jazz for thirteen years. In that time he has written for *Jazzwise, Jazz UK*, the *Independent*, the *Independent on Sunday, Avant, MOJO, Record Collector*, the French magazine *Improjazz, Jazz on CD*, and the Danish publication *Jazz Special*. His academic background is in the social sciences, and he holds honors degrees from North Staffordshire University and the Open University and a master's degree from the University of Leicester.

Until 2003 he worked in the British Probation and Prison Services, where he was responsible for the delivery of group work and drug programs and for child and public protection. In a rich and varied working life, he has worked in factories and warehouses, on farms, and in offices, and was at one time a long-distance truck driver. He says, however, that writing about jazz and the musicians that make it is simply the best job that anyone could possibly have.

APR 2 8 2010

14